5th Workshop on Online Abuse and Harms (WOAH 2021)

Held online due to COVID-19

Bangkok, Thailand
6 August 2021

ISBN: 978-1-7138-3391-8

Printed from e-media with permission by:

Curran Associates, Inc.
57 Morehouse Lane
Red Hook, NY 12571

CURRAN ASSOCIATES INC. proceedings.com

Some format issues inherent in the e-media version may also appear in this print version.

Association for Computational Linguistics
209 N. Eighth Street
Stroudsburg, Pennsylvania 18360

Phone: 1-570-476-8006
Fax: 1-570-476-0860

acl@aclweb.org

Additional copies of this publication are available from:

Curran Associates, Inc.
57 Morehouse Lane
Red Hook, NY 12571 USA
Phone: 845-758-0400
Fax: 845-758-2633
Email: curran@proceedings.com
Web: www.proceedings.com

WOAH 2021

The 5th Workshop on Online Abuse and Harms

Proceedings of the Workshop

August 6, 2021
Bangkok, Thailand (online)

Platinum Sponsors

facebook

Message from the Organisers

Digital technologies have brought myriad benefits for society, transforming how people connect, communicate and interact with each other. However, they have also enabled harmful and abusive behaviours to reach large audiences and for their negative effects to be amplified, including interpersonal aggression, bullying and hate speech. Already marginalised and vulnerable communities are often disproportionately at risk of receiving such abuse, compounding other social inequalities and injustices. The Workshop on Online Abuse and Harms (WOAH) convenes research into these issues, particularly work that develops, interrogates and applies computational methods for detecting, classifying and modelling online abuse.

Technical disciplines such as machine learning and natural language processing (NLP) have made substantial advances in creating more powerful technologies to stop online abuse. Yet a growing body of work shows the limitations of many automated detection systems for tackling abusive online content, which can be biased, brittle, low performing and simplistic. These issues are magnified by the lack of explainability and transparency. And although WOAH is collocated with ACL and many of our papers are rooted firmly in the field of machine learning, these are not purely engineering challenges, but raise fundamental social questions of fairness and harm. For this reason, we continue to emphasise the need for inter-, cross- and anti- disciplinary work by inviting contributions from a range of fields, including but not limited to: NLP, machine learning, computational social sciences, law, politics, psychology, network analysis, sociology and cultural studies. In this fifth edition of WOAH we direct the conversation at the workshop through our theme: Social Bias and Unfairness in Online Abuse Detection Systems. Continuing the tradition started in WOAH 4, we have invited civil society, in particular individuals and organisations working with women and marginalised communities, to submit reports, case studies, findings, data, and to record their lived experiences through our civil society track. Our hope is that WOAH provides a platform to facilitate the interdisciplinary conversations and collaborations that are needed to effectively and ethically address online abuse.

Speaking to the complex nature of the issue of online abuse, we are pleased to invite Leon Derczynski, currently an Associate Professor at ITU Copenhagen who works on a range of topics in Natural Language Processing; Deb Raji, currently a Research Fellow at Mozilla who researches AI accountability and auditing; Murali Shanmugavelan, currently a researcher at the Centre for Global Media and Communications at SOAS (London) to deliver keynotes. We are grateful to all our speakers for being available, and look forward to the dialogues that they will generate. On the day of WOAH the invited keynote speakers will give talks and then take part in a multi-disciplinary panel discussion to debate our theme and other issues in computational online abuse research. This will be followed by paper Q&A sessions, with facilitated discussions. Due to the virtual nature of this edition of the workshop, we have gathered papers into thematic panels to allow for more in-depth and rounded discussions.

In this edition of the workshop, we introduce our first official Shared Task for fine-grained detection of hateful memes, in recognition of the ever-growing complexity of human communication. Memes and their communicative intent can be understood by humans because we jointly understand the text and pictures. In contrast, most AI systems analyze text and image separately and do not learn a joint representation. This is both inefficient and flawed, and such systems are likely to fail when a non-hateful image is combined with non-hateful text to produce content that is nonetheless still hateful. For AI to detect this sort of hate it must learn to understand content the way that people do: holistically.

Continuing the success of past editions of the workshop, we received 48 submissions. Following a rigorous review process, we selected 24 submissions to be presented at the workshop. These include 13 long papers, 7 short papers, 3 shared-task system descriptions, and 1 extended abstract. The accepted papers cover a wide array of topics: Understanding the dynamics and nature of online abuse; BERTology: transformer-based modelling of online abuse; Datasets and language resources for online abuse; Fairness, bias and understandability of models; Analysing models to improve real-world performance; Resources for non-English languages. We are hugely excited about the discussions which will take place around these works. We are grateful to everyone who submitted their research and to our excellent team of reviewers.

With this, we welcome you to the Fifth Workshop on Online Abuse and Harms. We look forward to a day filled with spirited discussion and thought provoking research!

Aida, Bertie, Douwe, Lambert, Vinod and Zeerak.

Organizing Committee

Aida Mostafazadeh Davani, University of Southern California
Douwe Kiela, Facebook AI Research
Mathias Lambert, Facebook AI Research
Bertie Vidgen, The Alan Turing Institute
Vinodkumar Prabhakaran, Google Research
Zeerak Waseem, University of Sheffield

Program Committee

Syed Sarfaraz Akhtar, Apple Inc (United States)
Mark Alfano, Macquarie University (Australia)
Pinkesh Badjatiya, International Institute of Information Technology Hyderabad (India)
Su Lin Blodgett, Microsoft Research (United States)
Sravan Bodapati, Amazon (United States)
Andrew Caines, University of Cambridge (United Kingdom)
Tuhin Chakrabarty, Columbia University (United States)
Aron Culotta, Tulane University (United States)
Thomas Davidson, Cornell University (United States)
Lucas Dixon, Google Research (France)
Nemanja Djuric, Aurora Innovation (United States)
Paula Fortuna, "TALN, Pompeu Fabra University" (Portugal)
Lee Gillam, University of Surrey (United Kingdom)
Tonei Glavinic, Dangerous Speech Project (Spain)
Marco Guerini, Fondazione Bruno Kessler (Italy)
Udo Hahn, Friedrich-Schiller-Universität Jena (Germany)
Alex Harris, The Alan Turing Institute (United Kingdom)
Christopher Homan, Rochester Institute of Technology (United States)
Muhammad Okky Ibrohim, Universitas Indonesia (Indonesia)
Srecko Joksimovic, University of South Australia (Australia)
Nishant Kambhatla, Simon Fraser University (Canada)
Brendan Kennedy, University of Southern California (United States)
Ashiqur KhudaBukhsh, Carnegie Mellon University (United States)
Ralf Krestel, "Hasso Plattner Institute, University of Potsdam" (Germany)
Diana Maynard, University of Sheffield (United Kingdom)
Smruthi Mukund, Amazon (United States)
Isar Nejadgholi, National Research Council Canada (Canada)
Shaoliang Nie, Facebook Inc (United States)
Debora Nozza, Bocconi University (Italy)
Viviana Patti, "University of Turin, Dipartimento di Informatica" (Italy)
Matúš Pikuliak, Kempelen Institute of Intelligent Technologies (Slovakia)
Michal Ptaszynski, Kitami Institute of Technology (Japan)
Georg Rehm, DFKI (Germany)
Julian Risch, deepset.ai (Germany)
Björn Ross, University of Edinburgh (United Kingdom)
Paul Röttger, University of Oxford (United Kingdom)
Niloofar Safi Samghabadi, Expedia Inc. (United States)
Qinlan Shen, Carnegie Mellon University (United States)
Jeffrey Sorensen, Google Jigsaw (United States)

Laila Sprejer, The Alan Turing Institute (United Kingdom)
Sajedul Talukder, Southern Illinois University (United States)
Linnet Taylor, Tilburg University (Netherlands)
Tristan Thrush, Facebook AI Research (FAIR) (United States)
Sara Tonelli, FBK (Italy)
Dimitrios Tsarapatsanis, University of York (United Kingdom)
Avijit Vajpayee, Amazon (United States)
Joris Van Hoboken, Vrije Universiteit Brussel and University of Amsterdam (Belgium)
Ingmar Weber, Qatar Computing Research Institute (Qatar)
Jing Xu, Facebook AI (United States)
Seunghyun Yoon, Adobe Research (United States)
Aleš Završnik, Institute of criminology at the Faculty of Law Ljubljana (Slovenia)
Torsten Zesch, "Language Technology Lab, University of Duisburg-Essen" (Germany)

Table of Contents

Conference Program

August 6, 2021

August 6, 2021

15:00–15:10 ***Opening Remarks***

15:10–15:40 **Keynote Session I**

15:10–15:55 *Keynote I*
Leon Derczynski

15:55–16:40 *Keynote II*
Murali Shanmugavelan

16:40–16:45 ***Break***

16:45–18:10 **Paper Presentations**

16:45–17:10 ***1-Minute Paper Storm***

17:10–17:40 **Paper Q & A Panels I**

17:10–17:40 ***BERTology: transformer-based modelling of online abuse***

Exploiting Auxiliary Data for Offensive Language Detection with Bidirectional Transformers
Sumer Singh and Sheng Li

Modeling Profanity and Hate Speech in Social Media with Semantic Subspaces
Vanessa Hahn, Dana Ruiter, Thomas Kleinbauer and Dietrich Klakow

HateBERT: Retraining BERT for Abusive Language Detection in English
Tommaso Caselli, Valerio Basile, Jelena Mitrović and Michael Granitzer

[Findings] Generate, Prune, Select: A Pipeline for Counterspeech Generation against Online Hate Speech
Wanzheng Zhu, Suma Bhat

17:10–17:40 ***Analysing models to improve real-world performance***

Multi-Annotator Modeling to Encode Diverse Perspectives in Hate Speech Annotations
Aida Mostafazadeh Davani, Mark Díaz and Vinodkumar Prabhakaran

Memes in the Wild: Assessing the Generalizability of the Hateful Memes Challenge Dataset
Hannah Kirk, Yennie Jun, Paulius Rauba, Gal Wachtel, Ruining Li, Xingjian Bai, Noah Broestl, Martin Doff-Sotta, Aleksandar Shtedritski and Yuki M Asano

Measuring and Improving Model-Moderator Collaboration using Uncertainty Estimation
Ian Kivlichan, Zi Lin, Jeremiah Liu and Lucy Vasserman

[Findings] Detecting Harmful Memes and Their Targets
Shraman Pramanick, Dimitar Dimitrov, Rituparna Mukherjee, Shivam Sharma, Md. Shad Akhtar, Preslav Nakov, Tanmoy Chakraborty

[Findings] Survival text regression for time-to-event prediction in conversations
Christine De Kock, Andreas Vlachos

17:40–18:10 ***Resources for non-English languages***

DALC: the Dutch Abusive Language Corpus
Tommaso Caselli, Arjan Schelhaas, Marieke Weultjes, Folkert Leistra, Hylke van der Veen, Gerben Timmerman and Malvina Nissim

Offensive Language Detection in Nepali Social Media
Nobal B. Niraula, Saurab Dulal and Diwa Koirala

MIN_PT: An European Portuguese Lexicon for Minorities Related Terms
Paula Fortuna, Vanessa Cortez, Miguel Sozinho Ramalho and Laura Pérez-Mayos

August 6, 2021 (continued)

17:40–18:10 Paper Q & A Panels II

17:40–18:10 ***Fairness, bias and understandability of models***

Fine-Grained Fairness Analysis of Abusive Language Detection Systems with CheckList
Marta Marchiori Manerba and Sara Tonelli

Improving Counterfactual Generation for Fair Hate Speech Detection
Aida Mostafazadeh Davani, Ali Omrani, Brendan Kennedy, Mohammad Atari, Xiang Ren and Morteza Dehghani

Hell Hath No Fury? Correcting Bias in the NRC Emotion Lexicon
Samira Zad, Joshuan Jimenez and Mark Finlayson

Mitigating Biases in Toxic Language Detection through Invariant Rationalization
Yung-Sung Chuang, Mingye Gao, Hongyin Luo, James Glass, Hung-yi Lee, Yun-Nung Chen and Shang-Wen Li

Fine-grained Classification of Political Bias in German News: A Data Set and Initial Experiments
Dmitrii Aksenov, Peter Bourgonje, Karolina Zaczynska, Malte Ostendorff, Julian Moreno-Schneider and Georg Rehm

17:40–18:10 ***Datasets and language resources for online abuse***

Jibes & Delights: A Dataset of Targeted Insults and Compliments to Tackle Online Abuse
Ravsimar Sodhi, Kartikey Pant and Radhika Mamidi

Context Sensitivity Estimation in Toxicity Detection
Alexandros Xenos, John Pavlopoulos and Ion Androutsopoulos

A Large-Scale English Multi-Label Twitter Dataset for Cyberbullying and Online Abuse Detection
Semiu Salawu, Jo Lumsden and Yulan He

Toxic Comment Collection: Making More Than 30 Datasets Easily Accessible in One Unified Format
Julian Risch, Philipp Schmidt and Ralf Krestel

[Findings] CONDA: a CONtextual Dual-Annotated dataset for in-game toxicity understanding and detection
Henry Weld, Guanghao Huang, Jean Lee, Tongshu Zhang, Kunze Wang, Xinghong Guo, Siqu Long, Josiah Poon, Soyeon Caren Han

17:40–18:10 ***Understanding the dynamics and nature of online abuse***

When the Echo Chamber Shatters: Examining the Use of Community-Specific Language Post-Subreddit Ban
Milo Trujillo, Sam Rosenblatt, Guillermo de Anda Jáuregui, Emily Moog, Briane Paul V. Samson, Laurent Hébert-Dufresne and Allison M. Roth

Targets and Aspects in Social Media Hate Speech
Alexander Shvets, Paula Fortuna, Juan Soler and Leo Wanner

Abusive Language on Social Media Through the Legal Looking Glass
Thales Bertaglia, Andreea Grigoriu, Michel Dumontier and Gijs van Dijck

18:10–18:20 ***Break***

18:20–19:00 ***Multi-Word Expressions and Online Abuse Panel***

19:00–19:15 ***Break***

19:15–19:45 **Keynote Session II**

19:15–20:00 *Keynote III*
Deb Raji

20:00–20:45 *Keynote Panel*
Deb Raji, Murali Shanmugavelan, Leon Derczynski

20:45–21:00 ***Break***

August 6, 2021 (continued)

21:00–21:45 Shared Task Session

Findings of the WOAH 5 Shared Task on Fine Grained Hateful Memes Detection
Lambert Mathias, Shaoliang Nie, Aida Mostafazadeh Davani, Douwe Kiela, Vinodkumar Prabhakaran, Bertie Vidgen and Zeerak Waseem

VL-BERT+: Detecting Protected Groups in Hateful Multimodal Memes
Piush Aggarwal, Michelle Espranita Liman, Darina Gold and Torsten Zesch

Racist or Sexist Meme? Classifying Memes beyond Hateful
Haris Bin Zia, Ignacio Castro and Gareth Tyson

Multimodal or Text? Retrieval or BERT? Benchmarking Classifiers for the Shared Task on Hateful Memes
Vasiliki Kougia and John Pavlopoulos

21:45–22:00 ***Closing Remarks***

Exploiting Auxiliary Data for Offensive Language Detection with Bidirectional Transformers

Sumer Singh
University of Georgia
Athens, GA, USA
sumer.singh@uga.edu

Sheng Li
University of Georgia
Athens, GA, USA
sheng.li@uga.edu

Abstract

Offensive language detection (OLD) has received increasing attention due to its societal impact. Recent work shows that bidirectional transformer based methods obtain impressive performance on OLD. However, such methods usually rely on large-scale well-labeled OLD datasets for model training. To address the issue of data/label scarcity in OLD, in this paper, we propose a simple yet effective domain adaptation approach to train bidirectional transformers. Our approach introduces domain adaptation (DA) training procedures to ALBERT, such that it can effectively exploit auxiliary data from source domains to improve the OLD performance in a target domain. Experimental results on benchmark datasets show that our approach, ALBERT (DA), obtains the state-of-the-art performance in most cases. Particularly, our approach significantly benefits underrepresented and under-performing classes, with a significant improvement over ALBERT.

1 Introduction

In today's digital age, the amount of offensive and abusive content found online has reached unprecedented levels. Offensive content online has several detrimental effects on its victims, e.g., victims of cyberbullying are more likely to have lower self-esteem and suicidal thoughts (Vazsonyi et al., 2012). To reduce the impact of offensive online contents, the first step is to detect them in an accurate and timely fashion. Next, it is imperative to identify the type and target of offensive contents. Segregating by type is important, because some types of offensive content are more serious and harmful than other types, e.g., hate speech is illegal in many countries and can attract large fines and even prison sentences, while profanity is not that serious. To this end, offensive language detection (OLD) has been extensively studied in recent years, which is an active topic in natural language understanding.

Existing methods on OLD, such as (Davidson et al., 2017), mainly focus on detecting whether the content is offensive or not, but they can not identify the specific type and target of such content. Waseem and Hovy (2016) analyze a corpus of around 16k tweets for hate speech detection, make use of meta features (such as gender and location of the user), and employ a simple n-gram based model. Liu et al. (2019) evaluate the performance of some deep learning models, including BERT (Devlin et al., 2018), and achieve the state of the art results on a newly collected OLD dataset, OLID (Zampieri et al., 2019). Although promising progress on OLD has been observed in recent years, existing methods, especially the deep learning based ones, often rely on large-scale well-labeled data for model training. In practice, labeling offensive language data requires tremendous efforts, due to linguistic variety and human bias.

In this paper, we propose to tackle the challenging issue of data/label scarcity in offensive language detection, by designing a simple yet effective domain adaptation approach based on bidirectional transformers. Domain adaptation aims to enhance the model capacity for a target domain by exploiting auxiliary information from external data sources (i.e., source domains), especially when the data and labels in the target domain are insufficient (Pan and Yang, 2009; Wang and Deng, 2018; Lai et al., 2018; Li et al., 2017; Li and Fu, 2016; Zhu et al., 2021). In particular, we aim to identify not only if the content is offensive, but also the corresponding type and target. In our work, the offensive language identification dataset (OLID) (Zampieri et al., 2019) is considered as target domain, which contains a hierarchical multi-level structure of offensive contents.

Proceedings of the Fifth Workshop on Online Abuse and Harms, pages 1–5
August 6, 2021. ©2021 Association for Computational Linguistics

An external large-scale dataset on toxic comment (ToxCom) classification is used as source domain. ALBERT (Lan et al., 2019) is used in our approach owing to its impressive performance on OLD. A set of training procedures are designed to achieve domain adaptation for the OLD task. In particular, as the external dataset is not labelled in the same format as the OLID dataset, we design a separate predictive layer that helps align two domains. Extensive empirical evaluations of our approach and baselines are conducted. The main contributions of our work are summarized as follows:

- We propose a simple domain adaptation approach based on bidirectional transformers for offensive language detection, which could effectively exploit useful information from auxiliary data sources.
- We conduct extensive evaluations on benchmark datasets, which demonstrate the remarkable performance of our approach on offensive language detection.

2 Related Work

In this section, we briefly review related work on offensive language detection and transformers.

Offensive Language Detection. Offensive language detection (OLD) has become an active research topic in recent years (Araujo De Souza and Da Costa Abreu, 2020). Nikolov and Radivchev (2019) experimented with a variety of models and observe promising results with BERT and SVC based models. Han et al. (2019) employed a GRU based RNN with 100 dimensional glove word embeddings (Pennington et al., 2014). Additionally, they develop a Modified Sentence Offensiveness Calculation (MSOC) model which makes use of a dictionary of offensive words. Liu et al. (2019) evaluated three models on the OLID dataset, including logistic regression, LSTM and BERT, and results show that BERT achieves the best performance. The concept of transfer learning mentioned in (Liu et al., 2019) is closely related to our work, since the BERT model is also pretrained on external text corpus. However, different from (Liu et al., 2019), our approach exploits external data that are closely related to the OLD task, and we propose a new training strategy for domain adaptation.

Transformers. Transformers (Vaswani et al., 2017) are developed to solve the issue of lack of parallelization faced by RNNs. In particular, Transformers calculate a score for each word with respect to every other word, in a parallel fashion. The score between two words signifies how related they are. Due to the parallelization, transformers train rapidly on modern day GPUs. Some representative Transformer-based architectures for language modeling include BERT (Devlin et al., 2018), XL-NET (Yang et al., 2019) and ALBERT (Lan et al., 2019). BERT employs the deep bidirectional transformers architecture for model pretraining and language understanding (Devlin et al., 2018). However, BERT usually ignores the dependency between the masked positions and thus there might be discrepancy between model pretraining and fine-tuning. XL-NET is proposed to address this issue, which is a generalized autoregressive pretraining method (Yang et al., 2019). Another issue of BERT is the intensive memory consumption during model training. Recently, some improved techniques such as ALBERT (Lan et al., 2019) are proposed to reduce the memory requirement of BERT and therefore increases the training speed. In this paper, we leverage the recent advances on Transformers and design a domain adaptation approach for the task of offensive language detection.

Table 1: Details of OLID dataset.

A	B	C	Training	Test	Total
OFF	TIN	IND	2,407	100	2,507
OFF	TIN	OTH	395	35	430
OFF	TIN	GRP	1,074	78	1,152
OFF	UNT	—	524	27	551
NOT	—	—	8,840	620	9,460
ALL	—	—	13,240	860	14,100

3 Methodology

3.1 Preliminary

Target Domain. In this work, we focus on the offensive language detection task on the OLID dataset, which is considered as target domain. The OLID dataset consists of real-world tweets and has three interrelated subtasks/levels: (A) Detecting if a tweet is offensive (*OFF*) or not (*NOT*); (B) Detecting if *OFF* tweets are targeted (*TIN*) or untargeted (*UNT*) and; (C) Detecting if *TIN* tweets are targeted at an individual (*IND*), group (*GRP*) or miscellaneous entity (*OTH*). The details of OLID dataset are summarized in Table 1. The following strategies are used to preprocess the data. (1) *Hash-*

Table 2: Details of Toxcom Dataset.

Classification	# of instances
clean	143,346
toxic	15,294
obscene	8,449
insult	7,877
identity hate	1,405
severe toxic	1,595
threat	478

tag Segmentation. Hashtags are split up and the preceding hash symbol is removed. This is done using wordsegment[1]. (2) *Censored Word Conversion.* A mapping is created of offensive words and their commonly used censored forms. All the censored forms are converted to their uncensored forms. (3) *Emoji Substitution.* All emojis are converted to text using their corresponding language meaning. This is done using Emoji[2]. (4) *Class Weights.* The dataset is highly skewed at each level, thus a weighting scheme is used, as follows: Let the classes be $\{c_1, c_2, \cdots, c_k\}$ and number of samples in each class be $\{N_1, N_2, \cdots, N_k\}$, then class c_i is assigned a weight of $\frac{1}{N_i}$.

Source Domain. To assist the OLD task in target domain, we employ an external large-scale dataset on toxic comment (ToxCom) classification[3] as source domain. ToxCom consists of 6 different offensive classes. Samples that belong to none of the 6 classes are labelled as *clean*. The details of ToxCom dataset are shown in Table 2. The number of *clean* comments is disproportionately high and will lead to considerable training time. Thus, only 16,225 randomly sampled *clean* comments are employed.

3.2 Domain Adaptation Approach

We propose a simple yet effective domain adaptation approach to train an ALBERT model for offensive language detection, which fully exploits auxiliary information from source domain to assist the learning task in target domain. The effectiveness of using auxiliary text for language understanding has been discussed in literature (Rezayi et al., 2021).

Both the source and target domains contain rich information about offensive contents, which makes it possible to seek a shared feature space to facilitate the classification tasks. A naive solution is to combine source and target datasets and simply train a model on the merged dataset. This strategy, however, may lead to degraded model performance for two reasons. First, two datasets are labelled in different ways, so that they don't share the same label space. Second, the divergence of data distributions due to various data sources. In particular, the target domain contains tweets, while the source domain is collected from Wikipedia comments. The diverse data sources lead to a significant gap between two domains, and therefore simply merging data from two domains is not an effective solution.

To address these issues, we propose the following training procedures with three major steps. Let D_S denote the source data and D_T denote the target dataset. *First*, we pretrain the ALBERT model on the source domain (i.e., ToxCom dataset). The loss function of model training with source data is defined as:

$$\mathcal{L}_S = \underset{\Theta}{\operatorname{argmin}} \operatorname{ALBERT}(D_S; \Theta) \tag{1}$$

where L_s denotes the loss function, ALBERT$(\cdot)$ is the Transformer based ALBERT network, and Θ represents the model parameters. *Second*, we freeze all the layers and discard the final predictive layer. Since two datasets have different labels, the final predictive layer could not contribute to the task in target domain. *Third*, we reuse the frozen layers with a newly added predictive layer, and train the network on the target dataset. The loss function of model finetuning with target data is defined as:

$$\mathcal{L}_T = \underset{\hat{\Theta}}{\operatorname{argmin}} \operatorname{ALBERT}(D_T; \Theta, \hat{\Theta}), \tag{2}$$

where $\hat{\Theta}$ denotes the finetuned model parameters. There are several ways to treat the previously frozen layers in this step: (1) A feature extraction type approach in which all layers remain frozen; (2) A finetuning type approach in which all layers are finetuned; and (3) A combination of both in which some layers are finetuned while some are frozen. Finally, the updated model will be used to perform OLD task in the target domain.

Let L denote the number of layers (including the predictive layer), N_S denote the number of training samples in the source domain, and N_T denote the number of training samples in the target domain. K is the set of layers that remain frozen during training in the target domain.

[1] https://github.com/grantjenks/python-wordsegment

[2] https://github.com/carpedm20/emoji

[3] https://www.kaggle.com/c/jigsaw-toxic-comment-classification-challenge/data

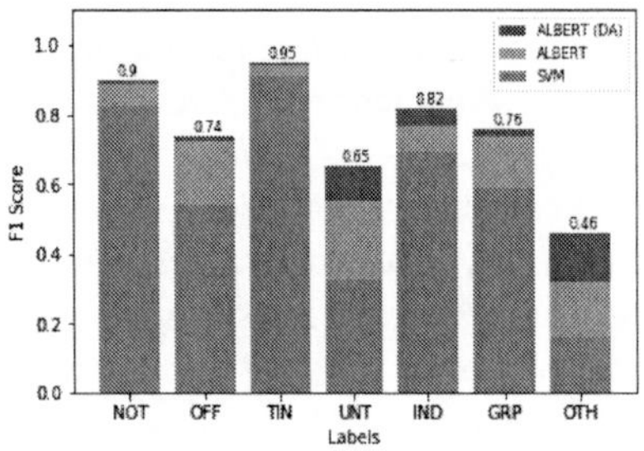

Figure 1: Classwise F1 Scores across three levels.

Table 3: Results. First three rows are previous state of the art results at each level.

Model	A	B	C
Liu et al. (2019)	**0.8286**	0.7159	0.5598
Han et al. (2019)	0.6899	0.7545	0.5149
Nikolov and Radivchev (2019)	0.8153	0.6674	0.6597
SVM	0.6896	0.6288	0.4831
CNN (UP)	0.7552	0.6732	0.4984
CNN	0.7875	0.7038	0.5185
CNN (CW)	0.8057	0.7348	0.5460
BERT	0.8023	0.7433	0.5936
ALBERT	0.8109	0.7560	0.6140
ALBERT (DA)	0.8241	**0.8108**	**0.6790**

4 Experiments

4.1 Baselines and Experimental Settings

In the experiments, four representative models are used as baselines, including the support vector machines (SVM), convolutional neural networks (CNN), BERT and ALBERT. We use the base version of BERT and the large version of ALBERT. The max sequence length is set to 32 and 64 for BERT and ALBERT, respectively. Training samples with length longer than max sequence length are discarded. Moreover, we compare our approach with three state-of-the-art methods (Liu et al., 2019; Han et al., 2019; Nikolov and Radivchev, 2019) on offensive language detection.

For domain adaptation, the finetuning and feature extraction approaches, discussed in Section 3.2, are tested. The feature extraction approach gives poor results on all three levels, with scores lower than ALBERT without domain adaptation. The third method is not used as it introduces a new hyperparameter, i.e., the number of trainable layers, which would have to be optimized with considerable computational costs. The finetuning type strategy gives good initial results and is used henceforth. The learning rate is set to 1.5×10^{-5} and 2×10^{-5} on the source data and target data, respectively. Following the standard evaluation protocol on the OLID dataset, the 9:1 training versus validation split is used. In each experiment (other than SVM), the models are trained for 3 epochs. The metric used here is macro F1 score, which is calculated by taking the unweighted average for all classes. Best performing models according to validation loss are saved and used for testing.

4.2 Results and Analysis

Table 3 shows the results of baselines and our domain adaptation approach, ALBERT (DA). For Task A, deep learning methods, including CNN, BERT and ALBERT, always outperform the classical classification method SVM. ALBERT achieves a macro F1 score of 0.8109, which is the highest score without domain adaptation. Task C is unique as it consists of three labels. All models suffer on the *OTH* class. This could be because the *OTH* class consists of very few training samples. Our approach, ALBERT (DA), achieves the state-of-the-art performance on Task C.

Figure 1 further breaks down the classwise scores for analysis. The most notable improvements are on *OTH* and *UNT* samples. ALBERT (DA) has an F1 score of 0.46, which is an improvement 43.75% over ALBERT on *OTH* samples. On *UNT* samples, ALBERT (DA) improves ALBERT's score of 0.55 to 0.65, which is an improvement of 18%. Conversely, performance on classes on which the ALBERT already has high F1-scores, such as *NOT* and *TIN*, do not see major improvements through domain adaptation. On *NOT* and *TIN* samples, ALBERT (DA) improves only 1.11% and 1.06% over ALBERT, respectively.

5 Conclusion

In this paper, we propose a simple yet effective domain adaptation approach to train bidirectional transformers for offensive language detection. Our approach effectively exploits external datasets that are relevant to offensive content classification to enhance the detection performance on a target dataset. Experimental results show that our approach, ALBERT (DA) obtains the state-of-the-art performance in most tasks, and it significantly benefits underrepresented and under-performing classes.

ACKNOWLEDGMENTS

We would like to thank the anonymous reviewers for their insightful comments. This research is supported in part by the U.S. Army Research Office Award under Grant Number W911NF-21-1-0109.

References

Gabriel Araujo De Souza and Marjory Da Costa Abreu. 2020. Automatic offensive language detection from twitter data using machine learning and feature selection of metadata.

Thomas Davidson, Dana Warmsley, Michael W. Macy, and Ingmar Weber. 2017. Automated hate speech detection and the problem of offensive language. *CoRR*, abs/1703.04009.

Jacob Devlin, Ming-Wei Chang, Kenton Lee, and Kristina Toutanova. 2018. Bert: Pre-training of deep bidirectional transformers for language understanding.

Jiahui Han, Shengtan Wu, and Xinyu Liu. 2019. jhan014 at SemEval-2019 task 6: Identifying and categorizing offensive language in social media. In *Proceedings of the 13th International Workshop on Semantic Evaluation*, pages 652–656, Minneapolis, Minnesota, USA. Association for Computational Linguistics.

Tuan Manh Lai, Trung Bui, Nedim Lipka, and Sheng Li. 2018. Supervised transfer learning for product information question answering. In *IEEE International Conference on Machine Learning and Applications*, pages 1109–1114.

Zhenzhong Lan, Mingda Chen, Sebastian Goodman, Kevin Gimpel, Piyush Sharma, and Radu Soricut. 2019. Albert: A lite bert for self-supervised learning of language representations.

Sheng Li and Yun Fu. 2016. Unsupervised transfer learning via low-rank coding for image clustering. In *International Joint Conference on Neural Networks*, pages 1795–1802.

Sheng Li, Kang Li, and Yun Fu. 2017. Self-taught low-rank coding for visual learning. *IEEE Transactions on Neural Networks and Learning Systems*, 29(3):645–656.

Ping Liu, Wen Li, and Liang Zou. 2019. NULI at SemEval-2019 task 6: Transfer learning for offensive language detection using bidirectional transformers. In *Proceedings of the 13th International Workshop on Semantic Evaluation*, pages 87–91, Minneapolis, Minnesota, USA. Association for Computational Linguistics.

Alex Nikolov and Victor Radivchev. 2019. Nikolov-radivchev at SemEval-2019 task 6: Offensive tweet classification with BERT and ensembles. In *Proceedings of the 13th International Workshop on Semantic Evaluation*, pages 691–695, Minneapolis, Minnesota, USA. Association for Computational Linguistics.

Sinno Jialin Pan and Qiang Yang. 2009. A survey on transfer learning. *IEEE Transactions on knowledge and data engineering*, 22(10):1345–1359.

Jeffrey Pennington, Richard Socher, and Christopher Manning. 2014. GloVe: Global vectors for word representation. In *Proceedings of the 2014 Conference on Empirical Methods in Natural Language Processing (EMNLP)*, pages 1532–1543, Doha, Qatar. Association for Computational Linguistics.

Saed Rezayi, Handong Zhao, Sungchul Kim, Ryan Rossi, Nedim Lipka, and Sheng Li. 2021. Edge: Enriching knowledge graph embeddings with external text. In *Proceedings of the 2021 Conference of the North American Chapter of the Association for Computational Linguistics: Human Language Technologies*, pages 2767–2776.

Ashish Vaswani, Noam Shazeer, Niki Parmar, Jakob Uszkoreit, Llion Jones, Aidan N. Gomez, Lukasz Kaiser, and Illia Polosukhin. 2017. Attention is all you need. *CoRR*, abs/1706.03762.

Alexander T. Vazsonyi, Hana Machackova, Anna Sevcikova, David Smahel, and Alena Cerna. 2012. Cyberbullying in context: Direct and indirect effects by low self-control across 25 european countries. *European Journal of Developmental Psychology*, 9(2):210–227.

Mei Wang and Weihong Deng. 2018. Deep visual domain adaptation: A survey. *Neurocomputing*, 312:135–153.

Zeerak Waseem and Dirk Hovy. 2016. Hateful symbols or hateful people? predictive features for hate speech detection on twitter. In *Proceedings of the NAACL student research workshop*, pages 88–93.

Zhilin Yang, Zihang Dai, Yiming Yang, Jaime G. Carbonell, Ruslan Salakhutdinov, and Quoc V. Le. 2019. Xlnet: Generalized autoregressive pretraining for language understanding. *CoRR*, abs/1906.08237.

Marcos Zampieri, Shervin Malmasi, Preslav Nakov, Sara Rosenthal, Noura Farra, and Ritesh Kumar. 2019. Predicting the Type and Target of Offensive Posts in Social Media. In *Proceedings of NAACL*.

Ronghang Zhu, Xiaodong Jiang, Jiasen Lu, and Sheng Li. 2021. Transferable feature learning on graphs across visual domains. In *IEEE International Conference on Multimedia and Expo*.

Modeling Profanity and Hate Speech in Social Media with Semantic Subspaces

Vanessa Hahn, Dana Ruiter, Thomas Kleinbauer, Dietrich Klakow
Spoken Language Systems Group
Saarland University
Saarbrücken, Germany
{vhahn|druiter|kleiba|dklakow}@lsv.uni-saarland.de

Abstract

Hate speech and profanity detection suffer from data sparsity, especially for languages other than English, due to the subjective nature of the tasks and the resulting annotation incompatibility of existing corpora. In this study, we identify profane subspaces in word and sentence representations and explore their generalization capability on a variety of similar and distant target tasks in a zero-shot setting. This is done monolingually (German) and cross-lingually to closely-related (English), distantly-related (French) and non-related (Arabic) tasks. We observe that, on both similar and distant target tasks and across all languages, the subspace-based representations transfer more effectively than standard BERT representations in the zero-shot setting, with improvements between F1 +10.9 and F1 +42.9 over the baselines across all tested monolingual and cross-lingual scenarios.

1 Introduction

Profanity and online hate speech have been recognized as crucial problems on social media platforms as they bear the potential to offend readers and disturb communities. The large volume of user-generated content makes manual moderation very difficult and has motivated a wide range of natural language processing (NLP) research in recent years. However, the issues are far from solved, and the automatic detection of profane and hateful contents in particular faces a number of severe challenges.

Pre-trained transformer-based (Vaswani et al., 2017) language models, e.g. BERT (Devlin et al., 2019), play a dominant role today in many NLP tasks. However, they work best when large amounts of training data are available. This is typically not the case for profanity and hate speech detection where few datasets are currently available (Waseem and Hovy, 2016; Basile et al., 2019; Struß et al., 2019) with moderate sizes at most. In addition, these tasks are known to be highly subjective (Waseem, 2016). Annotation protocols for hate speech and profanity often rely on different assumptions that make it non-trivial to combine multiple datasets. In addition, such datasets only exist for few languages besides English (Ousidhoum et al., 2019; Abu Farha and Magdy, 2020; Zampieri et al., 2020).

For such low-resource scenarios, few- and zero-shot transfer learning has seen an increased interest in the research community. One particular approach, using semantic subspaces to model specific linguistic aspects of interest (Rothe et al., 2016), has proven to be effective for representing contrasting semantic aspects of language such as e.g. positive and negative sentiment.

In this paper, we propose to learn **semantic subspaces to model profane language** on both the word and the sentence level. This approach is especially promising because of its ability to cope with sparse profanity-related datasets confined to very few languages. Profanity and hate speech often co-occur but are not equivalent, since not all hate speech is profane (e.g. *implicit* hate speech) and not all profanity is hateful (e.g. *colloquialisms*). Despite being *distantly related* tasks, we posit that modeling profane language via semantic subspaces may have a positive impact on downstream hate speech tasks.

We analyze the efficacy of the subspaces to encode the profanity (*neutral* vs. *profane* language) aspect and apply the resulting subspace-based representations to a **zero-shot transfer classification** scenario with both similar (*neutral/profane*) and distant (*neutral/hate*) target classification tasks. To study their ability to generalize across languages we evaluate the zero-shot transfer in both a **monolingual** (German) and a **cross-lingual** setting

Proceedings of the Fifth Workshop on Online Abuse and Harms, pages 6–16
August 6, 2021.

with closely-related[1] (English), distantly-related (French) and non-related (Arabic) languages.

We find that subspace-based representations outperform popular alternatives, such as BERT or word embeddings, by a large margin across all tested transfer tasks, indicating their strong generalization capabilities not only monolingually but also cross-lingually. We further show that semantic subspaces can be used for **word-substitution** tasks with the goal of generating automatic suggestions of neutral counterparts for the civil rephrasing of profane contents.

2 Related Work

Semantic subspaces have been used to identify gender (Bolukbasi et al., 2016) or multiclass ethnic and religious (Manzini et al., 2019) bias in word representations. Liang et al. (2020) identify multiclass (gender, religious) bias in sentence representations. Similarly, Niu and Carpuat (2017) identify a stylistic subspace that captures the degree of formality in a word representation. This is done using a list of minimal-pairs, i.e. pairs of words or sentences that only differ in the semantic feature of interest over which they perform principal component analysis (PCA). We take the same general approach in this paper (see Section 3).

Conversely, Gonen and Goldberg (2019) show that the methods in Bolukbasi et al. (2016) are not able to identify and remove the gender bias entirely. Following this, Ravfogel et al. (2020) argue that semantic features such as gender are encoded nonlinearly, and suggest an iterative approach to identifying and removing gender features from semantic representations entirely.

Addressing the issue of data sparseness, Rothe et al. (2016) use ultradense subspaces to generate task-specific representations that capture semantic features such as abstractness and sentiment and show that these are especially useful for low-resourced downstream tasks. While they focus on using small amounts of labeled data of a specific target task to learn the subspaces, we focus our study on learning a generic profane subspace and test its generalization capacity on similar and distant target tasks in a zero-shot setting.

Zero-shot transfer, where a model trained on a set of tasks is evaluated on a previously unseen task, has recently gained a lot of traction in NLP. Nowadays, this is done using large-scale transformer-based language models such as BERT, that share parameters between tasks. Multilingual varieties such as XLM-R (Conneau et al., 2020) enable the zero-shot cross-lingual transfer of a task. One example is sentence classification trained on a (high-resource) language being transferred into another (low-resource) language (Hu et al., 2020).

[1]Both English and German belong to the West-Germanic language branch, and are thus closely-related. French, on the other hand, is only distantly related to German via the Indo-European language family, while Arabic (Semitic language family) and German are not related.

w (profane)	ŵ (neutral)
Arschloch [asshole]	Mann [man]
Fotze [cunt]	Frau [woman]
Hackfresse [shitface]	Mensch [human]

Table 1: Examples of word-level minimal pairs.

3 Method: Semantic Subspaces

A common way to represent word-level semantic subspaces is based on a set P of so-called *minimal pairs*, i.e. N pairs of words $(w, \hat{w})$ that differ only in the semantic dimension of interest (Bolukbasi et al., 2016; Niu and Carpuat, 2017). Table 1 displays some examples of such word pairs for the profanity domain. Each word w is encoded as a word embedding $e(w)$:

$$P = \{(e(w_1), e(\hat{w}_1)), \ldots, (e(w_N), e(\hat{w}_N))\}$$

Then, each pair is normalized by a mean-shift:

$$\bar{P} = \{(e(w_i) - \mu_i, e(\hat{w}_i) - \mu_i) | 1 \leq i \leq N\}$$

where each $\mu_i = \frac{1}{2}(e(w_i) + e(\hat{w}_i))$.

Finally, PCA is performed on the set $\bar{P}$ and the most significant principal component (PC) is used as a representation of the semantic subspace.

We diverge from this approach in four ways:

Normalization We note that there is no convincing justification for the normalization step. As our experiments in the following sections show, we find that the profanity subspace is better represented by P than by $\bar{P}$. For our experiments, we thus distinguish three different types of representations:

- **BASE**: The raw featurized representation r.
- **PCA-RAW**: Featurized representation r projected onto the non-normalized subspace $S(P)$.

- **PCA-NORM**: Featurized representation r projected onto the normalized subspace $S(\bar{P})$.

Here, projecting a vector representation r onto a subspace is defined as the dot product $r \cdot S(P)$.

Number of Principal Components c The use of just a single PC as the best representation of the semantic subspace is not well motivated. This is recognized by Niu and Carpuat (2017) who experiment on the first $c = 1, 2, 4, \ldots, 512$ PC and report results on their downstream-task directly. However, a downside of their method for determining a good value for c is the requirement of a task-specific validation set which runs orthogonal to the assumption that a good semantic subspace should generalize well to many related tasks.

Instead, we propose the use of an *intrinsic evaluation* that requires no additional data to estimate a good value for c. Rothe et al. (2016) have shown that semantic subspaces are especially useful for classification tasks related to the semantic feature encoded in the subspace. Here, we argue the inverse: if a semantic subspace with c components yields the best performance on a related classification task, c should be an appropriate number of components to encode the semantic feature.

More specifically, we apply a classifier function $f(x) = y$, which learns to map a subspace-based representation $x = e \cdot S(P)$ to a label $y \in \{\text{profane}, \text{neutral}\}$. We learn $f(x)$ on the same set P used to learn the subspace. In order to evaluate on previously unseen entities, we employ 5-fold cross validation over the available list of minimal pairs P and evaluate Macro F1 on the held-out fold. Due to the simplicity of this intrinsic evaluation, the experiment can be performed for all values of c and the c yielding the highest average Macro F1 is selected as the final value. The above holds for P and $\bar{P}$ equally.

Sentence-Level Minimal Pairs We move the word-level approach to the sentence level. In this case, minimal pairs are made up of vector representations of sentences $(e(s), e(\hat{s}))$.

In order to standardize the approach and to focus the variation in the sentence representations on the profanity feature, sentence-level minimal pairs are constructed by keeping all words contained equivalent except for *significant words* that in themselves are minimal pairs for the semantic feature of interest. For instance, a sentence-level minimal pair for the *profanity* feature with significant words:

The food here is shitty.
The food here is disgusting.

Zero-Shot Transfer In order to evaluate how well profanity is encoded in the resulting word- and sentence-level subspaces, we test their generalization capabilities in a zero-shot classification setup. Given a subspace $S(P)$ (or $S(\bar{P})$), we train a classifier $f(x) = y$ to classify subspace-based representations $x = e \cdot S(P)$ as belonging to class $y \in \{\text{profane}|\text{neutral}\}$. The x used to train the classifier are the same entities in the minimal pairs used to learn $S(P)$. This classification task is the *source task* $\mathcal{T} = \{x, y\}$. As the classifier is learned on subspace-based representations, it should be able to generalize significantly better to previously unseen profanity-related tasks than a classifier learned on generic representations $x = e$ (Rothe et al., 2016). Given a previously unseen task $\bar{\mathcal{T}} = \{\bar{x}, \bar{y}\}$, we follow a **zero-shot transfer** approach and let classifier f, learned on source task $\mathcal{T}$ only, predict the new labels $\bar{y}$ given instances $\bar{x}$ without training it on data from $\bar{\mathcal{T}}$. The zero-shot generalization can be quantified by calculating the accuracy of the predicted labels $\hat{\bar{y}}$ given the gold labels $\bar{y}$. The extend of this zero-shot generalization capability can be tested by performing zero-shot classification on a variety of unseen tasks $\bar{\mathcal{T}}$ with variable task distances $\bar{\mathcal{T}} \Leftrightarrow \mathcal{T}$.

4 Experimental Setup

4.1 Data

Word Lists The minimal-pairs used in our experiments are derived from a German slur collection[2].

Fine-Tuning We use the German, English, French and Arabic portions of a large collection of tweets[3] collected between 2013–2018 to fine-tune BERT. For the German BERT model, all available German tweets are used, while the multilingual BERT is fine-tuned on a balanced corpus of 5M tweets per language. For validation during fine-tuning, we set aside $1k$ tweets per language.

Target Tasks We test our sentence-level representations, which are used to train a *neutral/profane* classifier on a subset of minimal pairs, on several hate speech benchmarks. For all four languages, we focus on a distant task DT (*neutral/hate*). For

[2] `www.hyperhero.com/de/insults.htm`
[3] `www.archive.org/details/twitterstream`

Corpus	# Sentences	# Tokens
Fine-Tuning		
Twitter-DE	5(9)M	45(85)M
Twitter-EN	5M	44M
Twitter-FR	5M	58M
Twitter-AR	5M	75M
Target Tasks		
DE-ST	111/111	1509/1404
DE-DT	2061/970	14187/9333
EN-ST	93/93	1409/1313
EN-DT	288/865	8032/3647
AR-ST	12/12	164/84
AR-DT	46/54	592/506
FR-DT	5822/302	49654/2660

Table 2: Number of sentences and tokens of the data used for fine-tuning BERT for the sentence-level experiments. Target task test sets are reported with their respective *neutral/hate* (DT) and *neutral/profane* (ST) distributions.

German, English and Arabic we additionally evaluate on a similar task ST (*neutral/profane*), for which we removed additional classes (*insult*, *abuse* etc.) from the original finer-grained data labels and downsampled to the minority class (*profane*).

For German (DE), we use the test sets of GermEval-2019 (Struß et al., 2019) Subtask 1 (*Other/Offense*) and Subtask 2 (*Other/Profanity*) for DT and ST respectively. For English (EN), we use the HASOC (Mandl et al., 2019) Subtask A (*NOT/HOF*) and Subtask B (*NOT/PRFN*) for DT and ST respectively. French (FR) is tested on the hate speech portion (*None/Hate*) of the corpus created by Charitidis et al. (2020) for DT only, while Arabic (AR) is tested on Mubarak et al. (2017) for DT (*Clean/Obscene+Offense*) and ST (*Clean/Obscene*). As AR has no official train/test splits, we use the last 100 samples for testing. The training data of these corpora is not used.

Table 2 summarizes the data used for fine-tuning as well as testing.

Pre-processing The Twitter corpora for fine-tuning were pre-processed by filtering out incompletely loaded tweets and duplicates. We also applied language detection using `spacy` to further remove tweets that consisted of mainly emojis or tweets that were written in other languages.

4.2 Model Specifications

To achieve good coverage of profane language, we use 300-dimensional German FastText embeddings (Deriu et al., 2017) trained on 50M German tweets for the word-level experiments in Section 5.

The BERT models (Devlin et al., 2019) used in Section 6 are `Bert-Base-German-Cased`[4] and `Bert-Base-Multilingual-Cased` for the monolingual and multilingual experiments respectively, since they pose strong baselines. We fine-tune on the Twitter data (Section 4.1) using the masked language modeling objective and early stopping over the evaluation loss ($\delta = 0$, patience $= 3$). All classification experiments use Linear Discriminant Analysis (LDA) as the classifier.

5 Word-Level Subspaces

Before moving to the lesser explored sentence-level subspaces, we first verify whether word-level semantic subspaces can also capture complex semantic features such as profanity.

5.1 Minimal Pairs

Staying within the general low-resource setting prevalent in hate speech and profanity domains, and to keep manual annotation effort low, we randomly sample a small amount of words from the German slur lists, namely 100, and manually map these to their neutral counterparts (Table 1). We focus this list on nouns describing humans.

Each word in our minimal pairs is featurized using its word embedding, this is our BASE representation. We learn PCA-RAW and PCA-NORM representations on the embedded minimal pairs.

5.2 Classification

We evaluate how well the resulting representations BASE, PCA-RAW and PCA-NORM encode information about the profanity of a word by focusing on a related word classification task where unseen words are classified as *neutral* or *profane*. To evaluate how efficient the subspaces can be learned in a low-resource setting, we downsample the list of minimal pairs to learn the subspace-based representations and the classification task to 10–100 word pairs. After the preliminary exploration of the number of principal components (PC) required to represent profanity, the number of PC for the final representations lie within a range of 15–111. Each experiment is run over 5 seeded runs and we report the average F1 Macro with standard error. As each seeded run resamples the training and test data, the standard error is also a good indicator

[4] `www.deepset.ai/german-bert`

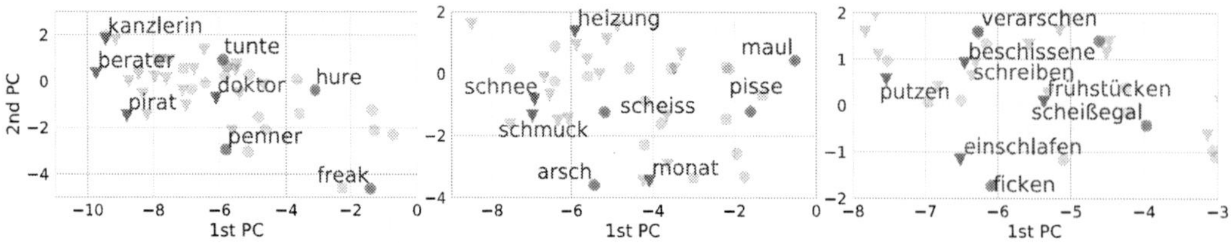

Figure 1: Projections of profane and neutral words from TL-1 (left), TL-2 (middle) and TL-3 (right) onto a word-level profane subspace learned by PCA-NORM on 10 minimal pairs (● Profane, ▼ Neutral).

of the variability of the method when trained on different subsets of minimal pairs.

Test Lists For this evaluation, we create three test lists (TL-{1,2,3}) of profane and neutral words. The contents of the three TLs are defined by their decreasing relatedness to the list of minimal pairs used for learning the subspace, which are nouns describing humans. TL-1 is thus also a list of nouns describing humans, TL-2 contains random nouns not describing humans, and TL-3 contains verbs and adjectives. The three TLs are created by randomly sampling from the word embeddings that underlie the subspace representations and adding matching words to TL-{1,2,3} until they each contain 25 profane and 25 neutral words, i.e. 150 in total.

Projecting the TLs onto the first and second PC of the PCA-NORM subspace learned on 10 minimal pairs suggests that a separation of profane and neutral words can be achieved for nouns describing humans (TL-1), while it is more difficult for less related words (TL-{2,3}) (Figure 1).

Results Across all TLs, the subspace-based representations outperform the generalist BASE representations (Figure 2), with PCA-NORM reaching F1-Macro scores of up to 96.0 (TL-1), 89.9 (TL-2) and 100 (TL-3) when trained on 90 word pairs. This suggests that they generalize well to unseen nouns describing humans as well as verbs and adjectives, while generalizing less to nouns not describing humans (TL-2). This may be due to TL-2 consisting of some less frequent compounds (e.g. Großmaul [big mouth]). PCA-NORM and PCA-RAW perform equally on TL-1 and TL-3, while PCA-NORM is slightly stronger on the mid-resource (50-90 pairs) range on TL-2. This suggests that the normalization step when constructing the profane subspace is only marginally beneficial. Even when the training data is very limited (10–40 pairs), the standard errors are decently small (F1 $\pm$1–5), indicating that the choice of minimal pairs has only a small impact on the downstream model performance. When more training data is available (80–100 pairs), the influence of a single minimal pair becomes less pronounced and thus the standard error decreases significantly.

5.3 Substitution

We use the profane subspace S_{prf} to substitute a profane word w with a neutral counterpart $\hat{w}$. We do this by removing S_{prf} from w,

$$\hat{w} = \frac{w - S_{\text{prf}}}{||w - S_{\text{prf}}||} \tag{1}$$

and replacing it by its new nearest neighbor $\text{NN}(\hat{w})$ in the word embeddings. Here, we focus on the PCA-NORM subspace learned on 10 minimal pairs only. We use this subspace to substitute all profane words in TL-{1,2,3}.

Human Evaluation To analyze the similarity and profanity of the substitutions, we perform a small human evaluation. Four annotators were asked to rate the similarity of profane words and their substitutions, and also to give a profanity score between 1 (not similar/profane) and 10 (very similar/profane) to words from a mixed list of slurs and substitutions.

Original profane words were rated with an average of 6.1 on the **profanity** scale, while substitutions were rated significantly lower, with an average rating of 1.9. Minor differences exist across TL splits, with TL-1 dropping from 6.8 to 1.3, TL-2 from 6.1 to 3.1 and TL-3 from 5.4 to 2.1.

The average **similarity** rating between profane words and their substitution differs strongly across different TLs. TL-1 has the lowest average rating of 2.8, while TL-2 has a rating of 3.3 and TL-3 a rating of 5.1. This is surprising, since the subspaces generalized well to TL-1 on the classification task.

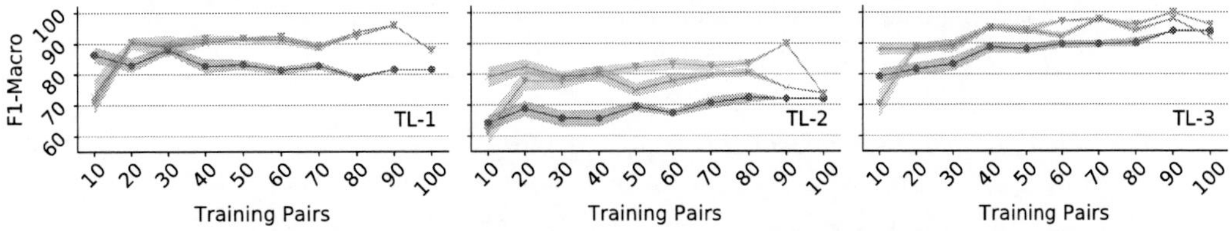

Figure 2: F1-Macro of the LDA models, using BASE or PCA-{RAW,NORM} representations on the word classification task based on 10 to 100 training word pairs (—•— BASE, —*— PCA-NORM, —*— PCA-RAW).

Word w	NN(w)	NN($\hat{w}$)
Scheisse [shit]	Scheiße, Scheissse, Scheissse04, Scheißee	schrecklich, augenscheinlich, schwerlich, schwesterlich [horrible, evidently, hardly, sisterly]
Spast [dumbass]	Kackspsst, Spasti, Vollspast, Dummerspast	Mann, Mensch, Familienmensch, Menschn [man, person, family person, people]
Bitch	x6bitch, bitchs, bitchin, bitchhh	Frau, Afrikanerin, Mann, Amerikanerin [woman, african, man, american]
Arschloch [asshole]	Narschloch, Arschlochs, Arschloc, learschloch	Mann, Frau, Lebenspartnerin, Menschwesen [man, woman, significant other, human creature]
Fresse [cakehole]	Fresser, Schnauze, Kackfufresse, Schnauzefresse	Frau, Mann, Lebensgefährtin, Rentnerin [woman, man, significant other, retiree]

Table 3: Profane words w with top 4 NNs before (NN(w)) and after (NN($\hat{w}$)) removal of the profane subspace.

Qualitative Analysis To understand the quality of the substitutions, especially on TL-1, which has obtained the lowest similarity score in the human evaluation, we perform a small qualitative analysis on 3 words sampled from TL-1 (*Spast, Bitch, Arschloch*) and 1 word sampled from TL-2 (*Fresse*) and TL-3 (*Scheiss*) each. Before removal, the nearest neighbors (NNs, Table 3) of the sampled offensive words were mostly orthographic variations (e.g. *Scheisse* [shit] vs. *Scheiße*) or compounds of the same word (e.g. *Spast* [dumbass] vs. *Vollspast* [complete dumbass]). After removal, the NNs are still negative but not profane (e.g. *Scheisse* →*schrecklich* [horrible]). While the first NNs are decent counterparts, later NNs introduce other (gender, ethnic, etc.) biases, possibly stemming from the word embeddings or from the minimal pairs used to learn the subspace. The counterparts to *Scheisse* [shit] seem to focus around the phonetics of the word (all words contain *sch*), which may also be due to the poor representation of adjectives in embedding spaces. *Fresse* [cakehole] is ambiguous[5], thus the subspace does not entirely capture it and the new NNs are neutral, but unrelated words.

While human similarity ratings on TL-1 were low, qualitative analysis shows that these can still be reasonable. The low rating on TL-1 may be due to annotators' reluctance to equate human-referencing slurs to neutral counterparts.

The ability to automatically find neutral alternatives to slurs may lead to practical applications such as the suggestion of alternative wordings.

6 Sentence-Level Subspaces

In Section 5, we identified profane subspaces on the word-level. However, abuse mostly happens on the sentence and discourse-level and is not limited to the use of isolated profane words. Therefore, we move this method to the sentence-level, exploring the two subspace-based representation types PCA-RAW and PCA-NORM. Concretely, we learn sentence-level profane subspaces that allow a context-sensitive representation and thus go beyond isolated profane words, and verify their efficacy to represent *profanity*. Similarly to the word-level experiments, we focus our analysis on the ability of the subspaces to generalize to similar (*neutral/profane*) and distant (*neutral/hate*) tasks. We compare their performance with a BERT-encoded BASE representation, which does not use a semantic subspace.

6.1 Minimal Pairs

Using the German slur collection, we identify tweets in Twitter-DE containing swearwords, from which we then take 100 random samples. We create a neutral counterpart by manually replacing significant words, i.e. swearwords, with a neutral

[5] *Fresse* can mean *shut up*, as well as being a pejorative for *face* and *eating*.

variation while keeping the rest of the tweet as is:

a) *ich darf das nicht verkacken!!!*
[I must not fuck this up!!!]]

b) *ich darf das nicht vermasseln!!!*
[I must not mess this up!!!]

6.2 Monolingual Zero-Shot Transfer

We validate the generalization of the German sentence-level subspaces to a similar (*profane*) and distant (*hate*) domain by zero-shot transferring them to unseen German target tasks and analyzing their performance.

6.2.1 Representation Types

We fine-tune `Bert-Base-German-Cased` on Twitter-DE (9M Tweets). Each sentence in our list of minimal pairs is then encoded using the fine-tuned German BERT and its sentence representation $s = \text{mean}(\{h_1, ..., h_T\})$ is the mean over the T encoder hidden states h. This is our BASE representation. We further train PCA-RAW and PCA-NORM on a subset of our minimal pairs. We chose 14–96 PCs for PCA-RAW and 9–94 PCs for PCA-NORM depending on the size of the subset of minimal pairs used to generate the subspace.

6.2.2 Results

We train the PCA-RAW and PCA-NORM representations on subsets of increasing size $(10, 20, \ldots, 100$ minimal pairs). For each subset and representation type (BASE, PCA-RAW, PCA-NORM), we train an LDA model to identify whether a sentence in the subset of minimal pairs is neutral or profane. These models are zero-shot transferred to the German similar task ST (*neutral/profane*) and distant task DT (*neutral/hate*). We report the average F1-Macro and standard error over 5 seeded runs, where each run resamples its train and test data.

ST: Similar Task Despite the fact that the LDA models were never trained on the target task data, the PCA-RAW and PCA-NORM representations yield high peaks in F1 when trained on 50 (F1 68.9, PCA-RAW) minimal pairs and tested on DE-ST (Figure 3). PCA-RAW outperforms PCA-NORM for almost all data sizes. PCA-RAW outperforms the BERT (BASE) representations especially on the very low-resource setting (10–60 pairs), with an increase of F1 $+14.2$ at 40 pairs. Once the training size reaches 70 pairs, the differences in F1 become smaller. The subspace-based representations are especially useful for the low-resource scenario.

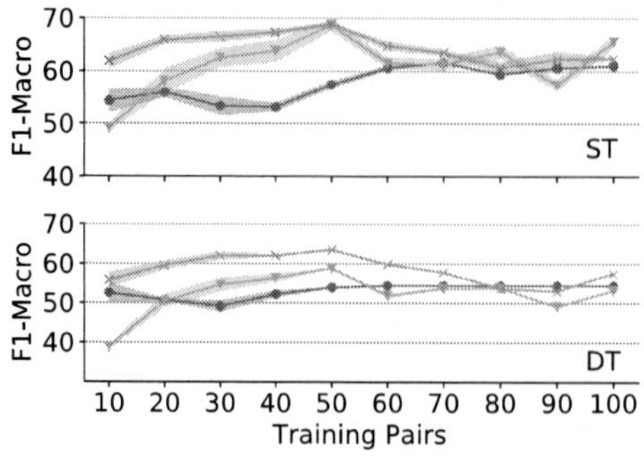

Figure 3: F1-Macro of the LDA models, zero-shot transferred to the similar (top) and distant (bottom) German tasks (BASE, PCA-NORM, PCA-RAW).

DT: Distant Task For the distant task DT, the general F1 scores are lower than for the similar task ST. However, PCA-RAW still reaches a Macro-F1 of 63.5 at 50 pairs for DE-DT. This indicates that the profane subspace found by PCA-RAW partially generalizes to a broader, offensive subspace. Similar to ST, the projected PCA-RAW representations are especially useful in the low-resource case up to 50 sentences. The F1 of the BERT baseline is well below the PCA-RAW representations when data is sparse, with a major gap of F1 $+10.9$ at 30 pairs for DE-DT. The classifier using BASE representations stays around F1 53.0 (DE-DT) and does not benefit from more data, indicating that these representations do not generalize to the target tasks. However, once normalization (PCA-NORM) is added, the generalization is also lost and we see a drop in performance around or below the baseline. As for ST, all three representation types level out once higher amounts of data (70–80 pairs) are reached.

The standard errors show a similar trend to those in the word-level experiments: we observe a small standard error when training data is sparse (10–40 pairs), indicating that the choice of minimal pairs has a small impact on the subspace quality, which decreases further when more minimal pairs are available for training (50–100 pairs).

6.3 Zero-Shot Cross-Lingual Transfer

To verify whether the subspaces also generalize to other languages, we zero-shot transfer and test the German BASE, PCA-RAW and PCA-NORM representations on the similar and distant tasks of closely-related (English), distantly-related (French) and non-related (Arabic) languages. For French, we only test on DT due to a lack of data for ST.

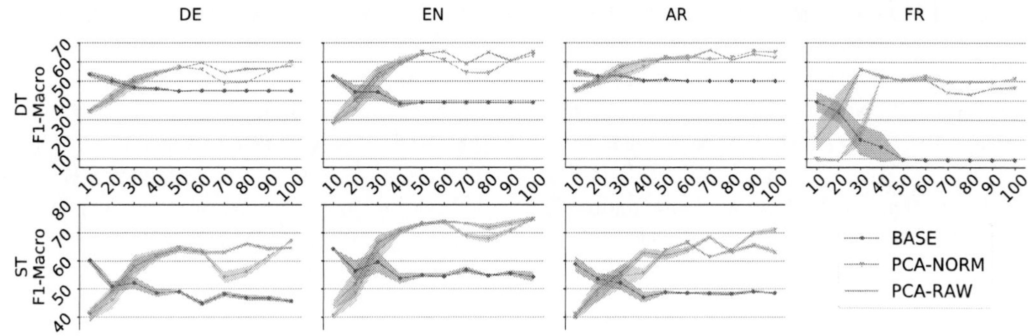

Figure 4: F1-Macro of the LDA model, using BASE or PCA-{RAW,NORM} representations, zero-shot transferred to the similar (bottom) and distant (top) German, English, Arabic and French tasks.

6.3.1 Representation Types

The setup is the same as in Section 6.2.1, except for using `Bert-Base-Multilingual-Cased` and fine-tuning it on a corpus consisting of the 5M {DE,EN,FR,AR} tweets. The resulting model is used to generate the hidden-representations needed to construct the BASE, PCA-RAW and PCA-NORM representations. After performing 5-fold cross validation, the optimal number of PC is determined. Depending on the number of minimal pairs, the resulting subspace sizes lie between 8–67 (PCA-RAW) and 10–44 (PCA-NORM).

6.3.2 Results

As in Section 6.2.2, we train on increasingly large subsets of the German minimal pairs.

ST: Similar Task We test the generalization of the German representations on the similar (*neutral/profane*) task on EN-ST and AR-ST as well as DE-ST for reference. Note that the LDA classifiers were trained on the German minimal pairs only, without access to target task data.

The trends on the three test sets are very similar to each other (Figure 4, bottom), indicating that the German profane subspaces transfer not only to the closely-related English, but also to the unrelated Arabic data. For all three languages, the PCA-{RAW,NORM} methods tend to grow in performance with increasing data until around 40 sentence pairs when the method seems to converge. This yields a performance of F1 66.1 on DE-ST at 80 pairs, F1 74.9 on EN-ST at 100 pairs and F1 68.4 on AR-ST at 70 pairs for PCA-RAW.

Overall, larger amounts of pairs are needed to reach top-performance in comparison to the monolingual case. This trend is also present when testing on DE-ST, leading us to posit that it is caused not by the cross-lingual transfer itself, but by the different underlying BERT models used to generate the initial representations. The differences in F1 between PCA-RAW and PCA-NORM are mere fluctuations between the two methods. The BASE representations are favorable only at 10 training pairs, with more data they overfit on the source task and are outperformed by the subspace representations, with differences of F1 +20.6 at 100 sentence pairs (PCA-RAW) on EN-ST, and F1 +22.4 at 100 sentence pairs (PCA-NORM) on AR-ST.

DT: Distant Task Similar trends to ST are observed on the distant (*neutral/hate*) tasks (Figure 4, top). While the BASE representations are strongest at 10 sentence pairs, they are outperformed by the subspace-based representations at around 30 pairs. PCA-RAW outperforms PCA-NORM and peaks at F1 59.6 (60 pairs), F1 65.6 (60 pairs), F1 66.2 (70 pairs) and F1 56.1 (30 pairs) for the German, English, Arabic and French test sets respectively.

We conclude that the German profane subspaces are transferable not only monolingually or to closely-related languages (English) but also to distantly-related (French) and non-related languages (Arabic), making a zero-shot transfer possible on both similar (neutral/profane) and distant tasks (neutral/hate). The BERT embeddings, on the other hand, were not able to perform the initial transfer, i.e. from minimal-pair training to similar and distant target tasks, thus making the transfer to other languages futile. Subspace-based representations are a powerful tool to fill this gap, especially for classifiers trained on small amounts of source target data and zero-shot transfer to related tasks.

External Comparison The transfer capabilities of our subspace-based models can be set into perspective by comparing them to state-of-the-art classification models that were trained directly on our target tasks. For **DT**, the top scoring team on EN-DT reaches higher levels of F1 (75.6) (Mandl et al., 2019) than our best PCA-RAW representations (F1 65.6). Similarly, the top scoring model on CHS-FR (Charitidis et al., 2020) lies at F1 82.0 and thus F1 +25.9 over PCA-RAW. However, PCA-RAW outperforms the best-performing model reported in Mubarak et al. (2017) (F1 60.0) by F1 +6.2. Note, however, that this comparison is vague, as there is no standard train-test split for AR. For ST, no direct comparison to SOTA models can be made, since the profane-neutral classification task is usually part of a larger multi-class classification task. Nevertheless, the success of simple subspace-based LDA models, trained on very small amounts of task-distant German data, at cross-lingually zero-shot transferring to various tasks underlines the generalization capability of our approach.

6.4 Qualitative Analysis

A qualitative per-task analysis of the errors of the best performing models (PCA-RAW) reveals that some of the gold labels are debatable. The subjectivity of hate speech is a well-known issue for automatic detection tasks. Here, it is especially observable for EN, AR and FR, where arguably offensive comments were annotated as neutral but classified as offensive by our model:

> *C'est toi la pute. Va voir ta mère*
> *[You are the whore. Go see your mom]*

We find that the models tend to over-blacklist tweets across languages as most errors stem from classifying neutrally-labeled tweets as offensive. This is triggered by negative words, e.g. *crime*, as well as words related to religion, race and politics, e.g.:

> *No Good Friday agreement, no deals with Trump.*

7 Conclusion and Future Work

In this work, we have shown that a complex feature such as *profanity* can be encoded using semantic subspaces on the word and sentence-level.

On the **word-level**, we found that the subspace-based representations are able to generalize to previously unseen words. Using the profane subspace, we were able to substitute previously unseen profane words with neutral counterparts.

On the **sentence-level**, we have tested the generalization of our subspace-based representations (PCA-RAW, PCA-NORM) against raw BERT representations (BASE) in a zero-shot transfer setting on both similar (*neutral/profane*) and distant (*neutral/hate*) tasks. While the BASE representations failed to zero-shot transfer to the target tasks, the subspace-based representations were able to perform the transfer to both similar and distant tasks, not only monolingually, but also to the closely-related (English), distantly-related (French) and non-related (Arabic) language tasks. We observe major improvements between F1 +10.9 (PCA-RAW on DE-DT) and F1 +42.9 (PCA-NORM on FR-DT) over the BASE representations in all scenarios. As our experiments have shown that the commonly used mean-shift normalization is not required, we plan to conduct further experiments using unaligned significant words/sentences.

The code, the fine-tuned models, and the list of minimal-pairs are made publicly available[6].

Acknowledgements

We want to thank the annotators Susann Boy, Dominik Godt and Fabian Gössl. We also thank Badr Abdullah, Michael Hedderich, Jyotsna Singh and the anonymous reviewers for their valuable feedback. The project on which this paper is based was funded by the DFG under the funding code WI 4204/3-1. Responsibility for the content of this publication is with the authors.

References

Ibrahim Abu Farha and Walid Magdy. 2020. Multi-task learning for Arabic offensive language and hate-speech detection. In *Proceedings of the 4th Workshop on Open-Source Arabic Corpora and Processing Tools, with a Shared Task on Offensive Language Detection*, pages 86–90, Marseille, France. European Language Resource Association.

Valerio Basile, Cristina Bosco, Elisabetta Fersini, Debora Nozza, Viviana Patti, Francisco Manuel Rangel Pardo, Paolo Rosso, and Manuela Sanguinetti. 2019. SemEval-2019 task 5: Multilingual detection of hate speech against immigrants and women in Twitter. In *Proceedings of the 13th International Workshop on Semantic Evaluation*, pages 54–63, Minneapolis, Minnesota, USA. Association for Computational Linguistics.

[6] `www.github.com/uds-lsv/profane_subspaces`

Tolga Bolukbasi, Kai-Wei Chang, James Zou, Venkatesh Saligrama, and Adam Kalai. 2016. Man is to computer programmer as woman is to homemaker? debiasing word embeddings. In *Proceedings of the 30th International Conference on Neural Information Processing Systems*, NIPS'16, page 4356–4364, Red Hook, NY, USA. Curran Associates Inc.

Polychronis Charitidis, Stavros Doropoulos, Stavros Vologiannidis, Ioannis Papastergiou, and Sophia Karakeva. 2020. Towards countering hate speech and personal attack in social media. *Online Social Networks and Media*, 17:100071.

Alexis Conneau, Kartikay Khandelwal, Naman Goyal, Vishrav Chaudhary, Guillaume Wenzek, Francisco Guzmán, Edouard Grave, Myle Ott, Luke Zettlemoyer, and Veselin Stoyanov. 2020. Unsupervised cross-lingual representation learning at scale. In *Proceedings of the 58th Annual Meeting of the Association for Computational Linguistics*, pages 8440–8451, Online. Association for Computational Linguistics.

Jan Deriu, Aurelien Lucchi, Valeria De Luca, Aliaksei Severyn, Simon Müller, Mark Cieliebak, Thomas Hofmann, and Martin Jaggi. 2017. Leveraging Large Amounts of Weakly Supervised Data for Multi-Language Sentiment Classification. In *WWW 2017 - International World Wide Web Conference*, page 1045–1052, Perth, Australia.

Jacob Devlin, Ming-Wei Chang, Kenton Lee, and Kristina Toutanova. 2019. BERT: Pre-training of deep bidirectional transformers for language understanding. In *Proceedings of the 2019 Conference of the North American Chapter of the Association for Computational Linguistics: Human Language Technologies, Volume 1 (Long and Short Papers)*, pages 4171–4186, Minneapolis, Minnesota. Association for Computational Linguistics.

Hila Gonen and Yoav Goldberg. 2019. Lipstick on a pig: Debiasing methods cover up systematic gender biases in word embeddings but do not remove them. In *Proceedings of the 2019 Conference of the North American Chapter of the Association for Computational Linguistics: Human Language Technologies, Volume 1 (Long and Short Papers)*, pages 609–614, Minneapolis, Minnesota. Association for Computational Linguistics.

Junjie Hu, Sebastian Ruder, Aditya Siddhant, Graham Neubig, Orhan Firat, and Melvin Johnson. 2020. Xtreme: A massively multilingual multi-task benchmark for evaluating cross-lingual generalization. *CoRR*, abs/2003.11080.

Paul Pu Liang, Irene Li, Emily Zheng, Yao Chong Lim, Ruslan Salakhutdinov, and Louis-Philippe Morency. 2020. Towards debiasing sentence representations. In *Proceedings of the 58th Annual Meeting of the Association for Computational Linguistics*, page 5502–5515, Online.

Thomas Mandl, Sandip Modha, Prasenjit Majumder, Daksh Patel, Mohana Dave, Chintak Mandlia, and Aditya Patel. 2019. Overview of the hasoc track at fire 2019: Hate speech and offensive content identification in indo-european languages. In *Proceedings of the 11th Forum for Information Retrieval Evaluation*, FIRE '19, page 14–17, New York, NY, USA. Association for Computing Machinery.

Thomas Manzini, Lim Yao Chong, Alan W Black, and Yulia Tsvetkov. 2019. Black is to criminal as caucasian is to police: Detecting and removing multiclass bias in word embeddings. In *Proceedings of the 2019 Conference of the North American Chapter of the Association for Computational Linguistics: Human Language Technologies, Volume 1 (Long and Short Papers)*, pages 615–621, Minneapolis, Minnesota. Association for Computational Linguistics.

Hamdy Mubarak, Kareem Darwish, and Walid Magdy. 2017. Abusive language detection on Arabic social media. In *Proceedings of the First Workshop on Abusive Language Online*, pages 52–56, Vancouver, BC, Canada. Association for Computational Linguistics.

Xing Niu and Marine Carpuat. 2017. Discovering stylistic variations in distributional vector space models via lexical paraphrases. In *Proceedings of the Workshop on Stylistic Variation*, pages 20–27, Copenhagen, Denmark. Association for Computational Linguistics.

Nedjma Ousidhoum, Zizheng Lin, Hongming Zhang, Yangqiu Song, and Dit-Yan Yeung. 2019. Multilingual and multi-aspect hate speech analysis. In *Proceedings of the 2019 Conference on Empirical Methods in Natural Language Processing and the 9th International Joint Conference on Natural Language Processing (EMNLP-IJCNLP)*, pages 4675–4684, Hong Kong, China. Association for Computational Linguistics.

Shauli Ravfogel, Yanai Elazar, Hila Gonen, Michael Twiton, and Yoav Goldberg. 2020. Null it out: Guarding protected attributes by iterative nullspace projection. In *Proceedings of the 58th Annual Meeting of the Association for Computational Linguistics*, pages 7237–7256, Online. Association for Computational Linguistics.

Sascha Rothe, Sebastian Ebert, and Hinrich Schütze. 2016. Ultradense word embeddings by orthogonal transformation. In *Proceedings of the 2016 Conference of the North American Chapter of the Association for Computational Linguistics: Human Language Technologies*, pages 767–777, San Diego, California. Association for Computational Linguistics.

Julia Maria Struß, Melanie Siegel, Josef Ruppenhofer, Michael Wiegand, and Manfred Klenner. 2019. Overview of germeval task 2, 2019 shared task on the identification of offensive language.

In *Preliminary proceedings of the 15th Conference on Natural Language Processing (KONVENS 2019), October 9 – 11, 2019 at Friedrich-Alexander-Universität Erlangen-Nürnberg*, pages 352 – 363, München [u.a.]. German Society for Computational Linguistics & Language Technology und Friedrich-Alexander-Universität Erlangen-Nürnberg.

Ashish Vaswani, Noam Shazeer, Niki Parmar, Jakob Uszkoreit, Llion Jones, Aidan N Gomez, Ł ukasz Kaiser, and Illia Polosukhin. 2017. Attention is all you need. In *Advances in Neural Information Processing Systems*, volume 30, pages 5998–6008. Curran Associates, Inc.

Zeerak Waseem. 2016. Are you a racist or am i seeing things? annotator influence on hate speech detection on twitter. In *Proceedings of the First Workshop on NLP and Computational Social Science*, pages 138–142, Austin, Texas. Association for Computational Linguistics.

Zeerak Waseem and Dirk Hovy. 2016. Hateful symbols or hateful people? predictive features for hate speech detection on twitter. In *Proceedings of the NAACL Student Research Workshop*, pages 88–93, San Diego, California. Association for Computational Linguistics.

Marcos Zampieri, Preslav Nakov, Sara Rosenthal, Pepa Atanasova, Georgi Karadzhov, Hamdy Mubarak, Leon Derczynski, Zeses Pitenis, and Çağrı Çöltekin. 2020. SemEval-2020 task 12: Multilingual offensive language identification in social media (OffensEval 2020). In *Proceedings of the Fourteenth Workshop on Semantic Evaluation*, pages 1425–1447, Barcelona (online). International Committee for Computational Linguistics.

HateBERT: Retraining BERT for Abusive Language Detection in English

Tommaso Caselli[♣], **Valerio Basile**[¶], **Jelena Mitrović**[♡], **Michael Granitzer**[♡]
[♣] University of Groningen [¶] University of Turin [♡] University of Passau
[♣] t.caselli@rug.nl [¶] valerio.basile@unito.it
[♡] {jelena.mitrovic, michael.granitzer}@uni-passau.de

Abstract

We introduce HateBERT, a re-trained BERT model for abusive language detection in English. The model was trained on RAL-E, a large-scale dataset of Reddit comments in English from communities banned for being offensive, abusive, or hateful that we have curated and made available to the public. We present the results of a detailed comparison between a general pre-trained language model and the retrained version on three English datasets for offensive, abusive language and hate speech detection tasks. In all datasets, HateBERT outperforms the corresponding general BERT model. We also discuss a battery of experiments comparing the portability of the fine-tuned models across the datasets, suggesting that portability is affected by compatibility of the annotated phenomena.

1 Introduction

The development of systems for the automatic identification of abusive language phenomena has followed a common trend in NLP: feature-based linear classifiers (Waseem and Hovy, 2016; Ribeiro et al., 2018; Ibrohim and Budi, 2019), neural network architectures (e.g., CNN or Bi-LSTM) (Kshirsagar et al., 2018; Mishra et al., 2018; Mitrović et al., 2019; Sigurbergsson and Derczynski, 2020), and fine-tuning pre-trained language models, e.g., BERT, RoBERTa, a.o., (Liu et al., 2019; Swamy et al., 2019). Results vary both across datasets and architectures, with linear classifiers qualifying as very competitive, if not better, when compared to neural networks. On the other hand, systems based on pre-trained language models have reached new state-of-the-art results. One issue with these pre-trained models is that the training language variety makes them well suited for general-purpose language understanding tasks, and it highlights their limits with more domain-specific language varieties. To address this, there is a growing interest in generating domain-specific BERT-like pre-trained language models, such as AlBERTo (Polignano et al., 2019) or TweetEval (Barbieri et al., 2020) for Twitter, BioBERT for the biomedical domain in English (Lee et al., 2019), FinBERT for the financial domain in English (Yang et al., 2020), and LEGAL-BERT for the legal domain in English (Chalkidis et al., 2020). We introduce HateBERT, a pre-trained BERT model for abusive language phenomena in social media in English.

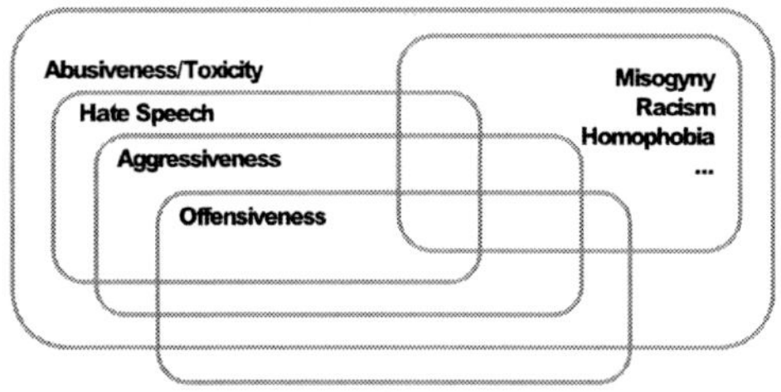

Figure 1: Abusive language phenomena and their relationships (adapted from Poletto et al. (2020)).

Abusive language phenomena fall along a wide spectrum including, a.o., microaggression, stereotyping, offense, abuse, hate speech, threats, and doxxing (Jurgens et al., 2019). Current approaches have focus on a limited range, namely offensive language, abusive language, and hate speech. The connections among these phenomena have only superficially been accounted for, resulting in a fragmented picture, with a variety of definitions, and (in)compatible annotations (Waseem et al., 2017). Poletto et al. (2020) introduce a graphical visualisation (Figure 1) of the connections among abusive language phenomena according to the definitions in previous work (Waseem and Hovy, 2016; Fortuna and Nunes, 2018; Malmasi and Zampieri, 2018; Basile et al., 2019; Zampieri et al., 2019). When it comes to offensive language, abusive language, and hate speech, the distinguishing factor is their level of specificity. This makes offensive language

Proceedings of the Fifth Workshop on Online Abuse and Harms, pages 17–25
August 6, 2021.

the most generic form of abusive language phenomena and hate speech the most specific, with abusive language being somewhere in the middle. Such differences are a major issue for the study of portability of models. Previous work (Karan and Šnajder, 2018; Benk, 2019; Pamungkas and Patti, 2019; Rizoiu et al., 2019) has addressed this task by conflating portability with generalizability, forcing datasets with different phenomena into homogenous annotations by collapsing labels into (binary) macro-categories. In our portability experiments, we show that the behavior of HateBERT can be explained by accounting for these difference in specificity across the abusive language phenomena.

Our key contributions are: (i.) additional evidence that further pre-training is a viable strategy to obtain domain-specific or language variety-oriented models in a fast and cheap way; (ii.) the release of HateBERT, a pre-trained BERT for abusive language phenomena, intended to boost research in this area; (iii.) the release of a large-scale dataset of social media posts in English from communities banned for being offensive, abusive, or hateful.

2 HateBERT: Re-training BERT with Abusive Online Communities

Further pre-training of transformer based pre-trained language models is becoming more and more popular as a competitive, effective, and fast solution to adapt pre-trained language models to new language varieties or domains (Barbieri et al., 2020; Lee et al., 2019; Yang et al., 2020; Chalkidis et al., 2020), especially in cases where raw data are scarce to generate a BERT-like model from scratch (Gururangan et al., 2020). This is the case of abusive language phenomena. However, for these phenomena an additional predicament with respect to previous work is that the options for suitable and representative collections of data are very limited. Directly scraping messages containing profanities would not be the best option as lots of potentially useful data may be missed. Graumas et al. (2019) have used tweets about controversial topics to generate offensive-loaded embeddings, but their approach presents some limits. On the other hand, Merenda et al. (2018) have shown the effectiveness of using messages from potentially abusive-oriented on-line communities to generate so-called *hate embeddings*. More recently, Papakyriakopoulos et al. (2020) have shown that biased word embeddings can be beneficial. We follow the idea of exploiting biased embeddings by creating them using messages from banned communities in Reddit.

RAL-E: the Reddit Abusive Language English dataset Reddit is a popular social media outlet where users share and discuss content. The website is organized into user-created and user-moderated communities known as *subreddits*, being *de facto* on-line communities. In 2015, Reddit strengthened its content policies and banned several subreddits (Chandrasekharan et al., 2017). We retrieved a large list of banned communities in English from different sources including official posts by the Reddit administrators and Wikipedia pages.[1] We then selected only communities that were banned for being deemed to host or promote offensive, abusive, and/or hateful content (e.g., expressing harassment, bullying, inciting/promoting violence, inciting/promoting hate). We collected the posts from these communities by crawling a publicly available collection of Reddit comments.[2] For each post, we kept only the text and the name of the community. The resulting collection comprises 1,492,740 messages from a period between January 2012 and June 2015, for a total of 43,820,621 tokens. The vocabulary of RAL-E is composed of 342,377 types and the average post length is 32.25 tokens. We further check the presence of explicit signals of abusive language phenomena using a list of offensive words. We selected all words with an offensiveness scores equal or higher than 0.75 from Wiegand et al. (2018)'s dictionary. We found that explicit offensive terms represent 1.2% of the tokens and that only 260,815 messages contain at least one offensive term. RAL-E is skewed since not all communities have the same amount of messages. The list of selected communities with their respective number of retrieved messages is reported in Table A.1 and the top 10 offensive terms are illustrated in Table A.2 in Appendix A.

Creating HateBERT From the RAL-E dataset, we used 1,478,348 messages (for a total of 43,379,350 tokens) to re-train the English BERT `base-uncased` model[3] by applying the Masked Language Model (MLM) objective. The remaining 149,274 messages (441,271 tokens) have been used as test set. We retrained for 100 epochs (al-

[1] https://en.wikipedia.org/wiki/Controversial_Reddit_communities

[2] https://www.reddit.com/r/datasets/comments/3bxlg7/i_have_every_publicly_available_reddit_comment/

[3] We used the pre-trained model available via the huggingface Transformers library - https://github.com/huggingface/transformers

most 2 million steps) in batches of 64 samples, including up to 512 sentencepiece tokens. We used Adam with learning rate `5e-5`. We trained using the huggingface code[4] on one Nvidia V100 GPU. The result is a shifted BERT model, HateBERT `base-uncased`, along two dimensions: (i.) language variety (i.e. social media); and (ii.) polarity (i.e., offense-, abuse-, and hate-oriented model).

Since our retraining does not change the vocabulary, we verified that HateBERT has shifted towards abusive language phenomena by using the MLM on five template sentences of the form "`[someone] is a(n)/ are [MASK]`". The template has been selected because it can trigger biases in the model's representations. We changed `[someone]` with any of the following tokens: "you", "she", "he", "women", "men" Although not exhaustive, HateBERT consistently present profanities or abusive terms as mask fillers, while this very rarely occurs with the generic BERT. Table 1 illustrates the results for "women".

BERT	HateBERT
"women"	
excluded (.075)	stu**d (.188)
encouraged (.032)	du*b (.128)
included (.027)	id***s (.075)

Table 1: MLM top 3 candidates for the templates "Women are [MASK.]".

3 Experiments and Results

To verify the usefulness of HateBERT for detecting abusive language phenomena, we run a set of experiments on three English datasets.

OffensEval 2019 (Zampieri et al., 2019) the dataset contains 14,100 tweets annotated for **offensive** language. According to the task definition, a message is labelled as offensive if "it contains any form of non-acceptable language (profanity) or a targeted offense, which can be veiled or direct." (Zampieri et al., 2019, pg. 76). The dataset is split into training and test, with 13,240 messages in training and 860 in test. The positive class (i.e. messages labeled as offensive) are 4,400 in training and 240 in test. No development data is provided.

AbusEval (Caselli et al., 2020) This dataset has been obtained by adding a layer of **abusive** language annotation to OffensEval 2019. Abusive language is defined as a specific case of offensive language, namely "hurtful language that a speaker uses to insult or offend another individual or a group of individuals based on their personal qualities, appearance, social status, opinions, statements, or actions." (Caselli et al., 2020, pg. 6197). The main difference with respect to offensive language is the exclusion of isolated profanities or untargeted messages from the positive class. The size of the dataset is the same as OffensEval 2019.The differences concern the distribution of the positive class which results in 2,749 in training and 178 in test.

HatEval (Basile et al., 2019) The English portion of the dataset contains 13,000 tweets annotated for **hate speech** against migrants and women. The authors define hate speech as "any communication that disparages a person or a group on the basis of some characteristic such as race, color, ethnicity, gender, sexual orientation, nationality, religion, or other characteristics." (Basile et al., 2019, pg. 54). Only hateful messages targeting migrants and women belong to the positive class, leaving any other message (including offensive or abusive against other targets) to the negative class. The training set is composed of 10,000 messages and the test contains 3,000. Both training and test contain an equal amount of messages with respect to the targets, i.e., 5,000 each in training and 1,500 each in test. This does not hold for the distribution of the positive class, where 4,165 messages are present in the training and 1,252 in the test set.

All datasets are imbalanced between positive and negative classes and they target phenomena that vary along the specificity dimension. This allows us to evaluate both the robusteness and the portability of HateBERT.

We applied the same pre-processing steps and hyperparameters when fine-tuning both the generic BERT and HateBERT. Pre-processing steps and hyperparameters (Table A.3) are more closely detailed in the Appendix B. Table 2 illustrates the results on each dataset (in-dataset evaluation), while Table 3 reports on the portability experiments (cross-dataset evaluation). The same evaluation metric from the original tasks, or paper, is applied, i.e., macro-averaged F1 of the positive and negative classes.

The in-domain results confirm the validity of the re-training approach to generate better models for detection of abusive language phenomena, with HateBERT largely outperforming the corre-

[4]`https://github.com/huggingface/transformers/tree/master/src/transformers`

Dataset	Model	Macro F1	Pos. class - F1
OffensEval 2019	BERT	.803±.006	.715±.009
	HateBERT	**.809±.008**	**.723±.012**
	Best	.829	.752
AbusEval	BERT	.727±.008	.552±.012
	HateBERT	**.765±.006**	**.623±.010**
	Caselli et al. (2020)	.716±.034	.531
HatEval	BERT	.480±.008	.633±.002
	HateBERT	**.516±.007**	**.645±.001**
	Best	.651	.673

Table 2: BERT *vs.* HateBERT: in-dataset. Best scores in bold. For BERT and HateBERT we report the average from 5 runs and its standard deviations. *Best* corresponds to the best systems in the original shared tasks. Caselli et al. (2020) is the most recent result for AbusEval.

Train	Model	OffensEval 2019	AbusEval	HatEval
OffensEval 2019	BERT	–	.726	.545
	HateBERT	.–	<u>.750</u>	<u>.547</u>
AbusEval	BERT	.710	–	.611
	HateBERT	<u>.713</u>	–	<u>.624</u>
HatEval	BERT	<u>.572</u>	<u>.590</u>	–
	HateBERT	.543	.555	–

Table 3: BERT *vs.* HateBERT: Portability. Columns show the dataset used for testing. Best macro F1 per training/test combination are underlined.

sponding generic model. A detailed analysis per class shows that the improvements affect both the positive and the negative classes, suggesting that HateBERT is more robust. The use of data from a different social media platform does not harm the fine-tuning stage of the retrained model, opening up possibilities of cross-fertilization studies across social media platforms. HateBERT beats the state-of-the-art for AbusEval, achieving competitive results on OffensEval and HatEval. In particular, HateBERT would rank #4 on OffensEval and #6 on HatEval, obtaining the second best F1 score on the positive class.

The portability experiments were run using the best model for each of the in-dataset experiments. Our results show that HateBERT ensures better portability than a generic BERT model, especially when going from generic abusive language phenomena (i.e., offensive language) towards more specific ones (i.e., abusive language or hate speech). This behaviour is expected and provides empirical evidence to the differences across the annotated phenomena. We also claim that HateBERT consistently obtains better representations of the targeted phenomena. This is evident when looking at the dif-

Train	Model	OffensEval 2019		AbusEval		HatEval	
		P	R	P	R	P	R
OffensEval 2019	BERT	–	–	.510	<u>.685</u>	.479	<u>.771</u>
	HateBERT	–	–	<u>.553</u>	.696	<u>.480</u>	.767
AbusEval	BERT	.776	<u>.420</u>	–	–	.545	<u>.571</u>
	HateBERT	<u>.836</u>	.404	–	–	<u>.565</u>	.567
HatEval	BERT	<u>.540</u>	<u>.220</u>	<u>.438</u>	<u>.241</u>	–	–
	HateBERT	.473	.183	.365	.191	–	–

Table 4: BERT *vs.* HateBERT: Portability - Precision and Recall for the positive class. Rows show the dataset used to train the model and columns the dataset used for testing. Best scores are underlined.

ferences in False Positives and False Negatives for the positive class, measured by means of Precision and Recall, respectively. As illustrated in Table 4, HateBERT always obtains a higher Precision score than BERT when fine-tuned on a generic abusive phenomenon and applied to more specific ones, at a very low cost for Recall. The unexpected higher Precision of HateBERT fine-tuned on AbusEval and tested on OffensEval 2019 (i.e., from specific to generic) is due to the datasets sharing same data distribution. Indeed, the results of the same model against HatEval support our analysis.

4 Conclusion and Future Directions

This contribution introduces HateBERT `base uncased`,[5] a pre-trained language model for abusive language phenomena in English. We confirm that further pre-training is an effective and cheap strategy to port pre-trained language models to other language varieties. The in-dataset evaluation shows that HateBERT consistently outperforms a generic BERT across different abusive language phenomena, such as offensive language (OffensEval 2019), abusive language (AbusEval), and hate speech (HatEval). The cross-dataset experiments show that HateBERT obtains robust representations of each abusive language phenomenon against which it has been fine-tuned. In particular, the cross-dataset experiments have provided (i.) further empirical evidence on the relationship among three abusive language phenomena along the dimension of specificity; (ii.) empirical support to the validity of the annotated data; (iii.) a principled explanation for the different performances of HateBERT and BERT.

[5]HateBERT, the fine-tuned model, and the RAL-E dataset are available at `https://osf.io/tbd58/?view_only=d90e681c672a494bb555de99fc7ae780`

A known issue concerning HateBERT is its bias toward the subreddit r/fatpeoplehate. To address this and other balancing issues, we retrieved an additional 1.3M messages. This has allowed us to add 712,583 new messages to 12 subreddits listed in Table A.1, and identify three additional ones (r/uncensorednews, r/europeannationalism, and r/farright), for a total of 597,609 messages. This new data is currently used to extend HateBERT.

Future work will focus on two directions: (i.) investigating to what extent the embedding representations of HateBERT are actually different from a general BERT pre-trained model, and (ii.) investigating the connections across the various abusive langauge phenomena.

Acknowledgements

SPONSORED BY THE

Federal Ministry of Education and Research

The project on which this report is based was funded by the German Federal Ministry of Education and Research (BMBF) under the funding code 01—S20049. The author is responsible for the content of this publication.

Ethical Statement

In this paper, the authors introduce HateBERT, a pre-trained language model for the study of abusive language phenomena in social media in English. HateBERT is unique because (i.) it is based on further pre-training of an existing pre-trained language model (i.e., BERT base-uncased) rather than training it from scratch, thus reducing the environmental impact of its creation; [6] (ii.) it uses a large collection of messages from communities that have been deemed to violate the content policy of a social media platform, namely Reddit, because of expressing harassment, bullying, incitement of violence, hate, offense, and abuse. The judgment on policy violation has been made by the community administrators and moderators. We consider this dataset for further pre-training more ecologically representative of the expressions of different abusive language phenomena in English than the use of manually annotated datasets.

The collection of banned subreddits has been retrieved from a publicly available collection of Reddit, obtained through the Reddit API and in compliance with Reddit's terms of use. From this collection, we generated the RAL-E dataset. RAL-E will be publicly released (it is accessible also at review phase in the Supplementary Materials). While its availability may have an important impact in boosting research on abusive language phenomena, especially by making natural interactions in online communities available, we are also aware of the risks of privacy violations for owners of the messages. This is one of the reasons why at this stage, we only make available in RAL-E the content of the message without metadata such as the screen name of the author and the community where the message was posted. Usernames and subreddit names have not been used to retrain the models. This reduces the risks of privacy leakage from the retrained models. Since the training material comes from banned community it is impossible and impracticable to obtain meaningful consent from the users (or redditers). In compliance with the Association for Internet Researchers Ethical Guidelines[7], we consider that: not making available the username and the specific community are the only reliable ways to protect users' privacy. We have also manually checked (for a small portion of the messages) whether it is possible to retrieve these messages by actively searching copy-paste the text of the message in Reddit. In none of the cases were we able to obtain a positive result.

There are numerous benefits from using such models to monitor the spread of abusive language phenomena in social media. Among them, we mention the following: (i.) reducing exposure to harmful content in social media; (ii.) contributing to the creation of healthier online interactions; and (iii.) promoting positive contagious behaviors and interactions (Matias, 2019). Unfortunately, work in this area is not free from potentially negative impacts. The most direct is a risk of promoting misrepresentation. HateBERT is an intrinsically biased pre-trained language model. The fine-tuned models that can be obtained are not overgenerating the positive classes, but they suffer from the biases in the manually annotated data, especially for the offensive language detection task (Sap et al., 2019;

[6]The Nvidia V100 GPU we used is shared and it has a maximum number of continuous reserved time of 72 hours. In total, it took 18 days to complete the 2 million retraining steps.

[7]https://aoir.org/reports/ethics3.pdf

Davidson et al., 2019). Furthermore, we think that such tools must always be used under the supervision of humans. Current datasets are completely lacking the actual context of occurrence of a message and the associated meaning nuances that may accompany it, labelling the positive classes only on the basis of superficial linguistic cues. The deployment of models based on HateBERT "in the wild" without human supervision requires additional research and suitable datasets for training.

We see benefits in the use of HateBERT in research on abusive language phenomena as well as in the availability of RAL-E. Researchers are encouraged to be aware of the intrinsic biased nature of HateBERT and of its impacts in real-world scenarios.

References

Francesco Barbieri, Jose Camacho-Collados, Luis Espinosa Anke, and Leonardo Neves. 2020. TweetEval: Unified benchmark and comparative evaluation for tweet classification. In *Findings of the Association for Computational Linguistics: EMNLP 2020*, pages 1644–1650, Online. Association for Computational Linguistics.

Valerio Basile, Cristina Bosco, Elisabetta Fersini, Debora Nozza, Viviana Patti, Francisco Manuel Rangel Pardo, Paolo Rosso, and Manuela Sanguinetti. 2019. SemEval-2019 task 5: Multilingual detection of hate speech against immigrants and women in twitter. In *Proceedings of the 13th International Workshop on Semantic Evaluation*, pages 54–63, Minneapolis, Minnesota, USA. Association for Computational Linguistics.

Michaela Benk. 2019. *Data Augmentation in Deep Learning for Hate Speech Detection in Lower Resource Settings*. Ph.D. thesis, Universität Zürich.

Tommaso Caselli, Valerio Basile, Jelena Mitrovic, Inga Kartoziya, and Michael Granitzer. 2020. I feel offended, don't be abusive! implicit/explicit messages in offensive and abusive language. In *Proceedings of The 12th Language Resources and Evaluation Conference*, pages 6193–6202, Marseille, France. European Language Resources Association.

Ilias Chalkidis, Manos Fergadiotis, Prodromos Malakasiotis, Nikolaos Aletras, and Ion Androutsopoulos. 2020. LEGAL-BERT: The muppets straight out of law school. In *Findings of the Association for Computational Linguistics: EMNLP 2020*, pages 2898–2904, Online. Association for Computational Linguistics.

Eshwar Chandrasekharan, Umashanthi Pavalanathan, Anirudh Srinivasan, Adam Glynn, Jacob Eisenstein, and Eric Gilbert. 2017. You can't stay here: The efficacy of reddit's 2015 ban examined through hate speech. *Proceedings of the ACM on Human-Computer Interaction*, 1:1–22.

Thomas Davidson, Debasmita Bhattacharya, and Ingmar Weber. 2019. Racial bias in hate speech and abusive language detection datasets. In *Proceedings of the Third Workshop on Abusive Language Online*, pages 25–35, Florence, Italy. Association for Computational Linguistics.

Paula Fortuna and Sérgio Nunes. 2018. A survey on automatic detection of hate speech in text. *ACM Computing Surveys (CSUR)*, 51(4):85.

Leon Graumas, Roy David, and Tommaso Caselli. 2019. Twitter-based Polarised Embeddings for Abusive Language Detection. In *2019 8th International Conference on Affective Computing and Intelligent Interaction Workshops and Demos (ACIIW)*, pages 1–7.

Suchin Gururangan, Ana Marasović, Swabha Swayamdipta, Kyle Lo, Iz Beltagy, Doug Downey, and Noah A. Smith. 2020. Don't stop pretraining: Adapt language models to domains and tasks. In *Proceedings of the 58th Annual Meeting of the Association for Computational Linguistics*, pages 8342–8360, Online. Association for Computational Linguistics.

Muhammad Okky Ibrohim and Indra Budi. 2019. Multi-label Hate Speech and Abusive Language Detection in Indonesian Twitter. In *Proceedings of the Third Workshop on Abusive Language Online*, pages 46–57.

David Jurgens, Libby Hemphill, and Eshwar Chandrasekharan. 2019. A just and comprehensive strategy for using NLP to address online abuse. In *Proceedings of the 57th Annual Meeting of the Association for Computational Linguistics*, pages 3658–3666, Florence, Italy. Association for Computational Linguistics.

Mladen Karan and Jan Šnajder. 2018. Cross-domain detection of abusive language online. In *Proceedings of the 2nd Workshop on Abusive Language Online (ALW2)*, pages 132–137, Brussels, Belgium. Association for Computational Linguistics.

Rohan Kshirsagar, Tyrus Cukuvac, Kathy McKeown, and Susan McGregor. 2018. Predictive embeddings for hate speech detection on twitter. In *Proceedings of the 2nd Workshop on Abusive Language Online (ALW2)*, pages 26–32, Brussels, Belgium. Association for Computational Linguistics.

Jinhyuk Lee, Wonjin Yoon, Sungdong Kim, Donghyeon Kim, Sunkyu Kim, Chan Ho So, and Jaewoo Kang. 2019. BioBERT: a pre-trained biomedical language representation model for biomedical text mining. *Bioinformatics*, 36(4):1234–1240.

Ping Liu, Wen Li, and Liang Zou. 2019. NULI at SemEval-2019 task 6: Transfer learning for offensive language detection using bidirectional transformers. In *Proceedings of the 13th International Workshop on Semantic Evaluation*, pages 87–91, Minneapolis, Minnesota, USA. Association for Computational Linguistics.

Shervin Malmasi and Marcos Zampieri. 2018. Challenges in discriminating profanity from hate speech. *Journal of Experimental & Theoretical Artificial Intelligence*, 30(2):187–202.

J Nathan Matias. 2019. Preventing harassment and increasing group participation through social norms in 2,190 online science discussions. *Proceedings of the National Academy of Sciences*, 116(20):9785–9789.

Flavio Merenda, Claudia Zaghi, Tommaso Caselli, and Malvina Nissim. 2018. Source-driven Representations for Hate Speech Detection. In *Proceedings of the 5th Italian Conference on Computational Linguistics (CLiC-it 2018)*, Turin, Italy.

Pushkar Mishra, Helen Yannakoudakis, and Ekaterina Shutova. 2018. Neural character-based composition models for abuse detection. In *Proceedings of the 2nd Workshop on Abusive Language Online (ALW2)*, pages 1–10, Brussels, Belgium. Association for Computational Linguistics.

Jelena Mitrović, Bastian Birkeneder, and Michael Granitzer. 2019. nlpUP at SemEval-2019 task 6: A deep neural language model for offensive language detection. In *Proceedings of the 13th International Workshop on Semantic Evaluation*, pages 722–726, Minneapolis, Minnesota, USA. Association for Computational Linguistics.

Endang Wahyu Pamungkas and Viviana Patti. 2019. Cross-domain and cross-lingual abusive language detection: A hybrid approach with deep learning and a multilingual lexicon. In *Proceedings of the 57th Annual Meeting of the Association for Computational Linguistics: Student Research Workshop*, pages 363–370.

Orestis Papakyriakopoulos, Simon Hegelich, Juan Carlos Medina Serrano, and Fabienne Marco. 2020. Bias in word embeddings. In *FAT* '20: Conference on Fairness, Accountability, and Transparency, Barcelona, Spain, January 27-30, 2020*, pages 446–457. ACM.

Fabio Poletto, Valerio Basile, Manuela Sanguinetti, Cristina Bosco, and Viviana Patti. 2020. Resources and Benchmark Corpora for Hate Speech Detection: a Systematic Review. *Language Resources and Evaluation*, 54(3):1–47.

Marco Polignano, Pierpaolo Basile, Marco de Gemmis, and Giovanni Semeraro. 2019. Hate speech detection through alberto italian language understanding model. In *Proceedings of the 3rd Workshop on Natural Language for Artificial Intelligence co-located with the 18th International Conference of the Italian Association for Artificial Intelligence (AIIA 2019), Rende, Italy, November 19th-22nd, 2019*, volume 2521 of *CEUR Workshop Proceedings*. CEUR-WS.org.

Manoel Horta Ribeiro, Pedro H Calais, Yuri A Santos, Virgílio AF Almeida, and Wagner Meira Jr. 2018. Characterizing and detecting hateful users on twitter. In *Twelfth International AAAI Conference on Web and Social Media*.

Marian-Andrei Rizoiu, Tianyu Wang, Gabriela Ferraro, and Hanna Suominen. 2019. Transfer learning for hate speech detection in social media. *arXiv preprint arXiv:1906.03829*.

Maarten Sap, Dallas Card, Saadia Gabriel, Yejin Choi, and Noah A. Smith. 2019. The risk of racial bias in hate speech detection. In *Proceedings of the 57th Annual Meeting of the Association for Computational Linguistics*, pages 1668–1678, Florence, Italy. Association for Computational Linguistics.

Gudbjartur Ingi Sigurbergsson and Leon Derczynski. 2020. Offensive Language and Hate Speech Detection for Danish. In *Proceedings of the 12th Language Resources and Evaluation Conference*. ELRA.

Steve Durairaj Swamy, Anupam Jamatia, and Björn Gambäck. 2019. Studying generalisability across abusive language detection datasets. In *Proceedings of the 23rd Conference on Computational Natural Language Learning (CoNLL)*, pages 940–950, Hong Kong, China. Association for Computational Linguistics.

Zeerak Waseem, Thomas Davidson, Dana Warmsley, and Ingmar Weber. 2017. Understanding abuse: A typology of abusive language detection subtasks. In *Proceedings of the First Workshop on Abusive Language Online*, pages 78–84.

Zeerak Waseem and Dirk Hovy. 2016. Hateful symbols or hateful people? predictive features for hate speech detection on twitter. In *Proceedings of the NAACL Student Research Workshop*, pages 88–93, San Diego, California. Association for Computational Linguistics.

Michael Wiegand, Josef Ruppenhofer, Anna Schmidt, and Clayton Greenberg. 2018. Inducing a lexicon of abusive words–a feature-based approach. In *Proceedings of the 2018 Conference of the North American Chapter of the Association for Computational Linguistics: Human Language Technologies, Volume 1 (Long Papers)*, pages 1046–1056.

Yi Yang, Mark Christopher Siy UY, and Allen Huang. 2020. Finbert: A pretrained language model for financial communications.

Marcos Zampieri, Shervin Malmasi, Preslav Nakov, Sara Rosenthal, Noura Farra, and Ritesh Kumar. 2019. SemEval-2019 task 6: Identifying and categorizing offensive language in social media (OffensEval). In *Proceedings of the 13th International Workshop on Semantic Evaluation*, pages 75–86, Minneapolis, Minnesota, USA. Association for Computational Linguistics.

Appendix A

Subreddit	Number of posts
apewrangling	5
beatingfaggots	3
blackpeoplehate	16
chicongo	15
chimpmusic	35
didntdonuffins	22
fatpeoplehate	1465531
funnyniggers	29
gibsmedat	24
hitler	297
holocaust	4946
kike	1
klukluxklan	1
milliondollarextreme	9543
misogyny	390
muhdick	15
nazi	1103
niggas	86
niggerhistorymonth	28
niggerrebooted	5
niggerspics	449
niggersstories	75
niggervideos	311
niglets	27
pol	80
polacks	151
sjwhate	10080
teenapers	23
whitesarecriminals	15

A.1: Distribution of messages per banned community composing the RAL-E dataset.

Profanity	Frequency
fucking	52,346
shit	49,012
fuck	44,627
disgusting	15,858
ass	15,789
ham	13,298
bitch	10,661
stupid	9,271
damn	7,873
lazy	7427

A.2: Top 10 profanities in RAL-E dataset.

Pre-processing before pre-training

- all users' mentions have been substituted with a placeholder (@USER);
- all URLs have been substituted with a with a placeholder (URL);
- emojis have been replaced with text (e.g. 🥺 → `:pleading_face:`) using Python `emoji` package;
- hashtag symbol has been removed from hasthtags (e.g. #kadiricinadalet → kadiricinadalet);
- extra blank spaces have been replac§ed with a single space;
- extra blank new lines have been removed.

Appendix B

Pre-processing before fine-tuning For each dataset, we have adopted minimal pre-processing steps. In particular:

- all users' mentions have been substituted with a placeholder (@USER);
- all URLs have been substituted with a with a placeholder (URL);
- emojis have been replaced with text (e.g. 🥺 → `:pleading_face:`) using Python `emoji` package;
- hashtag symbol has been removed from hasthtags (e.g. #kadiricinadalet → kadiricinadalet);
- extra blank spaces have been replaced with a single space.

Hyperparameter	Value
Learning rate	1e-5
Training Epoch	5
Adam epsilon	1e-8
Max sequence length	100
Batch size	32
Num. warmup steps	0

A.3: Hyperparamters for fine-tuning BERT and HateBERT.

Memes in the Wild: Assessing the Generalizability of the Hateful Memes Challenge Dataset

Hannah Rose Kirk[1†‡], **Yennie Jun**[1†], **Paulius Rauba**[1†], **Gal Wachtel**[1†], **Ruining Li**[2†], **Xingjian Bai**[2†], **Noah Broestl**[3†], **Martin Doff-Sotta**[4†], **Aleksandar Shtedritski**[4†], **Yuki M. Asano**[4†]

[1]Oxford Internet Institute, [2]Dept. of Computer Science, [3]Oxford Uehiro Centre for Practical Ethics

[4]Dept. of Engineering Science, [†] Oxford Artificial Intelligence Society

[‡]hannah.kirk@oii.ox.ac.uk

Abstract

Hateful memes pose a unique challenge for current machine learning systems because their message is derived from both text- and visual-modalities. To this effect, Facebook released the Hateful Memes Challenge, a dataset of memes with pre-extracted text captions, but it is unclear whether these synthetic examples generalize to 'memes in the wild'. In this paper, we collect hateful and non-hateful memes from Pinterest to evaluate out-of-sample performance on models pre-trained on the Facebook dataset. We find that memes in the wild differ in two key aspects: 1) Captions must be extracted via OCR, injecting noise and diminishing performance of multimodal models, and 2) Memes are more diverse than 'traditional memes', including screenshots of conversations or text on a plain background. This paper thus serves as a reality check for the current benchmark of hateful meme detection and its applicability for detecting real world hate.

1 Introduction

Hate speech is becoming increasingly difficult to monitor due to an increase in volume and diversification of type (MacAvaney et al., 2019). To facilitate the development of multimodal hate detection algorithms, Facebook introduced the Hateful Memes Challenge, a dataset synthetically constructed by pairing text and images (Kiela et al., 2020). Crucially, a meme's hatefulness is determined by the combined meaning of image and text. The question of likeness between synthetically created content and naturally occurring memes is both an ethical and technical one: Any features of this benchmark dataset which are not representative of reality will result in models potentially overfitting to 'clean' memes and generalizing poorly to memes in the wild. Thus, we ask the question: How well do Facebook's synthetic examples (`FB`) represent memes found in the real world? We use Pinterest memes (`Pin`) as our example of memes in the wild and explore differences across three aspects:

1. **OCR.** While `FB` memes have their text pre-extracted, memes in the wild do not. Therefore, we test the performance of several Optical Character Recognition (OCR) algorithms on `Pin` and `FB` memes.

2. **Text content**. To compare text modality content, we examine the most frequent n-grams and train a classifier to predict a meme's dataset membership based on its text.

3. **Image content and style**. To compare image modality, we evaluate meme types (traditional memes, text, screenshots) and attributes contained within memes (number of faces and estimated demographic characteristics).

After characterizing these differences, we evaluate a number of unimodal and multimodal hate classifiers pre-trained on `FB` memes to assess how well they generalize to memes in the wild.

2 Background

The majority of hate speech research focuses on text, mostly from Twitter (Waseem and Hovy, 2016; Davidson et al., 2017; Founta et al., 2018; Zampieri et al., 2019). Text-based studies face challenges such as distinguishing hate speech from offensive speech (Davidson et al., 2017) and counter speech (Mathew et al., 2018), as well as avoiding racial bias (Sap et al., 2019). Some studies focus on *multimodal* forms of hate, such as sexist advertisements (Gasparini et al., 2018), YouTube videos (Poria et al., 2016), and memes (Suryawanshi et al., 2020; Zhou and Chen, 2020; Das et al., 2020).

While the Hateful Memes Challenge (Kiela et al., 2020) encouraged innovative research on multimodal hate, many of the solutions may not generalize to detecting hateful memes at large. For

Proceedings of the Fifth Workshop on Online Abuse and Harms, pages 26–35

example, the winning team Zhong (2020) exploits a simple statistical bias resulting from the dataset generation process. While the original dataset has since been re-annotated with fine-grained labels regarding the target and type of hate (Nie et al., 2021), this paper focuses on the binary distinction of hate and non-hate.

3 Methods

3.1 Pinterest Data Collection Process

Pinterest is a social media site which groups images into collections based on similar themes. The search function returns images based on user-defined descriptions and tags. Therefore, we collect memes from Pinterest[1] using keyword search terms as noisy labels for whether the returned images are likely hateful or non-hateful (see Appendix A). For hate, we sample based on two heuristics: synonyms of hatefulness or specific hate directed towards protected groups (e.g., 'offensive memes', 'sexist memes') and slurs associated with these types of hate (e.g., 'sl*t memes', 'wh*ore memes'). For non-hate, we again draw on two heuristics: positive sentiment words (e.g., 'funny', 'wholesome', 'cute') and memes relating to entities excluded from the definition of hate speech because they are not a protected category (e.g., 'food', 'maths'). Memes are collected between March 13 and April 1, 2021. We drop duplicate memes, leaving 2,840 images, of which 37% belong to the hateful category.

3.2 Extracting Text- and Image-Modalities (OCR)

We evaluate the following OCR algorithms on the `Pin` and `FB` datasets: Tesseract (Smith, 2007), EasyOCR (Jaded AI) and East (Zhou et al., 2017). Previous research has shown the importance of prefiltering images before applying OCR algorithms (Bieniecki et al., 2007). Therefore, we consider two prefiltering methods fine-tuned to the specific characteristics of each dataset (see Appendix B).

3.3 Unimodal Text Differences

After OCR text extraction, we retain words with a probability of correct identification ≥ 0.5, and remove stopwords. A text-based classification task using a unigram Naïve-Bayes model is employed to discriminate between hateful and non-hateful memes of both `Pin` and `FB` datasets.

3.4 Unimodal Image Differences

To investigate the distribution of *types* of memes, we train a linear classifier on image features from the penultimate layer of CLIP (see Appendix C) (Radford et al., 2021). From the 100 manually examined `Pin` memes, we find three broad categories: 1) traditional memes; 2) memes consisting of just text; and 3) screenshots. Examples of each are shown in Appendix C. Further, to detect (potentially several) human faces contained within memes and their relationship with hatefulness, we use a pre-trained FaceNet model (Schroff et al., 2015) to locate faces and apply a pre-trained DEX model (Rothe et al., 2015) to estimate their ages, genders, races. We compare the distributions of these features between the hateful/non-hateful samples.

We note that these models are controversial and may suffer from algorithmic bias due to differential accuracy rates for detecting various subgroups. Alvi et al. (2018) show DEX contains erroneous age information, and Terhorst et al. (2021) show that FaceNet has lower recognition rates for female faces compared to male faces. These are larger issues discussed within the computer vision community (Buolamwini and Gebru, 2018).

3.5 Comparison Across Baseline Models

To examine the consequences of differences between the `FB` and `Pin` datasets, we conduct a preliminary classification of memes into hate and non-hate using benchmark models. First, we take a subsample of the `Pin` dataset to match Facebook's `dev` dataset, which contains 540 memes, of which 37% are hateful. We compare performance across three samples: (1) `FB` memes with 'ground truth' text and labels; (2) `FB` memes with Tesseract OCR text and ground truth labels; and (3) `Pin` memes with Tesseract OCR text and noisy labels. Next, we select several baseline models pretrained on `FB` memes[2], provided in the original Hateful Memes challenge (Kiela et al., 2020). Of the 11 pretrained baseline models, we evaluate the performance of five that do not require further preprocessing: Concat Bert, Late Fusion, MMBT-Grid, Unimodal Image, and Unimodal Text. We note that these models are not fine-tuned on

[1]We use an open-sourced Pinterest scraper, available at `https://github.com/iamatulsingh/pinterest-image-scrap`.

[2]These are available for download at `https://github.com/facebookresearch/mmf/tree/master/projects/hateful_memes`.

Pin memes but simply evaluate their transfer performance. Finally, we make zero-shot predictions using CLIP (Radford et al., 2021), and evaluate a linear model of visual features trained on the FB dataset (see Appendix D).

4 Results

4.1 OCR Performance

Each of the three OCR engines is paired with one of the two prefiltering methods tuned specifically to each dataset, forming a total of six pairs for evaluation. For both datasets, the methods are tested on 100 random images with manually annotated text. For each method, we compute the average cosine similarity of the joint TF-IDF vectors between the labelled and cleaned[3] predicted text, shown in Tab. 1. Tesseract with FB tuning performs best on the FB dataset, while Easy with Pin tuning performs best on the Pin dataset. We evaluate transferability by comparing how a given pair performs on both datasets. **OCR transferability is generally low**, but greater from the FB dataset to the Pin dataset, despite the latter being more general than the former. This may be explained by the fact that the dominant form of Pin memes (i.e. text on a uniform background outside of the image) is not present in the FB dataset, so any method specifically optimized for Pin memes would perform poorly on FB memes.

Table 1: Cosine similarity between predicted text and labelled text for various OCR engines and prefiltering pairs. Best result per dataset is bolded.

	FB	Pin	$\|\Delta\|$
Tesseract, FB tuning	**0.70**	0.36	0.34
Tesseract, Pin tuning	0.22	0.58	0.26
Easy, FB tuning	0.53	0.30	0.23
Easy, Pin tuning	0.32	**0.67**	0.35
East, FB tuning	0.36	0.17	0.19
East, Pin tuning	0.05	0.32	0.27

4.2 Unimodal Text Differences

We compare unigrams and bigrams across datasets after removing stop words, numbers, and URLs. The bigrams are topically different (refer to Appendix E). A unigram token-based Naïve-Bayes classifier is trained on both datasets separately to distinguish between hateful and non-hateful classes. The model achieves an accuracy score of 60.7% on FB memes and 68.2% on Pin memes (random guessing is 50%), indicating mildly different text distributions between hate and non-hate. In order to understand the differences between the type of language used in the two datasets, a classifier is trained to discriminate between FB and Pin memes (regardless of whether they are hateful) based on the extracted tokens. The accuracy is 77.4% on a balanced test set. The high classification performance might be explained by the OCR-generated junk text in the Pin memes which can be observed in a t-SNE plot (see Appendix F).

4.3 Unimodal Image Differences

While the FB dataset contains only "traditional memes"[4], we find this definition of 'a meme' to be too narrow: **the Pin memes are more diverse**, containing 15% memes with only text and 7% memes which are screenshots (see Tab. 2).

Table 2: Percentage of each meme type in Pin and FB datasets, extracted by CLIP.

Meme Type	FB	Pin	$\|\Delta\|$
Traditional meme	95.6%	77.3%	18.3%
Text	1.4%	15.3%	13.9%
Screenshot	3.0%	7.4%	4.4%

Tab. 3 shows the facial recognition results. **We find that Pin memes contain fewer faces than FB memes**, while other demographic factors broadly match. The DEX model identifies similar age distributions by hate and non-hate and by dataset, with an average of 30 and a gender distribution heavily skewed towards male faces (see Appendix G for additional demographics).

Table 3: Facial detection and demographic (gender, age) distributions from pre-trained FaceNet and DEX.

	FB		Pin	
metric	Hate	Non-Hate	Hate	Non-Hate
Images w/ Faces	72.8%	71.9%	52.0%	38.8%
Gender (M:F)	84:16	84:16	82:18	88:12
Age	$30.7_{\pm5.7}$	$31.2_{\pm6.3}$	$29.4_{\pm5.5}$	$29.9_{\pm5.4}$

4.4 Performance of Baseline Models

How well do hate detection pipelines generalize? Tab. 4 shows the F1 scores for the predictions of hate made by each model on the three samples: (1)

[3]The cleaned text is obtained with lower case conversion and punctuation removal.

[4]The misclassifications into other types reflect the accuracy of our classifier.

FB with ground-truth caption, (2) FB with OCR, (3) Pin with OCR.

Table 4: F1 scores for pretrained baseline models on three datasets. Best result per dataset is bolded.

Text from:	FB Ground-truth	FB OCR	Pin OCR
Multimodal Models			
Concat BERT	0.321	0.278	0.184
Late Fusion	0.499	0.471	0.377
MMBT-Grid	0.396	0.328	0.351
Unimodal Models			
Text BERT	0.408	0.320	0.327
Image-Grid*	0.226	0.226	0.351
CLIP Models			
$\text{CLIP}_{\text{Zero-Shot}}$*	0.509	0.509	0.543
$\text{CLIP}_{\text{Linear Probe}}$*	**0.556**	**0.556**	**0.569**

* these models do not use any text inputs so F1 scores repeated for ground truth and OCR columns.

Surprisingly, we find that the $\text{CLIP}_{\text{Linear Probe}}$ generalizes very well, performing best for all three samples, with superior performance on Pin memes as compared to FB memes. Because CLIP has been pre-trained on around 400M image-text pairs from the Internet, its learned features generalize better to the Pin dataset, even though it was fine-tuned on the FB dataset. Of the multimodal models, Late Fusion performs the best on all three samples. When comparing the performance of Late Fusion on the FB and Pin OCR samples, **we find a significant drop in model performance of 12 percentage points**. The unimodal text model performs significantly better on FB with the ground truth annotations as compared to either sample with OCR extracted text. This may be explained by the 'clean' captions which do not generalize to real-world meme instances without pre-extracted text.

5 Discussion

The key difference in text modalities derives from the efficacy of the OCR extraction, where messier captions result in performance losses in Text BERT classification. This forms a critique of the way in which the Hateful Memes Challenge is constructed, in which researchers are incentivized to rely on the pre-extracted text rather than using OCR; thus, the reported performance overestimates success in the real world. Further, the Challenge defines a meme as 'a traditional meme' but we question whether this definition is too narrow to encompass the diversity of real memes found in the wild, such as screenshots of text conversations.

When comparing the performance of unimodal and multimodal models, we find multimodal models have superior classification capabilities which may be because the combination of multiple modes create meaning beyond the text and image alone (Kruk et al., 2019). For all three multimodal models (Concat BERT, Late Fusion, and MMBT-Grid), the score for FB memes with ground truth captions is higher than that of FB memes with OCR extracted text, which in turn is higher than that of Pin memes. Finally, we note that CLIP's performance, for zero-shot and linear probing, surpasses the other models and is stable across both datasets.

Limitations Despite presenting a preliminary investigation of the generalizability of the FB dataset to memes in the wild, this paper has several limitations. Firstly, the errors introduced by OCR text extraction resulted in 'messy' captions for Pin memes. This may explain why Pin memes could be distinguished from FB memes by a Naïve-Bayes classifier using text alone. However, these errors demonstrate our key conclusion that the pre-extracted captions of FB memes are not representative of the appropriate pipelines which are required for real world hateful meme detection.

Secondly, our Pin dataset relies on noisy labels of hate/non-hate based on keyword searches, but this chosen heuristic may not catch subtler forms of hate. Further, user-defined labels introduce normative value judgements of whether something is 'offensive' versus 'funny', and such judgements may differ from how Facebook's community standards define hate (Facebook, 2021). In future work, we aim to annotate the Pin dataset with multiple manual annotators for greater comparability to the FB dataset. These ground-truth annotations will allow us to pre-train models on Pin memes and also assess transferability to FB memes.

Conclusion We conduct a reality check of the Hateful Memes Challenge. Our results indicate that there are differences between the synthetic Facebook memes and 'in-the-wild' Pinterest memes, both with regards to text and image modalities. Training and testing unimodal text models on Facebook's pre-extracted captions discounts the potential errors introduced by OCR extraction, which is required for real world hateful meme detection. We hope to repeat this work once we have annotations for the Pinterest dataset and to expand the analysis from comparing between the binary categories of hate versus non-hate to include a comparison across different types and targets of hate.

References

M. Alvi, Andrew Zisserman, and C. Nellåker. 2018. Turning a blind eye: Explicit removal of biases and variation from deep neural network embeddings. In *ECCV Workshops*.

Wojciech Bieniecki, Szymon Grabowski, and Wojciech Rozenberg. 2007. Image preprocessing for improving ocr accuracy. In *2007 international conference on perspective technologies and methods in MEMS design*, pages 75–80. IEEE.

Joy Buolamwini and Timnit Gebru. 2018. Gender shades: Intersectional accuracy disparities in commercial gender classification. In *Conference on fairness, accountability and transparency*, pages 77–91. PMLR.

Abhishek Das, Japsimar Singh Wahi, and Siyao Li. 2020. Detecting hate speech in multi-modal memes. *arXiv preprint arXiv:2012.14891*.

Thomas Davidson, Dana Warmsley, Michael Macy, and Ingmar Weber. 2017. Automated hate speech detection and the problem of offensive language. In *Proceedings of the International AAAI Conference on Web and Social Media*, volume 11.

Facebook. 2021. Community standards hate speech. `https://www.facebook.com/communitystandards/hate_speech`. Accessed on 12 June 2021.

Antigoni Founta, Constantinos Djouvas, Despoina Chatzakou, Ilias Leontiadis, Jeremy Blackburn, Gianluca Stringhini, Athena Vakali, Michael Sirivianos, and Nicolas Kourtellis. 2018. Large scale crowdsourcing and characterization of twitter abusive behavior. In *Proceedings of the International AAAI Conference on Web and Social Media*, volume 12.

Francesca Gasparini, Ilaria Erba, Elisabetta Fersini, and Silvia Corchs. 2018. Multimodal classification of sexist advertisements. In *ICETE (1)*, pages 565–572.

Jaded AI. Easy OCR. `https://github.com/JaidedAI/EasyOCR`.

Douwe Kiela, Hamed Firooz, Aravind Mohan, Vedanuj Goswami, Amanpreet Singh, Pratik Ringshia, and Davide Testuggine. 2020. The hateful memes challenge: Detecting hate speech in multimodal memes. *ArXiv*, abs/2005.04790.

Julia Kruk, Jonah Lubin, Karan Sikka, X. Lin, Dan Jurafsky, and Ajay Divakaran. 2019. Integrating text and image: Determining multimodal document intent in instagram posts. *ArXiv*, abs/1904.09073.

Sean MacAvaney, Hao-Ren Yao, Eugene Yang, Katina Russell, Nazli Goharian, and Ophir Frieder. 2019. Hate speech detection: Challenges and solutions. *PloS one*, 14(8):e0221152.

Binny Mathew, Navish Kumar, Pawan Goyal, Animesh Mukherjee, et al. 2018. Analyzing the hate and counter speech accounts on twitter. *arXiv preprint arXiv:1812.02712*.

Shaoliang Nie, Aida Davani, Lambert Mathias, Douwe Kiela, Zeerak Waseem, Bertie Vidgen, and Vinodkumar Prabhakaran. 2021. Woah shared task fine grained hateful memes classification. `https://github.com/facebookresearch/fine_grained_hateful_memes/`.

Pinterest. 2021. All about pinterest. `https://help.pinterest.com/en-gb/guide/all-about-pinterest`. Accessed on 12 June 2021.

Soujanya Poria, Erik Cambria, Newton Howard, Guang-Bin Huang, and Amir Hussain. 2016. Fusing audio, visual and textual clues for sentiment analysis from multimodal content. *Neurocomputing*, 174:50–59.

Alec Radford, Jong Wook Kim, Chris Hallacy, Aditya Ramesh, Gabriel Goh, Sandhini Agarwal, Girish Sastry, Amanda Askell, Pamela Mishkin, Jack Clark, Gretchen Krueger, and Ilya Sutskever. 2021. Learning transferable visual models from natural language supervision.

Rasmus Rothe, Radu Timofte, and Luc Van Gool. 2015. Dex: Deep expectation of apparent age from a single image. In *2015 IEEE International Conference on Computer Vision Workshop (ICCVW)*, pages 252–257.

Maarten Sap, Dallas Card, Saadia Gabriel, Yejin Choi, and Noah A Smith. 2019. The risk of racial bias in hate speech detection. In *Proceedings of the 57th annual meeting of the association for computational linguistics*, pages 1668–1678.

Florian Schroff, Dmitry Kalenichenko, and James Philbin. 2015. Facenet: A unified embedding for face recognition and clustering. In *2015 IEEE Conference on Computer Vision and Pattern Recognition (CVPR)*, pages 815–823.

Ray Smith. 2007. An overview of the tesseract ocr engine. In *Ninth international conference on document analysis and recognition (ICDAR 2007)*, volume 2, pages 629–633. IEEE.

Shardul Suryawanshi, Bharathi Raja Chakravarthi, Mihael Arcan, and Paul Buitelaar. 2020. Multimodal meme dataset (multioff) for identifying offensive content in image and text. In *Proceedings of the Second Workshop on Trolling, Aggression and Cyberbullying*, pages 32–41.

P. Terhorst, Jan Niklas Kolf, Marco Huber, Florian Kirchbuchner, N. Damer, A. Morales, Julian Fierrez, and Arjan Kuijper. 2021. A comprehensive study on face recognition biases beyond demographics. *ArXiv*, abs/2103.01592.

Laurens Van Der Maaten and Geoffrey Hinton. 2008. Visualizing Data using t-SNE. Technical report.

Zeerak Waseem and Dirk Hovy. 2016. Hateful symbols or hateful people? predictive features for hate speech detection on twitter. In *Proceedings of the NAACL student research workshop*, pages 88–93.

Marcos Zampieri, Shervin Malmasi, Preslav Nakov, Sara Rosenthal, Noura Farra, and Ritesh Kumar. 2019. Predicting the type and target of offensive posts in social media. *arXiv preprint arXiv:1902.09666*.

Xiayu Zhong. 2020. Classification of multimodal hate speech–the winning solution of hateful memes challenge. *arXiv preprint arXiv:2012.01002*.

Xinyu Zhou, Cong Yao, He Wen, Yuzhi Wang, Shuchang Zhou, Weiran He, and Jiajun Liang. 2017. East: an efficient and accurate scene text detector. In *Proceedings of the IEEE conference on Computer Vision and Pattern Recognition*, pages 5551–5560.

Yi Zhou and Zhenhao Chen. 2020. Multimodal learning for hateful memes detection. *arXiv preprint arXiv:2011.12870*.

A Details on Pinterest Data Collection

Tab. 5 shows the keywords we use to search for memes on Pinterest. The search function returns images based on user-defined tags and descriptions aligning with the search term (Pinterest, 2021). Each keyword search returns several hundred images on the first few pages of results. Note that Pinterest bans searches for 'racist' memes or slurs associated with racial hatred so these could not be collected. We prefer this method of 'noisy' labelling over classifying the memes with existing hate speech classifiers with the text as input because users likely take the multimodal content of the meme into account when adding tags or writing descriptions. However, we recognize that user-defined labelling comes with its own limitations of introducing noise into the dataset from idiosyncratic interpretation of tags. We also recognize that the memes we collect from Pinterest do not represent all Pinterest memes, nor do they represent all memes generally on the Internet. Rather, they reflect a sample of instances. Further, we over-sample non-hateful memes as compared to hateful memes because this distribution is one that is reflected in the real world. For example, the `FB` dev set is composed of 37% hateful memes. Lastly, while we manually confirm that the noisy labels of 50 hateful and 50 non-hateful memes (see Tab. 6), we also recognize that not all of the images accurately match the associated noisy label, especially for hateful memes which must match the definition of hate speech as directed towards a protected category.

Table 5: Keywords used to produce noisily-labelled samples of hateful and non-hateful memes from Pinterest.

Noisy Label	Keywords
Hate	"sexist", "offensive", "vulgar", "wh*re", "sl*t", "prostitute"
Non-Hate	"funny", "wholesome", "happy", "friendship", "cute", "phd", "student", "food", "exercise"

Table 6: Results of manual annotation for noisy labelling. Of 50 random memes with a noisy hate label, we find 80% are indeed hateful, and of 50 random memes with a noisy non-hate label, we find 94% are indeed non-hateful.

	Noisy Hate	Noisy Non-Hate
Annotator Hate	40	3
Annotator Non-Hate	10	47

B Details on OCR Engines

B.1 OCR Algorithms

We evaluate three OCR algorithms on the `Pin` and `FB` datasets. First, Tesseract (Smith, 2007) is Google's open-source OCR engine. It has been continuously developed and maintained since its first release in 1985 by Hewlett-Packard Laboratories. Second, EasyOCR (Jaded AI) developed by Jaded AI, is the algorithm used by the winner of the Facebook Hateful Meme Challenge. Third, East (Zhou et al., 2017) is an efficient deep learning algorithm for text detection in natural scenes. In this paper East is used to isolate regions of interest in the image in combination with Tesseract for text recognition.

B.2 OCR Pre-filtering

Figure 4 shows the dominant text patterns in `FB` (a) and `Pin` (b) datasets, respectively. We use a specific prefiltering adapted to each pattern as follows.

FB Tuning: `FB` memes always have a black-edged white Impact font. The most efficient prefiltering sequence consists of applying an RGB-to-Gray conversion, followed by binary thresholding, closing, and inversion. **Pin Tuning:** `Pin` memes are less structured than `FB` memes, but a commonly observed meme type is text placed outside of the image on a uniform background. For this pattern, the most efficient prefiltering sequence consists of an RGB-to-Gray conversion followed by Otsu's thresholding.

The optimal thresholds used to classify pixels in binary and Otsu's thresholding operations are found so as to maximise the average cosine similarity of the joint TF-IDF vectors between the labelled and predicted text from a sample of 30 annotated images from both datasets.

(a) (b)

Figure 1: Dominant text patterns in (a) Facebook dataset (b) Pinterest dataset.

C Classification of Memes into Types

C.1 Data Preparation

To prepare the data needed for training the ternary (i.e., traditional memes, memes purely consisting of text, and screenshots) classifier, we annotate the `Pin` dataset with manual annotations to create a balanced set of 400 images. We split the set randomly, so that 70% is used as the training data and the rest 30% as the validation data. Figure 2 shows the main types of memes encountered. The `FB` dataset only has traditional meme types.

a) b) c)

Figure 2: Different types of memes: (a) Traditional meme (b) Text (c) Screenshot.

C.2 Training Process

We use image features taken from the penultimate layer of CLIP. We train a neural network with two hidden layers of 64 and 12 neurons respectively with ReLU activations, using Adam optimizer, for 50 epochs. The model achieves 93.3% accuracy on the validation set.

D Classification Using CLIP

D.1 Zero-shot Classification

To perform zero-shot classification using CLIP (Radford et al., 2021), for every meme we use two prompts, "`a meme`" and "`a hatespeech meme`". We measure the similarity score between the image and text embeddings and use the corresponding text prompt as a label. Note we regard this method as neither multimodal nor uni-modal, as the text is not explicitly given to the model, but as shown in (Radford et al., 2021), CLIP has some OCR capabilities. In a future work we would like to explore how to modify the text prompts to improve performance.

D.2 Linear Probing

We train a binary linear classifier on the image features of CLIP on the FB train set. We train the classifier following the procedure outlined by (Radford et al., 2021). Finally, we evaluate the binary classifier of the FB dev set and the Pin dataset.

In all experiments above we use the pretrained ViT-B/32 model.

E Common Bigrams

The FB and Pin datasets have distinctively different bigrams after data cleaning and the removal of stop words.

The most common bigrams for hateful FB memes are: ['black people', 'white people', 'white trash', 'black guy', 'sh*t brains', 'look like']. The most common bigrams for non-hateful FB memes are: ['strip club', 'isis strip', 'meanwhile isis', 'white people', 'look like', 'ilhan omar']

The most common bigrams for hateful Pin memes are: 'im saying', 'favorite color', 'single white', 'black panthers', 'saying wh*res', and 'saying sl*t'. The most common bigrams for non-hateful Pin memes are: 'best friend', 'dad jokes', 'teacher new', 'black lives', 'lives matter', and 'let dog'.

F T-SNE Text Embeddings

The meme-level embeddings are calculated by (i) extracting a 300-dimensional embedding for each word in the meme, using fastText embeddings trained on Wikipedia and Common Crawl; (ii) averaging all the embeddings along each dimension. A T-SNE transformation is then applied to the full dataset, reducing it to two-dimensional space. After this reduction, 1000 text-embeddings from each category—FB and Pin — are extracted and visualized. The default perplexity parameter of 50 is used. Fig.3 presents the t-SNE plot (Van Der Maaten and Hinton, 2008), which indicates a concentration of multiple embeddings of the Pin memes within a region at the bottom of the figure. These memes represent those that have nonsensical word tokens from OCR errors.

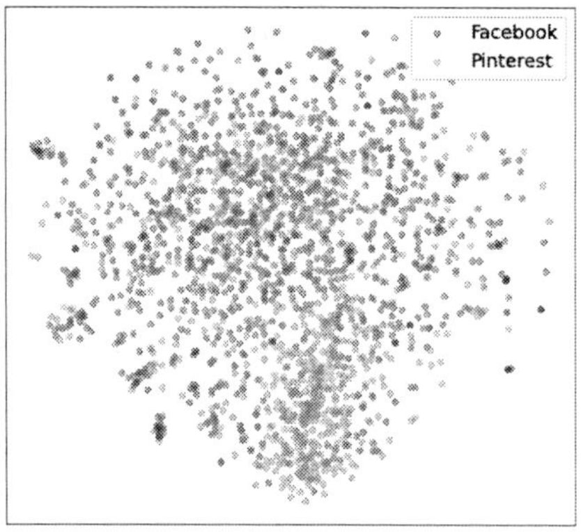

Figure 3: t-SNE of Facebook and Pinterest memes' text-embeddings for a random sample of 1000 each.

G Face Recognition

G.1 Multi-Faces Detection Method

To evaluate memes with multiple faces, we develop a self-adaptive algorithm to separate faces. For each meme, we enumerate the position of a cutting line (either horizontal or vertical) with fixed granularity, and run facial detection models on both parts separately. If both parts have a high probability of containing faces, we decide that each part has at least one face. Hence, we cut the meme along the line, and run this algorithm iteratively on both parts. If no enumerated cutting line satisfies the condition above, then we decide there's only one face in the meme and terminate the algorithm.

G.2 Additional Results on Facial Analysis

Table 7: Predicted ratio of emotion categories on faces from different datasets from pre-trained DEX model.

	FB		Pin	
categories	Hate	Non-Hate	Hate	Non-Hate
angry	10.6%	10.1%	9.0%	13.7%
disgust	0.3%	0.2%	0.7%	0.6%
fear	9.5%	10.2%	10.6%	13.0%
happy	35.1%	36.3%	34.2%	30.1%
neutral	23.1%	22.7%	23.4%	21.5%
sad	18.8%	18.7%	20.4%	18.6%
surprise	2.2%	1.7%	1.7%	1.8%

Table 8: Predicted ratio of racial categories of faces from different datasets from pre-trained DEX model.

	FB		Pin	
categories	Hate	Non-Hate	Hate	Non-Hate
asian	10.6%	10.8%	9.7%	13.9%
black	15.0%	15.3%	6.5%	11.0%
indian	5.9%	6.1%	3.2%	5.1%
latino hispanic	14.3%	14.5%	10.2%	11.7%
middle eastern	12.7%	11.2%	9.5%	10.1%
white	41.5%	42.1%	60.9%	48.1%

G.3 Examples of Faces in Memes

(a) FB Hate (b) FB Non-hate (c) Pin Hate (d) Pin Non-hate

Figure 4: Samples of faces in FB Hate, FB Non-hate, Pin Hate, and Pin Non-hate datasets, and their demographic characteristic predicted by the DEX model:
(a) Woman, 37, white, sad (72.0%); (b) Man, 27, black, happy (99.9%);
(c) Man, 36, middle eastern, angry (52.2%); (d) Man, 29, black, neutral (68.0%)

Measuring and Improving Model-Moderator Collaboration using Uncertainty Estimation

Ian D. Kivlichan* Jigsaw kivlichan@google.com
Zi Lin*† Google Research lzi@google.com
Jeremiah Liu* Google Research jereliu@google.com
Lucy Vasserman Jigsaw lucyvasserman@google.com

Abstract

Content moderation is often performed by a collaboration between humans and machine learning models. However, it is not well understood *how* to design the collaborative process so as to maximize the combined moderator-model system performance. This work presents a rigorous study of this problem, focusing on an approach that incorporates model uncertainty into the collaborative process. First, we introduce principled metrics to describe the performance of the collaborative system under capacity constraints on the human moderator, quantifying how efficiently the combined system utilizes human decisions. Using these metrics, we conduct a large benchmark study evaluating the performance of state-of-the-art uncertainty models under different collaborative review strategies. We find that an uncertainty-based strategy consistently outperforms the widely used strategy based on toxicity scores, and moreover that the choice of review strategy drastically changes the overall system performance. Our results demonstrate the importance of rigorous metrics for understanding and developing effective moderator-model systems for content moderation, as well as the utility of uncertainty estimation in this domain.[1]

1 Introduction

Maintaining civil discussions online is a persistent challenge for online platforms. Due to the sheer scale of user-generated text, modern content moderation systems often employ machine learning algorithms to automatically classify user comments based on their toxicity, with the goal of flagging a collection of likely policy-violating content for human experts to review (Etim, 2017). However, modern deep learning models have been shown to suffer from reliability and robustness issues, especially in the face of the rich and complex sociolinguistic phenomena in real-world online conversations. Examples include possibly generating confidently wrong predictions based on spurious lexical features (Wang and Culotta, 2020), or exhibiting undesired biases toward particular social subgroups (Dixon et al., 2018). This has raised questions about how current toxicity detection models will perform in realistic online environments, as well as the potential consequences for moderation systems (Rainie et al., 2017).

In this work, we study an approach to address these questions by incorporating model uncertainty into the collaborative model-moderator system's decision-making process. The intuition is that by using uncertainty as a signal for the likelihood of model error, we can improve the efficiency and performance of the collaborative moderation system by prioritizing the least confident examples from the model for human review. Despite a plethora of uncertainty methods in the literature, there has been limited work studying their effectiveness in improving the performance of human-AI collaborative systems with respect to application-specific metrics and criteria (Awaysheh et al., 2019; Dusenberry et al., 2020; Jesson et al., 2020). This is especially important for the content moderation task: real-world practice has unique challenges and constraints, including label imbalance, distributional shift, and limited resources of human experts; how these factors impact the collaborative system's effectiveness is not well understood.

In this work, we lay the foundation for the study of the uncertainty-aware collaborative content moderation problem. We first (1) propose rigorous met-

*Equal contribution; authors listed alphabetically.

†This work was done while Zi Lin was an AI resident at Google Research.

[1]Complete code including metric implementations and experiments is available at http://github.com/google/uncertainty-baselines/tree/master/baselines/toxic_comments.

Proceedings of the Fifth Workshop on Online Abuse and Harms, pages 36–53
August 6, 2021.

rics *Oracle-Model Collaborative Accuracy* (OC-Acc) and *AUC* (OC-AUC) to measure the performance of the overall collaborative system under capacity constraints on a simulated human moderator. We also propose *Review Efficiency*, a intrinsic metric to measure a model's ability to improve the collaboration efficiency by selecting examples that need further review. Then, (2) we introduce a challenging data benchmark, *Collaborative Toxicity Moderation in the Wild* (CoToMoD), for evaluating the effectiveness of a collaborative toxic comment moderation system. CoToMoD emulates the realistic train-deployment environment of a moderation system, in which the deployment environment contains richer linguistic phenomena and a more diverse range of topics than the training data, such that effective collaboration is crucial for good system performance (Amodei et al., 2016). Finally, (3) we present a large benchmark study to evaluate the performance of five classic and state-of-the-art uncertainty approaches on CoToMoD under two different moderation review approaches (based on the uncertainty score and on the toxicity score, respectively). We find that both the model's predictive and uncertainty quality contribute to the performance of the final system, and that the uncertainty-based review strategy outperforms the toxicity strategy across a variety of models and range of human review capacities.

2 Related Work

Our collaborative metrics draw on the idea of classification with a reject option, or learning with abstention (Bartlett and Wegkamp, 2008; Cortes et al., 2016, 2018; Kompa et al., 2021). In this classification scenario, the model has the option to reject an example instead of predicting its label. The challenge in connecting learning with abstention to OC-Acc or OC-AUC is to account for how many examples have already been rejected. Specifically, the difficulty is that the metrics we present are all dataset-level metrics, i.e. the "reject" option is not at the level of individual examples, but rather a set capacity over the entire dataset. Moreover, this means OC-Acc and OC-AUC can be compared directly with traditional accuracy or AUC measures. This difference in focus enables us to consider human time as the limiting resource in the overall model-moderator system's performance.

One key point for our work is that the best model (in isolation) may not yield the best performance in collaboration with a human (Bansal et al., 2021). Our work demonstrates this for a case where the collaboration procedure is decided over the full dataset rather than per example: because of this, Bansal et al. (2021)'s expected team utility does not easily generalize to our setting. In particular, the user chooses which classifier predictions to accept after receiving all of them rather than per example.

Robustness to distribution shift has been applied to toxicity classification in other works (Adragna et al., 2020; Koh et al., 2020), emphasizing the connection between fairness and robustness. Our work focuses on how these methods connect to the human review process, and how uncertainty can lead to better decision-making for a model collaborating with a human. Along these lines, Dusenberry et al. (2020) analyzed how uncertainty affects optimal decisions in a medical context, though again at the level of individual examples rather than over the dataset.

3 Background: Uncertainty Quantification for Deep Toxicity Classification

Types of Uncertainty Consider modeling a toxicity dataset $\mathcal{D} = \{y_i, x_i\}_{i=1}^N$ using a deep classifier $f_W(x)$. Here the x_i are example comments, $y_i \sim p^*(y|x_i)$ are toxicity labels drawn from a data generating process p^* (e.g., the human annotation process), and W are the parameters of the deep neural network. There are two distinct types of uncertainty in this modeling process: *data uncertainty* and *model uncertainty* (Sullivan, 2015; Liu et al., 2019). *Data uncertainty* arises from the stochastic variability inherent in the data generating process p^*. For example, the toxicity label y_i for a comment can vary between 0 and 1 depending on raters' different understandings of the comment or of the annotation guidelines. On the other hand, *model uncertainty* arises from the model's lack of knowledge about the world, commonly caused by insufficient coverage of the training data. For example, at evaluation time, the toxicity classifier may encounter neologisms or misspellings that did not appear in the training data, making it more likely to make a mistake (van Aken et al., 2018). While the *model uncertainty* can be reduced by training on more data, the *data uncertainty* is inherent to the data generating process and is irreducible.

Estimating Uncertainty A model that quantifies its uncertainty well should properly capture both the data and the model uncertainties. To this end, a learned deep classifier $f_W(x)$ describes the *data uncertainty* via its predictive probability, e.g.:

$$p(y|x, W) = \text{sigmoid}(f_W(x)),$$

which is conditioned on the model parameter W, and is commonly learned by minimizing the Kullback-Leibler (KL) divergence between the model distribution $p(y|x, W)$ and the empirical distribution of the data (e.g. by minimizing the cross-entropy loss (Goodfellow et al., 2016)). On the other hand, a deep classifier can quantify *model uncertainty* by using probabilistic methods to learn the posterior distribution of the model parameters:

$$W \sim p(W).$$

This distribution over W leads to a distribution over the predictive probabilities $p(y|x, W)$. As a result, at inference time, the model can sample model weights $\{W_m\}_{m=1}^M$ from the posterior distribution $p(W)$, and then compute the posterior sample of predictive probabilities $\{p(y|x, W_m)\}_{m=1}^M$. This allows the model to express its model uncertainty through the variance of the posterior distribution $\text{Var}\big(p(y|x, W)\big)$. Section 5 surveys popular probabilistic deep learning methods.

In practice, it is convenient to compute a single uncertainty score capturing both types of uncertainty. To this end, we can first compute the marginalized predictive probability:

$$p(y|x) = \int p(y|x, W)p(W)\, dW$$

which captures both types of uncertainty by marginalizing the data uncertainty $p(y|x, W)$ over the model uncertainty $p(W)$. We can thus quantify the overall uncertainty of the model by computing the predictive variance of this binary distribution:

$$u_{\text{unc}}(x) = p(y|x) \times (1 - p(y|x)). \quad (1)$$

Evaluating Uncertainty Quality A common approach to evaluate a model's uncertainty quality is to measure its *calibration* performance, i.e., whether the model's predictive uncertainty is indicative of the predictive error (Guo et al., 2017). As we shall see in experiments, traditional calibration metrics like the Brier score (Ovadia et al., 2019) do not correlate well with the model performance in collaborative prediction. One notable reason is that the collaborative systems use uncertainty as a ranking score (to identify possibly wrong predictions), while metrics like Brier score only measure the uncertainty's ranking performance indirectly.

		Uncertainty	
		Uncertain	Certain
Accuracy	Inaccurate	TP	FN
	Accurate	FP	TN

Figure 1: Confusion matrix for evaluating uncertainty calibration. We describe the correspondence in the text.

This motivates us to consider *Calibration AUC*, a new class of calibration metrics that focus on the uncertainty score $u_{\text{unc}}(x)$'s ranking performance. This metric evaluates uncertainty estimation by recasting it as a binary prediction problem, where the binary label is the model's prediction error $\mathbb{I}(f(x_i) \neq y_i)$, and the predictive score is the model uncertainty. This formulation leads to a confusion matrix as shown in Figure 1 (Krishnan and Tickoo, 2020). Here, the four confusion matrix variables take on new meanings: (1) True Positive (TP) corresponds to the case where the prediction is inaccurate and the model is uncertain, (2) True Negative (TN) to the accurate and certain case, (3) False Negative (FN) to the inaccurate and certain case (i.e., over-confidence), and finally (4) False Positive (FP) to the accurate and uncertain case (i.e., under-confidence). Now, consider having the model predict its testing error using model uncertainty. The precision (TP/(TP+FP)) measures the fraction of inaccurate examples where the model is uncertain, recall (TP/(TP+FN)) measures the fraction of uncertain examples where the model is inaccurate, and the false positive rate (FP/(FP+TN)) measures the fraction of under-confident examples among the correct predictions. Thus, the model's calibration performance can be measured by the area under the precision-recall curve (***Calibration AUPRC***) and under the receiver operating characteristic curve (***Calibration AUROC***) for this problem. It is worth noting that the calibration AUPRC is closely related to the intrinsic metrics for the model's collaborative effectiveness: we discuss this in greater detail for the *Review Efficiency* in Section 4.1 and Appendix A.2). This renders it especially suitable for evaluating model uncertainty in the context of collaborative content moderation.

4 The Collaborative Content Moderation Task

Online content moderation is a *collaborative* process, performed by humans working in conjunction with machine learning models. For example, the model can select a set of likely policy-violating posts for further review by human moderators. In this work, we consider a setting where a neural model interacts with an "oracle" human moderator with limited capacity in moderating online comments. Given a large number of examples $\{x_i\}_{i=1}^n$, the model first generates the predictive probability $p(y|x_i)$ and review score $u(x_i)$ for each example. Then, the model sends a pre-specified number of these examples to human moderators according to the rankings of the review score $u(x_i)$, and relies on its prediction $p(y|x_i)$ for the rest of the examples. In this work, we make the simplifying assumption that the human experts act like an oracle, correctly labeling all comments sent by the model.

4.1 Measuring the Performance of the Collaborative Moderation System

Machine learning systems for online content moderation are typically evaluated using metrics like accuracy or area under the receiver operating characteristic curve (AUROC). These metrics reflect the origins of these systems in classification problems, such as for detecting / classifying online abuse, harassment, or toxicity (Yin et al., 2009; Dinakar et al., 2011; Cheng et al., 2015; Wulczyn et al., 2017). However, they do not capture the model's ability to effectively collaborate with human moderators, or the performance of the resultant collaborative system.

New metrics, both extrinsic and intrinsic (Mollá and Hutchinson, 2003), are one of the core contributions of this work. We introduce extrinsic metrics describing the performance of the overall model-moderator collaborative system (Oracle-Model Collaborative Accuracy and AUC, analogous to the classic accuracy and AUC), and an intrinsic metric focusing on the model's ability to effectively collaborate with human moderators (Review Efficiency), i.e., how well the model selects the examples in need of further review.

Extrinsic Metrics: Oracle-model Collaborative Accuracy and AUC To capture the collaborative interaction between human moderators and machine learning models, we first propose ***Oracle-Model Collaborative Accuracy* (OC-Acc)**. OC-Acc measures the combined accuracy of this collaborative process, subject to a limited review capacity α for the human oracle (i.e., the oracle can process at most $\alpha \times 100\%$ of the total examples). Formally, given a dataset $D = \{(x_i, y_i)\}_{i=1}^n$, for a predictive model $f(x_i)$ generating a review score $u(x_i)$, the Oracle-Model Collaborative Accuracy for example x_i is

$$\text{OC-Acc}(x_i|\alpha) = \begin{cases} 1 & \text{if } u(x_i) > q_{1-\alpha} \\ \mathbb{I}(f(x_i) = y_i) & \text{otherwise} \end{cases},$$

Thus, over the whole dataset, OC-Acc(α) = $\frac{1}{n}\sum_{i=1}^n$ OC-Acc$(x_i|\alpha)$. Here $q_{1-\alpha}$ is the $(1-\alpha)^{\text{th}}$ quantile of the model's review scores $\{u(x_i)\}_{i=1}^n$ over the entire dataset. OC-Acc thus describes the performance of a collaborative system which defers to a human oracle when the review score $u(x_i)$ is high, and relies on the model prediction otherwise, capturing the real-world usage and performance of the underlying model in a way that traditional metrics fail to.

However, as an accuracy-like metric, OC-Acc relies on a set threshold on the prediction score. This limits the metric's ability in describing model performance when compared to threshold-agnostic metrics like AUC. Moreover, OC-Acc can be sensitive to the intrinsic class imbalance in the toxicity datasets, appearing overly optimistic for model predictions that are biased toward negative class, similar to traditional accuracy metrics (Borkan et al., 2019). Therefore in practice, we prefer the AUC analogue of Oracle-Model Collaborative Accuracy, which we term the ***Oracle-Model Collaborative AUC* (OC-AUC)**. OC-AUC measures the same collaborative process as the OC-Acc, where the model sends the predictions with the top $\alpha \times 100\%$ of review scores. Then, similar to the standard AUC computation, OC-AUC sets up a collection of classifiers with varying predictive score thresholds, each of which has access to the oracle exactly as for OC-Acc (Davis and Goadrich, 2006). Each of these classifiers sends the same set of examples to the oracle (since the review score $u(x)$ is threshold-independent), and the oracle corrects model predictions when they are incorrect given the threshold. The OC-AUC—both OC-AUROC and OC-AUPRC—can then be calculated over this set of classifiers following the standard AUC algorithms (Davis and Goadrich, 2006).

Intrinsic Metric: Review Efficiency The metrics so far measure the performance of the overall collaborative system, which combines both the model's predictive accuracy and the model's effectiveness in collaboration. To understand the source of the improvement, we also introduce ***Review Efficiency***, an intrinsic metric focusing solely on the model's effectiveness in collaboration. Specifically, *Review Efficiency* is the proportion of examples sent to the oracle for which the model prediction would otherwise have been incorrect. This can be thought of as the model's precision in selecting inaccurate examples for further review (TP/(TP+FP) in Figure 1).

Note that the system's overall performance (measured by the oracle-model collaborative accuracy) can be rewritten as a weighted sum of the model's original predictive accuracy and the Review Efficiency (RE):

$$\text{OC-Acc}(\alpha) = \text{Acc} + \alpha \times \text{RE}(\alpha) \quad (2)$$

where $\text{RE}(\alpha)$ is the model's review efficiency among all the examples whose review score $u(x_i)$ are greater than $q_{1-\alpha}$ (i.e., those sent to human moderators). Thus, a model with better predictive performance and higher review efficiency yields better performance in the overall system. The benefits of review efficiency become more pronounced as the review fraction α increases. We derive Eq. (2) in Appendix B.

4.2 CoToMoD: An Evaluation Benchmark for Real-world Collaborative Moderation

In a realistic industrial setting, toxicity detection models are often trained on a well-curated dataset with clean annotations, and then deployed to an environment that contains a more diverse range of sociolinguistic phenomena, and additionally exhibits systematic shifts in the lexical and topical distributions when compared to the training corpus.

To this end, we introduce a challenging data benchmark, ***Collaborative Toxicity Moderation in the Wild* (CoToMoD)**, to evaluate the performance of collaborative moderation systems in a realistic environment. CoToMoD consists of a set of *train*, *test*, and *deployment* environments: the *train* and *test* environments consist of 200k comments from Wikipedia discussion comments from 2004–2015 (the Wikipedia Talk Corpus (Wulczyn et al., 2017)), and the *deployment* environment consists of one million public comments appeared on approximately 50 English-language news sites across the world from 2015–2017 (the CivilComments dataset (Borkan et al., 2019)). This setup mirrors the real-world implementation of these methods, where robust performance under changing data is essential for proper deployment (Amodei et al., 2016).

Notably, CoToMoD contains two data challenges often encountered in practice: (1) *Distributional Shift*, i.e. the comments in the training and deployment environments cover different time periods and surround different topics of interest (Wikipedia pages vs. news articles). As the CivilComments corpus is much larger in size, it contains a considerable collection of long-tail phenomena (e.g., neologisms, obfuscation, etc.) that appear less frequently in the training data. (2) *Class Imbalance*, i.e. the fact that most online content is not toxic (Cheng et al., 2017; Wulczyn et al., 2017). This manifests in the datasets we use: roughly 2.5% (50,350 / 1,999,514) of the examples in the CivilComments dataset, and 9.6% (21,384 / 223,549) of the examples in Wikipedia Talk Corpus examples are toxic (Wulczyn et al., 2017; Borkan et al., 2019). As we will show, failing to account for class imbalance can severely bias model predictions toward the majority (non-toxic) class, reducing the effectiveness of the collaborative system.

5 Methods

Moderation Review Strategy In measuring model-moderator collaborative performance, we consider two review strategies (i.e. using different review scores $u(x)$). First, we experiment with a common toxicity-based review strategy (Jigsaw, 2019; Salganik and Lee, 2020). Specifically, the model sends comments for review in decreasing order of the predicted toxicity score (i.e., the predictive probability $p(y|x)$), equivalent to a review score $u_{\text{tox}}(x) = p(y|x)$. The second strategy is uncertainty-based: given $p(y|x)$, we use uncertainty as the review score, $u_{\text{unc}}(x) = p(y|x)(1 - p(y|x))$ (recall Eq. (1)), so that the review score is maximized at $p(y|x) = 0.5$, and decreases toward 0 as $p(x)$ approaches 0 or 1. Which strategy performs best depends on the toxicity distribution in the dataset and the available review capacity α.

Uncertainty Models We evaluate the performance of classic and the latest state-of-the-art probabilistic deep learning methods on the CoToMoD benchmark. We consider $\text{BERT}_{\texttt{base}}$ as the base model (Devlin et al., 2019), and select five methods based on their practical applicability for transformer models. Specifically, we consider (1) *Deterministic* which computes the sigmoid probability $p(x) = \text{sigmoid}(\text{logit}(x))$ of a vanilla BERT model (Hendrycks and Gimpel, 2017), (2) *Monte Carlo Dropout* (*MC Dropout*) which estimates uncertainty using the Monte Carlo average of $p(x)$ from 10 dropout samples (Gal and Ghahramani, 2016), (3) *Deep Ensemble* which estimates uncertainty using the ensemble mean of $p(x)$ from 10 BERT models trained in parallel (Lakshminarayanan et al., 2017), (4) *Spectral-normalized Neural Gaussian Process* (*SNGP*), a recent state-of-the-art approach which improves a BERT model's uncertainty quality by transforming it into an approximate Gaussian process model (Liu et al., 2020), and (5) *SNGP Ensemble*, which is the Deep Ensemble using SNGP as the base model.

Learning Objective To address class imbalance, we consider combining the uncertainty methods with *Focal Loss* (Lin et al., 2017). Focal loss reshapes the loss function to down-weight "easy" negatives (i.e. non-toxic examples), thereby focusing training on a smaller set of more difficult examples, and empirically leading to improved predictive and uncertainty calibration performance on class-imbalanced datasets (Lin et al., 2017; Mukhoti et al., 2020). We focus our attention on focal loss (rather than other approaches to class imbalance) because of how this impact on calibration interacts with our moderation review strategies.

6 Benchmark Experiments

We first examine the prediction and calibration performance of the uncertainty models alone (Section 6.1). For prediction, we compute the predictive accuracy (Acc) and the predictive AUC (both AUROC and AUPRC). For uncertainty, we compute the Brier score (i.e., the mean squared error between true labels and predictive probabilities, a standard uncertainty metric), and also the Calibration AUPRC (Section 3).

We then evaluate the models' collaboration performance under both the uncertainty- and the toxicity-based review strategies (Section 6.2). For each model-strategy combination, we measure the model's collaboration ability by computing Review Efficiency, and evaluate the performance of the overall collaborative system using Oracle-Model Collaborative AUROC (OC-AUROC). We evaluate all collaborative metrics over a range of human moderator review capacities, with their review fractions (i.e., fraction of total examples the model sends to the moderator for further review) ranging over $\{0.001, 0.005, 0.01, 0.02, 0.05, 0.1, 0.15, 0.20\}$.

Results on further uncertainty and collaboration metrics (Calibration AUROC, OC-Acc, OC-AUPRC, etc.) are in Appendix D.

6.1 Prediction and Calibration

Table 1 shows the performance of all uncertainty methods evaluated on the testing (the Wikipedia Talk corpus) and the deployment environments (the CivilComments corpus).

First, we compare the uncertainty methods based on the predictive and calibration AUC. As shown, for prediction, the ensemble models (both SNGP Ensemble and Deep Ensemble) provide the best performance, while the SNGP Ensemble and MC Dropout perform best for uncertainty calibration. Training with focal loss systematically improves the model prediction under class imbalance (improving the predictive AUC), while incurring a trade-off with the model's calibration quality (i.e. decreasing the calibration AUC).

Next, we turn to the model performance between the test and deployment environments. Across all methods, we observe a significant drop in predictive performance (~ 0.28 for AUROC and ~ 0.13 for AUPRC), and a less pronounced, but still noticeable drop in uncertainty calibration (~ 0.05 for Calibration AUPRC). Interestingly, focal loss seems to mitigate the drop in predictive performance, but also slightly exacerbates the drop in uncertainty calibration.

Lastly, we observe a counter-intuitive improvement in the non-AUC metrics (i.e., accuracy and Brier score) in the out-of-domain deployment environment. This is likely due to their sensitivity to class imbalance (recall that toxic examples are slightly less rare in CivilComments). As a result, these classic metrics tend to favor model predictions biased toward the negative class, and therefore are less suitable for evaluating model performance in the context of toxic comment moderation.

6.2 Collaboration Performance

Figure 2 and 3 show the Oracle-model Collaborative AUROC (OC-AUROC) of the overall collaborative system, and Figure 4 shows the Review Efficiency of uncertainty models. Both the toxicity-based (dashed line) and uncertainty-based review strategies (solid line) are included.

		Testing Env (Wikipedia Talk)					Deployment Env (CivilComments)				
	Model	AUROC ↑	AUPRC ↑	Acc. ↑	Brier ↓	Calib. AUPRC ↑	AUROC ↑	AUPRC ↑	Acc. ↑	Brier ↓	Calib. AUPRC ↑
XENT	Deterministic	0.9734	0.8019	0.9231	0.0548	0.4053	0.7796	0.6689	0.9628	0.0246	0.3581
	SNGP	0.9741	0.8029	0.9233	0.0548	0.4063	0.7695	0.6665	0.9640	0.0253	0.3660
	MC Dropout	0.9729	0.8006	**0.9274**	**0.0508**	0.4020	0.7806	0.6727	**0.9671**	**0.0241**	**0.3707**
	Deep Ensemble	0.9738	0.8074	0.9231	0.0544	0.4045	**0.7849**	**0.6741**	0.9625	0.0242	0.3484
	SNGP Ensemble	**0.9741**	**0.8045**	0.9226	0.0549	**0.4158**	0.7749	0.6719	0.9633	0.0248	0.3655
Focal	Deterministic	0.9730	0.8036	0.9476	0.0628	0.3804	0.8013	0.6766	**0.9795**	0.0377	0.3018
	SNGP	0.9736	0.8076	0.9455	0.0388	0.3885	0.8003	0.6820	0.9784	**0.0264**	0.3181
	MC Dropout	0.9741	0.8076	0.9472	0.0622	**0.3890**	0.8009	0.6790	0.9790	0.0360	0.3185
	Deep Ensemble	0.9735	0.8077	**0.9479**	0.0639	0.3840	**0.8041**	0.6814	**0.9795**	0.0381	0.3035
	SNGP Ensemble	**0.9742**	**0.8122**	0.9467	**0.0379**	0.3846	0.8002	**0.6827**	0.9790	0.0266	**0.3212**

Table 1: Metrics for models evaluated on the testing environment (the Wikipedia Talk corpus, left) and deployment environment (the CivilComments corpus, right). XENT (top) and Focal (bottom) indicate models trained with cross-entropy and focal losses, respectively. The best metric values for each loss function are shown in bold.

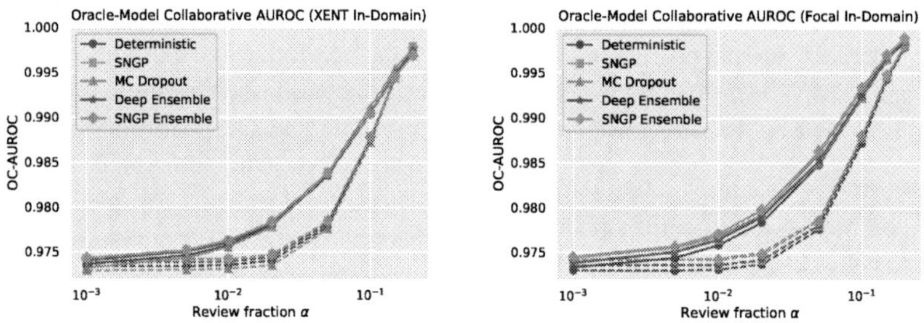

Figure 2: Semilog plot of oracle-model collaborative AUROC as a function of review fraction (the proportion of comments the model can send for human/oracle review), trained with cross-entropy (XENT, left) or focal loss (right) and evaluated on the Wikipedia Talk corpus (i.e., the in-domain testing environment). **Solid line:** uncertainty-based review strategy. **Dashed line:** toxicity-based review strategy. The best performing method is the SNGP Ensemble trained with focal loss and uses the uncertainty-based strategy.

Effect of Review Strategy For the AUC performance of the collaborative system, *the uncertainty-based review strategy consistently outperforms the toxicity-based review strategy*. For example, in the in-domain environment (Wikipedia Talk corpus), using the uncertainty- rather than toxicity-based review strategy yields larger OC-AUROC improvements than any modeling change; this holds across all measured review fractions. We see a similar trend for OC-AUPRC (Appendix Figure 7-8).

The trend in Review Efficiency (Figure 4) provides a more nuanced view to this picture. As shown, the efficiency of the toxicity-based strategy starts to improve as the review fraction increases, leading to a cross-over with the uncertainty-based strategy at high fractions. This is likely caused by the fact that in toxicity classification, the false positive rate exceeds the false negative rate. Therefore sending a large number of positive predictions eventually leads the collaborative system to capture more errors, at the cost of a higher review load on human moderators. We notice that this transition occurs much earlier out-of-domain on CivilComments (Figure 4 right). This highlights the impact of the toxicity distribution of the data on the best review strategy: because the proportion of toxic examples is much lower in CivilComments than in the Wikipedia Talk Corpus, the cross-over between the uncertainty and toxicity review strategies correspondingly occurs at lower review fractions. Finally, it is important to note that this advantage in review efficiency does not directly translate to improvements for the overall system. For example, the OC-AUCs using the toxicity strategy are still lower than those with the uncertainty strategy even for high review fractions.

Effect of Modeling Approach Recall that the performance of the overall collaborative system is the result of the model performance in both prediction and calibration, e.g. Eq. (2). As a result, the model performance in Section 6.1 translates to performance on the collaborative metrics. For example, the ensemble methods (SNGP Ensemble and Deep Ensemble) consistently outperform on the OC-AUC metrics due to their high performance in predictive AUC and decent performance in calibration (Table 1). On the other hand, MC Dropout has

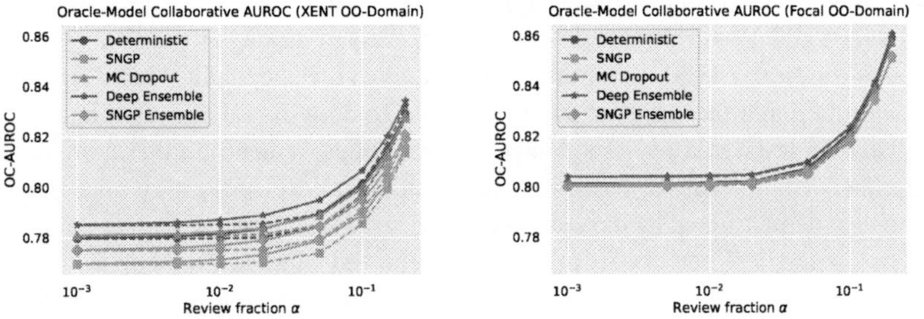

Figure 3: Semilog plot of oracle-model collaborative AUROC as a function of review fraction, trained with cross-entropy (XENT, left) or focal loss (right) and evaluated on CivilComments corpus (i.e., the out-of-domain deployment environment). **Solid line:** uncertainty-based review strategy. **Dashed line:** toxicity-based review strategy. Training with focal rather than cross-entropy loss yields a large improvement. The best performing method is the Deep Ensemble trained with focal loss and uses the uncertainty-based review strategy.

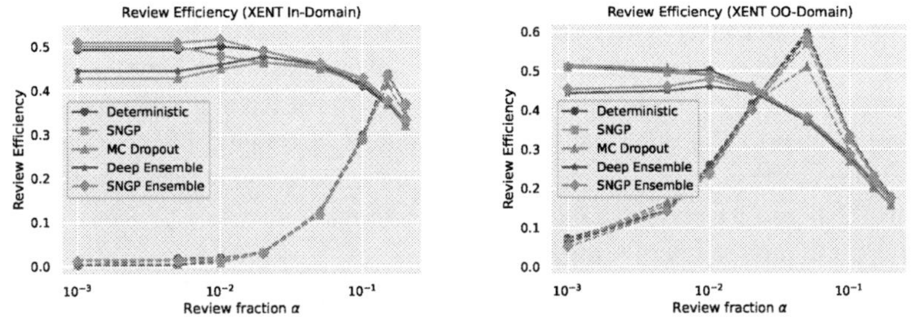

Figure 4: Semilog plot of review efficiency as a function of review fraction, trained with cross-entropy and evaluated on the Wikipedia Talk corpus (i.e., the in-domain testing environment, left) and CivilComments (i.e., the out-of-domain deployment environment, right). **Solid line:** uncertainty-based review strategy. **Dashed line:** toxicity-based review strategy.

good calibration performance but sub-optimal predictive AUC. As a result, it sometimes attains the best Review Efficiency (e.g., Figure 4, right), but never achieves the best overall OC-AUC. Finally, comparing between training objectives, the focal-loss-trained models tend to outperform their cross-entropy-trained counterparts in OC-AUC, due to the fact that focal loss tends to bring significant benefits to the predictive AUC (albeit at a small cost to the calibration performance).

7 Conclusion

In this work, we presented the problem of collaborative content moderation, and introduced *CoToMoD*, a challenging benchmark for evaluating the practical effectiveness of collaborative (model-moderator) content moderation systems. We proposed principled metrics to quantify how effectively a machine learning model and human (e.g. a moderator) can collaborate. These include *Oracle-Model Collaborative Accuracy* (OC-Acc) and *AUC* (OC-AUC), which measure analogues of the usual accuracy or AUC for interacting human-AI systems subject to limited human review capacity. We also proposed *Review Efficiency*, which quantifies how effectively a model utilizes human decisions. These metrics are distinct from classic measures of predictive performance or uncertainty calibration, and enable us to evaluate the performance of the full collaborative system as a function of human attention, as well as to understand how efficiently the collaborative system utilizes human decision-making. Moreover, though we focused here on measuring the combined system's performance through metrics analogous to accuracy and AUC, it is trivial to extend these to other classic metrics like precision and recall.

Using these new metrics, we evaluated the performance of a variety of models on the collaborative content moderation task. We considered two canonical strategies for collaborative review: one based on the toxicity scores, and a new one using model uncertainty. We found that the uncertainty-based review strategy outperforms the toxicity strategy across a variety of models and range of human review capacities, yielding a $>30\%$ absolute increase in how efficiently the model uses human decisions and ~ 0.01 and ~ 0.05 absolute increases in the collaborative system's AUROC and AUPRC, respectively. This merits further study and consideration of this strategy's use in content moderation. The interaction between the data distribution and best review strategy demonstrated by the crossover between the two strategies' performance out-of-domain) emphasizes the implicit trade-off between false positives and false negatives in the two review strategies: because toxicity is rare, prioritizing comments for review in order of toxicity reduces the false positive rate while potentially increasing the false negative rate. By comparison, the uncertainty-based review strategy treats false positives and negatives more evenly. Further study is needed to clarify this interaction. Our work shows that the choice of review strategy drastically changes the collaborative system performance: evaluating and striving to optimize only the model yields much smaller improvements than changing the review strategy, and misses major opportunities to improve the overall system.

Though the results presented in the current paper are encouraging, there remain important challenges for uncertainty modeling in the domain of toxic content moderation. In particular, dataset bias remains a significant issue: statistical correlation between the annotated toxicity labels and various surface-level cues may lead models to learn to overly rely on e.g. lexical or dialectal patterns (Zhou et al., 2021). This could cause the model to produce high-confidence mispredictions for comments containing these cues (e.g., reclaimed words or counter-speech), resulting in a degradation in calibration performance in the deployment environment (cf. Table 1). Surprisingly, the standard debiasing techniques we experimented in this work (specifically, focal loss (Karimi Mahabadi et al., 2020)) only exacerbated this decline in calibration performance. This suggests that naively applying debiasing techniques may incur unexpected negative impacts on other aspects of the moderation system. Further research is needed into modeling approaches that can achieve robust performance both in prediction and in uncertainty calibration under data bias and distributional shift (Nam et al., 2020; Utama et al., 2020; Du et al., 2021; Yaghoobzadeh et al., 2021; Bao et al., 2021; Karimi Mahabadi et al., 2020).

There exist several important directions for future work. One key direction is to develop better review strategies than the ones discussed here: though the uncertainty-based strategy outperforms the toxicity-based one, there may be room for further improvement. Furthermore, constraints on the moderation process may necessitate different review strategies: for example, if content can only be removed with moderator approval, we could experiment with a hybrid strategy which sends a mixture of high toxicity and high uncertainty content for human review. A second direction is to study how these methods perform with real moderators: the experiments in this work are computational and there may exist further challenges in practice. For example, the difficulty of rating a comment can depend on the text itself in unexpected ways. Finally, a linked question is how to communicate uncertainty and different review strategies to moderators: simpler communicable strategies may be preferable to more complex ones with better theoretical performance.

Acknowledgements

The authors would like to thank Jeffrey Sorensen for extensive feedback on the manuscript, and Nitesh Goyal, Aditya Gupta, Luheng He, Balaji Lakshminarayanan, Alyssa Lees, and Jie Ren for helpful comments and discussions.

References

Robert Adragna, Elliot Creager, David Madras, and Richard Zemel. 2020. Fairness and robustness in invariant learning: A case study in toxicity classification. *arXiv preprint arXiv:2011.06485*.

Betty van Aken, Julian Risch, Ralf Krestel, and Alexander Löser. 2018. Challenges for toxic comment classification: An in-depth error analysis. In *Proceedings of the 2nd Workshop on Abusive Language Online (ALW2)*, pages 33–42, Brussels, Belgium. Association for Computational Linguistics.

Dario Amodei, Chris Olah, Jacob Steinhardt, Paul Christiano, John Schulman, and Dan Mané. 2016. Concrete problems in ai safety. *arXiv preprint arXiv:1606.06565*.

Abdullah Awaysheh, Jeffrey Wilcke, François Elvinger, Loren Rees, Weiguo Fan, and Kurt L. Zimmerman. 2019. Review of Medical Decision Support and Machine-Learning Methods. *Veterinary Pathology*, 56(4):512–525.

Gagan Bansal, Besmira Nushi, Ece Kamar, Eric Horvitz, and Daniel S. Weld. 2021. Is the most accurate ai the best teammate? optimizing ai for teamwork. *Proceedings of the AAAI Conference on Artificial Intelligence*, 35(13):11405–11414.

Yujia Bao, Shiyu Chang, and Regina Barzilay. 2021. Predict then interpolate: A simple algorithm to learn stable classifiers. In *International Conference on Machine Learning*. PMLR.

Peter L. Bartlett and Marten H. Wegkamp. 2008. Classification with a reject option using a hinge loss. *Journal of Machine Learning Research*, 9(59):1823–1840.

Daniel Borkan, Lucas Dixon, Jeffrey Sorensen, Nithum Thain, and Lucy Vasserman. 2019. Nuanced metrics for measuring unintended bias with real data for text classification. *CoRR*, abs/1903.04561.

Justin Cheng, Michael Bernstein, Cristian Danescu-Niculescu-Mizil, and Jure Leskovec. 2017. Anyone can become a troll: Causes of trolling behavior in online discussions. In *Proceedings of the 2017 ACM Conference on Computer Supported Cooperative Work and Social Computing*, CSCW '17, page 1217–1230, New York, NY, USA. Association for Computing Machinery.

Justin Cheng, Cristian Danescu-Niculescu-Mizil, and Jure Leskovec. 2015. Antisocial behavior in online discussion communities. *Proceedings of the International AAAI Conference on Web and Social Media*, 9(1).

Corinna Cortes, Giulia DeSalvo, Claudio Gentile, Mehryar Mohri, and Scott Yang. 2018. Online learning with abstention. In *Proceedings of the 35th International Conference on Machine Learning*, volume 80 of *Proceedings of Machine Learning Research*, pages 1059–1067, Stockholmsmässan, Stockholm Sweden. PMLR.

Corinna Cortes, Giulia DeSalvo, and Mehryar Mohri. 2016. Learning with rejection. In *Algorithmic Learning Theory - 27th International Conference, ALT 2016, Proceedings*, Lecture Notes in Computer Science (including subseries Lecture Notes in Artificial Intelligence and Lecture Notes in Bioinformatics), pages 67–82. Springer Verlag. 27th International Conference on Algorithmic Learning Theory, ALT 2016 ; Conference date: 19-10-2016 Through 21-10-2016.

Jesse Davis and Mark Goadrich. 2006. The relationship between precision-recall and roc curves. In *Proceedings of the 23rd International Conference on Machine Learning*, ICML '06, page 233–240, New York, NY, USA. Association for Computing Machinery.

Jacob Devlin, Ming-Wei Chang, Kenton Lee, and Kristina Toutanova. 2019. BERT: Pre-training of deep bidirectional transformers for language understanding. In *Proceedings of the 2019 Conference of the North American Chapter of the Association for Computational Linguistics: Human Language Technologies, Volume 1 (Long and Short Papers)*, pages 4171–4186, Minneapolis, Minnesota. Association for Computational Linguistics.

Karthik Dinakar, Roi Reichart, and Henry Lieberman. 2011. Modeling the detection of textual cyberbullying. *Proceedings of the International AAAI Conference on Web and Social Media*, 5(1).

Lucas Dixon, John Li, Jeffrey Sorensen, Nithum Thain, and Lucy Vasserman. 2018. Measuring and mitigating unintended bias in text classification. In *Proceedings of the 2018 AAAI/ACM Conference on AI, Ethics, and Society*, AIES '18, page 67–73, New York, NY, USA. Association for Computing Machinery.

Mengnan Du, Varun Manjunatha, Rajiv Jain, Ruchi Deshpande, Franck Dernoncourt, Jiuxiang Gu, Tong Sun, and Xia Hu. 2021. Towards interpreting and mitigating shortcut learning behavior of NLU models. *CoRR*, abs/2103.06922.

Michael W. Dusenberry, Dustin Tran, Edward Choi, Jonas Kemp, Jeremy Nixon, Ghassen Jerfel, Katherine Heller, and Andrew M. Dai. 2020. Analyzing the role of model uncertainty for electronic health records. In *Proceedings of the ACM Conference on Health, Inference, and Learning*, CHIL '20, pages 204–213, New York, NY, USA. Association for Computing Machinery.

Bassey Etim. 2017. The times sharply increases articles open for comments, using google's technology. *The New York Times*, 13.

Yarin Gal and Zoubin Ghahramani. 2016. Dropout as a bayesian approximation: Representing model uncertainty in deep learning. In *Proceedings of The 33rd International Conference on Machine Learning*, volume 48 of *Proceedings of Machine Learning Research*, pages 1050–1059, New York, New York, USA. PMLR.

Ian Goodfellow, Yoshua Bengio, and Aaron Courville. 2016. *Deep Learning*. MIT Press. `http://www.deeplearningbook.org`.

Chuan Guo, Geoff Pleiss, Yu Sun, and Kilian Q. Weinberger. 2017. On calibration of modern neural networks. In *Proceedings of the 34th International Conference on Machine Learning*, volume 70 of *Proceedings of Machine Learning Research*, pages 1321–1330. PMLR.

Dan Hendrycks and Kevin Gimpel. 2017. A baseline for detecting misclassified and out-of-distribution examples in neural networks. In *5th International Conference on Learning Representations, ICLR 2017, Toulon, France, April 24-26, 2017, Conference Track Proceedings*. OpenReview.net.

Andrew Jesson, Sören Mindermann, Uri Shalit, and Yarin Gal. 2020. Identifying Causal-Effect Inference Failure with Uncertainty-Aware Models. In *Advances in Neural Information Processing Systems*, volume 33, pages 11637–11649. Curran Associates, Inc.

Jigsaw. 2019. How latin america's second largest social platform moderates more than 150k comments a month. https://medium.com/jigsaw/how-latin-americas-second-largest-social-platform-moderates-more-than-150k-comments-a-month-df0d8a3ac242. Accessed: 2021-04-26.

Rabeeh Karimi Mahabadi, Yonatan Belinkov, and James Henderson. 2020. End-to-end bias mitigation by modelling biases in corpora. In *Proceedings of the 58th Annual Meeting of the Association for Computational Linguistics*, pages 8706–8716, Online. Association for Computational Linguistics.

Pang Wei Koh, Shiori Sagawa, Henrik Marklund, Sang Michael Xie, Marvin Zhang, Akshay Balsubramani, Weihua Hu, Michihiro Yasunaga, Richard Lanas Phillips, Sara Beery, et al. 2020. Wilds: A benchmark of in-the-wild distribution shifts. *arXiv preprint arXiv:2012.07421*.

Benjamin Kompa, Jasper Snoek, and Andrew L. Beam. 2021. Second opinion needed: communicating uncertainty in medical machine learning. *npj Digital Medicine*, 4(1):4.

Ranganath Krishnan and Omesh Tickoo. 2020. Improving model calibration with accuracy versus uncertainty optimization. *Advances in Neural Information Processing Systems*.

Balaji Lakshminarayanan, Alexander Pritzel, and Charles Blundell. 2017. Simple and scalable predictive uncertainty estimation using deep ensembles. In *Advances in Neural Information Processing Systems*, volume 30. Curran Associates, Inc.

Tsung-Yi Lin, Priya Goyal, Ross Girshick, Kaiming He, and Piotr Dollar. 2017. Focal loss for dense object detection. In *Proceedings of the IEEE International Conference on Computer Vision (ICCV)*.

Jeremiah Liu, Zi Lin, Shreyas Padhy, Dustin Tran, Tania Bedrax Weiss, and Balaji Lakshminarayanan. 2020. Simple and principled uncertainty estimation with deterministic deep learning via distance awareness. In *Advances in Neural Information Processing Systems*, volume 33, pages 7498–7512. Curran Associates, Inc.

Jeremiah Liu, John Paisley, Marianthi-Anna Kioumourtzoglou, and Brent Coull. 2019. Accurate uncertainty estimation and decomposition in ensemble learning. In *Advances in Neural Information Processing Systems*, volume 32. Curran Associates, Inc.

Diego Mollá and Ben Hutchinson. 2003. Intrinsic versus extrinsic evaluations of parsing systems. In *Proceedings of the EACL 2003 Workshop on Evaluation Initiatives in Natural Language Processing: Are Evaluation Methods, Metrics and Resources Reusable?*, Evalinitiatives '03, page 43–50, USA. Association for Computational Linguistics.

Jishnu Mukhoti, Viveka Kulharia, Amartya Sanyal, Stuart Golodetz, Philip Torr, and Puneet Dokania. 2020. Calibrating deep neural networks using focal loss. In *Advances in Neural Information Processing Systems*, volume 33, pages 15288–15299. Curran Associates, Inc.

Mahdi Pakdaman Naeini, Gregory F. Cooper, and Milos Hauskrecht. 2015. Obtaining well calibrated probabilities using bayesian binning. In *Proceedings of the Twenty-Ninth AAAI Conference on Artificial Intelligence*, AAAI'15, page 2901–2907. AAAI Press.

Junhyun Nam, Hyuntak Cha, Sungsoo Ahn, Jaeho Lee, and Jinwoo Shin. 2020. Learning from failure: De-biasing classifier from biased classifier. In *Advances in Neural Information Processing Systems*, volume 33, pages 20673–20684. Curran Associates, Inc.

Yaniv Ovadia, Emily Fertig, Jie Ren, Zachary Nado, D. Sculley, Sebastian Nowozin, Joshua Dillon, Balaji Lakshminarayanan, and Jasper Snoek. 2019. Can you trust your model's uncertainty? evaluating predictive uncertainty under dataset shift. In *Advances in Neural Information Processing Systems*, volume 32. Curran Associates, Inc.

Lee Rainie, Janna Anderson, and Jonathan Albright. 2017. The Future of Free Speech, Trolls, Anonymity and Fake News Online.

Matthew J. Salganik and Robin C. Lee. 2020. To apply machine learning responsibly, we use it in moderation. https://open.nytimes.com/to-apply-machine-learning-responsibly-we-use-it-in-moderation-d001f49e0644/. Accessed: 2021-04-26.

T. J. Sullivan. 2015. *Introduction to uncertainty quantification*. Springer.

Prasetya Ajie Utama, Nafise Sadat Moosavi, and Iryna Gurevych. 2020. Towards debiasing NLU models from unknown biases. In *Proceedings of the 2020 Conference on Empirical Methods in Natural Language Processing (EMNLP)*, pages 7597–7610, Online. Association for Computational Linguistics.

Zhao Wang and Aron Culotta. 2020. Identifying spurious correlations for robust text classification. In *Findings of the Association for Computational Linguistics: EMNLP 2020*, pages 3431–3440, Online. Association for Computational Linguistics.

Ellery Wulczyn, Nithum Thain, and Lucas Dixon. 2017. Ex machina: Personal attacks seen at scale. In *Proceedings of the 26th International Conference on World Wide Web*, WWW '17, pages 1391–1399, Republic and Canton of Geneva, CHE. International World Wide Web Conferences Steering Committee.

Yadollah Yaghoobzadeh, Soroush Mehri, Remi Tachet des Combes, T. J. Hazen, and Alessandro Sordoni. 2021. Increasing robustness to spurious correlations using forgettable examples. In *Proceedings of the 16th Conference of the European Chapter of the Association for Computational Linguistics: Main Volume*, pages 3319–3332, Online. Association for Computational Linguistics.

Dawei Yin, Zhenzhen Xue, Liangjie Hong, Brian D Davison, April Kontostathis, and Lynne Edwards. 2009. Detection of harassment on web 2.0. *Proceedings of the Content Analysis in the WEB*, 2:1–7.

Xuhui Zhou, Maarten Sap, Swabha Swayamdipta, Yejin Choi, and Noah Smith. 2021. Challenges in automated debiasing for toxic language detection. In *Proceedings of the 16th Conference of the European Chapter of the Association for Computational Linguistics: Main Volume*, pages 3143–3155, Online. Association for Computational Linguistics.

A Details on Metrics

A.1 Expected Calibration Error

For completeness, we include a definition of the expected calibration error (ECE) (Naeini et al., 2015) here. We use the ECE as a comparison for the uncertainty calibration performance alongside the Brier score in the tables in Appendix D.

ECE can be computed by discretizes the probability range $[0, 1]$ into a set of B bins, and computes the weighted average of the difference between confidence (the mean probability within each bin) and the accuracy (the fraction of predictions within each bin that are correct),

$$\text{ECE} = \sum_{b=1}^{B} \frac{n_b}{N} |\text{conf}(b) - \text{acc}(b)|, \quad (3)$$

where $\text{acc}(b)$ and $\text{conf}(b)$ denote the accuracy and confidence for bin b, respectively, n_b is the number of examples in bin b, and $N = \sum_b n_b$ is the total number of examples.

A.2 Connection between Calibration AUPRC and Collaboration Metrics

As discussed in Section 3, Calibration AUPRC is an especially suitable metric for measuring model uncertainty in the context of collaborative content moderation, due to its close connection with the intrinsic metrics for the model's collaboration effectiveness.

Specifically, the *Review Efficiency* metric (introduced in Section 4.1) can be understood as the analog of **precision** for the calibration task. To see this, recall the four confusion matrix variables introduced in Figure 1: (1) True Positive (TP) corresponds to the case where the prediction is inaccurate and the model is uncertain, (2) True Negative (TN) to the accurate and certain case, (3) False Negative (FN) to the inaccurate and certain case (i.e., over-confidence), and finally (4) False Positive (FP) to the accurate and uncertain case (i.e., under-confidence).

Then, given a review capacity constraint α, we see that

$$\text{ReviewEfficiency}(\alpha) = \frac{TP_\alpha}{TP_\alpha + FP_\alpha},$$

which measures the proportion of examples that were sent to human moderator that would otherwise be classified incorrectly.

Similarly, we can also define the analog of **recall** for the calibration task, which we term *Review Effectiveness*:

$$\text{ReviewEffectiveness}(\alpha) = \frac{TP_\alpha}{TP_\alpha + FN_\alpha}.$$

Review Effectiveness is also a valid intrinsic metric for the model's collaboration effectivess. It measures the proportion of incorrect model predictions that were successfully corrected using the review strategy. (We visualize model performance in Review Effectiveness in Section D.)

To this end, the calibration AUPRC can be understood as the area under the Review Efficiency v.s. Review Effectiveness curve, with the usual classification threshold replaced by the review capacity α. Therefore, calibration AUPRC serves as a threshold-agnostic metric that captures the model's intrinsic performance in collaboration effectiveness.

A.3 Further Discussion

For the uncertainty-based review, an important question is whether classic uncertainty metrics like Brier score capture good model-moderator collaborative efficiency. The SNGP Ensemble's good performance contrasts with its poorer Brier score (Table 1). By comparison, the calibration AUPRC successfully captures this good performance, and is highest for that model. More generally, the low-review fraction review efficiency with cross-entropy is exactly captured by the calibration AUPRC (same ordering for the two measures). This correspondence is not perfect: though the SNGP Ensemble with focal loss has the highest review efficiency overall, its calibration AUPRC is lower than the MC Dropout or SNGP models (models with next highest review efficiencies). This may reflect the reshaping effect of focal loss on SNGP's calibration (explored in Appendix C). Overall, calibration AUPRC much better captures the relationship between collaborative ability and calibration than do classic calibration metrics like Brier score (or ECE, see Appendix D). This is because classic calibration metrics are population-level averages, whereas calibration AUPRC measures the ranking of the predictions, and is thus more closely linked to the review order problem.

B Connecting Review Efficiency and Collaborative Accuracy

In this appendix, we derive Eq. (2) from the main paper, which connects the Review Efficiency and Oracle-Collaborative Accuracy.

Given a trained toxicity model, a review policy and a dataset, let us denote r as the event that an example gets reviewed, and c as the event that model prediction is correct. Now, assuming the model sends $\alpha \times 100\%$ of examples for human review, we have:

$$\text{Acc} = P(c), \qquad \alpha = P(r).$$

Also, we can write:

$$\text{RE}(\alpha) = P(\neg c|r)$$

i.e., review efficiency $\text{RE}(\alpha)$ is the percentage of incorrect predictions among reviewed examples. Finally:

$$\text{OC-Acc}(\alpha) = P(c \cap \neg r) + P(c \cap r) + P(\neg c \cap r)$$

i.e., an example is predicted correctly by the collaborative system if either the model prediction itself is accurate ($c \cap \neg r$), or it was sent for human review ($c \cap r$ or $\neg c \cap r$).

The above expression of OC-Acc leads to two different decompositions of the OC-Acc. First,

$$\begin{aligned}\text{OC-Acc}(\alpha) &= P(c \cap \neg r) + P(r) \\ &= P(c|\neg r)P(\neg r) + P(r) \\ &= \text{Acc}(1-\alpha) * (1-\alpha) + \alpha,\end{aligned}$$

where $\text{Acc}(1-\alpha)$ is the accuracy among the $(1-\alpha) \times 100\%$ examples that are not sent to human for review.

Alternatively, we can write

$$\begin{aligned}\text{OC-Acc}(\alpha) &= P(c) + P(\neg c \cap r) \\ &= P(c) + P(\neg c|r)P(r) \\ &= \text{Acc} + \text{RE}(\alpha) * \alpha,\end{aligned}$$

which coincides with the expression in Eq. (2).

C Reliability Diagrams for Deterministic and SNGP models

We study the effect of focal loss on calibration quality for SNGP in further detail. We plot the reliability diagrams for the deterministic and SNGP models trained with cross-entropy and focal cross-entropy. Figure 5 shows the reliability diagrams in-domain and Figure 6 shows them out-of-domain. We see that focal loss fundamentally changes the models' uncertainty behavior, systematically shifting the uncertainty curves from overconfidence (the lower right, below the diagonal) and toward the calibration line (the diagonal). However, the exact pattern of change is model dependent. We find that the deterministic model with focal loss is over-confident for predictions under 0.5, and under-confident above 0.5, while the SNGP models are still over-confident, although to a lesser degree compared to using cross-entropy loss.

D Complete metric results

We give the results for the remaining collaborative metrics not included in the main paper in this appendix. These give a comprehensive summary of the collaborative performance of the models evaluated in the paper. Table 2 and Table 3 give values for all review fraction-independent metrics, both in- and out-of-domain, respectively. We did not include the ECE and calibration AUROC in the corresponding table in the main paper (Table 1) for simplicity. Similarly, Figures 9 and 7 show the in-domain results (the OC-Acc and OC-AUPRC), and the out-of-domain plots (in the same order, followed by Review Efficiency) are Figures 10 through 12.

The in- and out-of-domain OC-AUROC figures are included in the main paper as Figure 2 and Figure 3, respectively; the in-domain Review Efficiency is Figure 4. Additionally, we also report results on the Review Effectiveness metric (introduced in Section A.2) in Figures 13-14. Similiar to Review Efficiency, we find little difference in performance between different uncertainty models, and that the uncertainty-based policy outperforms toxicity-based policy especially in the low review capacity setting.

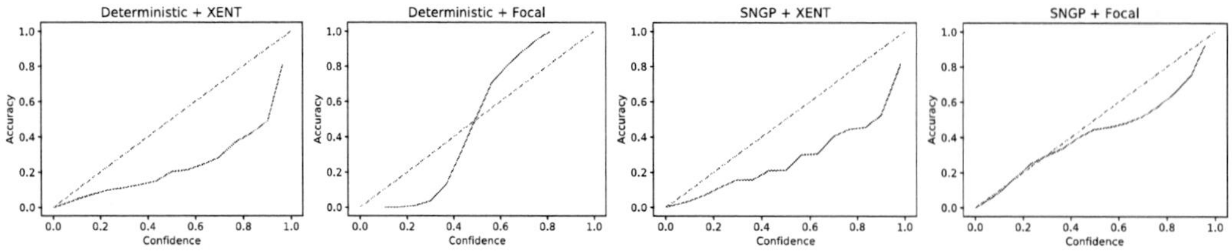

Figure 5: In-domain reliability diagrams for deterministic models and SNGP models with cross-entropy (XENT) and focal cross-entropy.

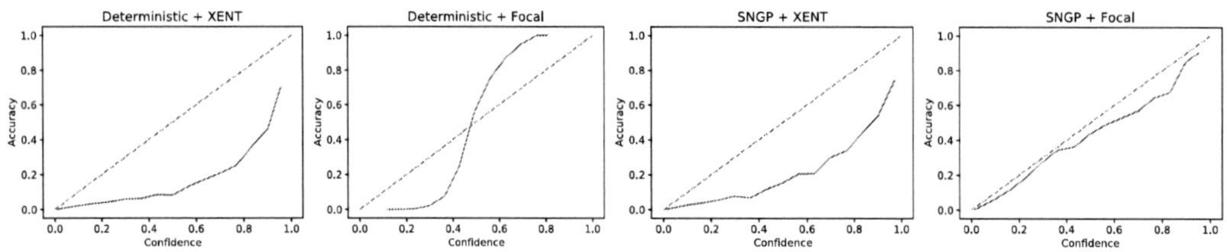

Figure 6: Reliability diagrams for deterministic models and SNGP models with cross-entropy (XENT) and focal cross-entropy on the CivilComments dataset.

	Model (Test)	AUROC ↑	AUPRC ↑	Acc. ↑	ECE ↓	Brier ↓	Calib. AUROC ↑	Calib. AUPRC ↑
XENT	Deterministic	0.9734	0.8019	0.9231	0.0245	0.0548	0.9230	0.4053
	SNGP	0.9741	0.8029	0.9233	0.0280	0.0548	0.9238	0.4063
	MC Dropout	0.9729	0.8006	**0.9274**	**0.0198**	**0.0508**	**0.9282**	0.4020
	Deep Ensemble	0.9738	**0.8074**	0.9231	0.0235	0.0544	0.9245	0.4045
	SNGP Ensemble	**0.9741**	0.8045	0.9226	0.0281	0.0549	0.9249	**0.4158**
Focal	Deterministic	0.9730	0.8036	0.9476	0.1486	0.0628	0.9405	0.3804
	SNGP	0.9736	0.8076	0.9455	0.0076	0.0388	0.9385	0.3885
	MC Dropout	0.9741	0.8076	0.9472	0.1442	0.0622	**0.9425**	**0.3890**
	Deep Ensemble	0.9735	0.8077	**0.9479**	0.1536	0.0639	0.9418	0.3840
	SNGP Ensemble	**0.9742**	**0.8122**	0.9467	**0.0075**	**0.0379**	0.9400	0.3846

Table 2: Metrics for models on the Wikipedia Talk corpus (in-domain testing environment), all numbers are averaged over 10 model runs. XENT and Focal indicate models trained with the cross-entropy and focal losses, respectively. The best metric values for each loss function are shown in bold.

	Model (Deployment)	AUROC ↑	AUPRC ↑	Acc. ↑	ECE ↓	Brier ↓	Calib. AUROC ↑	Calib. AUPRC ↑
XENT	Deterministic	0.7796	0.6689	0.9628	0.0128	0.0246	0.9412	0.3581
	SNGP	0.7695	0.6665	0.9640	**0.0070**	0.0253	0.9457	0.3660
	MC Dropout	0.7806	0.6727	**0.9671**	0.0136	**0.0241**	**0.9502**	**0.3707**
	Deep Ensemble	**0.7849**	**0.6741**	0.9625	0.0141	0.0242	0.9420	0.3484
	SNGP Ensemble	0.7749	0.6719	0.9633	0.0076	0.0248	0.9463	0.3655
Focal	Deterministic	0.8013	0.6766	**0.9795**	0.1973	0.0377	0.9444	0.3018
	SNGP	0.8003	0.6820	0.9784	0.0182	**0.0264**	0.9465	0.3181
	MC Dropout	0.8009	0.6790	0.9790	0.1896	0.0360	**0.9481**	0.3185
	Deep Ensemble	**0.8041**	0.6814	**0.9795**	0.1998	0.0381	0.9461	0.3035
	SNGP Ensemble	0.8002	**0.6827**	0.9790	**0.0176**	0.0266	**0.9481**	**0.3212**

Table 3: Metrics for models on the CivilComments corpus (out-of-domain deployment environment), all numbers are averaged over 10 model runs. XENT and Focal indicate models trained with the cross-entropy and focal losses, respectively. The best metric values for each loss function are shown in bold.

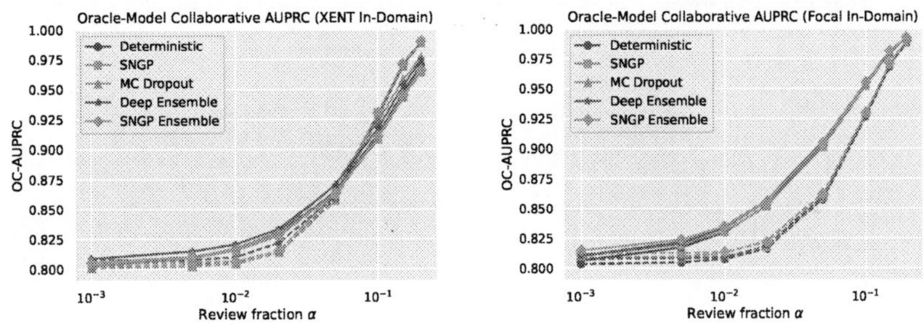

Figure 7: Oracle-model collaborative AUPRC as a function of review fraction, trained with cross-entropy (left) or focal loss (right) and evaluated on Wikipedia Toxicity corpus (in-domain test environment). **Solid Line**: uncertainty-based strategy. **Dashed Line**: toxicity-based strategy. Overall, the SNGP Ensemble with focal loss using the uncertainty review performs best across all α. Restricted to cross-entropy loss, the Deep Ensemble using uncertainty-based review performs best until $\alpha \approx 0.1$, when some of the toxicity-based reviews (e.g. SNGP Ensemble) begin to outperform it.

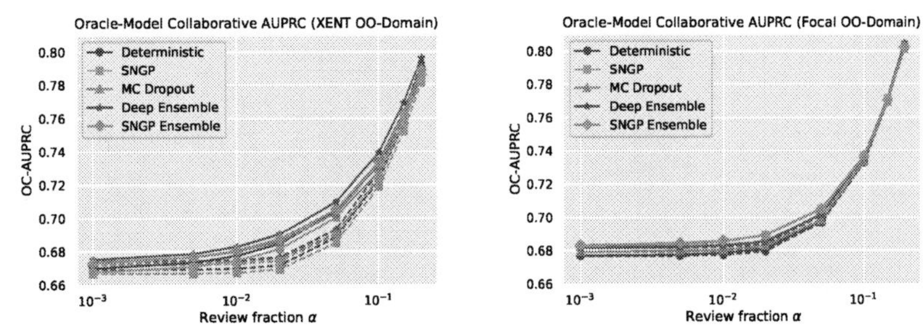

Figure 8: Oracle-model collaborative AUPRC as a function of review fraction, trained with cross-entropy (left) or focal loss (right) and evaluated on CivilComments corpus (out-of-domain deployment environment). **Solid Line**: uncertainty-based strategy. **Dashed Line**: toxicity-based strategy. Similar to the out-of-domain OC-AUROC results in Figure 3, of the models trained with cross-entropy loss the Deep Ensemble performs best. Training with focal loss yields a small baseline improvement, but surprisingly results in the SNGP Ensemble performing best. The uncertainty-based review strategy uniformly outperforms toxicity-based review, though the difference is small when training with focal loss.

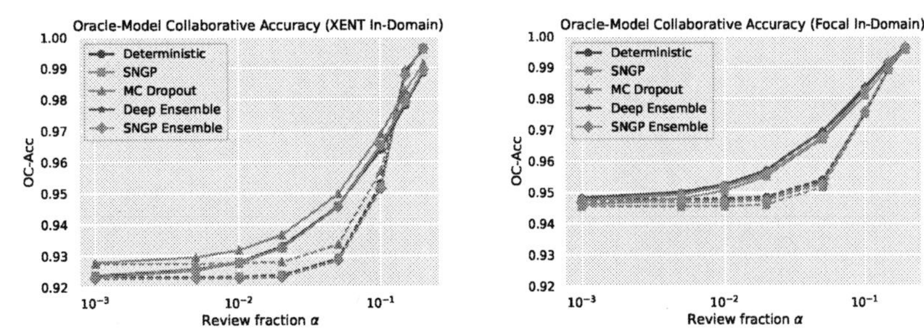

Figure 9: Oracle-model collaborative accuracy as a function of review fraction, trained with cross-entropy (left) or focal loss (right) and evaluated on Wikipedia Toxicity corpus (in-domain test environment). **Solid Line**: uncertainty-based strategy. **Dashed Line**: toxicity-based strategy. Focal loss yields a significant improvement, equivalent to using a 10% review fraction with cross-entropy. For most review fractions (below $\alpha = 0.1$), MC Dropout using the uncertainty review strategy performs trained with cross-entropy, while overall the Deep Ensemble with focal loss (again using the uncertainty review) performs best. For large review fractions ($\alpha > 0.1$), the toxicity-based review in fact outperforms the uncertainty review.

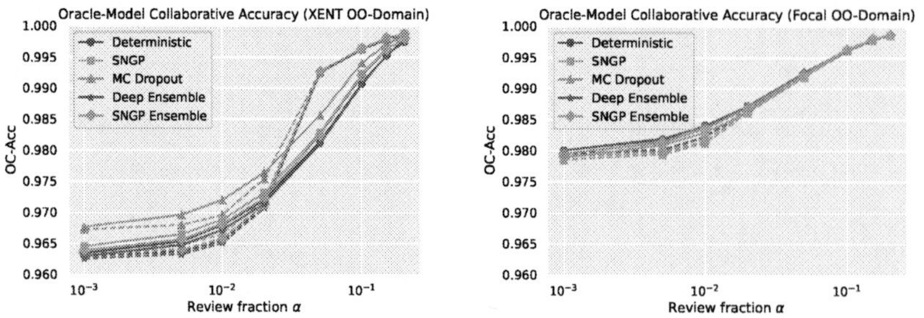

Figure 10: Oracle-model collaborative accuracy as a function of review fraction, trained with cross-entropy (left) or focal loss (right) and evaluated on CivilComments corpus (out-of-domain deployment environment). **Solid Line**: uncertainty-based strategy. **Dashed Line**: toxicity-based strategy. Training with cross-entropy, MC Dropout using uncertainty-based review performs best until the SNGP Ensemble using the toxicity-based review overtakes it at $\alpha = 0.05$. Training with focal loss gives significant baseline improvements (by mitigating the class imbalance problem); the Deep Ensemble is best for small α while the SNGP Ensemble is best for large α. Despite these baseline improvements, they appear to come at a cost of collaborative accuracy in the intermediate region around $\alpha \approx 0.05$, where the SNGP Ensemble trained with cross-entropy briefly performs best overall, apart from that region the models with focal loss and the uncertainty-based review perform best (Deep Ensemble for $\alpha \leq 0.02$, SNGP Ensemble for $\alpha \geq 0.1$).

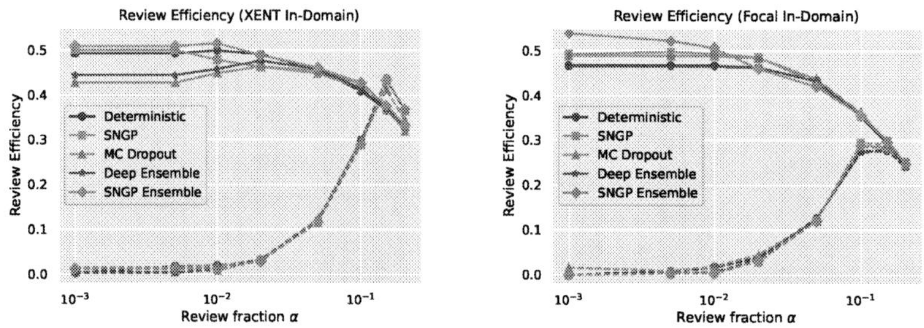

Figure 11: Review efficiency as a function of review fraction, trained with cross-entropy (left) or focal loss (right) and evaluated on Wikipedia Toxicity corpus (in-domain test environment). **Solid Line**: uncertainty-based strategy. **Dashed Line**: toxicity-based strategy. This is the only plot for which we observe a major crossover: training with cross-entropy, the efficiency for toxicity-based review spikes above the uncertainty-based review efficiency at $\alpha = 0.02$ before converging back toward it with increasing α. There is no corresponding crossover when training with focal loss; rather, the efficiencies of the two strategies converge at $\alpha = 0.02$ instead.

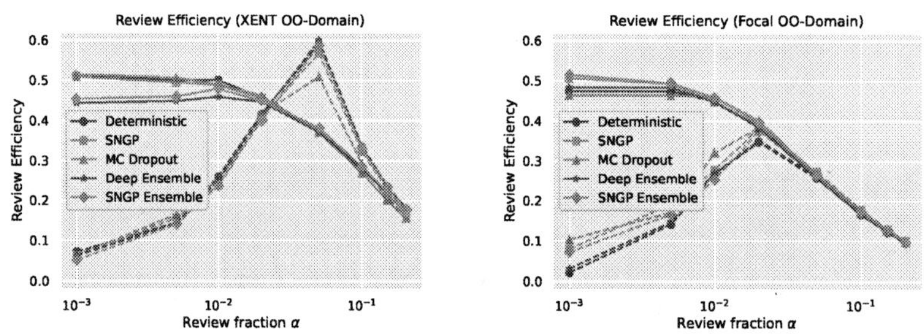

Figure 12: Review efficiency as a function of review fraction, trained with cross-entropy (left) or focal loss (right) and evaluated on CivilComments corpus (out-of-domain deployment environment). **Solid Line**: uncertainty-based strategy. **Dashed Line**: toxicity-based strategy. This is the only plot for which we observe a major crossover: training with cross-entropy, the efficiency for toxicity-based review spikes above the uncertainty-based review efficiency at $\alpha = 0.02$ before converging back toward it with increasing α. There is no corresponding crossover when training with focal loss; rather, the efficiencies of the two strategies converge at $\alpha = 0.02$ instead.

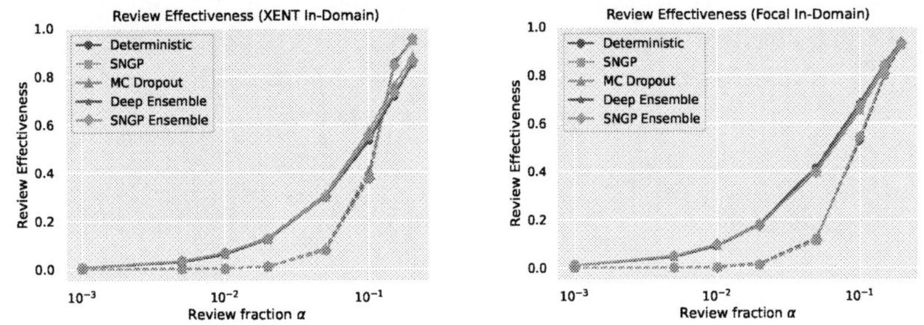

Figure 13: Review effectiveness as a function of review fraction, trained with cross-entropy (left) or focal loss (right) and evaluated on Wikipedia Toxicity corpus (in-domain test environment). **Solid Line**: uncertainty-based strategy. **Dashed Line**: toxicity-based strategy. There is little difference between models here: the uncertainty-based review strategy successfully catches more incorrect model decisions until $\alpha \approx 0.15$.

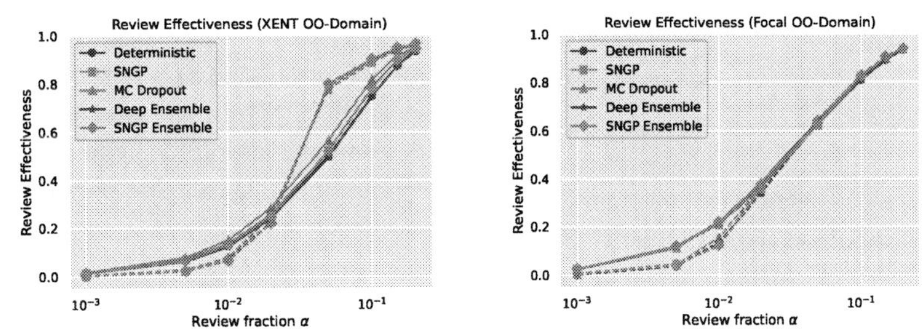

Figure 14: Review effectiveness as a function of review fraction, trained with cross-entropy (left) or focal loss (right) and evaluated on CivilComments corpus (out-of-domain deployment environment). **Solid Line**: uncertainty-based strategy. **Dashed Line**: toxicity-based strategy. Here, the uncertainty review performs better until a crossover at $\alpha \approx 0.02$, much lower than in Figure 4. The SNGP Ensemble performs best with either cross-entropy or focal loss (slightly better with cross-entropy).

DALC: the Dutch Abusive Language Corpus

Tommaso Caselli, Arjan Schelhaas, Marieke Weultjes, Folkert Leistra, Hylke van der Veen, Gerben Timmerman and Malvina Nissim
CLCG, University of Groningen
{t.caselli, m.nissim}@rug.nl
{a.j.schelhaas, m.i.weultjes }@student.rug.nl
{f.a.leistra,h.f.van.der.veen}@student.rug.nl
gerbentimmerman@protonmail.com

Abstract

As socially unacceptable language become pervasive in social media platforms, the need for automatic content moderation become more pressing. This contribution introduces the Dutch Abusive Language Corpus (DALC v1.0), a new dataset with tweets manually annotated for abusive language. The resource address a gap in language resources for Dutch and adopts a multi-layer annotation scheme modeling the explicitness and the target of the abusive messages. Baselines experiments on all annotation layers have been conducted, achieving a macro F1 score of 0.748 for binary classification of the explicitness layer and .489 for target classification.

1 Introduction

The growth of online user generated content poses challenges to manual content moderation efforts (Nobata et al., 2016). In a 2016 Eurobarometer survey, 75% of people who follow or participate in online discussions have witnessed or experienced abuse, threat, or hate speech.[1] The increasing polarization of online debates and conversations, together with the amount of associated toxic and abusive behaviors, call for some form of automatic content moderation. Currently, the mainstream approach in automatic content moderation uses reactive interventions, i.e., blocking or deleting 'bad' messages (Seering et al., 2019). There is an open debate on its efficacy (Chandrasekharan et al., 2017) and on the risks of perpetrating bias and discrimination (Sap et al., 2019). Alternative, less drastic, and more interactive methods have been proposed, such as the generation of counternarratives (Chung et al., 2019). In either case, the first step towards full or semi-automatic moderation is the detection of potentially abusive language. Such step relies on language-specific resources to train tools to distinguish the "good" messages from the harmful ones. As a contribution in this direction, we have developed the Dutch Abusive Language Corpus, or DALC v1.0, a manually annotated corpus of tweets for abusive language detection in Dutch.[2] The resource is unique in the Dutch-speaking panorama because of the approach used to collect the data, the annotation guidelines, and the final data curation.

DALC is compatible with previous work on abusive language in other languages (Waseem and Hovy, 2016a; Papegnies et al., 2017; Founta et al., 2018; Mishra et al., 2018; Davidson et al., 2019; Poletto et al., 2020) but presents innovations both with respect to the application of the label "abusive" to messages and the adoption of a multi-layered annotation to distinguish the explicitness of the abusive message and its target (Waseem et al., 2017).

Our contributions can be summarized as follows:

- the promotion of **a bottom-up approach to collect potentially abusive messages** combining multiple strategies in an attempt to minimize biases that may be introduced by developers;
- the release of a manually **annotated corpus for abusive language detection in Dutch**, DALC v1.0;
- a series of **baseline experiments** using different architectures (i.e., a dictionary based approach, a Linear SVM, a Dutch transformer-based language model) showing the complexity of the task.

[1] https://what-europe-does-for-me.eu/en/portal/2/H19

[2] The corpus, the annotation guidelines, and the baselines models are publicly available at https://github.com/tommasoc80/DALC

Proceedings of the Fifth Workshop on Online Abuse and Harms, pages 54–66
August 6, 2021.

2 Related Work

Previous work on abusive language phenomena and behaviors is extensive and varied. However, limitations exist and they mainly concentrate along three dimensions: (i) definitions; (ii) data sources and collection methods; and (iii) language diversity.

The development of automatic methods for detecting forms of abusive language has been rapid and has seen a boom of definitions, labels, and phenomena being investigated, including racism (Waseem and Hovy, 2016a; Davidson et al., 2017, 2019), hate speech (Alfina et al., 2017; Founta et al., 2018; Mishra et al., 2018; Basile et al., 2019), toxicity[3] and verbal aggression (Kumar et al., 2018), misogyny (Frenda et al., 2018; Pamungkas et al., 2020; Guest et al., 2021), and offensive language (Wiegand et al., 2018; Zampieri et al., 2019a; Rosenthal et al., 2020). Variations in definitions and in annotation guidelines have given rise to isolated datasets, limiting the portability of trained systems and reuse of resources (Swamy et al., 2019; Fortuna et al., 2021). Comprehensive frameworks that integrate and harmonize the variety of definitions and investigate the interactions across the annotated phenomena are still at early stages (Poletto et al., 2020). DALC v1.0 is compatible with existing definitions of abusive language and promotes a multi-layered annotation scheme compatible with previous initiatives, with a special attention to the reusability of datasets.

Collecting good representative data for abusive language is a challenging task. The majority of existing datasets focuses on messages from social media platforms, with Twitter being the most used Vidgen and Derczynski (2021). Unlike other language phenomena, e.g., named entities, abusive language is less widespread and cannot be easily captured by means of random sampling. Schematically, we identify three major methods to collect data: namely: (i) use of communities (Tulkens et al., 2016; Del Vigna et al., 2017; Merenda et al., 2018; Kennedy et al., 2018) which targets online communities known to be more likely to have abusive behaviors; (ii) use of keywords (Waseem and Hovy, 2016b; Alfina et al., 2017; Sanguinetti et al., 2018; ElSherief et al., 2018; Founta et al., 2018), where manually compiled lists of words corresponding either to potential targets (e.g, "women", "migrants", a.o.) or profanities are employed; (iii) use of seed users (Wiegand et al., 2018; Ribeiro et al., 2018), which collects messages from users that have been identified to post abusive texts via some heuristics. Each of these methods has advantages and disadvantages. For instance, the use of keywords may create denser datasets, but at the same time risks of developing biased data are very high (Wiegand et al., 2019). Furthermore, according to the specific platform used, some of the methods cannot be reliably applied. For instance, in a platform like Twitter targeting online communities is not trivial. Recently, refinements have been proposed to address limitations of each approach. In some cases controversial posts, videos or keywords are used as proxies for communities (Hammer, 2016; Graumans et al., 2019), in other cases hybrid approaches are proposed by combining keywords and seed users (Basile et al., 2019), others exploit platform pre-filtering functionalities (Zampieri et al., 2019a). DALC v1.0 integrates different bottom-up approaches to collect data providing a first cross-fertlization attempt across two social media platforms and paying attention to minimize the introduction of biases.

Vidgen and Derczynski (2021) provides a comprehensive survey covering 63 datasets all targeting a specific abusive phenomenon/behavior. The majority of them (25 datasets) is for English, with a long tail of other languages mostly belonging to the Indo-European family, although limited in their diversity. The lack of publicly available datasets for any Sino-Tibetan, Niger-Congo, or Afro-Asiatic languages is striking.

When it comes to abusive language datasets, Dutch is less-resourced. Notable previous work has been conducted by Tulkens et al. (2016) who developed a dataset and systems for detecting racist discourse in Dutch social media. DALC v1.0 differentiates because it is a "generic" resource for abusive language where all possible types of abusive phenomena are valid. This leaves room to refinement in the proposed corpus to investigate potential sub-types of abusive phenomena and their associated linguistic devices.

3 Data Collection

DALC v1.0 is based on a sample of a large ongoing collection of Twitter messages in Dutch at the University of Groningen (Tjong Kim Sang, 2011). For its construction, rather than focusing individually on any of the mentioned approaches,

[3] The Toxic Comment Clas- sification Challenge https://bit.ly/2QuHKD6

we propose a combination of three methods that only partially overlap with previous work.

Keyword extraction The first method is based on van Rosendaal et al. (2020), where keyword collection is refined via cross-fertilization between two social media platforms, namely Reddit and Twitter. Controversial posts from the subreddit `r/thenetherlands`, the biggest Reddit community in Dutch, at specific time periods are scraped, and a list of unigram keywords is extracted using TF-IDF. The top 50 unigrams are used as search terms in the corresponding time period in Twitter. This approach avoids the introduction of bias from the developers in the compilation of lists of search term. Obtaining them from controversial posts in Reddit may lead to denser samples of data in Twitter for abusive language phenomena.

We identified 8 different time periods between 2015 and 2020. We include both periods of time that may contain "historically significant events" (e.g., the Paris Attack in November 2015; the Dutch General Election in March 2017; the *Sinterklaas intocht* in December 20218; the Black Lives Matter protests after the killing of George Floyd in August 2020) and random time periods where no major events occurred, at least to our knowledge (e.g., April 2015; June 2018; May and September 2019). This results in a total of 12,884,560 retrieved tweets.

To ease the annotation process, we have sampled the retrieved data in smaller annotations batches. From each time period, we have generated samples of 10k messages composed as follows: 5k messages are randomly sampled, while the remaining 5k (non-overlapping) messages are extracted using two Dutch lexicon of potentially offensive/hateful terms, namely HADES (Tulkens et al., 2016) and HurtLex v1.2 (Bassignana et al., 2018). The actual manual annotation is performed on randomly extracted batches of 500 messages each. Table 1 provides an overview of the number of messages extracted per time period and the amount that has been manually annotated.

Geolocation The second method is inspired by previous work showing that in the Western areas of the (north hemisphere of the) world hatred messages tend to be more frequent in geographical areas that are economically depressed and where disenfranchised communities live (Medina et al., 2018; Gerstenfeld, 2017).[4] We use data from the Dutch *Centraal Bureau voor de Statistiek* (CBS) about unemployment to proxy such communities in the Netherlands, identifying two provinces: Zuid-Holland and Groningen.[5] We develop a set of heuristics, including the use of city names in these two provinces, to randomly collect messages from these areas. This is needed since the geolocation of the users is optional and does not have a fixed format. We managed to successfully extract 356,401 messages that can be reliably assigned to one of the two provinces. Similar to the keywords method, a sample of 5k messages is extracted using the lexicons and an additional 5k randomly. Four batches of 500 instances each have been manually annotated.

Seed users The last method uses seed users. We manually compile an ad-hoc list of 67 profanities, swearwords, and slurs by extending our lexicons. We then search for messages containing any of these elements in a ten-day window in December 2018 (namely 2018-11-12 – 2018-11-22). This results in a total of 3,105,833 messages. We rank each users according to the number of messages containing at least one of the target words. We select the top 50 users as seed users. We then extract for each of the selected user a maximum of 100 messages in a different time period, namely between May and June 2020, for a total of 5k tweets. Contrary to the other two methods, we directly created batches of 500 messages each for the manual annotation.

Since we are interested in original content, all messages sampled for the manual annotation do not contain retweets.

4 Annotation and Data Curation

DALC v1.0 has been manually annotated using internally developed guidelines. The guidelines provides the annotators with a definition of abusive language that refines proposals in previous work (Papegnies et al., 2017; Founta et al., 2018; Caselli et al., 2020). In particular, abusive language is defined as:

> *impolite, harsh, or hurtful language (that may contain profanities or vulgar language) that result in a debasement, harassment, threat, or*

[4]See also `https://bit.ly/3aDqoLd`.

[5]`https://bit.ly/2RPGSt5`

Time Period	Related Event	Extracted	Annotated
12-22 November 2015	Paris Attack	631,041	1,824
07-17 March 2017	Dutch Parliament Elections	265,256	1,824
April 2017	n/a	1,769,426	2,563
12-22 November 2018	*Intoch*[Arrival] Sinterklaas	377,007	526
June 2018	n/a	1,985,337	2,514
August 2020	Protests/BLM	733,985	3,128
May 20219	n/a	4,390,695	2,504
September 2019	n/a	2,731,813	2,504

Table 1: DALC v1.0 - Keywords: overview of the data collected and annotated

aggression of an individual or a (social) group, but not necessarily of an entity, an institution, an organization, or a concept.

Notably, this definition requires that an identifiable target must be present in the message to qualify as potentially abusive. This is a necessary requirement in our definition and it also helps us to discriminate abusive language from more generic phenomena like offensive language, forms of harsh criticism, and other socially unacceptable language phenomena. We have specifically introduced harsh criticism to restrict the application of the abusive language label. Indeed expressing heavy criticisms against an institution (e.g., the E.U. Commission, or a government) may result in inappropriate and offensive language but it does not entail being abusive. Exceptions, however, hold: cases of synecdoches where an institution, an entity, or a concept are used to attack the members of a social group are considered instances of abusive language.

Following Waseem et al. (2017) and Zampieri et al. (2019a) we perform a multi-layered annotation distinguishing the levels of **explicitness** of the abusive messages and the **targets**. Explicitness combines three factors: (i) the surface evidence of the message; (ii) the assumed intentions of the user (i.e., *is the message debasing someone?*); and (iii) its effects on the receiver(s) (i.e., *can the message be perceived as debasing by a targeted individual or a community?*). While the last two factors (intentions and effects) help to identify the abusiveness nature of the message, the surface forms is essential to distinguish overtly abusive messages from more subtle forms. A distinguishing criterion, in fact, is the presence of profanities, slurs, and offensive terms. We define three values:

- **Explicit** (EXP): A message is marked as explicit if it is interpreted as potentially abusive and if it contains a profanity or a slur;
- **Implicit** (IMP): A message is marked as implicit if it is interpreted as potentially abusive but it DOES NOT contain any identifiable profanity or slur;
- **Not abusive** (NOT): A message is marked as a not abusive if it is interpreted as lacking an intention of the user to debase/harass/threat a target and there is no debasing effect on the receiver. The mere presence of a profanity does not provide sufficient ground for annotating the message as abusive.

A further differentiating criteria is that all messages where the author debases or offends him-/herself (e.g., messages that contain the first person singular or plural pronoun) are considered as not abusive

The target layer makes explicit *to whom* the message is directed. We reuse the values and definitions from Zampieri et al. (2019a). In particular, we have:

- **Individual** (IND): any message that targets a person, being it named or unnamed, or a famous person;
- **Group** (GRP): any message that targets a group of people considered as a unity because of ethnicity, gender, political affiliation, religion, disabilities, or other common properties; and
- **Other** (OTH): any abusive message that addresses an organisation, an institution, or a concept. Instances of synecdoches are marked with this value rather than with group.

The annotation has been conducted in two phases. Phase 1 (March–May 2020) has seen five annotators, all bachelor students in Information Science. The students conducted the annotation of the data as part of their bachelor thesis project. Phase 2

(November–December 2020) has been conducted by one master student in Information Science with previous experience in this task. All annotators are native speakers of Dutch. More details are reported in the Data Statement A.

During Phase 1, we validate the annotation guidelines by means of a pairwise inter-annotator agreement (IAA) study on two independent subsets of 100 messages each. The first sample is obtained using the keyword method and the second using the geolocation. For the keywords sample, Cohen's kappa is 0.572 for the explicitness and 0.670 for the target. For the geolocation sample, the kappa for explicitness is comparable (0.522) although that for target is lower (0.466). The results are comparable previous work (Caselli et al., 2020) indicating substantial agreement. Cases of disagreement have been discussed between the annotators and resolved. The data used for the IAA has been integrated in DALC v1.0. No IAA has been computed for the messages collected using seed authors. In phase 2 we further expanded the initial data annotation.

The final corpus has been manually curated by one of the authors of this paper. The data curation phase focuses on the creation of the Train, Dev, Test splits in such a way that there is no overlap for time periods and, most importantly, users. Table 2 reports an overview of the data of each split and the number of annotated messages included.

Split	Data Source	Messages Included
Train	Paris Attack	1,051
	Dutch Parliament Election	996
	Protests/BLM	1,767
	Seed users	2,060 (+58)
Dev	Paris Attack	109
	Dutch Parliament Election	90
	Protests/BLM	156
	Seed users	196 (+6)
Test	*Intoch* Sinterklass	121
	April 2017	266
	June 2018	333
	May 2019	307
	September 2019	323
	Seed users	258 (+54)

Table 2: DALC v10: distribution of the sources across Train, Dev, Test. Numbers in parentheses indicate adjustments to prevent data overlap.

Overall, DALC v1.0 contains 8,156 tweets. In each split, the abusive messages correspond roughly to 1/3 of the messages. Maintaining this balance is not a trivial task. As it appears from Table 2, the different methods we used to collect the data results in different proportions of messages. Concerning the use of keywords, the combination of controversial keywords and historically relevant events works best, i.e., returns more densely annotated batches for the positive class, than the use of controversial keywords in random time periods. The geolocation method has been excluded due to the extremely low number of messages belonging to the positive class. Furthermore, a closer inspection revealed that these messages could be easily aggregated by their authors. We thus merge them with the seed users. Indeed, seed users results as the most successful method. Out of 5,000 messages collected, we managed to annotate and keep 2,520 of them. Excluding the merged users from the geolocation data, the Train/Dev split contains 38 unique users with an average of 54 messages each. On the other hand, the Test set contains 11 unique users and 23 messages each on average. To avoid any possibility of data overlap, we check that no message retrieved using the keyword method in one data split (e.g. Train) belongs to a seed users in a different data split (e.g., Test). For instance, we have found that 8 messages from the Paris Attack source have the same seed users of the test split. Only 118 messages were involved in these adjustments. In Table 2 we have marked these changes by showing the additional messages in parenthesis next to the seed users rows.

Table 3 shows DALC v1.0's label distribution per split. Overall, 1,879 messages have been annotated as containing forms of abusive language. The majority of them, 65.40%, has been classified as explicit. When focusing on the Train and Test splits, the most remarkable difference concerns the number of abusive messages labeled as implicit: 38.25% vs. 28.10%, respectively. As for the targets, the majority is realized by IND (55.18%) followed by GRP (34.64%) and OTH (10.69%). Interestingly, the distributions of the target is comparable to that of other datasets in other languages such as OLID (Zampieri et al., 2019a).

The average length of a message in DALC v1.0 is 25.94 words. Tokenization has been done by using the Dutch tokenizer available in SpaCy (Honnibal et al., 2020). In general, abusive messages are significantly[6] longer than the non abusive ones, with an average of 27.58 words compared to 22.77. While the differences between explicit and implicit

[6]Statistical test: Mann-Whitney Test; $p < 0.05$

Split	Explicitness			Target		
	EXP	IMP	NOT	IND	GRP	OTH
Train	699	443	4,564	634	399	109
Dev	72	38	439	62	33	15
Test	458	179	1,264	341	219	77
Total	1,229	660	6,267	1,037	651	201

Table 3: DALC v1.0: Distribution of Train, Dev, and Test splits for explicitness and target.

messages are basically non existent in the Train split, we observe significantly[7] longer implicit messages in the test data, with an average of 27.99 words against the 24.16 of the explicit ones. Standard deviations suggest that the length of the messages is skewed both in training and test for the three classes, with values ranging between 16.23 (EXPLICIT) and 13.71 (NOT) in Train, and 15.57 (IMPLICIT) and 14.03 (NOT) in Test.

We further investigate the composition of the DALC v1.0 by analysing the top 50 keywords per class between the Train and Test distributions by applying a TF-IDF approach. Table 4 illustrates a sample of the extracted keywords. As expected, clear instances of profanities and slurs appear in the EXP class. The IMP class does not present surface cues linked to specific lexical items. Actually, without knowing the class label and simply comparing the keywords, it is impossible to distinguish the IMP messages from those labeled as NOT. A further take-away of the keyword analysis is the lack of prevalence of any topic specific items (Wiegand et al., 2019). This, however, does not necessarily means that DALC v1.0 does not contain biases: indeed, the messages are not equally distributed across the time periods and seed users. On the other hand, our inspection of keywords has shown the lack of topic-specific keywords across the three classes.

We complete our analysis by exploring the similarities and differences between Train and Test splits. We investigate these aspects by means of two metrics: the Jensen-Shannon (J-S) divergence and the Out-of-Vocabulary rate (OOV). The J-S divergence assesses the similarity between two probability distributions, q and r. On the other hand, the OOV rate helps in assessing the differences between the Train and Test splits as it highlights the percentage of unknown tokens. We obtain a J-S score of 73% and an OOV rate of 64.6%. This means that while the Train and Test distributions are quite similar to each other, the gap in terms of lexical items between the two is quite large. This supports the validity of our data curation approach where overlap between Training and Test split is not allowed.

[7]Statistical test: Mann-Whitney Test; $p < 0.05$

5 Baselines

We present a set of baseline experiments that accompany the release of DALC v1.0 for the two annotation layers. For the explicitness layer, we first experiment a simplified setting by framing the problem as a binary classification task. In this setting the distinction between EXP and IMP labels is collapsed into a new unique value for all abusive messages (i.e., ABU). The follow-up experiment, on the other hand, maintains the fine-grained distinction in the three classes (i.e., EXP *vs.* IMP *vs.* NOT).

For the target layer no simplification of the labels is possible since each oh them identified a specific referent. Thus, target experiments preserve the original three labels (i.e., IND *vs.* GRP *vs.* OTH).

In all experiments we adopt a common preprocessing of the data. All user mentions and links to external web pages are replaced with dedicated placeholders symbols, respectively USER and URL. Emojis are replaced with their corresponding text using the `emoji` package. Hashtags symbols have been removed but we have not split hashtags composed by multiple words in separate tokens.

The models are trained on the Train split and evaluated on the held out Test set. The Dev split is used for parameter tuning. As illustrated in Table 3, the distributions of the labels in the classes for both annotation layers is unbalanced. We thus evaluate and compare our models using the macro-average F1. Furthermore, we report Precision and Recall for each class. In each annotation layer, we compare the models to a majority class baseline (MFC).

Abusive *vs.* Not Abusive This binary setting allows to test the classification abilities of different architectures in a simplified setting. It also provides evidence of the complexity of the task given the lack of overlap across time periods and seed users between Train and Test.

We experimented with three models. The first is a dictionary-based approach. The approach is very simple: given a reference dictionary of profanities,

Train			Test		
EXP	**IMP**	**NOT**	**EXP**	**IMP**	**NOT**
sod*****er	kansloze	schaambeek	spoort	ha	fashion******sisters
lelijkerd	huilie	onderbuikonzin	huilie	stap	boekenkast
ontslaan	nakijken	maradonny	arrogante	iek	hierzo
ha	lijk	jood	mal****	schaapskleren	tuu
st*****	slimste	haarpijn	la**e	aantonen	kúnnen
sowieso	dissel	geboorteplaats	blind	fuhrer	ouuuuttttttt
f***head	stem	huurauto	k*****stad	trapt	och
paras*****	binnenlaten	spinnend	gebruik	dommie	penny
k*t	jaily	leukkkk	k****r	verhaal	nieuwjaar
uitgemergelde	gestraft	afloopt	gebruikte	rollen	supermooi

Table 4: DALC v1.0: Top 10 keywords per class in Train and Test. Explicitly offensive/abusive content have been masked with $*$

abusive terms, slurs in Dutch, if any message contains one or more of the terms in the dictionary, then it is labeled as abusive (i.e., ABU). We have created a new lexicon of 847 potentially abusive term by refining the original Dutch entries in HurtLex v1.2 (Bassignana et al., 2018) and integrating the list with 256 culturally specific terms. In particular, most of the new entries concerned names of diseases (e.g., *kanker* [cancer]) that in Dutch are commonly used to debase or harass people. Each term has also been classified as belonging to one of two macro-categories, namely "negative stereotypes" (representing 45.1% of the entries) and "hate words and slurs beyond stereotypes" (including the remaining 54.9% of the entries). The list has not been extended with additional terms from the EXP messages in the Train split of DALC v1.0.

The second model is a Linear Support Vector Machine (SVM) model. We used the available implementation in `scikit-learn` (Pedregosa et al., 2011). Each message is represented by a TF-IDF vector combining word and character ngrams. We run a grid search to find the best ngram combination and parameter tuning. The final configuration uses bigrams and character ngrams in the range 3–5, a C values of 1.0, and removal of stopwords.

The last model is based on a monolingual Dutch pre-trained language model, BERTje (de Vries et al., 2019), available through the `Hugging Face` transformers library.[8] The model is fine tuned for five epochs, with a standard learning rate of 2e-5, AdamW optimizer (with `eps` equals to 1e-8), and batch size of 32.

The results of the experiments are reported in Table 5. All models outperform the MFC baseline,

System	Class	Precision	Recall	Macro-F1
MFC	ABU	0	0	0.399
	NOT	0.664	1.0	
Dictionary	ABU	0.716	0.433	0.685
	NOT	0.761	0.913	
SVM	ABU	0.858	0.323	0.655
	NOT	0.740	0.973	
BERTje	ABU	0.850	0.500	**0.748**
	NOT	0.791	0.955	

Table 5: DALC v1.0: Binary classification. Best scores in bold.

however, the task proves to be challenging. BERTje obtains by far the best results with a macro F1 of 0.748. Quite surprisingly, the Dictionary model has more competitive results than the SVM. The gap in scores can be explained by the large OOV rate between Train and Test split. SVMs usually are very competitive models but one of their shortcoming is the heavy dependence on a shared vocabulary between training and test distributions. A further element of attention is the low Recall that all models have for the positive class. While this behavior is expected due to the unbalanced distributions of the classes, we claim that this is an additional cue with respect to the data distribution of DALC v1.0.

To further confirm this intuition, we ran an additional set of experiments on a different data split. We maintained exactly the same amount of messages and distribution in the classes. On the other hand, we did allow for overlap across time periods and seed users. The OOV rate between Train and Test splits drops to 55.21%. At the same time, by re-running the experiments with the same settings for all models, the Dictionary model is the weakest, with a macro F1 of 0.680. On the other hand, the Linear SVM achieves competitive results when

[8] `https://huggingface.co/GroNLP/bert-base-dutch-cased`

compared to BERTje (macro F1 of 0.749 *vs.* 0.786, respectively).

Explicit *vs.* Implicit For the fine-grained classification, we compare only two architectures, the linear SVM and BERTje. As already stated, this is a more challenging setting namely due to a combination of factors such as the number of classes, the data distributions, and the class imbalance. The grid search for the SVM confirmed the same settings as for the binary experiment. We re-used the same settings for BERTje. Table 6 summarizes the results.

System	Class	Precision	Recall	Macro-F1
SVM	EXP	0.805	0.270	0.433
	IMP	0.461	0.033	
	NOT	0.719	0.986	
BERTje	EXP	0.759	0.447	**0.561**
	IMP	0.373	0.189	
	NOT	0.790	0.962	

Table 6: DALC v1.0: Explicitness classification. Best scores in bold.

BERTje is again the model achieving the best results, with a macro F1 of 0.561. Both models, however, struggle to correctly classify the IMP messages correctly. Observing the distribution of the errors for this class, both models tend to be misclassify the IMP messages as NOT, further confirming the observations from the keyword analysis. The increased granularity of the classes has a negative impact on the performance of the SVM also for the EXP messages. While Precision is comparable to the binary setting, the system largely suffers in Recall. This is not the case for BERTje, where Precision and Recall for the EXP and NOT classes are in line with the results of the binary setting. On the other hand, the results for the IMP classes are encouraging, although far from being satisfying.

Target Classification Models for this task are trained to distinguish among the three target classes: individuals (IND), group(s) (GRP), and other (OTH). For this experiment the amount of training data is smaller since only abusive messages have been used. We experimented with two models' architectures only: a Linear SVM and BERTje. The grid search for the SVM results in the same settings of for the explicitness layer. When it comes to BERTje, we apply the same settings: fine tuninig for five epochs, standard learning rate of 2e-5, AdamW optimizer (with `eps` equals to 1e-8), and batch size of 32. Results are reported in Table 7.

System	Class	Precision	Recall	Macro-F1
MFC	IND	0.535	1.00	0.232
	GRP	0	0	
	OTH	0	0	
SVM	IND	0.693	0.897	0.492
	GRP	0.698	0.602	
	OTH	0.285	0.026	
BERTje	IND	0.745	0.841	**0.498**
	GRP	0.634	0.730	
	OTH	1.0	0.012	

Table 7: DALC v1.0: Target classification. Best scores in bold.

Both models clearly outperform the MFC baseline. However, the gap between the two is very small differently than for the explicitness layer. Both models struggle with the OTH class. The lower amount of training examples for this class (only 109) is a factor the impact the performance. However, this class is also less homogeneous than the others. It contains different types of targets such as institutions, events, and entities that do not fit in the other two classes. When focusing on the results for the IND and OTH classes, it seems that models suffer less when compared to the explicitness layer. This suggest that there may be a reduced variation in the expressions of the targets. Finally, the results are in line with previous work on target detection in English (Zampieri et al., 2019b).

6 Conclusions and Future Work

This paper introduces DALC v1.0, the first "generic" resource for abusive language detection in Dutch. DALC v1.0 contains more thn 8k Twitter messages manually labeled using a multi-layer annotation scheme targeting the explicitness of the message and the targets. A further peculiarity of the dataset is the complete lack of overlap for time periods and users between Train and Test splits, making the task more challenging.

The combination of multiple data collection strategies aims at promoting new bottom-up approaches less prone to additional biases in the data other than those from the manual labeling.

DALC v1.0 adopts a definition of abusive language and an annotation philosophy compatible with previous work, paying attention to promote interoperability across language resources, languages, and abusive language phenomena.

The baseline experiments and systems that have been developed further indicate the challenges of this dataset. The best results are obtained with a fine tuned transformer-based pre-trained language model, BERTje. Fine-grained distinction for the explicitness layer is particularly difficult for implicitly abusive messages. Furthermore, target classification is a challenging task, with overall macro-F1 below 0.50.

Future work will focus on an in-depth investigation of the errors to identify easy and complex cases.

References

Ika Alfina, Rio Mulia, Mohamad Ivan Fanany, and Yudo Ekanata. 2017. Hate speech detection in the indonesian language: A dataset and preliminary study. In *2017 International Conference on Advanced Computer Science and Information Systems (ICACSIS)*, pages 233–238. IEEE.

Valerio Basile, Cristina Bosco, Elisabetta Fersini, Debora Nozza, Viviana Patti, Francisco Manuel Rangel Pardo, Paolo Rosso, and Manuela Sanguinetti. 2019. SemEval-2019 task 5: Multilingual detection of hate speech against immigrants and women in twitter. In *Proceedings of the 13th International Workshop on Semantic Evaluation*, pages 54–63, Minneapolis, Minnesota, USA. Association for Computational Linguistics.

Elisa Bassignana, Valerio Basile, and Viviana Patti. 2018. Hurtlex: A multilingual lexicon of words to hurt. In *5th Italian Conference on Computational Linguistics, CLiC-it 2018*, volume 2253, pages 1–6. CEUR-WS.

Tommaso Caselli, Valerio Basile, Jelena Mitrović, Inga Kartoziya, and Michael Granitzer. 2020. I feel offended, don't be abusive! implicit/explicit messages in offensive and abusive language. In *Proceedings of the 12th Language Resources and Evaluation Conference*, pages 6193–6202, Marseille, France. European Language Resources Association.

Eshwar Chandrasekharan, Umashanthi Pavalanathan, Anirudh Srinivasan, Adam Glynn, Jacob Eisenstein, and Eric Gilbert. 2017. You can't stay here: The efficacy of reddit's 2015 ban examined through hate speech. *Proceedings of the ACM on Human-Computer Interaction*, 1(CSCW):1–22.

Yi-Ling Chung, Elizaveta Kuzmenko, Serra Sinem Tekiroglu, and Marco Guerini. 2019. CONAN - COunter NArratives through nichesourcing: a multilingual dataset of responses to fight online hate speech. In *Proceedings of the 57th Annual Meeting of the Association for Computational Linguistics*, pages 2819–2829, Florence, Italy. Association for Computational Linguistics.

Thomas Davidson, Debasmita Bhattacharya, and Ingmar Weber. 2019. Racial bias in hate speech and abusive language detection datasets. In *Proceedings of the Third Workshop on Abusive Language Online*, pages 25–35, Florence, Italy. Association for Computational Linguistics.

Thomas Davidson, Dana Warmsley, Michael Macy, and Ingmar Weber. 2017. Automated hate speech detection and the problem of offensive language. In *Proceedings of the International AAAI Conference on Web and Social Media*, volume 11.

Fabio Del Vigna, Andrea Cimino, Felice Dell'Orletta, Marinella Petrocchi, and Maurizio Tesconi. 2017. Hate me, hate me not: Hate speech detection on facebook. In *Proceedings of the First Italian Conference on Cybersecurity (ITASEC17)*, pages 86–95.

Daria Denti and Alessandra Faggian. 2019. In *5th International Conference on Hate Studies*, Spokane, USA. non-archival. [link].

Mai ElSherief, Shirin Nilizadeh, Dana Nguyen, Giovanni Vigna, and Elizabeth Belding. 2018. Peer to peer hate: Hate speech instigators and their targets. In *Proceedings of the International AAAI Conference on Web and Social Media*, volume 12.

Paula Fortuna, Juan Soler-Company, and Leo Wanner. 2021. How well do hate speech, toxicity, abusive and offensive language classification models generalize across datasets? *Information Processing & Management*, 58(3):102524.

Antigoni Maria Founta, Constantinos Djouvas, Despoina Chatzakou, Ilias Leontiadis, Jeremy Blackburn, Gianluca Stringhini, Athena Vakali, Michael Sirivianos, and Nicolas Kourtellis. 2018. Large scale crowdsourcing and characterization of twitter abusive behavior. In *Twelfth International AAAI Conference on Web and Social Media.*

Simona Frenda, Ghanem Bilal, et al. 2018. Exploration of misogyny in spanish and english tweets. In *Third Workshop on Evaluation of Human Language Technologies for Iberian Languages (IberEval 2018)*, volume 2150, pages 260–267. Ceur Workshop Proceedings.

Phyllis B Gerstenfeld. 2017. *Hate crimes: Causes, controls, and controversies.* Sage Publications.

Leon Graumans, Roy David, and Tommaso Caselli. 2019. Twitter-based polarised embeddings for abusive language detection. In *2019 8th International Conference on Affective Computing and Intelligent Interaction Workshops and Demos (ACIIW)*. IEEE.

Ella Guest, Bertie Vidgen, Alexandros Mittos, Nishanth Sastry, Gareth Tyson, and Helen Margetts. 2021. An expert annotated dataset for the detection of online misogyny. In *Proceedings of the 16th Conference of the European Chapter of the Association for Computational Linguistics: Main Volume*, pages 1336–1350.

Hugo Lewi Hammer. 2016. Automatic detection of hateful comments in online discussion. In *International Conference on Industrial Networks and Intelligent Systems*, pages 164–173. Springer.

Matthew Honnibal, Ines Montani, Sofie Van Landeghem, and Adriane Boyd. 2020. spaCy: Industrial-strength Natural Language Processing in Python.

Brendan Kennedy, Mohammad Atari, Aida M Davani, Leigh Yeh, Ali Omrani, Yehsong Kim, Kris Coombs, Shreya Havaldar, Gwenyth Portillo-Wightman, Elaine Gonzalez, and et al. 2018. The gab hate corpus: A collection of 27k posts annotated for hate speech.

Ritesh Kumar, Atul Kr. Ojha, Shervin Malmasi, and Marcos Zampieri. 2018. Benchmarking aggression identification in social media. In *Proceedings of the First Workshop on Trolling, Aggression and Cyberbullying (TRAC-2018)*, pages 1–11, Santa Fe, New Mexico, USA. Association for Computational Linguistics.

Richard M Medina, Emily Nicolosi, Simon Brewer, and Andrew M Linke. 2018. Geographies of organized hate in america: a regional analysis. *Annals of the American Association of Geographers*, 108(4):1006–1021.

Flavio Merenda, Claudia Zaghi, Tommaso Caselli, and Malvina Nissim. 2018. Source-driven representations for hate speech detection. In *CLiC-it*.

Pushkar Mishra, Marco Del Tredici, Helen Yannakoudakis, and Ekaterina Shutova. 2018. Author profiling for abuse detection. In *Proceedings of the 27th International Conference on Computational Linguistics*, pages 1088–1098.

Chikashi Nobata, Joel Tetreault, Achint Thomas, Yashar Mehdad, and Yi Chang. 2016. Abusive language detection in online user content. In *Proceedings of the 25th International Conference on World Wide Web*, WWW '16, pages 145–153, Republic and Canton of Geneva, Switzerland. International World Wide Web Conferences Steering Committee.

Endang Wahyu Pamungkas, Valerio Basile, and Viviana Patti. 2020. Misogyny detection in twitter: a multilingual and cross-domain study. *Information Processing & Management*, 57(6):102360.

Etienne Papegnies, Vincent Labatut, Richard Dufour, and Georges Linarès. 2017. Detection of abusive messages in an on-line community. In *CORIA*.

Fabian Pedregosa, Gaël Varoquaux, Alexandre Gramfort, Vincent Michel, Bertrand Thirion, Olivier Grisel, Mathieu Blondel, Peter Prettenhofer, Ron Weiss, Vincent Dubourg, et al. 2011. Scikit-learn: Machine learning in python. *the Journal of machine Learning research*, 12:2825–2830.

Fabio Poletto, Valerio Basile, Manuela Sanguinetti, Cristina Bosco, and Viviana Patti. 2020. Resources and benchmark corpora for hate speech detection: a systematic review. *Language Resources and Evaluation*, pages 1–47.

Manoel Horta Ribeiro, Pedro H Calais, Yuri A Santos, Virgílio AF Almeida, and Wagner Meira Jr. 2018. Characterizing and detecting hateful users on twitter. In *Twelfth International AAAI Conference on Web and Social Media*.

Juliet van Rosendaal, Tommaso Caselli, and Malvina Nissim. 2020. Lower bias, higher density abusive language datasets: A recipe. In *Proceedings of the Workshop on Resources and Techniques for User and Author Profiling in Abusive Language*, pages 14–19, Marseille, France. European Language Resources Association (ELRA).

Sara Rosenthal, Pepa Atanasova, Georgi Karadzhov, Marcos Zampieri, and Preslav Nakov. 2020. A large-scale semi-supervised dataset for offensive language identification. *arXiv preprint arXiv:2004.14454*.

Manuela Sanguinetti, Fabio Poletto, Cristina Bosco, Viviana Patti, and Marco Stranisci. 2018. An Italian Twitter Corpus of Hate Speech against Immigrants. In *Proceedings of the Eleventh International Conference on Language Resources and Evaluation (LREC 2018)*, Miyazaki, Japan. European Language Resources Association (ELRA).

Maarten Sap, Dallas Card, Saadia Gabriel, Yejin Choi, and Noah A. Smith. 2019. The risk of racial bias in hate speech detection. In *Proceedings of the 57th Annual Meeting of the Association for Computational Linguistics*, pages 1668–1678, Florence, Italy. Association for Computational Linguistics.

Joseph Seering, Tony Wang, Jina Yoon, and Geoff Kaufman. 2019. Moderator engagement and community development in the age of algorithms. *New Media & Society*, 21(7):1417–1443.

Steve Durairaj Swamy, Anupam Jamatia, and Björn Gambäck. 2019. Studying generalisability across abusive language detection datasets. In *Proceedings of the 23rd Conference on Computational Natural Language Learning (CoNLL)*, pages 940–950.

Erik Tjong Kim Sang. 2011. Het gebruik van twitter voor taalkundig onderzoek. *TABU: Bulletin voor Taalwetenschap*, 39(1/2):62–72.

Stéphan Tulkens, Lisa Hilte, Elise Lodewyckx, Ben Verhoeven, and Walter Daelemans. 2016. The automated detection of racist discourse in dutch social media. *Computational Linguistics in the Netherlands Journal*, 6:3–20.

Bertie Vidgen and Leon Derczynski. 2021. Directions in abusive language training data, a systematic review: Garbage in, garbage out. *PLOS ONE*, 15.

Wietse de Vries, Andreas van Cranenburgh, Arianna Bisazza, Tommaso Caselli, Gertjan van Noord, and Malvina Nissim. 2019. Bertje: A dutch bert model. *arXiv preprint arXiv:1912.09582*.

Zeerak Waseem, Thomas Davidson, Dana Warmsley, and Ingmar Weber. 2017. Understanding abuse: A typology of abusive language detection subtasks. In *Proceedings of the First Workshop on Abusive Language Online*, pages 78–84.

Zeerak Waseem and Dirk Hovy. 2016a. Hateful symbols or hateful people? predictive features for hate speech detection on twitter. In *Proceedings of the NAACL Student Research Workshop*, pages 88–93, San Diego, California. Association for Computational Linguistics.

Zeerak Waseem and Dirk Hovy. 2016b. Hateful symbols or hateful people? predictive features for hate speech detection on twitter. In *Proceedings of the NAACL student research workshop*, pages 88–93.

Michael Wiegand, Josef Ruppenhofer, and Thomas Kleinbauer. 2019. Detection of Abusive Language: the Problem of Biased Datasets. In *Proceedings of the 2019 Conference of the North American Chapter of the Association for Computational Linguistics: Human Language Technologies, Volume 1 (Long and Short Papers)*, pages 602–608, Minneapolis, Minnesota. Association for Computational Linguistics.

Michael Wiegand, Josef Ruppenhofer, Anna Schmidt, and Clayton Greenberg. 2018. Inducing a lexicon of abusive words–a feature-based approach. In *Proceedings of the 2018 Conference of the North American Chapter of the Association for Computational Linguistics: Human Language Technologies, Volume 1 (Long Papers)*, pages 1046–1056.

Marcos Zampieri, Shervin Malmasi, Preslav Nakov, Sara Rosenthal, Noura Farra, and Ritesh Kumar. 2019a. Predicting the Type and Target of Offensive Posts in Social Media. In *Proceedings of NAACL*.

Marcos Zampieri, Shervin Malmasi, Preslav Nakov, Sara Rosenthal, Noura Farra, and Ritesh Kumar. 2019b. SemEval-2019 task 6: Identifying and categorizing offensive language in social media (OffensEval). In *Proceedings of the 13th International Workshop on Semantic Evaluation*, pages 75–86, Minneapolis, Minnesota, USA. Association for Computational Linguistics.

A Data Statement

Data set name: Dutch Abusive Language Corpus (DALC) v1.0
Data will be released to the public in compliance with GDPR and Twitter's Terms of Service.

A. CURATION RATIONALE The corpus is composed by tweets in Dutch extracted using different strategies and covering different time windows.

- **Keywords**: we have used a cross-platform approach to identify relevant keywords and reduce bias that may be introduced in manual selection of the data. We first identified a time window in Reddit, extracted all posts that received a controversial label. We then identified keywords (unigram) and retained the top 50 keywords per time window. We then used the keywords to extract tweets in corresponding periods. For each time period, we selected a sample 5,000 messages using two dictionaries containing know profanities in Dutch. An additional 5,000 messages are randomly selected. The messages are then re-shuffled and annotated.

- **Geolocation**: following Denti and Faggian (2019) that show the existence of a correlation between hateful messages and disenfranchised and economic poor areas, we selected two geo-graphical areas (Zuid-Holland and Groningen) that according to a 2015 study by the Ducth Buraeu of Statistics (CBS) have the highest unemployement rates of the country. We collected 706,044 tweets posted by users whose location was set to the two target areas. The amount of messages was further filtered by removing noise (i.e., messages containing URLs), dropping to 356,401 tweets. Similarly to the keywords approach, we further filtered 2,500 messages using one profanity dictionary and collected an additional 2,500 randomly.

- **Authors**: we looked for seed users, i.e., users that are likely to post/use abusive language in their tweets. We created an ad-hoc list of 67 profanities, swearwords, and slurs and then searched for messages containing any of these elements in a ten-day window in December 2018 (namely 2018-11-12 – 2018-11-22), corresponding to a moment of heated debate in the country about Zwarte Piet. We collected an initial amount of 3,105,833 tweets. We then selected as seed users the top 15, i.e., the top 15 users who most frequently use in their messages any of the 67 keywords. For each of them we further collected a maximum of 100 tweets randomly, summing up to a total of 1390 tweets

- **Dictionaries used**: HADES (Tulkens et al., 2016); HurtLex v1.2 (Bassignana et al., 2018)

Time periods (DD-MM-YYYY):

1 12-11-2015/22-11-2015 (November 2015 Paris attacks);

2 07-03-2017/17-03-2017 (2017 Dutch general election);

3 12-11-2018/22-11-2018 (Intocht Sinterklaas 2018);

4 2020-08 (protests in solidarity with the Black Lives Matter movement);

5 2015-04;

6 2018-06

7 2019-05

8 2019-09

B. LANGUAGE VARIETY/VARIETIES
BCP-47 language tag: `nl`
Language variety description: Netherlands and Belgium (Vlaams)

C. SPEAKER DEMOGRAPHIC N/A

D. ANNOTATOR DEMOGRAPHIC

- **Annotator #1**: Age: 21; Gender: female; Race/ethnicity: caucasian; Native language: Dutch; Socioeconomic status:n/a Training in linguistics/other relevant discipline: BA in Information science

- **Annotator #2**: Age: 21; Gender: male; Race/ethnicity: caucasian; Native language: Dutch; Socioeconomic status:n/a Training in linguistics/other relevant discipline: BA in Information science

- **Annotator #3**: Age: 21; Gender: male; Race/ethnicity: caucasian; Native language: Dutch; Socioeconomic status:n/a Training in linguistics/other relevant discipline: BA in Information science

- **Annotator #4**: Age: 21; Gender: male; Race/ethnicity: caucasian; Native language: Dutch; Socioeconomic status:n/a Training in linguistics/other relevant discipline: BA in Information science

- **Annotator #5**: Age: 23; Gender: male; Race/ethnicity: caucasian; Native language: Dutch; Socioeconomic status:n/a Training in linguistics/other relevant discipline: BA in Information science

- **Annotator #6**: Age: 24; Gender: male; Race/ethnicity: caucasian; Native language: Dutch; Socioeconomic status:n/a Training in linguistics/other relevant discipline: MA in Information science

E. SPEECH SITUATION N/A

F. TEXT CHARACTERISTICS Twitter messages; short messages of max. 280 characters; the original messages may contain multimedia materials, external URL links, and mentions of other users. For all experiments, URLs and users' mentions have been anonymized. Time period of collection illustrated in §A **Curation Rationale**.

G. RECORDING QUALITY N/A

Data Statements are from the University of Washington. Contact: datastatements@uw.edu. The markdown Data Statement we used is from June 4th, 2020. The Data Statement template is based on worksheets distributed at the 2020 LREC workshop on Data Statements, by Emily M. Bender, Batya Friedman, and Angelina McMillan-Major.

B Ethical considerations

Dual use DALC v1.0 and the accompanying models are exposed to risks of dual use from malevolent agents. However, we think that by making publicly available the resource, documenting the process behind its creation and the models, we may mitigate such risks.

Privacy Collection of data from Twitter's users has been conducted in compliance with Twitter's Terms of Service. Given the large amount of users that may be involved, we could not collect informed consent from each of them. To comply with this limitations, we have made publicly available only the tweet IDs. This will protect the users' rights to delete their messages or accounts. However, releasing only IDs exposes DALC to fluctuations in terms of potentially available messages, thus making replicability of experiments and comparison with future work impossible. To obviate to this limitation, we make available another version of the corpus, DALC Full Text. This version of the corpus allows users to access to the full text message of all 8,156 tweets. The DALC Full Text dataset is released with a BY-NC 4.0 licence. In this case, we make available only the text, removing any information related to the time periods or seed users. We have also anonymized all users' mentions and external URLs. The CC licence is extended with further restrictions explicitly preventing users to actively search for the text of the messages in any form. We deem these sufficient steps to protect users' privacy and rights to do research using internet material.

Offensive Language Detection in Nepali Social Media

Nobal B. Niraula*
Nowa Lab
Madison, Alabama, USA
nobal@nowalab.com

Saurab Dulal*
The University of Memphis
Memphis, Tennessee, USA
sdulal@memphis.edu

Diwa Koirala
Nowa Lab
Madison, Alabama, USA
diwa@nowalab.com

Abstract

Social media texts such as blog posts, comments, and tweets often contain offensive languages including racial hate speech comments, personal attacks, and sexual harassments. Detecting inappropriate use of language is, therefore, of utmost importance for the safety of the users as well as for suppressing hateful conduct and aggression. Existing approaches to this problem are mostly available for resource-rich languages such as English and German. In this paper, we characterize the offensive language in Nepali, a low-resource language, highlighting the challenges that need to be addressed for processing Nepali social media text. We also present experiments for detecting offensive language using supervised machine learning. Besides contributing the first baseline approaches of detecting offensive language in Nepali, we also release human annotated data sets to encourage future research on this crucial topic.

1 Introduction

User-generated content on social media and discussion forums has surged with the advent of technology and the availability of affordable mobile devices. Users interact on these platforms with natural language posts and comments on diverse topics. Such interactions may contain toxic comments or posts that are acutely insulting or harmful to other participants. Such content (foul language) typically consists of racial hate speech, personal attacks, and sexual harassment. Detection of inappropriate use of language is, therefore, of utmost importance. It keeps the discussion healthy by eliminating foul language and also enhances the security of the users by suppressing hateful conduct and aggression.

An approach to filter offensive content is to use human experts (e.g. moderators) and manually review the posts or comments as soon as they get posted. However, manual review is almost impractical and cost-prohibitive, especially when the systems having large user bases that generate a stream of content in a short period. In recent years, the computational linguistics and language technology communities are actively working on automating the detection process. Automated effort can prevent foul content from being posted. It can also flag suspicious content so that human experts monitoring the system can initiate corrective actions.

In this paper, we focus on detecting offensive language in Nepali. While numerous studies exist towards automatic detection of offensive content in resource-rich languages such as English (Gitari et al., 2015; Burnap and Williams, 2016; Davidson et al., 2017; Gambäck and Sikdar, 2017; Waseem, 2016) and German (Schneider et al., 2018; Wiedemann et al., 2018; Michele et al., 2018), to our knowledge, there is no prior work available for a resource-poor language Nepali. Some studies have been found for Hindi (Dalal et al., 2014; Bharti et al., 2017) which is written in the same Devanagari script as Nepali. However, due to the differences in vocabulary, grammar, culture, and ethnicity, systems developed for Hindi do not work for Nepali. Therefore, our novel work presented in this paper lays a foundation for detecting offensive content in Nepali.

The key contributions of this paper are listed as follows:

- We characterize the offensive languages commonly found in Nepali social media.
- We release a human labeled data sets for offensive language detection in Nepali social media which is available at https://github.com/nowalab/offensive-nepali.

*These authors contributed equally to this work

Proceedings of the Fifth Workshop on Online Abuse and Harms, pages 67–75
August 6, 2021.

- We prescribe novel preprocessing approaches for Nepali social media text.
- We provide baseline models for coarse-grained and fine-grained classifications of offensive language in Nepali.

2 Related Work

Detection of hate speech and offensive language across multiple languages is ramping up in recent years. This task is typically modeled as a supervised learning problem that requires a set of human-labeled training examples corresponding to different target classes. The target classes are the types of hate speech or offensive language under the study. Schmidt and Wiegand (2017) provides a comprehensive survey of the approaches in several aspects such as the features used, classification algorithms, and data sets and annotations.

As mentioned previously, majority of studies on hate speech and offensive language detection have been conducted in resource-rich languages such as English and German. Such research is further facilitated by recent competitions and shared tasks that make availability of gold training examples. Toxic Comment Classification Challenge by Kaggle[1], for example, provides thousands of human-labeled examples for detecting toxic behaviors in Wikipedia comments. Similarly, First Shared Task on Aggression Identification (Kumar et al., 2018) for Hindi and English, and Germeval (Wiegand et al., 2018) for German provide gold data sets for detecting offensive languages. The former contains 15000 aggression-annotated Facebook posts and comments each in Hindi and English and the latter contains over 8000 human annotated tweets for German.

An example of hate speech detection in English language is by Burnap and Williams (2016) who studied the detection in tweets with different categories: (a) race (ethnicity), (b) disability, (c) religion, and (c) sexual orientation and transgender status. Their data set consisted of 1803 tweets related to sexual orientation with 183 instances of offensive or antagonistic content, 1876 tweets related to race with 70 instances of offensive or antagonistic content, and 1914 tweets related to the disability with 51 instances of offensive or antagonistic content. The authors modeled the hate speech detection as a classification problem, achieving F-measures of 0.77, 0.75, 0.75, and 0.47 for religion, disability, race, and sexual orientation respectively. Davidson et al. (2017) differentiated hate speech from offensive languages. They classified each English tweet into (a) offensive (b) hate speech and (c) None using different classifiers. Thousands of tweets were labeled using CrowdFlower for the training examples. Several classifiers were trained using a one-versus-rest framework in which a separate classifier was trained for each class and the class label with the highest predicted probability across all classifiers was assigned to each tweet. Out of the several classifiers, logistic regression and support vector machine performed the best achieving the overall precision and recall as 0.91 and 0.90 respectively. However, the precision and recall scores for the hate class were low (precision of 0.44 and recall 0.61), suggesting that the classification of hate speech is challenging. Similarly, Gambäck and Sikdar (2017) trained Convolutional Neural Networks using 6655 Twitter hate-speech data-set originally created by Waseem (2016) to classify utterances into (a) Sexism, (b) Racism, (c) Sexism and Racism, and (d) Non-hate speech, achieving an overall precision, recall, and f-measure as 0.7287, 0.7775, and 0.7389, respectively.

Like in English, detecting offensive languages in German language has also been increased recently especially due to the shared tasks at Germeval 2018[2] and Germeval 2019[3]. Germeval 2018 provided 5009 categorized tweets as training data sets and 3532 as test data sets. It offered two tasks : (1) a coarse-grained binary classification with the categories OFFENSIVE and OTHER and (2) a fine-grained classification with the four categories PROFANITY, INSULT, ABUSE, and OTHER. The training data set consists of 66.3% tweets as OTHER, 20.4% as ABUSE, and 11.9% as INSULT, and only 1.4% as PROFANITY. The best performing system in task 1, TUWienKBS (Montani, 2018), received overall precision, recall, and F-measure of 0.71, 0.65, and 0.68 for OFFENSIVE and 0.82, 0.86, and 0.84 for OTHER respectively. The best performing system, uhhLT(Wiedemann et al., 2018), for the fine-grained task (task 2) achieved average precision, recall, and f-measure as 0.56, 0.49, and 0.52, respectively.

[1]https://www.kaggle.com/c/jigsaw-toxic-comment-classification-challenge

[2]https://projects.fzai.h-da.de/iggsa/germeval-2018/

[3]https://projects.fzai.h-da.de/iggsa/

The closest work to ours is the study of linguistic taboos and euphemisms in Nepali by Niraula et al. (2020). The authors presented how the offensive contents are formed in Nepali and also created a resource containing a list of common offensive terms in Nepali. However, they have not addressed the detection of offensive content itself.

3 Offensive Language in Nepali Social Media

Hate speech is a communication that disparages a person or a group based on some characteristic such as race, color, ethnicity, gender, sexual orientation, nationality, religion, or other characteristic (Schmidt and Wiegand, 2017). Hate speech can have strong cultural implications (Schmidt and Wiegand, 2017) and thus an utterance can be perceived as offensive or not depending on the observer's cultural background. Besides, the distribution of hate speech can be different in different countries. For example, a country with a mix of religions most likely contains more hate speech related to religions than a country having a singly dominant religion. Therefore, in this section, we discuss different kinds of offensive languages that we observed in Nepali social media.

We reviewed several social media posts and comments on Twitter, YouTube, Facebook, Blogs, and News Portals and identified the common hate speech types. We listed the common types in Table 1 with two examples for each. RACIST (OR), SEXIST(OS), and Other Offensive (OO) (e.g. attack to an individual or organization) are the most commonly observed offensive language types in Nepali social media posts. RACIST (OR) and SEXIST (OS) both are specific cases of offensive content. We noticed an enormous amount of offensive content (OOs) that is not SEXIST or RACIST.

We can expect more of RACIST comments because Nepali society is a mix of several ethnic groups, casts and regions (*pahade* - people live in hilly region; *madheshi* - people live in the south; *ethnic groups* - gurung, magar; *casts* - bahun, chhetri, dalit, etc.). The social tensions among these races and ethnic groups are reflected in the posts and comments.

Hate speeches related to gender and religion are also observed. Interestingly, we observed the hate speech towards females the most when compared with males and the third gender. Targets to Hinduism, Islam, Christianity, and Buddhism are the most common hate speech related to religions. Furthermore, several cases of use of swear words, violent rhetoric, and personal attack towards individuals or organizations are also observed. We categorized them as Other Offensive.

3.1 Challenges in Processing Nepali Social Media Text

Social media text in any language is very noisy and contains ad-hoc typos, abbreviations, acronyms, and hashtags that require a significant amount of preprocessing. In addition to these challenges, Nepali natural language processing requires many other issues to be handled. First, the content can be written in four different ways as shown in Table 1: (a) Nepali text in Devanagari script (b) Nepali text in Roman script, pronunciation-based, (c) pure English text, and (d) Mixed script text that contains both Devanagari and Roman scripts. In addition, cases of *Neglish* in which the user switches between Nepali and English languages are also found. Furthermore, some interesting cases of code-switching were also found, mostly among Hindi, Nepali, Maithili, and English: "सही बोला भाई" (Translation: *rightly said brother*), "गुड night" (Translation: *good night*)

Second, even when the script is written in Devanagari (or Roman), there are several orthographic writing issues one has to deal with while processing Nepali natural language text. The same word (such as चोक्सी) can be written in so many different ways in Devanagari (or in Roman) as they are pronounced almost the same (refer to Table 2).

Third, Nepali is morphologically rich and complex. The same base verb, मार्नु (to kill) for instance, have different forms (मार्छु, मार्छस्, मार्छौं, मार्छेस, मारिन्छ, मारिवक्सिन्छ, मारिनेछ, मारिएला, मारेछ, मारिछे, मारेछन्, मारिएको, मरेको, मारिन्छ, नमार, नमार्नु, etc.) depending on gender, number, honor and tense, giving diverse forms for the same base token. Handling this issue is very crucial for processing Nepali text.

Fourth, Nepali is a low-resource language because Nepali natural language processing is in its infancy. There aren't adequate resources available to process the language. For example, there is not even a list of standard vocabulary words available to use. Lemmatization of morphologically rich languages is crucial but currently is not possible for Nepali. There is no reliable public or commercial parts-of-speech tagger available.

S.N	Content	Type
1	Nepali (Devanagari): मासाला पागल भए जस्तो छ! Translation: “massala” it seems he got mad	OO
2	Nepali (Transliterated): sale khate aphu matra educated thhanndo rahexa Translation: “sale” “khate” (pejorative term for people living in urban slum dwellers) thinks he is the only educated	OO
3	Nepali (Devanagari): पागल् बाहुन् Translation: lunatic “bahun” (an upper cast)	OR
4	Nepali (Transliterated): Rajako kaam chhodi kamiko dewali Translation: Going to kami’s festival over king’s assignment – a traditionally non-tabooed idiom that is considered racist now	OR
5	Nepali (Transliterated): Pothi baseko suhaudaina Translation: It does not suit a woman to raise her voice (sexist idiom)	OS
6	Nepali (Mixed): पैसामा बीक्छन के टी हरू sala Translation: girls get sold with money *sala*	OS
7	Nepali (Transliterated): ma pani bahun hu tara tapaaik ko kuro chhita bujhena Translation: I am also a bramhin, but I am dissatisfied with your words	NO
8	Nepali (Devanagari): यो भालु हो सर Translation: Sir, this is a bear	NO

Table 1: Examples of common offensive languages found in Nepali social media. Note that they could be typed in (a) *Romanized* (2, 4, 5, 7) (b) *Devanagari Script* (1, 3, 8) and (c) *Mixed* i.e. Romanized + Devanagari (6). OO = Other-Offensive, OR = Offensive Racist, OS = Offensive Sexist, NO = Non-offensive

Script	Content
English	mad witch
Romanized - 1	pagal boksi
Romanized - 2	pagal bokshi
Devanagari - 1	पागल वोक्सी
Devanagari - 2	पागल वोक्सि
Devanagari - 3	पागल वोक्सी
Devanagari - 4	पागल बोक्सि
Devanagari - 5	पागल बोक्शी
Devanagari - 6	पागल बोक्शि
Mixed -1	पागल boksi
Mixed -2	पागल bokshi
Mixed -3	pagal वोक्सी

Table 2: Different orthographic forms of writing the text “mad witch”

Fifth, translation of data sets or resources from other languages to Nepali is not straightforward. Commercially available language translation services are poor in translating contents from other languages to Nepali. All of these issues make the processing of Nepali text very challenging.

4 Methodology

In this section, we describe the data collection, data annotation, and our system to detect offensive languages in Nepali text.

4.1 Data Collection

Our goal is to create a labeled data set of hate speech of different types and train machine learning models using it. Since hate speech appears relatively less in social media, annotating a large sample gives just a few offensive contents, making the annotation process very laborious and expensive. To address this problem, researchers apply different strategies to improve the distribution of offensive content Zampieri et al. (2019). Following these strategies, we made a pool of comments and posts from the sources in social media that have higher chances of containing hate speech. Our pool consists of over 15000 comments and posts from diverse social media platforms such as Facebook, Twitter, YouTube, Nepali Blogs, and News Portals.

For Facebook, we first made a list of potentially controversial posts posted to a general audience in open groups and public pages between 2017 and 2019. We then extracted around 7000 comments corresponding to those posts. For Twitter, we followed a bootstrapping approach as done by prior arts (Zampieri et al., 2019). For this, we first created a small list of Nepali words (in both Devanagari and Romanized forms) that have higher chances of being used in hate speech. The words themselves are not explicitly offensive but can appear in hate speech depending on the context of their use. For example, the words "बाहुन" (*bahun* - an upper cast in Nepali society) and "भालु" (*bhalu* - bear) are non-offensive by themselves but can appear in offensive contexts. Offensively, *bahun* can be used to insult someone racially based on their cast, and *bhalu* can be used to call someone a prostitute. Using the list of keywords, we performed a targeted search on Twitter and collected about 4000 tweets, approximately 50 tweets per word. These tweets enhanced the pool with diverse and context-sensitive posts. For YouTube, similar to Facebook, we manually created a list of potentially controversial, non-controversial, and neutral videos, and extracted approximately 3500 comments. Video contents are highly engaging. A good length video – especially a controversial one – contained diverse emotions and attributes such as anger, happiness, low and high pitch, etc., and was scrutinized by the viewers. The YouTube video comments also helped to maintain the diversity of data set in the writing form as they were typed in transliterated, mixed, and pure Devanagari font and fulfill our categorical requirements. Besides, they captured the inputs from the diversity of people commenting on the posts. Finally, the rest of the comments, about 500, were gathered from several Nepali blogs and news websites.

Source	NO	OO	OR	OS	Total
Twitter	1214	802	39	22	2077
Facebook	2313	853	168	27	3361
YouTube	908	846	56	36	1846
Other	117	51	6	3	177
Total	4552	2552	269	88	7462

Table 3: The pool of social medial data set.

4.2 Data Annotation and Data Set

After constructing the pool of comments and posts, we randomized the records for annotation. To ensure the quality, we used two annotators and asked them to annotate each record into four categories: SEXIST, RACIST, OTHER-OFFENSIVE, and NON-OFFENSIVE. We computed the inter-rater reliability (IRR) between each pair of ratings using Cohen's kappa (k) (McHugh, 2012). IRR scores were computed for both fine-grained (considering all four labels) and coarse-grained (offensive or non-offensive) cases. For the coarse-grained, we considered the three offensive categories SEXIST, RACIST, and OTHER-OFFENSIVE as offensive. The Cohen's kappa coefficients obtained for fine-grained and coarse-grained cases were 0.71 and 0.78, respectively, suggesting substantial agreements between the raters. We observed most of the disagreements between human annotators in borderline cases. For example, *Kati milyo Parti bat Dr. Sab lai* (How much/many did you get from the party[4], Dr. Sab?) was marked as offensive by one while non-offensive by the other. This comment could be a personal attack for corruption in certain contexts while non-offensive in some other e.g. receiving compensation or votes. The disagreements were reviewed by the third annotator and resolved on consensus.

	NO	OO	OR	OS	Total
Train	3562	1950	218	68	5798
Test	896	486	49	19	1450

Table 4: Training and Testing Data Sets

Additionally, the social media posts and comments often contained personally identifiable information such as person names, organization names, and phone numbers. To anonymize the comments, we replace the person/organization names with unique random yet real person/organization names. Since gender information carries vital linguistic properties in the language, we tried preserving the gender as much as possible during the name replacement process. A name with a known gender (i.e. male or female) is replaced with another random name of the same gender.

The annotators annotated 7462 records altogether. The distribution of the annotation across different categories is presented in Table 3. We removed the duplicated examples from the annotated corpus and performed 80-20 split randomly to create the training and test data sets. The statistics of these data sets are shown in Table 4. To encourage the research community for addressing this important task of offensive language detection in Nepali, we have released these gold data sets at `https://github.com/nowalab/offensive-nepali`.

[4]Party here specifically refers to political organization

4.3 Preprocessing

As described in Section 3.1, the social media comments and posts came in different forms: comments purely in Devanagari script, transliteration using Roman letters, pure English, or their combinations. In fact, more than 50% of the comments in our pool are written in transliterated or mixed forms. We speculate, due to the ease of writing, this pattern will continue. These observations reiterate the need for text normalization while processing Nepali social media texts. To this end, we consider two different text normalization schemes:

(A) Dirghikaran (Prep_Dir): Because multiple characters have the same sound, inconsistencies appear even for the same word written in Devanagari script. We use the following mappings to normalize the character variants: ि -> ी, ु -> ू, स -> श, ष -> श, व -> ब, उ -> ऊ, ्री -> ृ, ्रि -> ्री, इ -> ई, ं -> ँ, न -> ण, ं -> ङ्. This converts the words with different orthographic forms to a normalized form, e.g., कितावं, and किताब both map to कीताब. This approach does not affect the tokens that are already transliterated in Romanized form or written in English.

(B) Romanization (Prep_Rom): With this scheme, we convert (transliterate) each Nepali word written in Devanagari script to its Romanized form using a number of rules. This rule-based system takes care of the orthographic variants as well. For instance, it converts all किताव, किताब, कीताब, and कीताव to *kitab*. We could have done the reverse way i.e. converting transliterated text in Romanized form to Devanagari script (e.g. *kitab* -> किताव) but we found that converting Devanagari text to Romanized using the rules is relatively easier. After this preprocessing, all the comments will be in Romanized forms. This powerful preprocessing technique has not been employed in any of the prior arts and is one of our novel contributions in this paper.

4.4 Features

Nepali, as illustrated in Section 3.1, is a morphologically rich language. A verb, for example, can take different forms depending upon gender, number, honor, tense, and their combinations. Therefore, character-based and sub-word features are expected to be useful in classifying offensive languages. For that reason, we considered both word (Unigrams and Bigrams) and character (Character Trigrams) features for our experiments.

4.5 Experiments

We performed experiments to see the effect of preprocessing scheme and classification model, and coarse and fine-grained classification. In all experiments, we reduced the features down to 10000 using KBest algorithm with chi-squared stat.

Prep.	Non-Offensive			Offensive		
	Pre.	Rec.	F_1	Pre.	Rec.	F_1
A	0.71	0.94	0.81	0.80	0.39	0.52
B	0.71	0.94	0.81	0.81	0.39	0.53
C	0.76	0.94	0.84	0.85	0.51	0.64
D	0.76	0.95	0.84	0.85	0.51	0.64
A	0.78	0.94	0.85	0.84	0.56	0.68
B	0.78	0.92	0.85	0.83	0.58	0.68
C	0.79	0.91	0.84	0.81	0.60	0.69
D	0.79	0.92	0.85	0.83	0.59	0.69
A	0.78	0.93	0.85	0.83	0.57	0.68
B	0.79	0.92	0.85	0.83	0.60	0.69
C	0.79	0.92	0.85	0.81	0.60	0.69
D	0.79	0.93	0.85	0.83	0.61	0.70

Table 5: Effect of prepossessing techniques and features on binary classification. Preprocessing techniques: (A) No Preprocessing (Prep_None) (B) Dirghikaran (Prep_Dir), (C) Romanization (Prep_Rom), and (D) Prep_Dir + Prep_Rom. The **first block** uses word only, the **second block** uses character only and the **last block** uses both word and character features.

Models	Non-Offensive			Offensive		
	Pre.	Rec.	F_1	Pre.	Rec.	F_1
Baseline	0.74	0.73	0.73	0.57	0.58	0.58
LR	0.80	0.93	0.87	0.86	0.63	0.72
SVM	0.78	0.95	0.85	0.87	0.56	0.68
RF	0.81	0.93	0.86	0.85	0.64	0.73
M-BERT	0.74	0.90	0.81	0.75	0.49	0.59

Table 6: Binary classification using different machine learning models.

4.6 Effect of Preprocessing

We trained a Logistic Regression classifier for binary classification using four different preprocessing schemes: A. No preprocessing (Prep_None), B. Dirghikaran (Prep_Dir), C. Romanization (Prep_Rom), and D. Both Prep_Dir + Prep_Rom, where + means string concatenation. We considered positive examples as the records with OO, OR, and OS from Table 4. This yielded the train data set with 3562 negative and 2236 positive examples and the test data set with 896 positive and 554 negative examples.

We reported the results using the test data in Table 5. The top, middle, and bottom blocks contain the results corresponding to word only, character only, and both word and character features, respectively. The results in the middle block are significantly better than the results in the top block, demonstrating that character-based features are extremely useful. It is expected because Nepali is morphologically very rich and the social media text is very noisy. Adding both word and character features further slightly improved the results (the bottom block).

Within each block, i.e. given a feature type, the results are better in the order: D > C > B > A, where A is no preprocessing. The preprocessing technique B, "Dirghikaran", improved the performance of the classifier compared to A. But the margin of improvement by C, "Romanization", is typically higher than that by B. It is especially significant when the word only features are used. This is because Dirghikaran only normalizes the terms written in the Devanagari script but it does not transliterate the text. Romanization, however, transliterates the text written in Devanagari script and makes it uniform with other already transliterated user posts. Combining texts using both Romanization and Dirghikaran, marked with D, slightly improved the results over C.

4.7 Coarse-grained Classification

For coarse-grained (i.e. binary) classification, we experimented with four machine learning classifiers that are most often used for offensive language detection. Specifically, we used: (A) **Logistic Regression (LR)**: Linear LR with L2 regularization constant 1 and limited-memory BFGS optimization, (B) **Support Vector Machine (SVM)**: Linear SVM with L2 regularization constant 1 and logistic loss function, (C) **Random Forests (RF)**: Averaging probabilistic predictions of 100 randomized decision trees. (D) **Multilingual BERT (M-BERT)**: Current best performing models for offensive language detection utilize BERT (Devlin et al., 2018) based models (Liu et al., 2019; Mozafari et al., 2019; Baruah et al., 2020). Although there is no BERT model available for Nepali yet, Nepali is included in M-BERT[5] which is trained using the entire Wikipedia dump for each language. We used Hugging Face Transformer library (Wolf et al., 2020) to build the M-BERT classifier.

In addition, we constructed a **baseline** model using the list of Nepali offensive terms collected by Niraula et al. (2020) and is available at GitHub[6]. This data set contains 1078 offensive terms, their transliterated forms, and interestingly their offensiveness scores. The offensiveness score ranges from 1 (slightly offensive) to 5 (absolute offensive e.g. taboo terms). For a given post, our baseline scans for the tokens present in the dictionary and sums the corresponding offensiveness scores. If the sum is 5 or more, it declares the post as offensive.

For baseline and traditional machine learning models (LR, SVM, and RF), as suggested by the experiments in Section 4.6, we chose the Romanization + Dirghikaran preprocessing strategy and both word and character-based features. In addition, we computed and utilized the indicator features, for each post, by scanning the preprocessed tokens and looking them up in the offensive dictionary. As before, we reduced the features using KBest to 10000 for both train and test data sets.

We trained the models and evaluated them using the binary train and test data sets constructed as described in Section 4.6. The evaluation results are presented in Table 6. The baseline model which is based on a dictionary obtained the F_1 scores of 0.58 and 0.73 for offensive and non-offensive categories. All machine learning models performed very well compared to the baseline model. Interestingly, M-BERT model did not perform well compared to the traditional models. This could be because M-BERT model is trained using Wikipedia content which is different from the social media text. Also, the size of Wikipedia for low-resource language Nepali is not huge and thus it is under-represented in the M-BERT model. Logistic Regression and Random Forrest models were the top-performing models, with the latter having a slightly higher F_1 score on the offensive category. For this reason, we chose the Random Forrest classifier for the fine-grained classification which we describe next.

4.8 Fine-grained classification

Fine-grained classification can be done by directly training a multi-class classifier over the labeled training data set. However, we followed the principle proposed by Park and Fung (2017) that performed better for this specific task. Following this, we trained a Random Forrest classifier for coarse-grained classification as in Section 4.7. We trained

[5]https://github.com/google-research/bert/blob/master/multilingual.md

[6] https://github.com/nowalab/offensive-nepali

	None			Other Offensive			Racist			Sexist		
	Pre.	Rec.	F_1	Pre.	Rec.	F_1	Pre.	Rec.	F_1	Pre.	Rec.	F_1
RF	0.81	0.93	0.87	0.79	0.64	0.71	0.76	0.32	0.45	0.9	0.05	0.01

Table 7: Results for detecting different offensive categories

another Random Forrest classifier using only the training data set with labels OO (other offensive), OR (offensive racist), and OS (offensive sexist). During testing, we applied the second classifier only to those test records that the first classifier predicted as offensive to get their fine-grained categories. We assigned a non-offensive label (NO) to each test record for which the first classifier predicted as non-offensive.

We reported the experiment results in Table 7. The F_1 scores for Non-Offensive, Other Offensive, Racist, and Sexist were 0.87, 0.71, 0.45, and 0.01 respectively. The lower performance for the sexist category was mainly due to the fewer training examples available for this category compared to the other categories (see Table 4). Gathering these fine-grained labels is a major challenge in the field than obtaining labels with simply offensive and non-offensive (Park and Fung, 2017). This is more evident in the low-resource language like Nepali.

4.9 Error Analysis

Most of the errors were due to the lack of world and contextual knowledge to the classifier and is always a challenge for offensive language detection in any language. For instance, *thamel ma bhalu ko bigbigi* (literal translation: *Abundant bears in Thamel*) is offensive while *jungle ma bhalu ko bigbigi* (literal meaning: *Abundant bears in jungle*) is non-offensive although both of these sentences have the same tokens everywhere except one i.e. *Thamel* vs. *Jungle*. *Thamel* is a famous tourist area in Kathmandu that also has a negative connotation as a brothel and *bhalu* is a contextually offensive term that can mean a *bear* or a *prostitute* depending on the context.

5 Conclusion

In this paper, we presented a systematic study of offensive language detection in Nepali, a topic that has not been explored for this low resource language. We collected diverse social media posts and generated a labeled data set by manually annotating 7248 posts with fine-grained labels. The data set is available at `https://github.com/nowalab/offensive-nepali`.

We presented different challenges that need to be addressed to process noisy social media posts in Nepali. We proposed three different preprocessing methods and provided detailed evaluations demonstrating their effectiveness on the model performance. We reported detailed experiments for coarse-grained detection of offensive languages using several conventional machine learning and recent deep learning models and features. We also provided a fine-grained classification of offensive comments using a two-step approach for Nepali language.

Our data set and baseline algorithms provide foundation for future research in this area to fight against cyberbullying and hate speech, which has been widespread in recent days. We would like to caution to those who use our work (e.g. data sets and algorithms) to avoid over-reliance on keywords and machine learning models. We remind everyone to keep the context in the forefront, and encourage using human review to the ones flagged by the machine learning systems as offensive, especially in cases of false positives.

Future work includes detecting the targets of the offensive comments, which could be an individual organization/person or a group. Leveraging offensive language data sets from other languages to Nepali, e.g. by translation and transfer learning as done by Sohn and Lee (2019), is another interesting future direction.

Acknowledgments

We would like acknowledge Ms. Monika Shah, professor Dr. Kumar Prasad Koirala, and Mr. Suraj Subedi for their continued support, helpful discussions and encouragements.

References

Arup Baruah, Kaushik Das, Ferdous Barbhuiya, and Kuntal Dey. 2020. Aggression identification in english, hindi and bangla text using bert, roberta and svm. In *Proceedings of the Second Workshop on Trolling, Aggression and Cyberbullying*, pages 76–82.

Santosh Kumar Bharti, Korra Sathya Babu, and Sanjay Kumar Jena. 2017. Harnessing online news for sarcasm detection in hindi tweets. In *International Conference on Pattern Recognition and Machine Intelligence*, pages 679–686. Springer.

Pete Burnap and Matthew L Williams. 2016. Us and them: identifying cyber hate on twitter across multiple protected characteristics. *EPJ Data Science*, 5(1):11.

Chetan Dalal, Shivyansh Tandon, and Amitabha Mukerjee. 2014. Insult detection in hindi. Technical report, Technical report on Artificial Intelligence, 18.

Thomas Davidson, Dana Warmsley, Michael Macy, and Ingmar Weber. 2017. Automated hate speech detection and the problem of offensive language. In *Proceedings of the 11th International Conference on Web and Social Media*.

Jacob Devlin, Ming-Wei Chang, Kenton Lee, and Kristina Toutanova. 2018. Bert: Pre-training of deep bidirectional transformers for language understanding. *arXiv preprint arXiv:1810.04805*.

Björn Gambäck and Utpal Kumar Sikdar. 2017. Using convolutional neural networks to classify hate-speech. In *Proceedings of the First Workshop on Abusive Language Online*, pages 85–90.

Njagi Dennis Gitari, Zhang Zuping, Hanyurwimfura Damien, and Jun Long. 2015. A lexicon-based approach for hate speech detection. *International Journal of Multimedia and Ubiquitous Engineering*, 10(4):215–230.

Ritesh Kumar, Atul Kr Ojha, Shervin Malmasi, and Marcos Zampieri. 2018. Benchmarking aggression identification in social media. In *Proceedings of the First Workshop on Trolling, Aggression and Cyberbullying (TRAC-2018)*, pages 1–11.

Ping Liu, Wen Li, and Liang Zou. 2019. Nuli at semeval-2019 task 6: Transfer learning for offensive language detection using bidirectional transformers. In *Proceedings of the 13th international workshop on semantic evaluation*, pages 87–91.

Mary L McHugh. 2012. Interrater reliability: the kappa statistic. *Biochemia medica*, 22(3):276–282.

Corazza Michele, Stefano Menini, Arslan Pinar, Rachele Sprugnoli, Cabrio Elena, Sara Tonelli, and Villata Serena. 2018. Inriafbk at germeval 2018: Identifying offensive tweets using recurrent neural networks. In *GermEval 2018*, pages 80–84.

Joaquın Padilla Montani. 2018. Tuwienkbs at germeval 2018: German abusive tweet detection. *Austrian Academy of Sciences, Vienna September 21, 2018*.

Marzieh Mozafari, Reza Farahbakhsh, and Noel Crespi. 2019. A bert-based transfer learning approach for hate speech detection in online social media. In *International Conference on Complex Networks and Their Applications*, pages 928–940. Springer.

Nobal B Niraula, Saurab Dulal, and Diwa Koirala. 2020. Linguistic taboos and euphemisms in nepali. *arXiv preprint arXiv:2007.13798*.

Ji Ho Park and Pascale Fung. 2017. One-step and two-step classification for abusive language detection on twitter. *arXiv preprint arXiv:1706.01206*.

Anna Schmidt and Michael Wiegand. 2017. A survey on hate speech detection using natural language processing. In *Proceedings of the Fifth International Workshop on Natural Language Processing for Social Media*, pages 1–10.

Julian Moreno Schneider, Roland Roller, Peter Bourgonje, Stefanie Hegele, and Georg Rehm. 2018. Towards the automatic classification of offensive language and related phenomena in german tweets. *Austrian Academy of Sciences, Vienna September 21, 2018*.

Hajung Sohn and Hyunju Lee. 2019. Mc-bert4hate: Hate speech detection using multi-channel bert for different languages and translations. In *2019 International Conference on Data Mining Workshops (ICDMW)*, pages 551–559. IEEE.

Zeerak Waseem. 2016. Are you a racist or am i seeing things? annotator influence on hate speech detection on twitter. In *Proceedings of the first workshop on NLP and computational social science*, pages 138–142.

Gregor Wiedemann, Eugen Ruppert, Raghav Jindal, and Chris Biemann. 2018. Transfer learning from lda to bilstm-cnn for offensive language detection in twitter. *Austrian Academy of Sciences, Vienna September 21, 2018*.

Michael Wiegand, Melanie Siegel, and Josef Ruppenhofer. 2018. Overview of the germeval 2018 shared task on the identification of offensive language. *Austrian Academy of Sciences, Vienna September 21, 2018*.

Thomas Wolf, Julien Chaumond, Lysandre Debut, Victor Sanh, Clement Delangue, Anthony Moi, Pierric Cistac, Morgan Funtowicz, Joe Davison, Sam Shleifer, et al. 2020. Transformers: State-of-the-art natural language processing. In *Proceedings of the 2020 Conference on Empirical Methods in Natural Language Processing: System Demonstrations*, pages 38–45.

Marcos Zampieri, Shervin Malmasi, Preslav Nakov, Sara Rosenthal, Noura Farra, and Ritesh Kumar. 2019. Predicting the type and target of offensive posts in social media. pages 1415–1420.

MIN_PT: An European Portuguese Lexicon for Minorities Related Terms

Paula Fortuna[1], **Vanessa Cortez**[2], **Miguel Sozinho Ramalho**[3], **Laura Pérez-Mayos**[1]
[1]NLP Group, Pompeu Fabra University,
[2]University of Minho,[3]University of Porto,
paula.fortuna@upf.edu|vanessalcl@gmail.com|m.ramalho@fe.up.pt|laura.perezm@upf.edu

Abstract

Hate speech-related lexicons have been proved to be useful for many tasks such as data collection and classification. However, existing Portuguese lexicons do not distinguish between European and Brazilian Portuguese, and do not include neutral terms that are potentially useful to detect a broader spectrum of content referring to minorities. In this work, we present MIN_PT, a new European Portuguese Lexicon for Minorities-Related Terms specifically designed to tackle the limitations of existing resources. We describe the data collection and annotation process, discuss the limitation and ethical concerns, and prove the utility of the resource by applying it to a use case for the Portuguese 2021 presidential elections.

1 Introduction

Dictionaries and lexicons are commonly used in the field of hate speech automatic detection (Fortuna and Nunes, 2018), with applications ranging from data collection (Silva et al., 2016) to feature extraction (Dadvar et al., 2013) and classification (Tulkens et al., 2016b) by applying some matching function with dictionary terms. However, even though such resources have been proved to be useful in numerous applications, lexical knowledge for hate speech classification has received little attention in literature (Bassignana et al., 2018). This work takes up this demand and focuses on presenting a new European Portuguese Lexicon for Minorities-Related Terms. The need for annotating a new resource derives from two different issues: lack of explicit European Portuguese lexicon, and the need for neutral terms.

Lack of European Portuguese lexicon The existent resources, e.g Hurtlex (Bassignana et al., 2018) or Hatebase[1], do not always distinguish European from Brazilian Portuguese. Both languages are similar and such simplification may serve the purpose of some applications. However, when addressing a nuanced and social phenomenon such as hate speech, the ethnographic differences between Portugal and Brazil require a more fine-grained annotation (e.g words such as "bicha" –fag– or "fufa" –dyke– refer to male and female homosexual individuals only in Portugal and not in Brazil).

Need for neutral terms The annotation of neutral terms in hate speech-related lexicons is not common, specially for low represented languages such as European Portuguese. This limits the application of such resources as those terms open new research venues. First, neutral terms can impact data collection stages as it is possible to identify a broader spectrum of online content referring to minorities. Second, it is possible to use neutral terms for bias detection and control if such terms are present equally in all the classes in a dataset. To overcome this limitation, we collect both offensive and non-offensive minorities' terms.

In what follows, Section 2 provides some background on existing annotated lexicons and their limitations. Section 3 describes the data collection and annotation process, and Section 4 presents the new lexicon. Section 5 presents a use case of the lexicon for the Portuguese 2021 presidential elections. Section 6 addresses some limitations and ethical concerns, and Section 7 summarizes the implications of our work for the automatic hate speech detection field.

2 Related Work

Lexicons can be analyzed in terms of how the data is generated and annotated. While some works have been manually annotated by humans, and others rely on automatic procedures where data is compiled by computational methods, other works

[1]https://hatebase.org/

Proceedings of the Fifth Workshop on Online Abuse and Harms, pages 76–80
August 6, 2021.

conjugate both methods by manually curating the automatically compiled data.

Hatebase is one of the widely used lexicons in the field. It corresponds to a broad multilingual vocabulary manually annotated in terms of different categories (e.g nationality, gender) with data across 95 languages and 175 countries. However, the containing words and phrases have been compiled by non-trained crowdsourced internet volunteers, and therefore the quality of the annotation can not be guaranteed. Moreover, the lexicon does not differentiate Portuguese and Brazilian content. Several works have been using Hatebase terms as keywords for content search in social media platforms, e.g (Davidson et al., 2017; Founta et al., 2018; Radfar et al., 2020). One of these works has contributed particularly to enrich the lexicon English content (Davidson et al., 2017). The authors expand the initial term list with n-grams from the extracted messages when searching with the keywords and finally manually remove irrelevant terms.

Tulkens et al. (2016a) presents another lexicon created to detect racist discourse in dutch social media. Starting with a list of words from the LIWC (Linguistic Inquiry and Word Count) (Tausczik and Pennebaker, 2010), the authors compile a set of terms by applying successive automatic expansions and manual annotation phases.

Hurtlex (Bassignana et al., 2018) is a multilingual lexicon automatically expanded and manually validated with 17 different dimensions such as: negative stereotypes ethnic slurs; professions and occupations; etc. In the set of the discussed lexicons, Hurtlex presents the more complete and complex taxonomy. However, for the purpose of our study, this taxonomy also misses neutral terms to refer to minorities, such as "mulheres" –women– or "muçulmanos" –muslim–, that can help to identify less explicit insults and also positive content. If we focus on the Hurtlex Portuguese subset of terms, we find again no distinction between Brazilian and Portuguese contexts.

Even though the discussed lexicons rely on automatic methods to compile an initial set of terms, they all require manual validation procedures to confirm relevant terms. In this procedure, annotators guarantee that terms match the taxonomy classification rules, which highlights the importance of human annotators to assure higher-quality resources. Accordingly, in this work we also rely on a manual enumeration and annotation of terms to create a new European Portuguese Lexicon for Minorities-Related Terms, containing both offensive and non-offensive terms. Our approach also aligns with the recommendation for synthetic data creation as the compiled data is generated, annotated and validated by experts in an attempt to mimic real behaviour (Vidgen and Derczynski, 2020).

3 Methodology

This section describes the data collection and annotation procedure followed to build MIN_PT, a European Portuguese Lexicon for Minorities Related Terms. We followed a qualitative approach with successive iterations and annotators' participation, as recommended in Vidgen and Derczynski (2020). Starting with and initial set of terms (Section 3.1), the annotators worked individually and collectively in successive iterations to create new annotation rules, remove undesired terms and expand the existent terms with new ones (Section 3.2). Then, two annotators discussed the lexicon terms to reach a consensus on a set of definitions and instructions, deciding which terms are kept and which terms must be eliminated (Section 3.3). The curated list of terms and their classification is available in a public GitHub repository[2].

3.1 Initial data source

For initial data seed, we rely on the Hatebase[3] for Portuguese hate terms; cf. Section 2. While it misses many terms, specially neutral, and mixes Brazilian and European Portuguese, it provides 319 terms and is a good starting point for our new lexicon.

3.2 Data Curation and Enrichment

Starting from the Hatebase for Portuguese hate terms, two annotators curated the list in three individual sessions and two collective sessions with the clear objective of achieving an exhaustive lexicon. The main discussions revolved around clarifying the meaning of diverse terms and deciding on ambiguous terms. The final annotation rules can be described as:

- Remove words that do not match vocabulary from Portugal, e.g. "sangue ruim" –mudblood–, "sapatão" –dyke–.

[2]https://github.com/paulafortuna/Portuguese-minority-terms

[3]https://hatebase.org/

- Enumerate all possible terms. An exhaustive list is achieved by manually: adding synonyms for the same term in case they exist; assuring all terms are present in singular, plural, masculine or feminine, in case such declensions apply; and adding all the known terms for all minority groups.

- Remove ambiguous terms that can have double meaning when the most common usage does not refer to minorities (e.g "preto´´, –black– may be used as an insult but is also a color, tea flavor, etc).

3.3 Data Annotation

After generating a curated list of terms, the annotators classified all terms into the following minorities-related categories: roma, LGBT, migrants, women, people based in religion, people based in ethnicity, and refugees. All the terms were further classified as being an insult (1) or not (0). It is important to notice that terms that can be used as both insults and in a neutral way were classified as not insults. This is the case for certain minority names that can also be used for name-calling (e.g "cigano" –gypsy–).

3.4 Annotators' Description

The two annotators of the MIN_PT lexicon are native Portuguese speakers –one for European and another for Brazilian Portuguese– living in Portugal and aware of the social context. Both identify as cis-gender women and correspond to two authors of the work with previous annotation experience.

4 Results

The MIN_PT European Portuguese Lexicon for Minorities Related Terms is composed of 155 carefully curated terms (cf. Section 3) related to 7 minority groups, as described in Table 1.

Even though our new lexicon contains much less terms than Hurtlex (Bassignana et al., 2018), 155 vs 3902 terms, it is worth noticing that only 23% of the terms in MIN_PT are present in Hurtlex. Therefore, the new lexicon presented in this work will prove to be a valuable resource for hate-speech detection, either on its own or in combination with other resources.

Minority group	Total	Insults
LGBT	44	20
People based on ethnicity	44	30
Women	29	24
Migrants	22	0
No minority	9	9
Roma	8	4
Religious people	6	0
Refugees	2	0

Table 1: MIN_PT lexicon terms frequency per class.

5 Lexicon Application: The case of Portuguese 2021 Presidential Elections

The annotation of this lexicon was motivated by the will to conduct an analysis on the Portuguese 2021 presidential elections twittersphere, aiming at understanding whether and how candidates' speeches and replies would tackle minority topics. The analyzed data is a subset from the *Portuguese Presidential Elections, Jan 24th 2021* (Ramalho, 2021) and corresponds to 35,101 tweets from September 2nd, 2020 to November 22th, 2020.

For the six candidates using Twitter, we performed a keyword matching with the terms in the MIN_PT lexicon to compute the percentage of tweets (Figure 1) and their replies (Figure 2) referring to minorities. Marisa Matias (*mmatias_*), André Ventura (*AndreCVentura*) and Ana Gomes (*AnaMartinsGomes*) are the candidates tackling a higher percentage of minorities topics. However, the targeted minorities are distinct depending on the candidate. While Ana Gomes focused more uniformly on the different groups, Marisa Matias discussed more refugees and women issues and André Ventura focused on Roma and people based on ethnicity, i.e racism issues. Comparing both figures, it is also interesting to see that the candidates' audience does not exactly resonate with the candidate in terms of mentioned minority topics. Moreover, while none of the candidates mentions any of the explicit insults in our lexicon, they were present in the audience.

While our lexicon proved to be valuable for an initial topic analysis, a more in depth analysis should be performed to get further insights on how politicians are referring to minorities.

6 Limitations and Ethical Concerns

Lexicons are static resources that can not mimic the contextual and mutating nature of language, and certain terms may refer to minorities, be considered as insults or just be neutral words depending on the

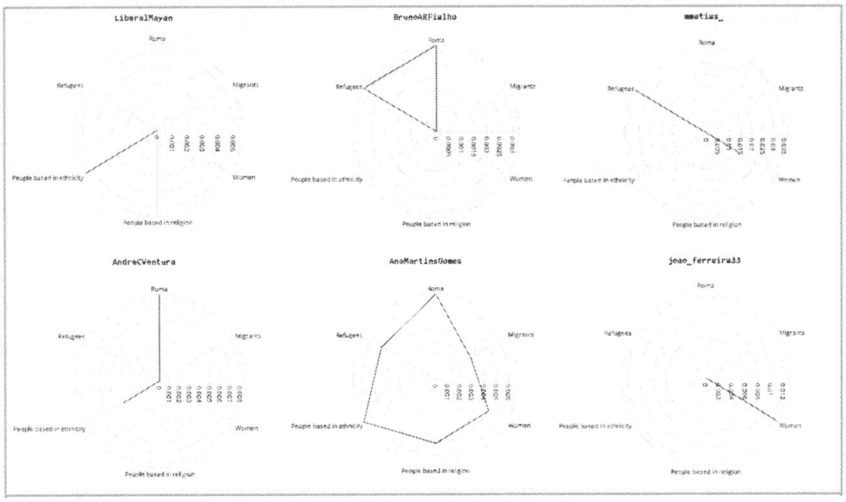

Figure 1: Relative frequencies of minority mentions in candidates' tweets.

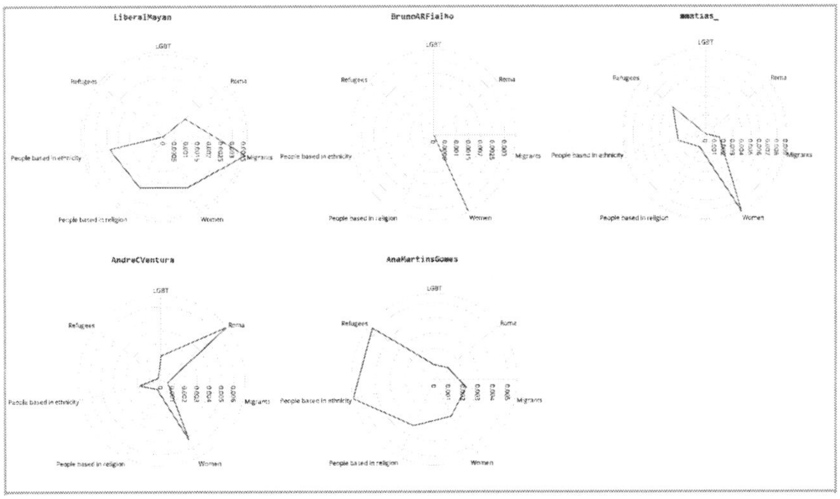

Figure 2: Relative frequencies of minority mentions in replies to candidates.

context in which they are used. Our annotation was done with the objective of analyzing politicians discourses and interactions on Twitter, and we explicitly removed ambiguous terms from the lexicon. Therefore, future users must be warned that the terms should be validated when used with other datasets and contexts.

Finally, even though the presence of the terms in our lexicon may imply hate speech against minorities, it should not be used for direct hate speech classification with keyword matching. Depending on the context and the data author, such terms may have a neutral and even positive meaning.

7 Conclusions

We presented MIN_PT, a new European Portuguese Lexicon for Minorities-Related Terms. We discussed existing annotated lexicons, grounding the need for a new lexicon. Following a qualitative approach, we produced a high-quality lexicon containing also neutral words and specific for European Portuguese. We also presented a use case of the lexicon on the analysis of Portuguese politicians' tweets. Future iterations of this work would benefit from the contribution of more annotators to increase the diversity of the available vocabulary.

Acknowledgements

Paula Fortuna is supported by the research grant SFRH/BD/143623/2019, provided by the Portuguese national funding agency for science, research and technology, Fundação para a Ciência e a Tecnologia (FCT), within the scope of Operational Program *Human Capital* (POCH), supported by the European Social Fund and by national funds from MCTES.

References

Elisa Bassignana, Valerio Basile, and Viviana Patti. 2018. Hurtlex: A multilingual lexicon of words to hurt. In *Proceedings of the Fifth Italian Conference on Computational Linguistics (CLiC-it 2018), Torino, Italy, December 10-12, 2018*, volume 2253 of *CEUR Workshop Proceedings*. CEUR-WS.org.

Maral Dadvar, Dolf Trieschnigg, Roeland Ordelman, and Franciska de Jong. 2013. Improving cyberbullying detection with user context. In *Advances in Information Retrieval*, pages 693–696, Berlin, Heidelberg. Springer Berlin Heidelberg.

Thomas Davidson, Dana Warmsley, Michael W. Macy, and Ingmar Weber. 2017. Automated hate speech detection and the problem of offensive language. In *Proceedings of the Eleventh International Conference on Web and Social Media, ICWSM 2017, Montréal, Québec, Canada, May 15-18, 2017*, pages 512–515. AAAI Press.

Paula Fortuna and Sérgio Nunes. 2018. A survey on automatic detection of hate speech in text. *ACM Computing Survey*, 51(4).

Antigoni-Maria Founta, Constantinos Djouvas, Despoina Chatzakou, Ilias Leontiadis, Jeremy Blackburn, Gianluca Stringhini, Athena Vakali, Michael Sirivianos, and Nicolas Kourtellis. 2018. Large scale crowdsourcing and characterization of twitter abusive behavior. In *Proceedings of the Twelfth International Conference on Web and Social Media, ICWSM 2018, Stanford, California, USA, June 25-28, 2018*, pages 491–500. AAAI Press.

Bahar Radfar, Karthik Shivaram, and Aron Culotta. 2020. Characterizing variation in toxic language by social context. In *Proceedings of the Fourteenth International AAAI Conference on Web and Social Media, ICWSM 2020, Held Virtually, Original Venue: Atlanta, Georgia, USA, June 8-11, 2020*, pages 959–963. AAAI Press.

Miguel Sozinho Ramalho. 2021. High-level approaches to detect malicious political activity on twitter.

Leandro Araújo Silva, Mainack Mondal, Denzil Correa, Fabrício Benevenuto, and Ingmar Weber. 2016. Analyzing the targets of hate in online social media. In *Proceedings of the Tenth International Conference on Web and Social Media, Cologne, Germany, May 17-20, 2016*, pages 687–690. AAAI Press.

Yla R. Tausczik and James W. Pennebaker. 2010. The psychological meaning of words: Liwc and computerized text analysis methods. *Journal of Language and Social Psychology*, 29(1):24–54.

Stéphan Tulkens, Lisa Hilte, Elise Lodewyckx, Ben Verhoeven, and Walter Daelemans. 2016a. The automated detection of racist discourse in dutch social media. *Computational Linguistics in the Netherlands Journal*, 6(1):3–20.

Stéphan Tulkens, Lisa Hilte, Elise Lodewyckx, Ben Verhoeven, and Walter Daelemans. 2016b. A dictionary-based approach to racism detection in Dutch social media. In *Proceedings of the LREC 2016 Workshop on Text Analytics for Cybersecurity and Online Safety (TA-COS)*. European Language Resources Association (ELRA).

Bertie Vidgen and Leon Derczynski. 2020. Directions in abusive language training data, a systematic review: Garbage in, garbage out. *Plos one*, 15(12):e0243300.

Fine-Grained Fairness Analysis of Abusive Language Detection Systems with CheckList

Marta Marchiori Manerba
Department of Philology, Literature and Linguistics
University of Pisa, Italy
martamarchiori96@gmail.com

Sara Tonelli
Fondazione Bruno Kessler
Trento, Italy
satonelli@fbk.eu

Abstract

Current abusive language detection systems have demonstrated unintended bias towards sensitive features such as nationality or gender. This is a crucial issue, which may harm minorities and underrepresented groups if such systems were integrated in real-world applications. In this paper, we create ad hoc tests through the CheckList tool (Ribeiro et al., 2020) to detect biases within abusive language classifiers for English. We compare the behaviour of two BERT-based models, one trained on a generic abusive language dataset and the other on a dataset for misogyny detection. Our evaluation shows that, although BERT-based classifiers achieve high accuracy levels on a variety of natural language processing tasks, they perform very poorly as regards fairness and bias, in particular on samples involving implicit stereotypes, expressions of hate towards minorities and protected attributes such as race or sexual orientation. We release both the notebooks implemented to extend the Fairness tests and the synthetic datasets usable to evaluate systems bias independently of CheckList.

1 Introduction

At every stage of a supervised learning process, biases can arise and be introduced in the pipeline, ultimately leading to harm (Suresh and Guttag, 2020; Dixon et al., 2018). When it comes to systems whose goal is to automatically detect abusive language, this issue becomes particularly serious, since unintended bias towards sensitive attributes such as gender, sexual orientation or nationality can harm underrepresented groups. Sap et al. (2019), for example, show that annotators tend to label messages in Afro-American English more frequently than when annotating other messages, which could lead to the training of a system reproducing the same kind of bias.

The role of the datasets used to train these models is crucial: as pointed out by (Wiegand et al., 2019a), there may be multiple reasons why a dataset is biased, e.g. due to skewed sampling strategies, prevalence of a specific subject (*topic bias*) or of content written by a specific author (*author bias*). Mitigation strategies may involve assessing which terms are frequent in the presence of certain labels and implementing techniques to balance the data by including neutral samples containing those same terms to prevent the model from learning inaccurate correlations (Wiegand et al., 2019a). Furthermore, it is important to distinguish between different types of hatred, depending on the target group addressed: for example, misogynistic expressions show different linguistic peculiarities than racist ones. It is therefore crucial to create specialised datasets addressing different phenomena of abusive language, so that systems can be tuned to the complex and nuanced scenario of online speech.

Given the sensitive context in which abusive language detection systems are deployed, a robust value-oriented evaluation of the model's fairness is necessary, in order to assess unintended biases and avoid, as far as possible, explicit harm or the amplification of pre-existing social biases. However, this bias-assessment process is complicated by the partial effectiveness of proposed methods that only work with certain definitions of bias and fairness, as well as by the limited availability of recognised benchmark datasets (Ntoutsi et al., 2020).

Concerning the different definitions of fairness, they have been collected and organised both in (Suresh and Guttag, 2020) and (Mehrabi et al., 2019), with the awareness that a single definition is not sufficient to address the multi-faceted problem of fairness in its entirety. In this work, we adopt a definition for fairness that is strongly contextual to abusive language detection. We define

Proceedings of the Fifth Workshop on Online Abuse and Harms, pages 81–91
August 6, 2021.

unfairness as the sensitivity of an abusive language detection classifier with respect to the presence in the record to be classified of entities belonging to protected groups or minorities. Specifically, a classifier is considered unfair or biased if the prediction changes according to the identities present, i.e. in similar sentences, the degree of hate is increased if terms such as *white* or *straight* are replaced by adjectives such as *black* or *non-binary*, revealing imbalances, possibly resulting from skewed and unrepresentative training data. *Fairness*, on the other hand, is defined as the behaviour of producing similar predictions for similar protected mentions, i.e. regardless of the specific value assumed by sensitive attributes like race and gender, without disadvantaging minorities or amplifying pre-existing social prejudices.

We deploy the *CheckList* tool (Ribeiro et al., 2020), which was originally created to evaluate general linguistic capabilities of NLP models, extending it to test fairness of abusive language detection systems. Embracing CheckList systematic framework, we create tests from hand-coded templates, reproducing stereotyped opinions and social biases, such as sexism and racism. The aim is to assess the performances of these models identifying the most frequent errors and detecting a range of unintended biases towards sensitive categories and topics. This last objective is motivated by evidence (Nozza et al., 2019) that NLP systems tend, in certain contexts, to rely for the classification on identity terms and sensitive attributes, as well as to generalize misleading correlations learnt from training datasets. As ultimate goal, the analysis of the failures could therefore lead to a general overview of the models' fairness: the ideal outcome would be to establish a proactive pipeline that allows the improvement of the systems, having highlighted the shortages through CheckList ad hoc synthetic testing. To the best of our knowledge, there has not yet been any work carried out with CheckList in this research direction.

2 Related work

Several tools and approaches have been proposed to identify the most frequent errors done by NLP tools. For example, Errudite (Wu et al., 2019) is a tool that allows interactive error analysis through counterfactuals generation, but it is limited to the tasks of Question Answering and Visual Question Answering.

TextAttack (Morris et al., 2020) – which, among other packages, deploys CheckList – is a model-agnostic framework useful for the expansion of the datasets and the increase of models robustness through adversarial attacks. Compared to CheckList, however, it is more complicated to handle and deploy for users with little NLP skills. An interesting aspect is that TextAttack includes in the package the so-called "recipes", i.e. attacks from the literature ready to run, that build a common ground for the assessment and comparison of models' performances.

As outlined in (Ribeiro et al., 2020), some methods to identify errors by NLP systems are task-specific, such as (Ribeiro et al., 2019) or (Belinkov and Bisk, 2018), while others focus on particular NLP components such as word embeddings, as in (Tsvetkov et al., 2016) or (Rogers et al., 2018). Compared to existing approaches, one of CheckList's major strengths lies in including the testing phase within a comprehensive framework. The evaluation, conducted through adaptable templates and a range of relevant linguistic capabilities, is on one hand more granular than overall measures such as accuracy; on the other hand it is more versatile, because it leaves liberty to the developer to enrich and expand the tests within new and more suitable capabilities, depending on the task and model under consideration.

On the topic of fairness and biases, (Kiritchenko et al., 2020) conduct an in-depth discussion on NLP works dealing with ethical issues and challenges in automatic abusive language detection. Among others, a perspective analyzed is the principle of fairness and non-discrimination throughout every stage of supervised machine learning processes. A recent survey by (Blodgett et al., 2020) also analyzes and criticizes the formalization of *bias* within NLP systems, revealing inconsistency, lack of normativity and common rationale in several works. Furthermore, the visibility reached by corporate tools, such as IBM AI Fairness 360 or Amazon SageMaker Clarify, which are designed and promoted by large IT companies, raises several questions: is self-regulation right? What would be the advantages and risks of conducting independent external auditing? Several metrics[1], generic tools and python packages[2] are available. Nevertheless, no consensus related to the above questions has

[1]Among others: Equal Accuracy, Equal Opportunity (Hardt et al., 2016), Demographic Parity.

[2]Fairlearn, Dalex, InterpretML, FAT Forensics, Captum.

been reached yet among the involved players.

Concerning existing datasets specifically designed to assess biases within Machine Learning models, (Mehrabi et al., 2019) list several of the widely used ones, which differ according to size, type of records (numerical, images, texts) and tackled domain (e.g. financial, facial recognition, etc.). The only language dataset cited is WiNoBias, (Zhao et al., 2018) [3] also used in this work as a lexical resource, which pertains to the field of co-reference resolution. Our contribution instead aims to broaden fairness evaluation, specifically testing biases in abusive language detection systems through CheckList facilities.

Concerning abusive language detection, a number of approaches has been proposed to perform both coarse-grained (i.e. binary) and fine-grained classification. 87 systems participated in the last Offenseval competition for English (Zampieri et al., 2020), which included a binary task on offensive language identification, one on offensive language categorization and another on target identification. As reported by the organisers, the majority of teams used some kind of pre-trained embeddings such as contextualized Transformers (Vaswani et al., 2017) and ELMo (Peters et al., 2018) embeddings. The most popular Transformers were BERT (Devlin et al., 2019) and RoBERTa (Liu et al., 2019b), which showed to achieve state-of-the-art results for English, especially when used in ensemble configurations. For this reason, we use BERT also in the experiments presented in the following sections.

3 Introduction to CheckList

Usually, the generalization capability of NLP models is evaluated based on the performance obtained on a held-out dataset, by measuring F1 or accuracy. This process, although widely adopted by the NLP community as a way to compare systems performances and approaches, lacks informativeness since it does not provide insights into how to improve the models through the analysis of errors.

In order to tackle this issue, *CheckList* (Ribeiro et al., 2020) was developed as a comprehensive task-agnostic framework, inspired by behavioral testing, in order to encourage more robust checking and to facilitate the assessment of models' general linguistic capabilities. The package allows the generation of data through the construction of different ad hoc tests by generalizations from templates and lexicons, general-purpose perturbations, tests expectations on the labels and context-aware suggestions using RoBERTa fill-ins (Liu et al., 2019b) as prompter for specific masked tokens. The tests created can be saved, shared and utilized for different systems.

CheckList includes three test types and a number of linguistic capabilities to be tested. The three types of tests are:

1. **Minimum Functionality Test** (MFT): the basic type of test, involving the standard classification of records with the corresponding labels. Each group of MFTs is designed to prove and explore how the model handles specific challenges related to a language capability, e.g. vocabulary, negation, etc.;

2. **Invariance Test** (INV): verifies that model predictions do not change significantly with respect to a record and its variants, generated by altering the original sentence through the replacement of specific terms with similar expressions;

3. **Directional Expectation Test** (DIR): verifies that model predictions change as a result of the record perturbation, i.e. the score should raise or fall according to the modification applied.

Concerning linguistic capabilities, CheckList covers a number of aspects that are usually relevant when evaluating NLP systems, such as robustness, named entity recognition, temporal awareness of the models and negation. While we also evaluated these aspects, our main focus here is models **Fairness**, which verifies that systems predictions do not change as a function of protected features. While the Fairness capability already proposed in CheckList involved the perturbation of sensitive attributes, namely expressions referring to gender, sexual orientation, nationality or religion, we first extend it by adding "professions" as protected attribute in order to assess whether predictions change if a male or a female assumes a specific job role. We then enrich the capability designing hand-coded templates, belonging to the MFT test type, resulting from the exploration of representative constructions and stereotypes annotated in the Social Bias Inference Corpus (Sap et al., 2020). The resulting samples exemplify several sexist, racist and ableist comments

[3] https://github.com/uclanlp/corefBias/tree/master/WinoBias/wino

and opinions: all of them are new aspects compared to the suites released by the authors (Ribeiro et al., 2020).

As described in the introduction, CheckList provides built-in tools to assist users in the creation of tests. Among others, WordNet allows the selection of synonyms, antonyms, hypernyms, etc. for a given expression. CheckList's templates take shape from these sets of semantically related words. We develop a further extension of the tool by integrating *SentiWordNet* (Baccianella et al., 2010), a lexical resource in which WordNet synsets have been associated with a sentiment score (negative, neutral or positive). In this way, CheckList can benefit from the sentiment-dimension of SentiWordNet. Indeed, during the development of templates and the perturbations of the records, SentiWordNet enables the selection of suitable linguistic substitutions for a given term, according to the label of the sentence to be created. An example: seeking a synonym that has a similar connotation as the adjective *happy* for the phrase "*The girl is happy*", the results returned include *glad*, with a positive denotations of 0.5. In this case, through SentiWordNet, it is possible to select a synonym term with a similar polarity, in order to create variants of the original sentence that preserve a similar semantic content and to assess how the model behaves with slightly different terms.

4 A Suite for Abusive Language Detection

Suites are objects designed by CheckList authors (Ribeiro et al., 2020) that enable users to organise, combine and save sets of tests, in order to reuse them several times and to aggregate results (i.e. failure rates) in a single run. Once a test is designed, it is added to the suite, specifying the test type (MFT, INV or DIR), a name, the language capability within which it is situated and a brief description. The suite will thus be composed of one or more capabilities, each of which is assessed through several tests. After the suite is created, it can be run to evaluate the output of a given classifier, provided that the system has been previously launched to label the records created for each test providing for each record a class and the respective probabilities. The results of the run of the suite are displayed through a visual and interactive summary, which reports misclassified samples and the various failure percentages obtained in each test (see Fig. 1 for an example).

The core of our work takes off from the notebooks released by CheckList authors (Ribeiro et al., 2020), specifically from the suite for the task of Sentiment Analysis[4], that builds a series of tests consisting in tweets about airline companies. In order to target a different task, which relies on binary decisions, we modify all the templates adjusting them for the task of abusive language detection. Our main contribution is the extension of the Fairness capability, which we enrich with several tests addressing diverse abuse targets and dealing with different types of biases.

4.1 Fairness tests

The tests developed for analysing **Fairness** deal with social biases towards specific different targets and topics, such as sexism, racism and ableism. With respect to the three test types available within CheckList, we have only utilized MFT and INV, because the third type, DIR, tests for a change in prediction as a result of sentence modifications, whereas for the definition of Fairness we adopt we intend to assess the opposite, i.e. that the prediction does not change as a function of perturbations of protected attributes.

The Fairness tests developed are grouped into categories which we have previously identified through the manual inspection of representative constructions and stereotypes annotated in the Social Bias Inference Corpus (Sap et al., 2020). The samples chosen are mainly abusive, and the assigned labels are the same as the examples from which we have generalised within the dataset. The groups of biases are not exhaustive, but they are still representative, as resulting also by exploring the most frequently occurring abuse targets in datasets for abusive language detection systems such as (Waseem and Hovy, 2016), (Golbeck et al., 2017), (Founta et al., 2018) and (Basile et al., 2019). We briefly describe the tests designed, grouping them by target and reporting between brackets the test type of each:

Misogyny, gender and sexual orientation:

- *Perturbing gender and sexual orientation* (INV): changing mentions of the protected attributes with similar values, i.e. replacing "gay" with "non-binary";

[4]For reference, the notebook on Sentiment Analysis at `https://github.com/marcotcr/checklist/blob/master/notebooks/Sentiment.ipynb`.

- *Stereotyped female vs male work roles* and *Stereotyped male vs. female work roles* (INV): perturbing stereotyped professions connected to the "unconventional" gender[5], i.e. "Jane is a driver" and "John is a secretary";
- *Unintended bias in misogyny detection* (MFT): extracting random records from the dataset of (Nozza et al., 2019), testing unintended biases within automatic misogyny identification;
- *Gender stereotypes* (MFT): simulating hateful sexist comments and opinions;
- *Body image stereotypes* (MFT): reporting common biases on body image;
- *Toxic masculinity stereotypes* (MFT): reporting common biases on toxic masculinity;
- *Neutral statements feminism-related* (MFT): generating neutral statements where an individual is identified as feminist, i.e. "Jane is feminist" or "John is feminist".

Race, nationality and religion:

- *Perturbing race* (INV): changing mentions of the protected attributes with similar values, i.e. replacing "white" with "black";
- *Perturbing nationality* (INV): changing mentions of the protected attributes with similar values, i.e. replacing "English" with "Italian";
- *Perturbing religion* (INV): changing mentions of the protected attributes with similar values, i.e. replacing "christian" with "jew";
- *Racial stereotypes* (MFT): simulating hateful racist comments and opinions.

Disability:

- *Ableist stereotypes* (MFT): simulating hateful ableist comments and opinions.

The hand-coded templates about body image and toxic masculinity, belonging to the **MFT test type**, do not always use explicitly hateful terms: occasionally prejudices are expressed in a more subtle way that models are often not able to handle. Sample records for the body image topic are "Janet is blonde, that's why she is not smart" and "Never let a `[offensive woman expression]` with no make-up on tell you what to `[verb]`". Examples of toxic masculinity are found in "Harry, you're not a real man if you don't have muscles" and "John, you're not a real man if you don't have a job". Regarding examples of insults toward a specific nationality or religion, the examples crafted consist in sentences like "Nobody really like `[nationality]`, they are `[offensive expression]`" and "Stop givin' money to them, `[offensive expression] [nationality]`". Stereotypes about disability, homeless people and old people, are obtained from templates like "All `[offensive term towards homeless]` are a burden to the society", "All `[offensive term towards disabled]` aren't capable of doing anything" and "Being `[offensive term to old people]` is funny after all, what are they complaining about?".

The **INVariance test type** involves assessing whether changing the value of sensitive attributes causes also a change in the label predicted or in the probabilities (i.e. without reason, revealing biases). Race, gender, sexual orientation, religion and nationality are examples of sensitive features. From simple templates like "`[name]` is `[nationality]`" are generated records as "Jane is Chinese", "Jane is Egyptian" and similar (for each test, it is possible to specify the exact number of instances to produce). Using instead the keys *gender* and *sexual orientation* will result in "Jane is asexual", "Jane is queer" and more. Applying this same procedure for the other sensitive keys will result in simplified (because the sentences are very similar) but very targeted synthetic data (see Section 4.2). The tests involving the perturbation of race, nationality, religion, gender and sexual orientation are those developed by CheckList's authors; we extend them by adding "professions" as protected attribute, in order to assess whether predictions change if a male or a female assumes a specific job role.

4.2 Synthetic datasets generation

After constructing the tests[6], we export the records created through the templates to make them available and usable independently of CheckList framework: in fact, this additional step, i.e. creating

[5]The list used to identify the "swapped" professions is `https://github.com/uclanlp/corefBias/tree/master/WinoBias/wino`.

[6]Data Statement (Bender and Friedman, 2018): templates and related labels were manually defined by the first author, a non-native English speaker.

datasets, is separate from the standard CheckList process, which instead requires the creation of data within the tests, framed in the capabilities and executed during the suite run. Specifically, we export the test records together with their corresponding labels, when applicable. In fact, only the MFT test type features a precise label, whereas the other two types (INV and DIR) involve an expectation of whether or not the probabilities will change and therefore cannot be conceptually formalised in a dataset, where labels are required.

The exported data results in the creation of three synthetic datasets covering different types of bias grouped by target (listed in 4.1), namely sexism, racism and ableism. The reason for distinguishing the records by abuse targets is due to the need for specialised datasets addressing different phenomena of abusive language with a fine-grained approach. The resulting data do not contain samples from datasets under license: the contents we release are therefore freely available[7].

Briefly, the first dataset on sexism contains 1,200 non-hateful and 4,423 hateful samples; the second one on racism contains 400 non-hateful and 1,500 hateful records; the last one on ableism contains 220 hateful sentences. The label distribution is radically different from traditional abusive language datasets, where the prevalent class is non-hateful. This choice is motivated by the fact that we want to mainly focus on the phenomena surrounding social prejudices providing realistic and diverse examples, with the aim of exploring in depth the language used to convey biases.

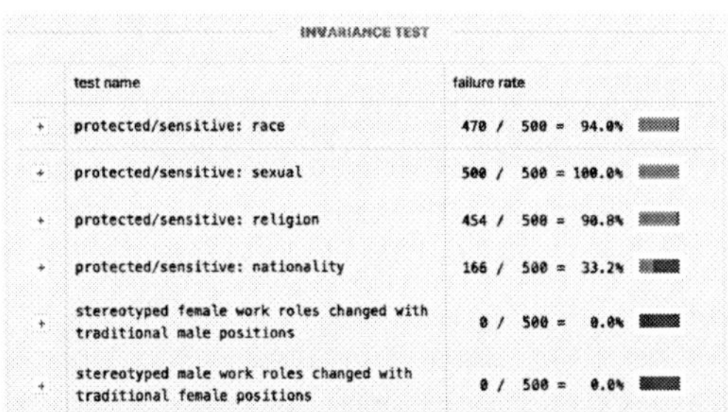
INVARIANCE TEST

	test name	failure rate
+	protected/sensitive: race	470 / 500 = 94.0%
+	protected/sensitive: sexual	500 / 500 = 100.0%
+	protected/sensitive: religion	454 / 500 = 90.8%
+	protected/sensitive: nationality	166 / 500 = 33.2%
+	stereotyped female work roles changed with traditional male positions	0 / 500 = 0.0%
+	stereotyped male work roles changed with traditional female positions	0 / 500 = 0.0%

Figure 1: CheckList visual summary of the performances obtained by the generic Abusive Language classifier on the INVariance tests within Fairness capability

[7]All the data and the Jupyter notebooks implemented to run the tests are available at `https://github.com/MartaMarchiori/Fairness-Analysis-with-CheckList`

5 System description

We run our evaluation using a standard BERT-based classifier for English, a language representation model developed by Google Research (Devlin et al., 2019), whose deep learning architecture obtained state-of-the-art results in several natural language processing tasks including sentiment analysis, natural language inference, textual entailment (Devlin et al., 2019) and hate speech detection (Liu et al., 2019a). BERT can be fine-tuned and adapted to specific tasks by adding just one additional output layer to the neural network. We use this approach because language models like BERT, or variants like ALBERT and RoBERTa (Wiedemann et al., 2020), have been used by the vast majority of participants in the last Offenseval campaign (Zampieri et al., 2020), yielding a very good performance on English (> 0.90 F1). For our experiments, we use the base model of BERT for English[8], trained on 3.3 billion words, which is made available on the project website (`https://github.com/google-research/bert`). We train two different classifiers in order to compare their behaviour w.r.t. biases. The first one is for generic abusive language detection, and is obtained by fine-tuning BERT on the (Founta et al., 2018) corpus. This dataset includes around 100K tweets annotated with four labels: hateful, abusive, spam or none. Differently from the other datasets, this was not created starting from a set of predefined offensive terms or hashtags to reduce bias, which is a main issue in abusive language datasets (Wiegand et al., 2019a). This should make this dataset more challenging for classification. For our experiments, we removed the spam class, and we mapped both hateful and abusive tweets to the abusive class, based on the assumption that hateful messages are the most serious form of abusive language and that the term 'abusive' is more appropriate to cover the cases of interest for our study (Caselli et al., 2020). The second model is trained with the AMI 2018 dataset (Fersini et al., 2018), which contains 4,000 tweets manually annotated as misogynistic or not. The purpose of this comparison is to assess potential changes in bias recognition, once a system has been specifically exposed to data dealing with these sensitive issues. Although BERT and similar language models may already encode biases (Bender et al., 2021), fine-tuning on different datasets may

[8]Uncased, 12-layer, 768-hidden, 12-heads, 110M parameters.

Fairness tests	Abusive Lang. Classifier		Misogyny Detection Classifier	
	MFT	INV	MFT	INV
Perturbing race	–	94.0	–	14.8
Perturbing nationality	–	33.2	–	5.0
Perturbing religion	–	90.8	–	1.6
Perturbing gender and sex. orient.	–	100.0	–	54.0
Stereotyped female vs male work roles	–	0		62.0
Stereotyped male vs. female work roles	–	0	–	0
Unintended bias in misogyny detec.	33.6	–	37.0	–
Gender stereotypes	49.0	–	42.2	–
Body image stereotypes	92.8	–	8.6	–
Toxic masculinity stereotypes	99.2	–	100	–
Neutral statements feminism-related	0	–	76.5	–
Racial stereotypes	30.2	–	88.2	–
Ableist stereotypes	43.2	–	97.7	–

Table 1: Performance of Abusive Language classifier and Misogyny Detection classifier on Fairness tests. Each cell contains the failure rate expressed in percentage for each test type. Each test involves 500 records randomly extracted from a larger subset, except for neutral statements feminism-related (200) and ableist stereotypes (220).

indeed lead to a change in classification behaviour and therefore in its implicit biases.

6 Evaluation

In Table 1, we report a general overview of the performance of the two trained models on fairness tests. Each test involves 500 records randomly extracted from a larger subset, except for neutral statements feminism-related (200) and ableist stereotypes (220): the total number of records, considering all tests, amounts to 5,920. The metric computed by CheckList framework and reported in the table is the *failure rate*, i.e. the percentage of the records misclassified over the total number of records for that specific test[9]. Unlike metrics such as accuracy, the lower the failure rate (i.e. the closer to 0%) the better the model performs. In general, we notice that the overall failures are extremely high.

6.1 Fairness in Abusive Language Detection

Using the generic classifier trained on the dataset by (Founta et al., 2018), we observe that the hand-coded templates about body image and toxic masculinity, belonging to the MFT test type, are the most misclassified (respectively 92.8% and 99.2%). Regarding examples of insults toward a specific nationality or religion, the failure rate is of 30.2%. On stereotypes about disability, homeless people and old people, the model performs worse, reaching a failure rate of 43.2%.

With respect to the samples related to the perturbation of stereotyped professions connected to the "unconventional" gender, verified with the INVariance test type, the model shows zero failure. The issues arise when the sensitive features involved are *race, gender, sexual orientation* and *religion* (respectively 94%, 100% and 90.8% failures). This result means that overall the model is sensitive to alterations in these categories: probably this is caused by skewed training data, where e.g. the words "asexual" or "jew" in neutral, non-offensive contexts are not frequently attested. In addition, some sensitivity is demonstrated in changing the value of the protected attribute *nationality* (33.2% failure).

6.2 Fairness in Misogyny Detection

Using the model trained on the AMI dataset (Fersini et al., 2018), we observe some differences with respect to the generic abusive language model, as reported in in Table 1. The case where the change is most notable concerns stereotypes related to body image, for which the error drops from 92.8% to 8.6%. Analysing the perturbations of race, gender, sexual orientation and religion, we report a large decrease in errors: respectively from 94.0%, 100% and 90.8% for the first model to 14.8%, 54.0% and 1.6% for the second one. Surprisingly, comparing to the zero failures of the original model with respect to the perturbation of stereotyped professions, this last model reports 62% failures for stereotyped female work roles changed with "traditional" male positions. The same outcome is obtained for neutral identification statements related to feminism, where the first model reports

[9]Other significant metrics could be computed to strengthen the statistics obtained. Since this work is deeply rooted in CheckList framework, we focus our analysis on the options provided by the tool.

zero failures, while the second one achieves 76.5% failure.

This could be partially motivated by the fact that the Misogyny Classifier could have generalized a stereotyped conception of reality from skewed data on Misogyny Detection, e.g. learning to associate a high degree of toxicity with neutral posts containing terms such as *feminist* or negative correlation about women in positions of responsibility, since we can hypothesise that most of the examples the system was trained on contained references to these identities in offensive context.

7 Discussion and Conclusions

The approach that CheckList proposes should complement the evaluation of NLP models carried out by applying standard metrics such as F1 and accuracy. Indeed, in addition to the traditional held-out datasets, the creation of ad hoc examples, from the most basic ones to the most complex, contribute to highlight weaknesses that cannot be easily detected through large existing datasets. Furthermore, CheckList provides a way to explore the models' dynamics: through the analysis of the errors, we can infer which linguistic phenomena the system has not yet acquired from the data. However, in order to enable this fine-grained evaluation, several specific tests and templates should be created that, like in our case, may contain a small amount of examples because of the difficulty to create or retrieve a varied sample of records covering specific phenomena, e.g. feminist and ableist stereotypes.

A significant drawback, closely related to CheckList deployment on abusive language detection systems, concerns the difficulty of including and dealing with contextual information (Menini et al., 2021). Sensitive real-world statements often acquire a different connotation w.r.t. the degree of hatred if a certain race, gender, or nationality is present, due to historical or social references (Sap et al., 2019). In our work, we temporarily avoid such risks using synthetic templates strongly polarized on the one hand towards offensiveness, on the other towards neutrality. Perturbing real-world data would seriously require taking into account these nuances by implementing a more flexible and accurate inspection of prediction variations.

Although state-of-the-art models such as BERT-based models achieve high accuracy levels on a variety of natural language processing tasks, including abusive language detection, we have shown through diverse tests that these systems perform very poorly concerning bias on samples involving implicit stereotypes and sensitive features such as gender or sexual orientation. Whether these biases in BERT-based systems emerge from the classification algorithm, the pretraining phase or the training data will have to be investigated and further explored in the future. As a preliminary analysis, our results show that training sets play a relevant role in this, as already highlighted in previous works (Wiegand et al., 2019b). For some phenomena, such as body image stereotypes or feminism-related statements, different training sets make the classifier behave very differently, in a way that we were able to quantify through our approach. Moreover, the notebooks through which we built the suite are made available and the tests are easily editable and adaptable to specific data or linguistic aspects to be investigated.

A future direction of this work might be to expand the package integrating other linguistic resources, such as emotion or sentiment lexica. Concerning linguistic capabilities, for Fairness other stereotypes from a wider range of datasets could be more thoroughly explored and formalised into templates. It would be also interesting to analyse whether classification that takes into account the broader discourse context (Menini et al., 2021) is less prone to biases. Suites for other languages could be built as well, given that datasets for abusive language detection are available in many languages beyond English (Corazza et al., 2020).

As suggested in (Dobbe et al., 2018), proposing a contribution within the Machine Learning domain responsibly and consciously means foremost acknowledging our own biases. In particular, we are referring to the implementation of hand-coded templates, that we generalized within the CheckList framework starting from real-user examples. The selection and the way in which the tests have been built certainly shaped the results.

Surely, this paper is not a complete or comprehensive work: for example, a direct interaction with the targeted users and the different stake-holders affected could have enriched the perspective and the insights retrieved. Furthermore, it is important to be aware that any solely technological solution will be partial, as not considering the broader social issue that is the source of these biases means simplifying and "fixing" only on the surface (Ntoutsi et al., 2020).

Regardless, we strongly believe that abusive language classifiers need a robust value-sensitive evaluation, in order to assess unintended biases and avoid, as far as possible, explicit harm or the amplification of pre-existing social biases, trying to ultimately build systems that contributes in a beneficial way to the society and all its citizens.

Acknowledgments

Part of this work has been funded by the KID_ACTIONS REC-AG project (n. 101005518) on "Kick-off preventIng and responDing to children and AdolesCenT cyberbullyIng through innovative mOnitoring and educatioNal technologieS", `https://www.kidactions.eu/`.

References

Stefano Baccianella, Andrea Esuli, and Fabrizio Sebastiani. 2010. SentiWordNet 3.0: An enhanced lexical resource for sentiment analysis and opinion mining. In *Proceedings of the Seventh International Conference on Language Resources and Evaluation (LREC'10)*, Valletta, Malta. European Language Resources Association (ELRA).

Valerio Basile, Cristina Bosco, Elisabetta Fersini, Debora Nozza, Viviana Patti, Francisco Manuel Rangel Pardo, Paolo Rosso, and Manuela Sanguinetti. 2019. SemEval-2019 task 5: Multilingual detection of hate speech against immigrants and women in Twitter. In *Proceedings of the 13th International Workshop on Semantic Evaluation*, pages 54–63, Minneapolis, Minnesota, USA. Association for Computational Linguistics.

Yonatan Belinkov and Yonatan Bisk. 2018. Synthetic and natural noise both break neural machine translation.

Emily M Bender and Batya Friedman. 2018. Data statements for natural language processing: Toward mitigating system bias and enabling better science. *Transactions of the Association for Computational Linguistics*, 6:587–604.

Emily M. Bender, Timnit Gebru, Angelina McMillan-Major, and Shmargaret Shmitchell. 2021. On the dangers of stochastic parrots: Can language models be too big? In *Proceedings of the 2021 ACM Conference on Fairness, Accountability, and Transparency*, FAccT '21, page 610–623, New York, NY, USA. Association for Computing Machinery.

Su Lin Blodgett, Solon Barocas, Hal Daumé III, and Hanna Wallach. 2020. Language (technology) is power: A critical survey of bias in nlp. *arXiv preprint arXiv:2005.14050*.

Tommaso Caselli, Valerio Basile, Jelena Mitrović, Inga Kartoziya, and Michael Granitzer. 2020. I feel offended, don't be abusive! implicit/explicit messages in offensive and abusive language. In *Proceedings of the 12th Language Resources and Evaluation Conference*, pages 6193–6202, Marseille, France. European Language Resources Association.

Michele Corazza, Stefano Menini, Elena Cabrio, Sara Tonelli, and Serena Villata. 2020. A multilingual evaluation for online hate speech detection. *ACM Trans. Internet Techn.*, 20(2):10:1–10:22.

Jacob Devlin, Ming-Wei Chang, Kenton Lee, and Kristina Toutanova. 2019. BERT: Pre-training of deep bidirectional transformers for language understanding. In *Proceedings of the 2019 Conference of the North American Chapter of the Association for Computational Linguistics: Human Language Technologies, Volume 1 (Long and Short Papers)*, pages 4171–4186, Minneapolis, Minnesota. Association for Computational Linguistics.

Lucas Dixon, John Li, Jeffrey Sorensen, Nithum Thain, and Lucy Vasserman. 2018. Measuring and mitigating unintended bias in text classification. In *Proceedings of the 2018 AAAI/ACM Conference on AI, Ethics, and Society*, AIES '18, page 67–73, New York, NY, USA. Association for Computing Machinery.

Roel Dobbe, Sarah Dean, T. Gilbert, and Nitin Kohli. 2018. A broader view on bias in automated decision-making: Reflecting on epistemology and dynamics. *ArXiv*, abs/1807.00553.

Elisabetta Fersini, Debora Nozza, and Paolo Rosso. 2018. Overview of the evalita 2018 task on automatic misogyny identification (ami). *EVALITA Evaluation of NLP and Speech Tools for Italian*, 12:59.

Antigoni-Maria Founta, Constantinos Djouvas, Despoina Chatzakou, Ilias Leontiadis, Jeremy Blackburn, Gianluca Stringhini, Athena Vakali, Michael Sirivianos, and Nicolas Kourtellis. 2018. Large scale crowdsourcing and characterization of twitter abusive behavior. In *11th International Conference on Web and Social Media, ICWSM 2018*. AAAI Press.

Jennifer Golbeck, Zahra Ashktorab, Rashad O Banjo, Alexandra Berlinger, Siddharth Bhagwan, Cody Buntain, Paul Cheakalos, Alicia A Geller, Quint Gergory, Rajesh Kumar Gnanasekaran, et al. 2017. A large labeled corpus for online harassment research. In *Proceedings of the 2017 ACM on Web Science Conference*, pages 229–233. ACM.

Moritz Hardt, Eric Price, and Nathan Srebro. 2016. Equality of opportunity in supervised learning. *arXiv preprint arXiv:1610.02413*.

Svetlana Kiritchenko, Isar Nejadgholi, and Kathleen C Fraser. 2020. Confronting abusive language online: A survey from the ethical and human rights perspective. *arXiv preprint arXiv:2012.12305*.

Ping Liu, Wen Li, and Liang Zou. 2019a. NULI at SemEval-2019 task 6: Transfer learning for offensive language detection using bidirectional transformers. In *Proceedings of the 13th International Workshop on Semantic Evaluation*, pages 87–91, Minneapolis, Minnesota, USA. Association for Computational Linguistics.

Yinhan Liu, Myle Ott, Naman Goyal, Jingfei Du, Mandar Joshi, Danqi Chen, Omer Levy, Mike Lewis, Luke Zettlemoyer, and Veselin Stoyanov. 2019b. Roberta: A robustly optimized BERT pretraining approach. *CoRR*, abs/1907.11692.

Ninareh Mehrabi, Fred Morstatter, Nripsuta Saxena, Kristina Lerman, and Aram Galstyan. 2019. A survey on bias and fairness in machine learning.

Stefano Menini, Alessio Palmero Aprosio, and Sara Tonelli. 2021. Abuse is contextual, what about nlp? the role of context in abusive language annotation and detection. *CoRR*, abs/2103.14916.

John X. Morris, Eli Lifland, Jin Yong Yoo, Jake Grigsby, Di Jin, and Yanjun Qi. 2020. Textattack: A framework for adversarial attacks, data augmentation, and adversarial training in nlp.

Debora Nozza, Claudia Volpetti, and Elisabetta Fersini. 2019. Unintended bias in misogyny detection. In *IEEE/WIC/ACM International Conference on Web Intelligence*, WI '19, page 149–155, New York, NY, USA. Association for Computing Machinery.

Eirini Ntoutsi, Pavlos Fafalios, Ujwal Gadiraju, Vasileios Iosifidis, Wolfgang Nejdl, Maria-Esther Vidal, Salvatore Ruggieri, Franco Turini, Symeon Papadopoulos, Emmanouil Krasanakis, Ioannis Kompatsiaris, Katharina Kinder-Kurlanda, Claudia Wagner, Fariba Karimi, Miriam Fernandez, Harith Alani, Bettina Berendt, Tina Kruegel, Christian Heinze, Klaus Broelemann, Gjergji Kasneci, Thanassis Tiropanis, and Steffen Staab. 2020. Bias in data-driven artificial intelligence systems—An introductory survey. *WIREs Data Mining and Knowledge Discovery*, 10(3):e1356.

Matthew Peters, Mark Neumann, Mohit Iyyer, Matt Gardner, Christopher Clark, Kenton Lee, and Luke Zettlemoyer. 2018. Deep contextualized word representations. In *Proceedings of the 2018 Conference of the North American Chapter of the Association for Computational Linguistics: Human Language Technologies, Volume 1 (Long Papers)*, pages 2227–2237.

Marco Tulio Ribeiro, Carlos Guestrin, and Sameer Singh. 2019. Are red roses red? evaluating consistency of question-answering models. In *Proceedings of the 57th Annual Meeting of the Association for Computational Linguistics*, pages 6174–6184, Florence, Italy. Association for Computational Linguistics.

Marco Tulio Ribeiro, Tongshuang Wu, Carlos Guestrin, and Sameer Singh. 2020. Beyond accuracy: Behavioral testing of NLP models with CheckList. In *Proceedings of the 58th Annual Meeting of the Association for Computational Linguistics*, pages 4902–4912, Online. Association for Computational Linguistics.

Anna Rogers, Shashwath Hosur Ananthakrishna, and Anna Rumshisky. 2018. What's in your embedding, and how it predicts task performance. In *Proceedings of the 27th International Conference on Computational Linguistics*, pages 2690–2703, Santa Fe, New Mexico, USA. Association for Computational Linguistics.

Maarten Sap, Dallas Card, Saadia Gabriel, Yejin Choi, and Noah A. Smith. 2019. The risk of racial bias in hate speech detection. In *Proceedings of the 57th Annual Meeting of the Association for Computational Linguistics*, pages 1668–1678, Florence, Italy. Association for Computational Linguistics.

Maarten Sap, Saadia Gabriel, Lianhui Qin, Dan Jurafsky, Noah A Smith, and Yejin Choi. 2020. Social bias frames: Reasoning about social and power implications of language. In *ACL*.

Harini Suresh and John V. Guttag. 2020. A framework for understanding unintended consequences of machine learning.

Yulia Tsvetkov, Manaal Faruqui, and Chris Dyer. 2016. Correlation-based intrinsic evaluation of word vector representations. In *Proceedings of the 1st Workshop on Evaluating Vector-Space Representations for NLP*, pages 111–115, Berlin, Germany. Association for Computational Linguistics.

Ashish Vaswani, Noam Shazeer, Niki Parmar, Jakob Uszkoreit, Llion Jones, Aidan N. Gomez, undefinedukasz Kaiser, and Illia Polosukhin. 2017. Attention is all you need. In *Proceedings of the 31st International Conference on Neural Information Processing Systems*, NIPS'17, page 6000–6010, Red Hook, NY, USA. Curran Associates Inc.

Zeerak Waseem and Dirk Hovy. 2016. Hateful Symbols or Hateful People? Predictive Features for Hate Speech Detection on Twitter. In *Proceedings of the NAACL Student Research Workshop*, pages 88–93, San Diego, California.

Gregor Wiedemann, Seid Muhie Yimam, and Chris Biemann. 2020. UHH-LT at SemEval-2020 task 12: Fine-tuning of pre-trained transformer networks for offensive language detection. In *Proceedings of the Fourteenth Workshop on Semantic Evaluation*, pages 1638–1644, Barcelona (online). International Committee for Computational Linguistics.

Michael Wiegand, Josef Ruppenhofer, and Thomas Kleinbauer. 2019a. Detection of Abusive Language: the Problem of Biased Datasets. In *Proceedings of the 2019 Conference of the North American Chapter of the Association for Computational Linguistics:*

Human Language Technologies, Volume 1 (Long and Short Papers), pages 602–608, Minneapolis, Minnesota. Association for Computational Linguistics.

Michael Wiegand, Maximilian Wolf, and Josef Ruppenhofer. 2019b. Detecting Derogatory Compounds – An Unsupervised Approach. In *Proceedings of the 2019 Conference of the North American Chapter of the Association for Computational Linguistics: Human Language Technologies, Volume 1 (Long and Short Papers)*, pages 2076–2081, Minneapolis, Minnesota. Association for Computational Linguistics.

Tongshuang Wu, Marco Tulio Ribeiro, Jeffrey Heer, and Daniel Weld. 2019. Errudite: Scalable, reproducible, and testable error analysis. In *Proceedings of the 57th Annual Meeting of the Association for Computational Linguistics*, pages 747–763, Florence, Italy. Association for Computational Linguistics.

Marcos Zampieri, Preslav Nakov, Sara Rosenthal, Pepa Atanasova, Georgi Karadzhov, Hamdy Mubarak, Leon Derczynski, Zeses Pitenis, and Çağrı Çöltekin. 2020. SemEval-2020 task 12: Multilingual offensive language identification in social media (OffensEval 2020). In *Proceedings of the Fourteenth Workshop on Semantic Evaluation*, pages 1425–1447, Barcelona (online). International Committee for Computational Linguistics.

Jieyu Zhao, Tianlu Wang, Mark Yatskar, Vicente Ordonez, and Kai-Wei Chang. 2018. Gender bias in coreference resolution: Evaluation and debiasing methods. In *Proceedings of the 2018 Conference of the North American Chapter of the Association for Computational Linguistics: Human Language Technologies, Volume 2 (Short Papers)*, pages 15–20, New Orleans, Louisiana. Association for Computational Linguistics.

Improving Counterfactual Generation for Fair Hate Speech Detection

Aida Mostafazadeh Davani, Ali Omrani, Brendan Kennedy, Mohammad Atari,
Xiang Ren, Morteza Dehghani
University of Southern California
{mostafaz, aomrani, btkenned, atari, xiangren, mdehghan}@usc.edu

Abstract

Bias mitigation approaches reduce models' dependence on sensitive features of data, such as social group tokens (SGTs), resulting in equal predictions across the sensitive features. In hate speech detection, however, equalizing model predictions may ignore important differences among targeted social groups, as hate speech can contain stereotypical language specific to each SGT. Here, to take the specific language about each SGT into account, we rely on *counterfactual fairness* and equalize predictions among counterfactuals, generated by changing the SGTs. Our method evaluates the similarity in sentence likelihoods (via pre-trained language models) among counterfactuals, to treat SGTs equally only within interchangeable contexts. By applying logit pairing to equalize outcomes on the restricted set of counterfactuals for each instance, we improve fairness metrics while preserving model performance on hate speech detection.

1 Introduction

Hate speech classifiers have high false-positive error rates in documents mentioning specific social group tokens (SGTs; *e.g.*, "*Asian*", "*Jew*"), due in part to the high prevalence of SGTs in instances of hate speech (Wiegand et al., 2019; Mehrabi et al., 2019). When propagated into social media content moderation, this *unintended bias* (Dixon et al., 2018) leads to unfair outcomes, *e.g.*, mislabeling mentions of protected social groups as hate speech.

For prediction tasks in which SGTs do not play any special role (e.g., in sentiment analysis), unintended bias can be reduced by optimizing group-level fairness metrics such as *equality of odds*, which statistically equalizes model performance across all social groups (Hardt et al., 2016; Dwork et al., 2012). However, in hate speech detection, this is not the case, with SGTs providing key information for the task (see Fig. 1). Instead, bias

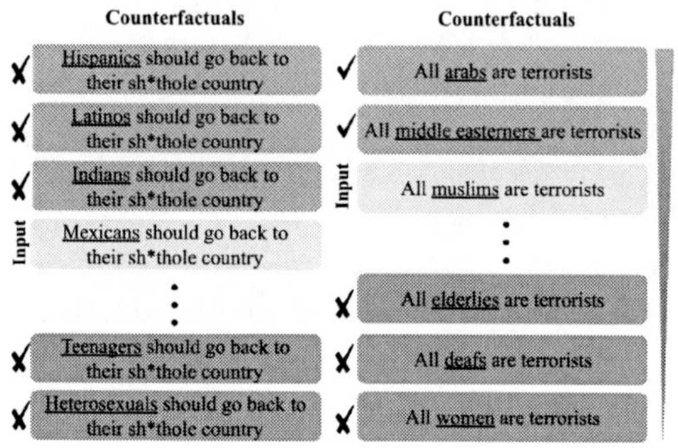

Figure 1: Two input sentences and their counterfactuals ranked by likelihood. Our method ensures similar outputs only for counterfactuals with higher likelihood.

mitigation in hate speech detection benefits from relying on individual-level fairness metrics such as *counterfactual fairness*, which assess the output variation resulting from changing the SGT in individual sentences (Garg et al., 2019; Kusner et al., 2017). Derived from causal reasoning, a counterfactual applies the slightest change to the actual world to assess the consequences in a similar world (Stalnaker, 1968; Lewis, 1973).

Accordingly, existing approaches for reducing bias in hate speech detection using counterfactual fairness learn robust models whose outputs are not affected by changing the SGT in the input (Garg et al., 2019). However, a drawback of such approaches is the lack of semantic analysis of the input to identify whether changing the SGT leads to a small enough change that preserves the hate speech label (Kasirzadeh and Smart, 2021). For instance, in a hateful statement, "*mexicans should go back to their sh*thole countries*", substituting "*mexicans*" with "*women*" changes the hate speech label, while using "*Hispanics*" should preserve the output. Here, we aim to create counterfactuals that *maximally* preserve the sentence and disregard counterfactuals that violate the requirement for be-

Proceedings of the Fifth Workshop on Online Abuse and Harms, pages 92–101
August 6, 2021.

ing the "*closest possible world*" (Fig. 1).

To this end, we develop a counterfactual generation method which filters candidate counterfactuals based on their difference in likelihood from the actual sentence, estimated by a pre-trained language model with known stereotypical correlations (Sheng et al., 2019). Intuitively, our method provides outputs that are robust with regard to the context and are not causally dependent on the presence of specific SGTs. This use of sentence likelihood is inspired by Nadeem et al. (2020) as it captures the similarity of an SGT and its surrounding words to prevent unlikely SGT substitutions. As a result, only counterfactuals with equal or higher likelihoods compared with the original ("closest possible worlds") are used during training. To enforce robust outputs for similar counterfactuals, we apply logit pairing (Kannan et al., 2018) on outputs for sentence-counterfactual pairs, adding their average differences to the classification loss. Our method (1) effectively identifies semantically similar counterfactuals and (2) improves fairness metrics while preserving classification performance, compared with other strategies for generating counterfactuals.

2 Related Work

Unintended bias in classification is defined as differing model performance on subsets of datasets that contain particular SGTs (Dixon et al., 2018; Mehrabi et al., 2019). To mitigate this bias, data augmentation approaches are proposed to create balanced labels for each SGT or to prevent biases from propagating to the learned model (Dixon et al., 2018; Zhao et al., 2018; Park et al., 2018). Other approaches apply regularization of post-hoc token importance (Kennedy et al., 2020b), or adversarial learning for generating fair representations (Madras et al., 2018; Zhang et al., 2018) to minimize the importance of protected features.

By altering sensitive features of the input and assessing the changes in the model prediction, counterfactual fairness (Kusner et al., 2017) seeks causal associations between sensitive features and other data attributes and outputs. Similarly, counterfactual token fairness applies counterfactual fairness to tokens in textual data (Garg et al., 2019).

Counterfactual fairness presupposes that the counterfactuals are close to the original world. However, previous work has yet to quantify this similarity in textual data. Key to our proposed framework is evaluating the semantic similarity between the original and the synthetically generated instances to only consider counterfactuals that convey similar sentiment. Consequently, our method prevents synthetic counterfactuals unlikely to exist in real-world samples which (1) decrease classification accuracy by adding noise into the training process and (2) misdirect fairness evaluation by introducing unexpected criteria.

3 Method

We propose a method for improving individual fairness in hate speech detection by considering the interchangeable role of SGTs in each specific context. Given instance $x \in X$, and a set of SGTs S, we seek to equalize outputs of a classifier f for x and its counterfactuals x_{cf} generated by substituting the SGT mentioned in x.

First, we provide the definition of *counterfactual token fairness* (CTF), which can be evaluated for a model over a dataset of sentences and their counterfactuals (Sec. 3.1). Next, we specify how *counterfactual logit pairing* (CLP) regularizes CTF in a classification task (Sec. 3.2). Lastly, we introduce our counterfactual generation method for Assessing Counterfactual Likelihoods (ACL, Sec. 3.3), which is driven by linguistic analysis of stereotype language in sentences.

3.1 Counterfactual Token Fairness (CTF)

Given instance $x \in X$, and a set of counterfactuals x_{cf}, generated by perturbing mentioned SGTs, the CTF for a classifier $f = \sigma(g(x))$ is:

$$\mathrm{CTF}(X, f) = \sum_{x \in X} \sum_{x' \in x_{cf}} |g(x) - g(x')|$$

where $g(x)$ returns the logits for x (Garg et al., 2019). Lower CTF indicates similar (i.e., fairer) outputs for sentences and their counterfactuals.

3.2 Counterfactual Logit Pairing (CLP)

To reduce CTF while training a hate speech classifier, we apply counterfactual logit pairing (CLP) (Kannan et al., 2018) to all instances and their counterfactuals. CLP penalizes prediction divergence among inputs and their counterfactuals by adding the average absolute difference in logits of the inputs and their counterfactuals to the training loss:

$$\sum_{x \in X} \ell_c(f(x), y) + \lambda \sum_{x \in X} \sum_{x' \in x_{cf}} |g(x) - g(x')|$$

where ℓ_c calculates the classification loss for an output $f(x)$ and its correct label y and λ tunes the

Stereotypical Sentences (from Gab)
Communists and dictators are desperate to get rid of god. His blessing overcomes the fearful evils of this fallen world.
Dumb ass n**** don't realize you actually have to work your ass off on a farm. It doesn't just magically happen now that they've stolen the land from **Whites**.
Israel and the Islamist conspiracy to deny **Jews** their land.
Women. lie. about. rape.

Table 1: **Sample stereotypical sentences** from Gab, for which changing the SGT (bolded) decreases the likelihood.

influence of the counterfactual fairness loss, the impact of which is discussed in the Appendix.

3.3 Counterfactual Generation

Rather than simplifying the model training by restricting CLP loss to all counterfactuals created by perturbing the SGTs in non-hate sentences (Garg et al., 2019), we identify similar counterfactuals based on likelihood analysis of each sentence. Our aim is to generate counterfactuals that preserve the likelihood of the original sentence.

In stereotypical sentences that target specific social groups, expecting equal outputs when changing the SGT leads to ignoring how specific vulnerable groups are targeted in text (Haas, 2012). Quantifying the change in a sentence as a result of perturbing SGTs has already been studied for detecting stereotypical language (Nadeem et al., 2020); similarly to Nadeem et al., we apply a generative language model (GPT2; Radford et al., 2019) to evaluate the change in sentence likelihood caused by substituting an SGT — e.g., we expect the language model to predict decrease in likelihood for a sentence about terrorism when it is paired with "*Muslim*" or "*Arab*" versus other SGTs.

Since GPT-2 uses the left context to predict the next word, for each word x_i in the sentence, the likelihood of x_i, $P(x_i|x_0 \dots x_{i-1})$, is approximated by the softmax of x_i with respect to the vocabulary. Therefore, the log-likelihood of a sentence $x_0, x_1, \dots x_{n-1}$ is computed with: $\lg P(x) = \sum_i^n \lg P(x_i|x_0, .., x_{i-1})$

We identify correct counterfactuals by comparing their log-likelihood to that of the original sentence and create the set of all correct counterfactuals $\boldsymbol{x}_{cf}$ by including counterfactuals with equal or higher likelihood compared with $\boldsymbol{x}$:

$$x_{cf} = \{x' | x' \in \text{substitute}(x, S), P(x) \leq P(x')\}$$

in which substitute(x, S) creates the set of all perturbed instance by substituting the SGT in x, with another SGT from the list of all SGTs S, which in this paper is a list of 77 SGTs (see Appendix), compiled from Dixon et al. (2018) and extended using WordNet synsets (Fellbaum, 2012).

Rank	# Items	# Choices	Accuracy(mean)	Agreement
1	500	4	74.88%	58.43
>1	250	2	63.07%	70.81

Table 2: Annotators' averaged accuracy and agreement (Fleiss, 1971) on sentences with different likelihood rankings.

4 Experiments

Here, we apply our method for generating counterfactuals (Sec. 3.3) to a large corpus to explore the method's ability to identify similar counterfactuals. Then, we apply CLP (Sec. 3.2) with different strategies for counterfactual generation and compare them to our approach, introduced in Sec. 3.3.

4.1 Evaluation of Generated Counterfactuals

Data. We randomly sampled 15 million posts from a corpus of social media posts from Gab (Gaffney, 2018), and selected all English posts that mention one SGT ($N \approx$ 2M). The log-likelihood of each post and its candidate counterfactuals were computed. The primary outcome was the original instance's *rank* in log-likelihood amongst its counterfactuals. Higher rank for a mentioned SGT indicates the stereotypical content of the sentence.

We conducted two qualitative analyses with human annotators to evaluate the generated counterfactuals. First, we selected sentences in which the highest ranks were assigned to the original SGTs and asked annotators to predict the mentioned SGT in a fill-in-the-blank test. If our method correctly ranks SGTs based on the context, we expect annotators to predict the original SGTs in such sentences. Then, we randomly selected a set of sentences and evaluated our method on finding the preferable counterfactual among a pair of candidates by comparing the choices to those of the annotators'.

Human annotators were from the authors of the paper, with backgrounds in computer science and social science. All annotators had previous experience with annotating hate speech content. However, they did not have any experience with the exact sentences in the evaluated dataset, given that the sentences were randomly selected from a dataset of 1.8M posts, collected by other researchers cited in the paper.

We preferred expert annotators over novice coders in this specific case, because previous stud-

	GHC						*Storm*					
	Hate	**EOO**			**CTF**		**Hate**	**EOO**			**CTF**	
	F1(↑)	TP(↓)	TN(↓)	FPR(↓)	DC(↓)	SC(↓)	F1(↑)	TP(↓)	TN(↓)	FPR(↓)	DC(↓)	SC(↓)
BERT	73.30±.2	38.3	23.0	6.6	2.22	1.99	78.52±.2	**40.8**	25.3	11.5	0.96	1.16
MASK	71.24±.2	39.0	20.3	2.5	1.78	1.99	70.91±.2	43.4	25.9	8.3	0.96	1.16
CLP+SG	62.10±.2	38.4	23.2	**0.2**	0.97	2.24	80.31±.2	41.8	25.4	9.8	0.71	1.06
CLP+Rand	66.45±.2	41.3	20.4	2.7	0.98	1.24	80.62±.2	43.7	25.8	**1.6**	0.83	0.99
CLP+GV	68.50±.2	38.3	23.0	3.1	1.01	1.25	79.28±.2	40.7	30.6	3.4	0.76	0.93
CLP+NEG	70.02±.2	39.6	**20.1**	7.7	0.76	1.98	77.62±.2	42.5	26.2	5.0	0.56	0.98
CLP+ACL	**73.31±.2**	**37.5**	20.5	2.4	**0.75**	**0.87**	**81.99±.2**	42.8	**23.1**	2.0	**0.42**	**0.53**

Table 3: **Results on GHC and Storm.** Baseline BERT model, and fine-tuned BERT masking SGTs, and five counterfactual logit pairing models (CLP) with counterfactual generation based on similar social groups (CLP+SG), random word substitution (CLP+Rand), GloVe similarity (CLP+GL), baseline approach (CLP+NEG; Garg et al., 2019), and our approach for Assessing Counterfactual Likelihoods (CLP+ACL), trained in 5-fold cross validation and tested on 20% of the datasets. Group-level fairness (true positive, true negative and false positive ratio) and counterfactual fairness are evaluated.

ies have indicated expert coder higher performance in hate speech annotation (Waseem, 2016). Moreover, annotators' cognitive biases and perceived stereotypes can greatly impact their judgments in detecting hate speech (Sap et al., 2019). Therefore, we preferred to have expert annotators with a shared understanding of the definition of stereotypes and hate speech, who are consequently less subjective in their judgments.

Results. In 2.9% of sentences the original SGT achieves the highest ranking. In 86.03% of the posts where the original SGT is ranked second, the top-ranked SGT is from the same *social category* (e.g., both SGTs referred to race or gender). We randomly selected 500 original posts with highest likelihood among their counterfactuals (Table 1 shows such samples) to qualitatively assess their stereotypicality in a fill-in-the-blank style test with human subjects. Three annotators, on average, identified the correct SGT from 4 random choices for 74.88% of posts. In a second evaluation, given sentences and two counterfactuals, annotators were asked to identify which SGT substitution preserves the hate speech and likelihood of the sentence. On average, annotators agreed with the model's choice in 63.07% of the test items. Table 2 demonstrates accuracy and agreement scores of annotators.

4.2 Fair Hate Speech Detection

We apply our counterfactuals generation method to hate speech detection, and equalize model outputs for sentences and their similar counterfactuals.

Compared Methods. We fine-tined BERT (Devlin et al., 2019) classifiers with CLP loss, using five approaches for generating counterfactuals: 1) **CLP+ACL** applies our approach for Assessing Counterfactual Likelihoods (Sec. 3.3), 2) **CLP+NEG** considers all counterfactuals for negative instances (Garg et al., 2019), 3) **CLP+SG** substitutes SGTs from the same social categories (inspired by Sec. 4.1), e.g., it replaces a racial group with other racial groups, 4) **CLP+Rand** substituting SGTs with random words, and 5) **CLP+GV** substitutes SGTs with ten most similar SGTs based on their GloVe word embeddings (Pennington et al., 2014). As baseline models we consider a vanilla fine-tuned BERT (**BERT**), and a fine-tuned BERT model that masks the SGTs (**MASK**)[1].

Data. We trained models on the Gab Hate Corpus (**GHC**; Kennedy et al., 2020a) and Stormfront dataset (**Storm**; de Gibert et al., 2018), including approximately 27k and 11k social media posts respectively. Both datasets are annotated based on typologies that define hate speech as targeting individuals or groups based on their group associations.

Evaluation Metrics. We compute CTF on two datasets of counterfactuals. (1) Similar Counterfactuals (SC; collected from Dixon et al. (2018)) includes synthetic, non-stereotypical instances based on templates (e.g., <You are a `ADJ SGT`>). In such instances, the sentence is not explicit to the SGT, and the model prediction should solely depend on the `ADJ`s so smaller values of CTF are indicative of a fairer models. (2) Dissimilar Counterfactuals (DC; from Nadeem et al. (2020)) includes stereotypical sentences and their counterfactuals generated by perturbing SGTs. Since instances are stereotypical, we expect all counterfactuals to be ignored by a fair model and lower CTF scores.

We also report group fairness metrics (equality of odds). The standard deviation of true positive (TP) and true negative (TN) rates across SGTs are

[1] Implementation details are provided in the Appendix

reported for a preserved test set (20% of the dataset) and instances generated by perturbing the SGTs. The standard deviation of false positive ratio (FPR) for different SGTs are also reported for a dataset of non-hateful New York Times sentences. Lower standard deviations indicate higher group fairness.

Results. Table 3 shows the results of these experiments on **GHC** and **Storm**. Evidently, our model (highlighted in Table 3) for generating counterfactuals enhances CTF while improving or preserving classification performance and group fairness (TP, TN, and FPR) on both datasets. The increase in classification performance demonstrates our method's capability in filtering noisy synthetic samples. These results call for further explorations of when fair models should treat SGTs equally. Rather than expecting equal results over all instances, fair predictions should be based on contextual information embedded in the sentences.

5 Conclusion

Our method treats social groups equally only within interchangeable contexts by applying logit pairing on a restricted set of counterfactuals. We demonstrated that biased pre-trained language models could enhance counterfactual fairness by identifying stereotypical sentences. Our method improved counterfactual token fairness and classification accuracy by filtering unlikely counterfactuals. Future work may explore semantic-based techniques for creating counterfactuals in domains other than hate speech detection, e.g., crime prediction, to better contextualize definitions of social group equality.

Broader Impact Statement

Our paper investigates bias mitigation in hate speech detection. This task is of great sensitivity because of the impact of online hate speech on minority social groups. While most discussions in the field of Ethics of AI focus on equalizing biases against different social groups from pre-trained language models, we make use of this bias to identify stereotypical or conspiratorial hate speech in social media and to ensure that hate speech detection models learn these linguistic association of stereotypes for protecting social groups from rhetoric that is explicitly targeting them.

Acknowledgments

This research was sponsored in part by NSF CAREER BCS-1846531 to Morteza Dehghani.

References

Martín Abadi, Paul Barham, Jianmin Chen, Zhifeng Chen, Andy Davis, Jeffrey Dean, Matthieu Devin, Sanjay Ghemawat, Geoffrey Irving, Michael Isard, et al. 2016. Tensorflow: A system for large-scale machine learning. In *12th {USENIX} symposium on operating systems design and implementation ({OSDI} 16)*, pages 265–283.

Amy J. C. Cuddy, Susan T Fiske, Virginia SY Kwan, Peter Glick, Stephanie Demoulin, Jacques-Philippe Leyens, Michael Harris Bond, Jean-Claude Croizet, Naomi Ellemers, Ed Sleebos, et al. 2009. Stereotype content model across cultures: Towards universal similarities and some differences. *British Journal of Social Psychology*, 48(1):1–33.

J. Devlin, Ming-Wei Chang, Kenton Lee, and Kristina Toutanova. 2019. Bert: Pre-training of deep bidirectional transformers for language understanding. In *NAACL-HLT*.

Lucas Dixon, John Li, Jeffrey Sorensen, Nithum Thain, and Lucy Vasserman. 2018. Measuring and mitigating unintended bias in text classification. In *Proceedings of the 2018 AAAI/ACM Conference on AI, Ethics, and Society*, pages 67–73.

Cynthia Dwork, Moritz Hardt, Toniann Pitassi, Omer Reingold, and Richard Zemel. 2012. Fairness through awareness. In *Proceedings of the 3rd innovations in theoretical computer science conference*, pages 214–226.

Christiane Fellbaum. 2012. Wordnet. *The encyclopedia of applied linguistics*.

Joseph L Fleiss. 1971. Measuring nominal scale agreement among many raters. *Psychological bulletin*, 76(5):378.

Gavin Gaffney. 2018. Pushshift gab corpus. `https://files.pushshift.io/gab/`. Accessed: 2019-5-23.

Sahaj Garg, Vincent Perot, Nicole Limtiaco, Ankur Taly, Ed H Chi, and Alex Beutel. 2019. Counterfactual fairness in text classification through robustness. In *Proceedings of the 2019 AAAI/ACM Conference on AI, Ethics, and Society*, pages 219–226. ACM.

Ona de Gibert, Naiara Perez, Aitor García-Pablos, and Montse Cuadros. 2018. Hate speech dataset from a white supremacy forum. *arXiv preprint arXiv:1809.04444*.

Anthony G Greenwald and Mahzarin R Banaji. 1995. Implicit social cognition: attitudes, self-esteem, and stereotypes. *Psychological review*, 102(1):4.

Rainer Greifeneder, Herbert Bless, and Klaus Fiedler. 2017. *Social cognition: How individuals construct social reality*. Psychology Press.

John Haas. 2012. Hate speech and stereotypic talk. *The handbook of intergroup communication*, pages 128–140.

Moritz Hardt, Eric Price, Nati Srebro, et al. 2016. Equality of opportunity in supervised learning. In *Advances in neural information processing systems*, pages 3315–3323.

Harini Kannan, Alexey Kurakin, and Ian Goodfellow. 2018. Adversarial logit pairing. *arXiv preprint arXiv:1803.06373*.

Atoosa Kasirzadeh and Andrew Smart. 2021. The use and misuse of counterfactuals in ethical machine learning. In *Proceedings of the 2021 ACM Conference on Fairness, Accountability, and Transparency*, pages 228–236.

Brendan Kennedy, Mohammad Atari, Aida M Davani, Leigh Yeh, Ali Omrani, Yehsong Kim, Kris Coombs Jr., Shreya Havaldar, Gwenyth Portillo-Wightman, Elaine Gonzalez, Joe Hoover, Aida Azatian, Gabriel Cardenas, Alyzeh Hussain, Austin Lara, Adam Omary, Christina Park, Xin Wang, Clarisa Wijaya, Yong Zhang, Beth Meyerowitz, and Morteza Dehghani. 2020a. The gab hate corpus: A collection of 27k posts annotated for hate speech.

Brendan Kennedy, Xisen Jin, Aida Mostafazadeh Davani, Morteza Dehghani, and Xiang Ren. 2020b. Contextualizing hate speech classifiers with post-hoc explanation. *Annual Conference of the Association for Computational Linguistics (ACL)*.

Matt J Kusner, Joshua Loftus, Chris Russell, and Ricardo Silva. 2017. Counterfactual fairness. In *Advances in Neural Information Processing Systems*, pages 4066–4076.

David Lewis. 1973. Counterfactuals and comparative possibility. In *Ifs*, pages 57–85. Springer.

David Madras, Elliot Creager, Toniann Pitassi, and Richard Zemel. 2018. Learning adversarially fair and transferable representations. *arXiv preprint arXiv:1802.06309*.

Ninareh Mehrabi, Fred Morstatter, Nripsuta Saxena, Kristina Lerman, and Aram Galstyan. 2019. A survey on bias and fairness in machine learning. *arXiv preprint arXiv:1908.09635*, 0.

Moin Nadeem, Anna Bethke, and Siva Reddy. 2020. Stereoset: Measuring stereotypical bias in pretrained language models. *arXiv preprint arXiv:2004.09456*.

Ji Ho Park, Jamin Shin, and Pascale Fung. 2018. Reducing gender bias in abusive language detection. *arXiv preprint arXiv:1808.07231*.

Jeffrey Pennington, Richard Socher, and Christopher D. Manning. 2014. Glove: Global vectors for word representation. In *Empirical Methods in Natural Language Processing (EMNLP)*, pages 1532–1543.

Alec Radford, Jeffrey Wu, Rewon Child, David Luan, Dario Amodei, and Ilya Sutskever. 2019. Language models are unsupervised multitask learners. *OpenAI Blog*, 1(8):9.

Maarten Sap, Dallas Card, Saadia Gabriel, Yejin Choi, and Noah A Smith. 2019. The risk of racial bias in hate speech detection. In *Proceedings of the 57th Annual Meeting of the Association for Computational Linguistics*, pages 1668–1678.

Emily Sheng, Kai-Wei Chang, Premkumar Natarajan, and Nanyun Peng. 2019. The woman worked as a babysitter: On biases in language generation. *arXiv preprint arXiv:1909.01326*.

Robert C Stalnaker. 1968. A theory of conditionals. In *Ifs*, pages 41–55. Springer.

Zeerak Waseem. 2016. Are you a racist or am i seeing things? annotator influence on hate speech detection on twitter. In *Proceedings of the first workshop on NLP and computational social science*, pages 138–142.

Michael Wiegand, Josef Ruppenhofer, and Thomas Kleinbauer. 2019. Detection of abusive language: the problem of biased datasets. In *Proceedings of the 2019 Conference of the North American Chapter of the Association for Computational Linguistics: Human Language Technologies, Volume 1 (Long and Short Papers)*, pages 602–608.

Thomas Wolf, Lysandre Debut, Victor Sanh, Julien Chaumond, Clement Delangue, Anthony Moi, Pierric Cistac, Tim Rault, Remi Louf, Morgan Funtowicz, Joe Davison, Sam Shleifer, Patrick von Platen, Clara Ma, Yacine Jernite, Julien Plu, Canwen Xu, Teven Le Scao, Sylvain Gugger, Mariama Drame, Quentin Lhoest, and Alexander Rush. 2020. Transformers: State-of-the-art natural language processing. In *Proceedings of the 2020 Conference on Empirical Methods in Natural Language Processing: System Demonstrations*, pages 38–45, Online. Association for Computational Linguistics.

Brian Hu Zhang, Blake Lemoine, and Margaret Mitchell. 2018. Mitigating unwanted biases with adversarial learning. In *Proceedings of the 2018 AAAI/ACM Conference on AI, Ethics, and Society*, pages 335–340. ACM.

Jieyu Zhao, Tianlu Wang, Mark Yatskar, Vicente Ordonez, and Kai-Wei Chang. 2018. Gender bias in coreference resolution: Evaluation and debiasing methods. *arXiv preprint arXiv:1804.06876*.

A Appendix

All data is uploaded to dropbox[2]

A.1 Social Group Tokens

Our social group terms include: heterosexual, catholic, queer, latinx, younger, christian, latin american, jewish, jew, democrat, republican, indian, trans, canadian, white, bisexual, female, men, man, women, woman, gay, paralytic, blind, aged, spanish, taiwanese, taoist, protestant, paralyzed, liberal, deaf, buddhist, chinese, african, older, elder, deafen, latino, straight, latina, english, asian, male, amerind, old, american, conservative, japanese, muslim, homosexual, nonbinary, lesbian, protestant, ashen, sikh, lgbt, teenage, middle eastern, hispanic, bourgeois, lgbtq, european, millenial, transgender, african, young, elderly, paralyze, middle aged, black, mexican, arab, immigrant, migrant, and communist

A.2 Study 1: Qualitative Analysis

Implementation Details To compute perplexity scores of the counterfactuals, we used 41 Google cloud virtual machine instances with the following configuration. All the instances used the Google n1-standard-4 (4 vCPUs, 15 GB memory). We had 1 x NVIDIA Tesla P100 Virtual Workstation, 15 x NVIDIA Tesla P4 Virtual Workstation, and 25 x NVIDIA Tesla K80. In addition we used one local machine with 1 x NVIDIA GeForce RTX 2080 SUPER, AMD Ryzen Threadripper 1920X CPU and 128 GB memory.

For each data point, the runtime of generating 64 counterfactuals along with their perplexity scores was about 1.5 seconds on instances with NVIDIA Tesla P4 Virtual Workstations and NVIDIA GeForce RTX 2080 SUPER and about 2.6 seconds on instances with NVIDIA Tesla K80 GPUs.

Hyper parameters We used the pre-trained GPT-2 model from the transformers library by hugging face [3] with 12-layer, 768-hidden, 12-heads, 117M parameters.

Dataset We downloaded the public dump of Gab posts [4] which contains more than 34 million posts from August 2016 to October 2018. After dropping posts with small number of English tokens (non-English posts) and malformed records, We got near 15 million posts referred to as **SGT-Gab**. Data can be found in the accompanied zip file.

A.3 Study 2

Implementation Details Each of the seven models were trained on 80% of the given dataset (either **GHC** or **Storm**), (*dataset*_train.csv file) and tested on the remaining 20% (*dataset*_test.csv file). The models were run on a single NVIDIA GeForce GTX 1080 GPU, where each epoch takes 3 seconds. Models were built in Python 3.6 and Tensorflow-GPU (Abadi et al., 2016).

Data cleaning was performed by applying the **BertTokenizer** tokenizer (Wolf et al., 2020), and models were trained by fine-tuning **Bert-For-Sequence-Classification** initialized with pre-trained "bert-base-uncased"[5] with 12-layers, 768-hidden, 12-heads, and 117M parameters (Wolf et al., 2020). The λ coefficient was set to 0.2 for all models to specify the same counterfactual loss in all models.

Hate Speech Datasets Here we provide detail on the two training datasets from our experiments. The Gab Hate Corpus (**GHC**; Kennedy et al., 2020a) is an annotated corpus of English social media posts from the far-right network "Gab." Labels were generated by majority vote between all provided annotations labels of "CV" (Call for Violence) and "HD" (Human Degradation) which are two sub-types of hate speech. Final dataset include 2254 positive labels of hate among 27557 items. Secondly, de Gibert et al. (2018) provide an annotated corpus of English (**Storm**). We used posts included in "all_files",[6] and generated our own train and test subset. The final dataset includes 1196 positive labels among 10944 items.

For each dataset, the train and test set were split based on maintaining the same ratio of SGTs in both sets. Similarly, in each fold of cross validation 20% of the train set was selected for validation purposes based on maintaining the same ratio of hate labels.

Fairness Evaluation Datasets

We used three out-of-domain datasets for evaluating fairness: First, an existing dataset of stereotypes in English ("Dissimilar Counterfactuals";

[2] https://www.dropbox.com/s/awjvtt5op43ewr6/Data.zip?dl=0

[3] https://huggingface.co/transformers/pretrained_models.html

[4] https://files.pushshift.io/gab/

[5] https://huggingface.co/bert-base-uncased

[6] https://github.com/Vicomtech/hate-speech-dataset

DC) collected by Nadeem et al. (2020) was applied, which contains two types of stereotype: *intersentence* instances consisted of a base sentence provided for a target group and a stereotypical sentence generated by annotators for the same group, while *intrasentence* instances were single sentences annotated as stereotypes. For each sentence, we substitute the target group with all our SGTs, resulting in 25565 samples.

Second, "Similar Counterfactuals" (SC) consists of 77k synthetic English sentences generated by Dixon et al. (2018). After removing sentences with less that 4 tokens, we ended up with 3200 sentences.

Third, following Kennedy et al. (2020b) we use a corpus of New York Times (NYT) articles to measure false positive rate. Specifically, for each SGT in our list (see Section A.1), we sampled 500 articles containing a mention of this SGT (and no other SGT mentions). This produced a balanced random sample of SGTs, which are heuristically assumed to have no hate speech (excepting rare occurrences, e.g., quotations).

Evaluation For evaluating the Counterfactual Token Fairness (CTF) among a sentence and the list of its counterfactuals, we computed the cosine similarity of the 2D logits, produced as the output of **Bert-For-Sequence-Classification** model. We then calculated the average of these similarities to get a CTF value for the sentence and computed the average of CTFs over the dataset.

Analysis of the Regularization Coefficient As mentioned in Section 3.2, the regularization coefficient λ controls the extent to which counterfactual logit pairing formulation affects the training process. A larger value of λ is expected to increases the importance of bias mitigation, while decreasing the essential classification performance. While in our experiments in Section 4.2 we set the same value for λ for all counterfactual pairing approaches, here we discuss λ as it creates a trade-off between classification accuracy and counterfactual token fairness.

Figure 2 and 3 demonstrate the effect of λ on the three main approaches evaluated on **GHC** and **Storm** datasets; 1) our approach for counterfactual generation (**CLP+ACL**), 2) Garg et al. (2019)'s approach which considers all counterfactuals of non-hate samples (**CLP+NEG**), and 3) counterfactual generation based on similar social categories (**CLP+SG**). As the plots denote, higher value of λ corresponds with lower classification accuracy and lower (more desirable) counterfactual token fairness. These results also denotes that our proposed method **CLP+ACL**, achieves higher accuracy and fairness compared to the other approaches with different values of λ. In our experiments reported in Table 3, λ is set to 0.2 for all approaches that are based on counterfactual pairing (**CLP+***). We chose this value, since based on the observed results in 2 and 3, it demonstrates the effect of counterfactual pairing loss on improving the fairness metrics while preserving classification accuracy. Future applications of our approach should rely on fine-tuning λ during training.

A.4 Glossary

Unintended bias: When a model is biased with respect to a feature that it was not intended to be (e.g. race in Toxicity classifier).

Group Fairness: Fairness defintions that treat different groups equally (e.g. equality of odds, equality of opportunity.)

Individual Fairness: Fairness definitions that ensure similar predictions to similar individuals (e.g. counterfactual fairness.)

Equality of Odds: "A predictor $\hat{Y}$ satisfies equalized odds with respect to protected attribute A and outcome Y, if $\hat{Y}$ and A are independent conditional on Y. $P(\hat{Y} = 1|A = 0, Y = y) = P(\hat{Y} = 1|A = 1, Y = y), y \in \{0, 1\}$", (Hardt et al., 2016)

Equality of Opportunity: "A binary predictor $\hat{Y}$ satisfies equal opportunity with respect to A and Y if $P(\hat{Y} = 1|A = 0, Y = 1) = P(\hat{Y} = 1|A = 1, Y = 1)$", (Hardt et al., 2016)

Counterfactual: Counterfactual conditionals are conditional sentences that assess the outcome under different circumstances. Here we use (Garg et al., 2019) definition of counterfactual questions, "How would the prediction change if the sensitive attribute referenced in the example were different?" with SGT as the sensitive attribute

Counterfactual reasoning: The process of inferences from counterfactual conditionals compared to regular conditionals.

Stereotype: Stereotyping is a cognitive bias, deeply rooted in human nature (Cuddy et al., 2009) and omnipresent in everyday life through which humans can promptly assess whether an outgroup is a threat or not. Stereotyping, along with other cognitive biases, impacts how individuals create their subjective social reality as a basis for social judgements and behaviors (Greifeneder et al., 2017). Stereotypes are often studied in terms of the associations that automatically influence judgement and behavior when relevant social categories are activated (Greenwald and Banaji, 1995).

	Non-hate Sample	Hate Sample
(Garg et al., 2019)	All Counterfactuals	No Counterfactuals
Issues	Adding noisy synthetic data into the model since SGTs cannot interchangeably appear in all contexts	Not supporting fairness for specific SGTs with high association with hate speech (Dixon et al., 2018)
Current approach	Counterfactuals with higher likelihood	
Improvement	Preventing counterfactuals with lower sentence likelihood, that can be noisy instances	Equalizing outputs for current instances and their more stereotypical counterfactuals

Table 4: The through comparison of the proposed approach with Garg et al. (2019), based on their solutions for positive and negative instances of hate speech

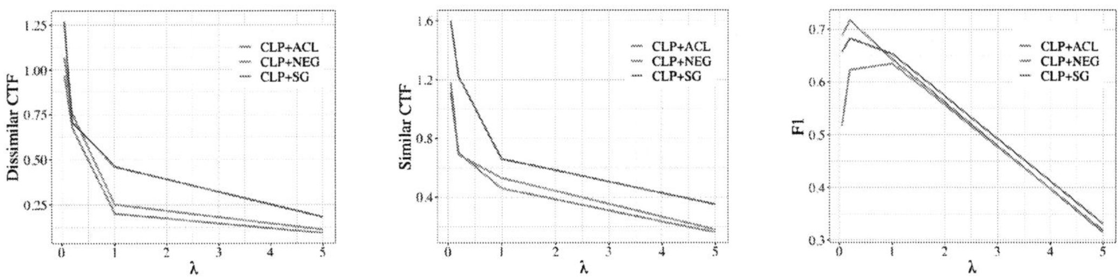

Figure 2: Changing the value of λ while training models on the **GHC** dataset demonstrated the tradeoff between accuracy and counterfactual token fairness (evaluated on two datasets of dissimilar and similar counterfactuals).

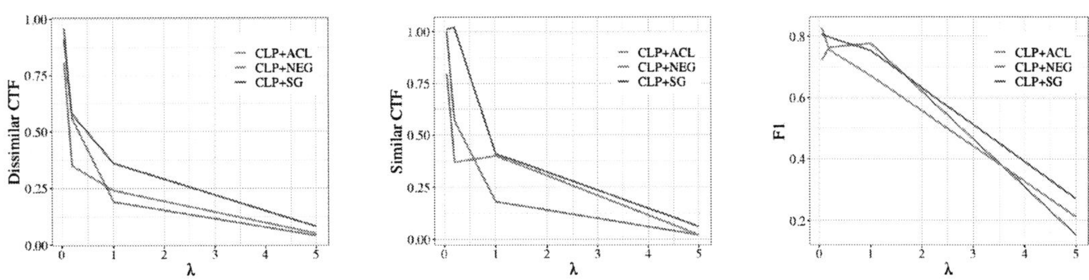

Figure 3: Changing the value of λ while training models on the **Storm** dataset demonstrated the tradeoff between accuracy and counterfactual token fairness (evaluated on two datasets of dissimilar and similar counterfactuals).

Hell Hath No Fury? Correcting Bias in the NRC Emotion Lexicon

Samira Zad, Joshuan Jimenez, & Mark A. Finlayson
Knight Foundation School of Computing and Information Sciences
Florida International University
11200 SW 8th Street, Miami, FL
{szad001,jjime178,markaf}@fiu.edu

Abstract

There have been several attempts to create an accurate and thorough emotion lexicon in English, which identifies the emotional content of words. Of the several commonly used resources, the NRC emotion lexicon (Mohammad and Turney, 2013b) has received the most attention due to its availability, size, and its choice of Plutchik's expressive 8-class emotion model. In this paper we identify a large number of troubling entries in the NRC lexicon, where words that should in most contexts be emotionally neutral, with no affect (e.g., *lesbian*, *stone*, *mountain*), are associated with emotional labels that are inaccurate, nonsensical, pejorative, or, at best, highly contingent and context-dependent (e.g., *lesbian* labeled as DISGUST and SADNESS, *stone* as ANGER, or *mountain* as ANTICIPATION). We describe a procedure for semi-automatically correcting these problems in the NRC, which includes disambiguating POS categories and aligning NRC entries with other emotion lexicons to infer the accuracy of labels. We demonstrate via an experimental benchmark that the quality of the resources is thus improved. We release the revised resource and our code to enable other researchers to reproduce and build upon results[1].

1 Introduction

Emotion detection is an NLP task that has long been of interest to the field (Hancock et al., 2007; Danisman and Alpkocak, 2008; Agrawal and An, 2012), and is usually conceived as a single- or multi-label classification in which zero (or more) emotion labels are assigned to variously defined semantic or syntactic subdivisions of the text. The importance of this task has only grown as the amount of available affective text has increased: social media, in particular, has made it especially convenient for people around the world to express their feelings and emotions regarding events large and small.

There are generally two ways to express emotions in textual data (Al-Saqqa et al., 2018). First, emotions can be expressed using *emotive* vocabulary: words directly referring to emotional states (*surprise*, *sadness*, *joy*). Second, emotions can be expressed using *affective* vocabulary: words whose emotional content depends on the context, without direct reference to emotional states, for example, interjections (*ow!*, *ouch!*, *ha-ha!*).

An *emotion lexicon* is a specific type of linguistic resource that maps the emotive or affective vocabulary of a language to a fixed set of emotion labels (e.g. Plutchik's eight-emotion model), where each entry in the lexicon associates a word with zero or more emotion labels. Because this information is difficult to find elsewhere, emotion lexicons are often used as one of the key components of affective text mining systems (Yadollahi et al., 2017). However, as is usual with linguistic resources, creating an emotion lexicon is a time-consuming, costly, and sometimes impractical part of the task. The difficulty is only accentuated when one considers the many affective uses of words, in which the emotional content is context dependent. Such context dependency underlines the utility of General-Purpose (context-independent) Emotion Lexicons (GPELs), which captures the mostly fixed emotive content of words, and which can serve as a foundation for more context-dependent systems.

In this paper, we analyze and improve one of the most commonly used GPELs, namely, the NRC lexicon (National Research Council of Canada; also known as the Emolex emotion lexicon Mohammad and Turney, 2013b,a, 2010). The NRC used Macquarie's Thesaurus (Bernard, 1986) as the source for terms, retaining only words that are repeated more than 120,000 times in Google n-gram corpus (Michel et al., 2011). The NRC maps each word to zero or more labels drawn from Plutchik's 8-

[1] https://doi.org/10.34703/gzx1-9v95/PO3YGX

Proceedings of the Fifth Workshop on Online Abuse and Harms, pages 102–113
August 6, 2021.

emotion psychological model (Plutchik, 1980), and provides labels for 14,182 individual words.

While the NRC has been used extensively across the emotion mining literature (Tabak and Evrim, 2016; Abdaoui et al., 2017; Rose et al., 2018; Lee et al., 2019; Ljubešić et al., 2020; Zad et al., 2021), close inspection reveals a large number of incorrect, non-sensical, pejorative, or otherwise troubling entries. While we provide more examples later in the paper, to give a flavor of the problem, the NRC provides emotion labels for many generic nouns (*tree*→ANGER), common verbs (*dance*→TRUST), colors (*white*→ANTICIPATION), places (*mosque*→ANGER), relations (*aunt*→TRUST), and adverbs (*scarcely*→SADNESS). Furthermore, the NRC suffers from significant ambiguity because it does not include part of speech categories for the terms: for example, while *console* implies SADNESS in its most common verb sense (as the NRC indicates), in its most common noun sense means a small side table, which probably should have no emotive content. In our analysis, many of these problematic entries seem to stem from a conflation of *emotive* (context-independent) and *affective* (context-dependent) emotion language use: it is as if, during the annotation of Shakespeare's *Macbeth*, the annotators of the NRC marked *hell*→ANGER and *woman*→ANGER because of the bard's highly contextualized statement "Hell hath no fury like a woman scorned": while it is true that this statement is often cited to support an assertion that women are angry people in general, and such a lexicon entry would help in correct marking of the affective implication of this specific statement in this particular context, it does not generalize to all, or even most, uses of the word *woman*. Therein lies the rub.

We begin the paper with a brief review of psychological models of emotion, available emotion lexicons, and datasets of emotion labeled text (§2). We then discuss in detail the deficiencies of the NRC, giving a variety of problematic examples, and speculating as to how these entries were included (§3). Next we describe a semi-automatic procedure designed to filter out many of these deficiencies (§4), after which we evaluate the effectiveness of the filtering procedure by integrating the corrected version of the NRC into an emotion detection system (§5). We conclude with a list of our contributions (§6).

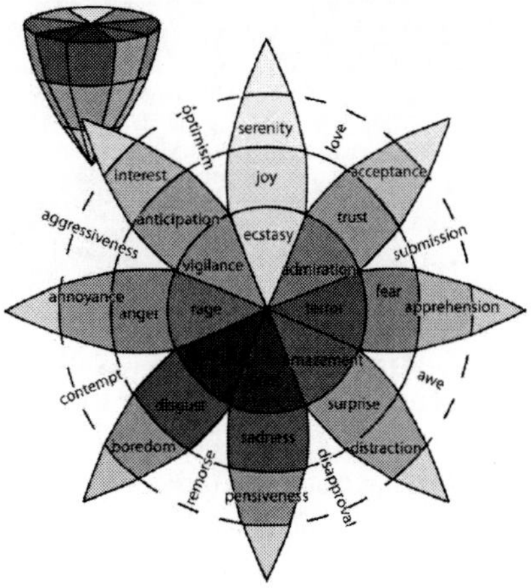

Figure 1: Plutchik's emotions wheel, Plutchik and Conte (1997). Figure taken from (Maupome and Isyutina, 2013), with permission.

2 Literature Review

2.1 Psychological Emotion Model

Emotion detection tasks are fundamentally predicated on a particular conception of what emotions exist. There are three broad classes of psychological theories of emotion: *discrete*, *dimensional*, and *hybrid*. Discrete psychological models represent basic emotions as individual, distinct categories, e.g., Oatley and Johnson-Laird (1987) with five emotions, Ekman (1992); Shaver et al. (1987) with six, Parrott (2001) with six basic emotions in the first level of a tree structure, Panksepp et al. (1998) with seven emotions, and Izard (2007) with ten. Dimensional psychological models, in contrast, propose that emotions are best described as lying in multi-dimensions space, e.g., the models of Russell (1980); Scherer (2005); Cambria (2016) with two dimensions, (Lövheim, 2012) with three, and Ortony et al. (1990); Fontaine et al. (2007); Cambria et al. (2012) with four. Hybrid models combine the two approaches by arranging categorical emotions along various dimensions, e.g., Plutchik's model (1980; 1984; 2001) with eight basic emotion categories (ANGER, FEAR, SADNESS, JOY, DISGUST, TRUST, SURPRISE, ANTICIPATION) arranged in two or three dimensions, as illustrated in Figure 1.

2.2 Emotion Lexicons

Emotion lexicons take a specific emotional theory and associate the labels or values in that theory with specific lexical entries. If the emotion lexi-

Author, Year	Lexicon	Size (words)	Set of Emotions
(Mohammad and Turney, 2010)	NRC	14,182	ANGER, FEAR, ANTICIPATION, TRUST, SURPRISE, SADNESS, JOY, DISGUST
(Mohammad and Turney, 2013b)	NRC hashtag	16,862	ANGER, FEAR, ANTICIPATION, TRUST, SURPRISE, SADNESS, JOY, DISGUST
(Stone et al., 1966)	General Enquirer	11,788	PLEASURE, AROUSAL, FEELING, PAIN
(Strapparava and Valitutti, 2004)	WordNet Affect	289	A HIERARCHY OF EMOTIONS
(Pennebaker et al., 2007)	LIWC	2,300	AFFECTIVE OR NOT, POSITIVE, NEGATIVE, ANXIETY, ANGER, SADNESS

Table 1: Comparison of emotion lexicons

con identifies emotive and affective uses tied to a specific context, then it is referred to as a *domain-specific emotion lexicon* (DSEL). In contrast, an emotion lexicon that seeks to represent the context-independent emotional meaning of words is referred to as a General Purpose Emotion Lexicon (GPEL). There are a variety of GPELs available, which we describe below.

The NRC lexicon (National Research Council of Canada; also known as the Emolex emotion lexicon) is one of the most commonly used lexicons. It comprises 14,182 words labeled according to Plutchik's psychological model. The NRC was created via a crowd-sourcing, and used Roget's Thesaurus as the source for terms (Mohammad and Turney, 2010, 2013a,b). Because we focus on the NRC lexicon in this paper, we discuss it in detail in the next section.

The WordNet Affect Lexicon (WNA or WAL Strapparava and Valitutti, 2004) is an emotion lexicon based on WordNet (Fellbaum, 1998). WNA arranges 289 noun synsets into an emotion hierarchy and associates 1,191 verbs, adverbs, and adjectives synsets to those emotion terms to WordNet.

NRC Hashtag Emotion Lexicon (Mohammad, 2012) comprises 16,862 words, drawn from Twitter hashtags, that are labeled with a strength of association (from 0 to infinity) for each of six emotion classes. It was created automatically by extracting tweets that contains `#joy`, `#sadness`, `#surprise`, `#disgust`, `#fear`, and `#anger`. Mohammad (2012) showed that the NRC Hashtag emotion lexicon provides better performance on Twitter Emotion Corpus than the WordNet-Affect emotion lexicon, but not as good as the original NRC emotion lexicon. Mohammad and Kiritchenko (2015) extended this work by expanding the hashtag word list to 585 emotion words, producing 15,825 labeled entries, with performance on headline data set again better than WNA.

The General Enquirer lexicon, while not specifically designed as an emotion lexicon, comprises 11,788 concepts labeled with 182 category labels that includes certain affect categories (e.g., pleasure, arousal, feeling, and pain) in addition to positive/negative semantic orientation for concepts (Stone et al., 1966).

Linguistic Inquiry and Word Count (LIWC Pennebaker et al., 2001, 2007) is a text analysis program that includes a lexicon comprising 2,300 entries spread across 73 categories, many of which are emotive or have sentiment, including NEGATION, ANGER, ANXIETY, SADNESS, etc.

There are lexicons which are related to emotion, but not themselves emotion lexicons. For example, Staiano and Guerini (2014) described the DepecheMood lexicon, which was an automatically generated, general-purpose, and mood lexicon with 37K terms. It includes eight mood-related labels (*don't care*, *amused*, *annoyed*, *inspired*, *anger*, *sadness*, *fear*, and *joy*) based on Rappler's mood meter (obtained by crawling the `rappler.com` social news network). Kušen et al. (2017) compared the four labels shared between NRC and DepecheMood (anger, sadness, fear, and joy), and showed that NRC had the highest recall. NRC performed better at capturing fear, anger, and joy, and DepecheMood performed better at recognize sadness. Araque et al. (2019) created the extended DepecheMood++ (DM++) for English on Rappler news and Italian on Corriere news (`corriere.it`, an online Italian newspaper).

Table 1 lists the main emotion lexicons in details. As can be seen, the NRC is one of the largest resources and uses one of the more expressive emotion ontologies, hence researchers' preference for it in their work.

2.3 Data Set

Annotated corpora of emotion-laden language go hand-in-hand with emotion lexicons. This is because one of the first tests of the utility of a lexicon is how well a system that uses the lexicon performs on automatic labeling. In general, data annotation is a crucial part of most machine learning research and affects the quality of the work substantially. As is commonly known, in the case of linguistic annotation, manually labeling large amounts of text is expensive and time consuming; further, in most cases, assigning labels can be subjective and dependent on the personality, emotions, background, and point of view of the annotator; and finally, unbalanced label frequency creates challenges for training various learning algorithms.

There are several text corpora annotated with emotional categorical models (Yadollahi et al., 2017; Sailunaz et al., 2018; Acheampong et al., 2020). For example, the International Survey on Emotion Antecedents and Reactions (ISEAR) corpus Scherer and Wallbott (1994) comprises 7,665 sentences drawn from 3,000 students from 37 countries were asked to report as a sentense or paragraph situations in which they had experienced FEAR, SADNESS, JOY, ANGER, SHAME, GUILT, and DISGUST emotions. ISEAR data set is annotated by authors and labeled by seven emotions (FEAR, SADNESS, JOY, ANGER, SHAME, GUILT, and DISGUST). Similarly, Aman's corpus Aman and Szpakowicz (2007) comprises of 1,466 sentences from blogs and labeled by seven emotions (SADNESS, SURPRISE, ANGER, FEAR, DISGUST, HAPPINESS, and MIXED EMOTIONS). The Semantic Evaluations (SemEval) corpus (Rosenthal et al., 2019) includes 1,250 news headlines and labeled by Ekman's six basic emotions (ANGER, DISGUST, SURPRISE, FEAR, JOY, and SADNESS). These are just three examples of many.

For evaluation we use Alm's fairy tale corpus (Alm, 2008, 2010) which contains 15,302 sentences from 176 children's fairy tales from classic collections by Beatrix Potter, the Brother's Grimm's, and Hans C. Andersen. We chose this corpus because of the ready availability of an emotion detection system (Zad and Finlayson, 2020) that uses this corpus for evaluation. Two annotators marked both the emotion and mood of each sentence in the corpus (i.e., two separate judgements by both annotators, for a total of four labels per sentence), using Ekman's six emotions (JOY, FEAR, SADNESS, SURPRISE, ANGER, and DISGUST). 1,167 sentences in the corpus had "high annotation agreement" which Alm defined as all four labels being the same, and there are a total of 4,627 other sentences which annotators have all labeled them as neutral. One reason to focus on only the high agreement sentences is because the overall Cohen's Kappa for the dataset agreement is a quite poor -0.2086. If we focus only on high agreement, the Cohen's Kappa is perfect. Emotion annotation is notoriously difficult, and very few emotion annotation projects have achieved high agreement. This suggests that most of the approaches to emotion annotation have suffered from lack of conceptual clarity.

3 Problems with the NRC

In our close inspection of the entries in the NRC, we noted three main problems. First, the NRC does not indicate the part of speech of terms labeled with emotion. This obviously causes a great deal of ambiguity as to whether a particular emotion label should apply to a particular use of a word form. Second, the NRC contains numerous incorrect, inaccurate, nonsensical, or pejorative associations, most of which can be ascribed to an apparent conflation of the distinction between emotive and affective emotional language, i.e., ignoring the importance of context for emotional semantics. Third, and finally, there are emotion markings in the lexicon for which we can find no support in Keyword-in-Context (KWIC) databases for any sense; we count these as simple errors.

3.1 Missing Parts of Speech

As Mohammad and Turney (2010) noted, the NRC includes some of the most frequent English nouns, verbs, adjectives, and adverbs. Problematically, however, the NRC does not indicate the part of speech for any entry. For example, the wordform *bombard* is labeled as ANGER|FEAR; however, in WordNet the gloss for the first sense of *bombard* as a noun is "a large shawm[2] ; the bass member of the shawm family". On the other hand, the gloss of the first sense of the verb form of *bombard* is "cast, hurl, or throw repeatedly with some missile", which is more compatible with the emotion ANGER|FEAR. Another example is the word *console*. The NRC marks *console*→SADNESS, but the primary sense of the noun form refers to "a small table fixed to a wall or designed to stand against a wall." Clearly there is no context-independent emotional inflection to this sense. The SADNESS label is more appropriate for the first verb sense "to give moral or emotional strength to", usually to a sad person.

Despite Araque et al. (2019) claims that adding POS tags to lexicons may decrease the performance of emotion detection mechanisms, we observe that lack of POS tagging has caused considerable ambi-

[2]a *shawm* is a type of musical intstrument

guity which negatively affects our emotion detection system performance.

Table 2 lists a small selection of NRC wordform labels that are problematic because of part-of-speech-related ambiguity. Although we did not count the number of NRC entries suffering this particular part-of-speech ambiguity problem, our best guess is that it affects roughly several thousand entries, about a third of the non-neutral portion of the lexicon.

3.2 Context Dependency

In general-purpose emotion lexicons (GPELs), words are generally marked with an emotion (one or more labels) if there is a dominant sense of the word, and it has emotion semantics. In domain-specific emotion lexicons (DSELs), by contrast, assignment of an emotion label is based on the common sense of each term in a specific domain (Bandhakavi et al., 2017). For example, the noun "shot" in a DSEL tailored for *sports*, referring taking a shot at a goal, might be plausibly marked as (*shot*→ANTICIPATION|JOY), while in a medical DSEL, referring to a injection, might be marked as (*shot*→ANTICIPATION|FEAR). Similarly, the adjective "crazy" in sports might be marked according to the sense in the statement "that goal was crazy!" (*crazy*→JOY|SURPRISE) while in the behavioral domain, it might be (*crazy*→DISGUST|FEAR). Table 3 gives a small selection of NRC entries where each label is appropriate only in a limited context, not corresponding to the literal meaning of the word in its dominant sense. The extreme version of this problem can be seen with words like *abundance* which have a multitude of labels that conflict (DISGUST|JOY|TRUST|ANTICIPATION). Overall this is a problem with regards to NRC because it is explicitly presented as a GPEL. In our evaluation of the NRC, while again we did not count exactly how many entries suffered from this issue, we estimate at least 600 or so entries, or 10% of the NRC, fall into this category.

3.3 Simple Errors

The NRC has a large number of terms, and as with any resource of this size there are bound to be minor faults or errors. Since human annotators provided the data needed to create the resource, we can assume that certain terms were given labels that are not appropriate and that some small number of these errors would have escaped notice of any manual error correcting procedures. We define these sorts of errors as those where the provided emotional labels do not make sense in any context supported by Keyword-in-Context (KWIC) indicies (iWeb, 2021; Davies and Kim, 2019). Table 4 lists a small selection of examples of seemingly simple errors in labels, for example *architecture*→TRUST. Some markings, furthermore, might be reflective of relatively obvious biases, which in light of recent work demonstrating the built-in biases of various AI and NLP resources (Bolukbasi et al., 2016; Bender and Friedman, 2018; Mehrabi et al., 2019; Blodgett et al., 2020), it would be good to try to correct for. Examples of the latter case include the entries *fat*→DISGUST |SADNESS, *lesbian*→DISGUST|SADNESS, or *mosque*→ANGER. We estimate that the number of entries affected by simple errors or biases is at least a few hundred, or roughly 5% of the NRC.

3.4 Problems with the NRC Annotation Process

Some aspects of the NRC annotation process go part of the way toward explaining some of the above problems. As discussed by Mohammad and Turney (2013a), the annotation process relied upon approximately 2,000 native and fluent speakers of English who answered a series of questions regarding the emotion terms. The directions were made ambiguous on purpose to minimize biasing the subject's judgements. The concern with this method is that the annotators could have been shown a term that is not familiar to them. This was circumvented by asking the individual to associate the term with a certain word similar in meaning amongst three non-viable options.

After selecting the most similar word, the annotator could continue annotating even when they do not really know the meaning of a word. This could have happened by the annotator quickly looking up the definition online. The annotators were told not to look up the words[3], but there is no guarantee that they did so, and much work has shown that crowdworkers are often unreliable (Ipeirotis et al., 2010; Vuurens et al., 2011).

Another concern with the annotation process was question wording. Questions 4–11 in particular raise specific concerns. These asked, for all combinations of a term X and each of the eight emotions Y, "How much is X associated with the emotion

[3] Annotators were instructed "please skip HIT if you do not know the meaning of the word"

Word	POS	Original NRC Labels	First Sense in WordNet	Corrected Label
awful	RB	ANGER|DISGUST|FEAR|SADNESS	used as a verbal intensifier	NEUTRAL
belt	NN	ANGER|FEAR	endless loop of flexible material between two rotating shafts or pulleys	NEUTRAL
bias	JJ	ANGER	slanting diagonally across the grain of a fabric	NEUTRAL
bloody	RB	ANGER|DISGUST|FEAR|SADNESS	extremely	NEUTRAL
board	VB	ANTICIPATION	get on board of (trains, buses, ships, aircraft, etc.)	NEUTRAL
boil	VB	DISGUST	come to the boiling point and change from a liquid to vapor	NEUTRAL
buffet	NN	ANGER	a piece of furniture that stands at the side of a dining room; has shelves and drawers	NEUTRAL
bully	JJ	ANGER|FEAR	very good	SURPRISE|JOY
cage	NN	SADNESS	an enclosure made or wire or metal bars in which birds or animals can be kept	NEUTRAL
case	NN	FEAR|SADNESS	an occurrence of something	NEUTRAL
collateral	JJ	TRUST	descended from a common ancestor but through different lines	NEUTRAL
console	NN	SADNESS	a small table fixed to a wall or designed to stand against a wall	NEUTRAL
desert	NN	ANGER|DISGUST|FEAR|SADNESS	arid land with little or no vegetation	NEUTRAL
kind	NN	JOY|TRUST	a category of things distinguished by some common characteristic or quality	NEUTRAL
rail	NN	ANTICIPATION|ANGER	a barrier consisting of a horizontal bar and supports	NEUTRAL

Table 2: Examples of NRC terms paired with parts of speech (first two columns) whose emotional labels in NRC are inappropriate. The last column shows the proposed correction.

Term	NRC Labels	Term	NRC Labels
abundance	DISGUST|JOY |TRUST|ANTICIPATION	monk	TRUST
baby	JOY	oblige	TRUST
count	TRUST	recreation	JOY|ANTICIPATION
create	JOY	remedy	JOY
explain	TRUST	remove	ANGER|FEAR |SADNESS
fact	TRUST	saint	ANTICIPATION|JOY |TRUST|SURPRISE
fall	SADNESS	save	JOY
fee	ANGER	score	ANTICIPATION|JOY |SURPRISE
fire	FEAR	star	ANTICIPATION|JOY |TRUST
gain	JOY|ANTICIPATION	understand	TRUST
grow	ANTICIPATION|JOY|TRUST	unnatural	DISGUST|FEAR
larger	DISGUST|SURPRISE|TRUST		
leader	TRUST		
mate	TRUST		

Table 3: Examples of context dependency

Term	Labels	Term	Labels
abacus	TRUST	cabinet	TRUST
alb	TRUST	calculation	ANTICIPATION
ambulance	FEAR|TRUST	coyote	FEAR
ammonia	DISGUST	critter	DISGUST
anaconda	DISGUST|FEAR	crypt	FEAR|SADNESS
aphid	DISGUST	fat	DISGUST|SADNESS
archaeology	ANTICIPATION	fee	ANGER
architecture	TRUST	iron	TRUST
assembly	TRUST	lamb	JOY|TRUST
association	TRUST	mill	ANTICIPATION
asymmetry	DISGUST	mountain	ANTICIPATION
atherosclerosis	FEAR|SADNESS	mosque	ANGER
baboon	DISGUST	machine	TRUST
backbone	ANGER|TRUST	organ	ANTICIPATION|JOY
balm	ANTICIPATION|JOY	pine	SADNESS
basketball	ANTICIPATION|JOY	rack	SADNESS
bee	ANGER|FEAR	ravine	FEAR
belt	ANGER|FEAR	ribbon	ANTICIPATION|JOY |ANGER
bier	FEAR|SADNESS		
biopsy	FEAR	rod	TRUST |FEAR
birthplace	ANGER	spine	ANGER
blackness	FEAR|SADNESS	stone	ANGER
bran	DISGUST	title	TRUST
infant	ANTICIPATION |FEAR|JOY |SURPRISE	tree	ANTICIPATION|JOY |DISGUST|TRUST |SURPRISE|ANGER

Table 4: Examples of simple errors.

Y?" Posing this in only the positive formulation potentially biased annotators to find confirmatory evidence. A more balanced procedure would have been to ask annotators to imagine not only how much of emotion Y was associated X, but also how much Y *wasn't* associated with X, prompting them to consider disconfirmatory evidence. Because of this confirmation bias in the collection procedure we posit that many of the terms in the NRC were associated with particular emotions even when those terms do not bring those emotions to mind when mentioned in isolation in normal usage.

Another way of addressing this bias would have been to show words in specific contexts; this avoids the need for an annotator to think up their own evidence to support their label, which may have been limited by the annotators's time, attention, creativity, or knowledge of English usage. Such an approach would no doubt have been costlier, but it perhaps would have produced higher quality labels.

When it came to validating the NRC, the authors compared their crowdsourced labels with labels from the WNA lexicon to see how close the judgements were. In the one earlier paper (Mohammad and Turney, 2013a), when the NRC had 10,000 entries, the authors reported that only 6.5% of the entries could be matched with those in WNA. Later, when the NRC was expanded to 14,182 entries, the authors did not report the percentage overlap. We measured this ourselves, and found the overlap between the full NRC and WNA is 2,328 (16%). This is a concern because this means most of the data could not be independently validated to see how accurate the annotations were, and so a majority were not subject to any rigorous or systematic quality control check.

4 Semi-Automatic Correction of the NRC

The NRC includes 14,182 entries made up of a unigram (single token wordforms) associated with a

Term	Label	Term	Label	Term	Label
arm	NEUTRAL	diversity	NEUTRAL	office	NEUTRAL
buy	NEUTRAL	endpoint	NEUTRAL	road	NEUTRAL
carrier	NEUTRAL	flat	NEUTRAL	weather	NEUTRAL
clothes	NEUTRAL	filter	NEUTRAL	yeast	NEUTRAL

Table 5: Examples of neutral words

selection of Plutchik's emotions eight (SADNESS, JOY, FEAR, ANGER, SURPRISE, TRUST, DISGUST, and ANTICIPATION), NEUTRAL, and two sentiments; as noted, no words had part of speech tags. After removing 9,719 wordforms marked neutral, examples of which are shown in Table 5, 4,463 wordforms remained. In the remainder of the paper we refer to this set as `NRC.orig`. We developed a procedure to semi-automatically correct the problems discussed in prior section. First, we assigned part-of-speech tags to entries. Second, we developed an automatic emotional word test leveraging both the original version of WNA and the larger WordNet resource. Finally, we manually checked all entries for correctness.

4.1 Assigning Part of Speech to NRC words

We began by constructing an expanded list of wordforms in NRC, each associated with a valid part of speech (POS). To determine whether a POS applied to a wordform, we looking up each wordform in WordNet under each of the main open class POS tags—Verb (VB), Adjective (JJ), Noun (NN), and Adverb (RB)—so each wordform could potentially have been associated with up to four POS tags. Every wordform was present in WordNet under at least one POS. If a WordNet sense was found for a POS, we consider that a valid tags for the wordform. After this step, our list contained has 6,166 entries of wordform-POS pairs (4,463 unique wordforms). We call this set `NRC.v1`.

4.2 Emotional Word Test

In the second step, we sought to automatically determine, on the one hand, which wordform-POS pairs likely had an emotional sense (whether emotive or affective), and on the other, pairs for which we had no direct evidence of emotional semantics. To do this, we performed the following comparisons with WNA and WordNet—if any one returned true, the pair was presumed emotional; otherwise, it was marked "unknown".

1. Is the wordform-POS pair labeled as non-neutral in WNA?
2. Is the first sense of the wordform-POS pair have a synonym labeled as non-neutral in WNA?
3. Does the WordNet gloss of the first sense of the wordform-POS pair contain words that are marked as emotional in WNA?
    (a) Find the first sense in WordNet for the wordform-POS pair.
    (b) Tokenize the gloss of the first sense.
    (c) Lemmatize the gloss.
    (d) Check if the lemmas are labeled as non-neutral in WNA.

Tokenization and lemmatization were performed with `nltk` (Loper and Bird, 2002). The above procedure identified 2,328 out of 6,166 pairs as "presumed emotional", leaving 3,838 pairs as "unknown." In the rest of this paper, we will refer to the lexicon of 2,328 pairs "presumed affective" pairs as `NRC.v2`.

4.3 Manual Checking

With NRC entries now organized as to whether or not they are presumed emotional (according to WNA or WordNet), we proceeded to manually check all entries. We used WNA only to remove the emotion label of some NRC wordforms. Since the number of synsets in WNA is 2,328 and the number of wordforms in NRC.v1 is 6,166 there must exist many wordforms that are not associated to WNA synsets and therefore will fail the Emotional Word Test. We did not rely soly on WNA when correcting bias in NRC, as we manually annotated every wordform in `NRC.v1` regardless of its Emotional Word Test result. The first two authors of the paper performed the below checks on all 6,166 entries in `NRC.v1`. We used the Cohen's Kappa metric to assess inter-annotator agreement (Landis and Koch, 1977), which we measured as 0.928, which represents near-perfect agreement. Notably, this emotion annotation task has much higher agreement than the sentence-level annotation emotion tasks discussed in Section 2.3. We suspect that this is the case for at least three reasons. First, focusing on words is an easier because sentences often have complex emotion valence: there might multiple emotions in a sentence. Second, the NRC words that are retained at this stage are clearly emotional, they are selected to be such, and so are less emotionally ambiguous than neutral words: there are no borderline cases. Finally, we defined a clear set of procedures for identifying the emotion, which were

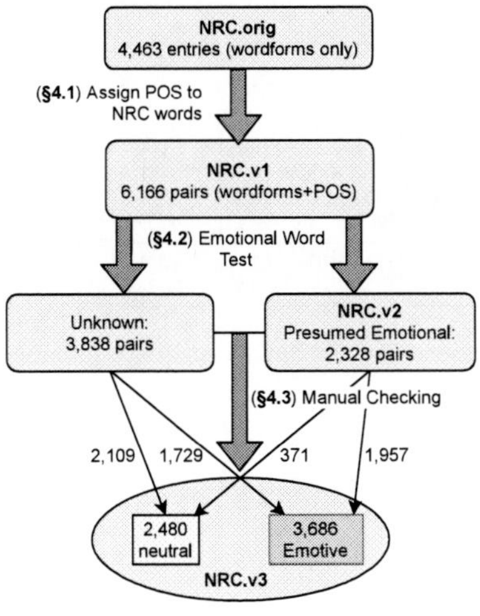

Figure 2: The semi-automatic procedure for correcting the NRC.

developed during several rounds of pilot annotation, following best practice in linguistic annotation.

- **Presumed Emotional:** For each wordform-POS pair, we examined the first sense in WordNet, any labels in WNA, and the labels in `NRC.orig` to determine if they were compatible, focusing on identified emotional words and synonyms. If there were disagreements between the WNA and `NRC.orig` we examined the Keyword-in-Context index for that POS. In cases where it was ambiguous whether `NRC.orig`, WNA, or WordNet was the correct analysis, we defaulted to `NRC.orig`. Out of 2,328 presumed emotional pairs, 1,957 were ultimately kept as having at least one emotion label.

- **Unknown:** Pairs in this group were distinguished from the Presumed Emotional group by the lack of obvious emotional words in the WordNet glosses of the pair or its synonyms. While we examined the WordNet entries for these pairs carefully, we spent more time examining the Keyword-in-Context index to look for emotional senses. Out of 3,838 unknown pairs, ultimately 1,729 were marked as having at least one emotion label.

Figure 2 shows the outline of the process to construct final, corrected version of the NRC, which we refer to as `NRC.v3` in the rest of the paper.

5 Evaluation of the Corrected Resource

In order to compare and evaluate the outcome of the correction procedure, we ran the emotion detection model developed by Zad and Finlayson (2020) using `NRC.v1`, `NRC.v2`, and `NRC.v3` as the emotion lexicon. We chose this model because the code was helpfully provided in full, and the model uses a single emotion lexicon with wordform-POS pairs to drive its emotion detection. In this section, we discuss the details of this comparison.

The emotion detection system of Zad and Finlayson originally used WNA as the emotion lexicon (leveraging wordform+POS pairs), and tested on Alm's fairy tale dataset (Alm, 2008). While the system is convenient as an experimental testbed because the full code is available, Alm's dataset uses only six emotions (ANGER, FEAR, SADNESS, SURPRISE, DISGUST, and JOY), as opposed to Plutchick's eight used by the NRC. This means we needed to trim our NRC versions down to six labels for compatibility (we dropped ANTICIPATION and TRUST). This makes the evaluation of the NRC using this experimental setup at best an approximation for the quality of our procedure. One would imagine that, if we had an experimental testbed that used all eight of Plutchik's emotions, performance would be correspondingly higher.

As described below, we also experimented with reducing the number of labels, following the experimental procedure outlined in Zad and Finlayson (2020). Further, following the same procedure, we conducted our emotion detection comparisons on the subset of Alm's dataset which represented "high agreement", namely, only sentences for which the annotators fully agreed with each other.

5.1 Comparing `NRC.v1`, `NRC.v2`, and `NRC.v3`

Table 6 shows the precision, recall and F_1 measurements of the emotion detection system when substituting the three different versions of the NRC in experimental setup for WNA, using just the six emotions present in Alm's data (dropping all the labels of ANTICIPATION and TRUST). The first three columns result gives a baseline for performance of what is effectively the original NRC in the Zad and Finlayson (2020) experimental setup.

The next two groups show `NRC.v2` and `NRC.v3`, respectively. As can be seen, overall micro-average performance rises from 0.435 for `NRC.v1` to 0.460 for `NRC.v2` and 0.484 for

	NRC.v1			NRC.v2			NRC.v3		
Emotion label	p	r	F_1	p	r	F_1	p	r	F_1
JOY	0.738	0.570	0.643	0.805	0.577	0.672	0.855	0.572	0.686
ANGER	0.359	0.253	0.297	0.347	0.226	0.274	0.432	0.240	0.308
SURPRISE	0.151	0.263	0.192	0.144	0.254	0.184	0.178	0.254	0.209
DISGUST	0.095	0.324	0.147	0.124	0.353	0.183	0.137	0.500	0.215
FEAR	0.407	0.212	0.279	0.589	0.200	0.299	0.535	0.327	0.406
SADNESS	0.632	0.417	0.502	0.661	0.473	0.552	0.717	0.451	0.553
macro-Avg.	0.397	0.340	0.343	0.445	0.347	0.361	0.476	0.391	**0.396**
micro-Avg.	0.466	0.408	0.435	0.510	0.418	0.460	0.545	0.435	**0.484**

Table 6: Result of using different, corrected versions of the NRC to the Zad and Finlayson (2020) emotion detection system on Alm's fairy tales.

	w SURPRISE			w/o SURPRISE			Avg.
	(1) w/ DISGUST	(2) w/o DISGUST	(3) DISGUST+ANGER	(4) w/ DISGUST	(5) w/o DISGUST	(6) DISGUST+ANGER	
NRC.v1	0.343	0.421	0.402	0.421	0.533	0.513	0.439
NRC.v2	0.361	0.439	0.429	0.451	0.573	0.551	0.467
NRC.v3	0.396	0.462	0.463	0.489	0.594	0.583	0.498
NRC.v1	0.435	0.481	0.461	0.545	0.603	0.577	**0.517**
NRC.v2	0.460	0.505	0.491	0.585	0.644	0.622	**0.551**
NRC.v3	0.484	0.520	0.517	0.607	0.655	0.637	**0.570**

Table 7: Comparing the macro-average (top three rows) and micro-average (bottom three rows) F_1-scores of using the three corrected versions of NRC with Zad and Finlayson's emotion detection system on Alm's fairy tales using different emotion label sets.

NRC.v3. This provides solid evidence that our correction procedure improved the quality of the resource.

While one might expect that the recall in Table 6 might strictly go down moving from NRC.v1 to NRC.v3, because we are removing terms, we are in fact correcting labels continuously in these revisions, which results in an improvement in recall and overall performance.

5.2 Varying the Label Sets

Alm's "high agreement" dataset only contains 148 sentences with DISGUST and SURPRISE labels, a highly imbalanced distribution. To investigate the impact of this imbalance on the results, we repeated the emotion detection experiment six times for each of the three version of the NRC, once for each of the reduced label sets shown in Table 7, which also shows how varying the label sets affects the performance of the emotion detection system for different version of the NRC. In all cases our corrected verisons of the NRC improve performance, anywhere from 5.3 to 7 points of F_1.

6 Contributions

We noted three categories of error in the popular NRC emotion lexicon, including a large number of seemingly biased entries. We developed and applied a semi-automatic procedure to generate three different corrected version of the NRC, and showed via experiment that these new versions improved the performance of an existing emotion-lexicon-based emotion detection system. This work shows the utility of careful error checking of lexical resources, especially with attention to correcting for unintended biases. Finally, we release the revised resource and our code to enable other researchers to reproduce and build upon results[4].

Acknowledgments

This material is based upon work supported by the U.S. Department of Homeland Security under Grant Award Number, 2017-ST-062-000002. The views and conclusions contained in this document are those of the authors and should not be interpreted as necessarily representing the official policies, either expressed or implied, of the U.S. Department of Homeland Security.

References

Amine Abdaoui, Jérôme Azé, Sandra Bringay, and Pascal Poncelet. 2017. Feel: a french expanded emotion lexicon. *Language Resources and Evaluation*, 51(3):833–855.

Francisca Adoma Acheampong, Chen Wenyu, and Henry Nunoo-Mensah. 2020. Text-based emotion detection: Advances, challenges, and opportunities. *Engineering Reports*, 2(7):e12189.

[4]https://doi.org/10.34703/gzx1-9v95/PO3YGX

Ameeta Agrawal and Aijun An. 2012. Unsupervised emotion detection from text using semantic and syntactic relations. In *Proceedings of the 2012 IEEE/WIC/ACM International Conferences on Web Intelligence and Intelligent Agent Technology*, volume 1, pages 346–353, Macau, China.

Samar Al-Saqqa, Heba Abdel-Nabi, and Arafat Awajan. 2018. A survey of textual emotion detection. In *2018 8th International Conference on Computer Science and Information Technology (CSIT)*, pages 136–142, Los Alamitos, CA.

Cecilia Ovesdotter Alm. 2010. Characteristics of high agreement affect annotation in text. In *Proceedings of the 4th Linguistic Annotation Workshop*, pages 118–122, Uppsala, Sweden.

Ebba Cecilia Ovesdotter Alm. 2008. *Affect in *Text and Speech*. Ph.D. thesis, University of Illinois at Urbana-Champaign, Urbana-Champaign, IL.

Saima Aman and Stan Szpakowicz. 2007. Identifying expressions of emotion in text. In *Proceedings of the 10th International Conference on Text, Speech and Dialogue (TSD)*, pages 196–205, Pilsen, Czech Republic.

Oscar Araque, Lorenzo Gatti, Jacopo Staiano, and Marco Guerini. 2019. DepecheMood++: A bilingual emotion lexicon built through simple yet powerful techniques. *IEEE Transactions on Affective Computing*, pages 1–1.

Anil Bandhakavi, Nirmalie Wiratunga, Deepak Padmanabhan, and Stewart Massie. 2017. Lexicon based feature extraction for emotion text classification. *Pattern Recognition Letters*, 93:133–142.

Emily M Bender and Batya Friedman. 2018. Data statements for natural language processing: Toward mitigating system bias and enabling better science. *Transactions of the Association for Computational Linguistics*, 6:587–604.

J. Bernard, editor. 1986. *The Macquarie Thesaurus*. Macquarie Library, Sydney, Australia.

Su Lin Blodgett, Solon Barocas, Hal Daumé III, and Hanna Wallach. 2020. Language (technology) is power: A critical survey of" bias" in nlp. *arXiv preprint arXiv:2005.14050*.

Tolga Bolukbasi, Kai-Wei Chang, James Zou, Venkatesh Saligrama, and Adam Kalai. 2016. Man is to computer programmer as woman is to homemaker? debiasing word embeddings. *arXiv preprint arXiv:1607.06520*.

Erik Cambria. 2016. Affective computing and sentiment analysis. *IEEE Intelligent Systems*, 31(2):102–107.

Erik Cambria, Andrew Livingstone, and Amir Hussain. 2012. The hourglass of emotions. In Anna Esposito, Antonietta M. Esposito, Alessandro Vinciarelli, Rüdiger Hoffmann, and Vincent Müller, editors, *Cognitive Behavioural Systems*, pages 144–157. Springer, Berlin. Published as Volume 7403, Lecture Notes in Computer Science (LNCS).

Taner Danisman and Adil Alpkocak. 2008. Feeler: Emotion classification of text using vector space model. In *Proceedings of the AISB 2008 Symposium on Affective Language in Human and Machine*, volume 1, page 53, Aberdeen, Scotland.

Mark Davies and Jong-Bok Kim. 2019. The advantages and challenges of "big data": Insights from the 14 billion word iWeb corpus. *Linguistic Research*, 36(1):1–34.

Paul Ekman. 1992. An argument for basic emotions. *Cognition & Emotion*, 6(3-4):169–200.

Christiane Fellbaum. 1998. Towards a representation of idioms in wordnet. In *Proceedings of the Workshop on the Use of WordNet in Natural Language Processing Systems*, pages 52–57, Montreal, Canada.

Johnny RJ Fontaine, Klaus R Scherer, Etienne B Roesch, and Phoebe C Ellsworth. 2007. The world of emotions is not two-dimensional. *Psychological Science*, 18(12):1050–1057.

Jeffrey T Hancock, Christopher Landrigan, and Courtney Silver. 2007. Expressing emotion in text-based communication. In *Proceedings of the SIGCHI conference on Human factors in computing systems*, pages 929–932, San Jose, CA.

Panagiotis G Ipeirotis, Foster Provost, and Jing Wang. 2010. Quality management on amazon mechanical turk. In *Proceedings of the ACM SIGKDD workshop on human computation*, pages 64–67, Washington, DC.

iWeb. 2021. The iWeb Corpus. `https://www.english-corpora.org/iweb/`. Last accessed on April 25, 2021.

Carroll E Izard. 2007. Basic emotions, natural kinds, emotion schemas, and a new paradigm. *Perspectives on Psychological Science*, 2(3):260–280.

Ema Kušen, Giuseppe Cascavilla, Kathrin Figl, Mauro Conti, and Mark Strembeck. 2017. Identifying emotions in social media: Comparison of word-emotion lexicons. In *Proceeedings of the 5th International Conference on Future Internet of Things and Cloud (FiCloud)*, pages 132–137, Prague, Czech Republic.

J Richard Landis and Gary G Koch. 1977. The measurement of observer agreement for categorical data. *Biometrics*, 33(1):159–174.

Young-Jun Lee, Chan-Yong Park, and Ho-Jin Choi. 2019. Word-level emotion embedding based on semi-supervised learning for emotional classification in dialogue. In *Proceedings of the IEEE International Conference on Big Data and Smart Computing (BigComp)*, pages 1–4, Kyoto, Japan.

Nikola Ljubešić, Ilia Markov, Darja Fišer, and Walter Daelemans. 2020. The lilah emotion lexicon of croatian, dutch and slovene. In *Proceedings of the 3rd Workshop on Computational Modeling of People's Opinions, Personality, and Emotion's in Social Media*, pages 153–157, Barcelona, Spain (Online).

Edward Loper and Steven Bird. 2002. Nltk: The natural language toolkit. *arXiv preprint cs/0205028*.

Hugo Lövheim. 2012. A new three-dimensional model for emotions and monoamine neurotransmitters. *Medical Hypotheses*, 78(2):341–348.

Gerardo Maupome and Olga Isyutina. 2013. Dental students' and faculty members' concepts and emotions associated with a caries risk assessment program. *Journal of Dental Education*, 77(11):1477–1487.

Ninareh Mehrabi, Fred Morstatter, Nripsuta Saxena, Kristina Lerman, and Aram Galstyan. 2019. A survey on bias and fairness in machine learning. *arXiv preprint arXiv:1908.09635*.

Jean-Baptiste Michel, Yuan Kui Shen, Aviva Presser Aiden, Adrian Veres, Matthew K Gray, Joseph P Pickett, Dale Hoiberg, Dan Clancy, Peter Norvig, Jon Orwant, et al. 2011. Quantitative analysis of culture using millions of digitized books. *Science*, 331(6014):176–182.

Saif Mohammad. 2012. # emotional tweets. In *Proceedings of the 1st Joint Conference on Lexical and Computational Semantics (*SEM)*, pages 246–255, Montreal, Canada.

Saif Mohammad and Peter Turney. 2010. Emotions evoked by common words and phrases: Using mechanical turk to create an emotion lexicon. In *Proceedings of the NAACL HLT 2010 workshop on computational approaches to analysis and generation of emotion in text*, pages 26–34, Los Angeles, CA.

Saif M Mohammad and Svetlana Kiritchenko. 2015. Using hashtags to capture fine emotion categories from tweets. *Computational Intelligence*, 31(2):301–326.

Saif M Mohammad and Peter D Turney. 2013a. Crowdsourcing a word–emotion association lexicon. *Computational intelligence*, 29(3):436–465.

Saif M Mohammad and Peter D Turney. 2013b. Nrc emotion lexicon. *National Research Council, Canada*, 2.

Keith Oatley and Philip N Johnson-Laird. 1987. Towards a cognitive theory of emotions. *Cognition and Emotion*, 1(1):29–50.

Andrew Ortony, Gerald L Clore, and Allan Collins. 1990. *The Cognitive Structure of Emotions*. Cambridge University Press, Cambridge, UK.

Jaak Panksepp, Brian Knutson, and Douglas L Pruitt. 1998. Toward a neuroscience of emotion. In Michael F. Mascolo and Sharon Griffin, editors, *What develops in emotional development?*, pages 53–84. Springer, Berlin, Germany.

W Gerrod Parrott. 2001. *Emotions in Social Psychology: Essential Readings*. Psychology Press, London.

James W Pennebaker, Roger J Booth, and Martha E Francis. 2007. Linguistic inquiry and word count: LIWC [computer software].

James W Pennebaker, Martha E Francis, and Roger J Booth. 2001. Linguistic inquiry and word count: LIWC 2001 [computer software].

Robert Plutchik. 1980. A general psychoevolutionary theory of emotion. In Robert Plutchik, editor, *Theories of Emotion*, pages 3–33. Elsevier, Amsterdam, The Netherlands.

Robert Plutchik. 1984. Emotions and imagery. *Journal of Mental Imagery*, 8:105–111.

Robert Plutchik. 2001. The nature of emotions: Human emotions have deep evolutionary roots, a fact that may explain their complexity and provide tools for clinical practice. *American Scientist*, 89(4):344–350.

Robert Ed Plutchik and Hope R Conte. 1997. *Circumplex Models of Personality and Emotions*. American Psychological Association, Washington, DC.

S Lovelyn Rose, R Venkatesan, Girish Pasupathy, and P Swaradh. 2018. A lexicon-based term weighting scheme for emotion identification of tweets. *International Journal of Data Analysis Techniques and Strategies*, 10(4):369–380.

Sara Rosenthal, Noura Farra, and Preslav Nakov. 2019. Semeval-2017 task 4: Sentiment analysis in twitter. *arXiv preprint arXiv:1912.00741*.

James A Russell. 1980. A circumplex model of affect. *Journal of Personality and Social Psychology*, 39(6):1161–1178.

Kashfia Sailunaz, Manmeet Dhaliwal, Jon Rokne, and Reda Alhajj. 2018. Emotion detection from text and speech: a survey. *Social Network Analysis and Mining*, 8(1):1–26.

Klaus R Scherer. 2005. What are emotions? and how can they be measured? *Social Science Information*, 44(4):695–729.

Klaus R Scherer and Harald G Wallbott. 1994. Evidence for universality and cultural variation of differential emotion response patterning. *Journal of Personality and Social Psychology*, 66(2):310.

Phillip Shaver, Judith Schwartz, Donald Kirson, and Cary O'connor. 1987. Emotion knowledge: Further exploration of a prototype approach. *Journal of Personality and Social Psychology*, 52(6):1061–1086.

Jacopo Staiano and Marco Guerini. 2014. DepecheMood: A lexicon for emotion analysis from crowd-annotated news. *arXiv preprint arXiv:1405.1605*.

Philip James Stone, Dexter Colboyd Dunphy, Daniel M Ogilvie, and Marshall S Smith. 1966. *The General Inquirer: a Computer Approach to Content Analysis*. MIT Press, Cambridge, MA.

Carlo Strapparava and Alessandro Valitutti. 2004. Wordnet affect: An affective extension of wordnet. In *Proceedings of the 4th International Conference on Language Resources and Evaluation (LREC)*, pages 1083–1086, Lisbon, Portugal.

Feride Savaroğlu Tabak and Vesile Evrim. 2016. Comparison of emotion lexicons. In *Proceedings of the 13th Interntaional Symposium on Smart Microgrids for Sustainable Energy Sources Enabled by Photonics and IoT Sensors (HONET-ICT)*, pages 154–158, Nicosia, Cyprus.

Jeroen Vuurens, Arjen P de Vries, and Carsten Eickhoff. 2011. How much spam can you take? an analysis of crowdsourcing results to increase accuracy. In *Proceedings of the ACM SIGIR Workshop on Crowdsourcing for Information Retrieval (CIR'11)*, pages 21–26, Beijing, China.

Ali Yadollahi, Ameneh Gholipour Shahraki, and Osmar R Zaiane. 2017. Current state of text sentiment analysis from opinion to emotion mining. *ACM Computing Surveys (CSUR)*, 50(2):1–33.

Samira Zad and Mark Finlayson. 2020. Systematic evaluation of a framework for unsupervised emotion recognition for narrative text. In *Proceedings of the 1st Joint Workshop on Narrative Understanding, Storylines, and Events*, pages 26–37, Online.

Samira Zad, Maryam Heidari, James H Jr Jones, and Ozlem Uzuner. 2021. Emotion detection of textual data: An interdisciplinary survey. In *Proceedings of the IEEE World AI IoT Congress (AIIoT 2021)*, Seattle, WA.

Mitigating Biases in Toxic Language Detection through Invariant Rationalization

Yung-Sung Chuang[1,2] **Mingye Gao**[2] **Hongyin Luo**[2]
James Glass[2] **Hung-yi Lee**[1] **Yun-Nung Chen**[1] **Shang-Wen Li**[3*]
[1]National Taiwan University, [2]MIT CSAIL, [3]Amazon AI
{yungsung, mingye, hyluo, glass}@mit.edu,
hungyilee@ntu.edu.tw, y.v.chen@ieee.org, shangwel@amazon.com

Abstract

Automatic detection of toxic language plays an essential role in protecting social media users, especially minority groups, from verbal abuse. However, biases toward some attributes, including gender, race, and dialect, exist in most training datasets for toxicity detection. The biases make the learned models unfair and can even exacerbate the marginalization of people. Considering that current debiasing methods for general natural language understanding tasks cannot effectively mitigate the biases in the toxicity detectors, we propose to use invariant rationalization (INVRAT), a game-theoretic framework consisting of a rationale generator and predictors, to rule out the spurious correlation of certain syntactic patterns (e.g., identity mentions, dialect) to toxicity labels. We empirically show that our method yields lower false positive rate in both lexical and dialectal attributes than previous debiasing methods.[1]

1 Introduction

As social media becomes more and more popular in recent years, many users, especially the minority groups, suffer from verbal abuse and assault. To protect these users from online harassment, it is necessary to develop a tool that can automatically detect the toxic language in social media. In fact, many toxic language detection (TLD) systems have been proposed in these years based on different models, such as support vector machines (SVM) (Gaydhani et al., 2018), bi-directional long short-term memory (BiLSTM) (Bojkovský and Pikuliak, 2019), logistic regression (Davidson et al., 2017) and fine-tuning BERT (d'Sa et al., 2020).

However, the existing TLD systems exhibit some problematic and discriminatory behaviors (Zhou et al., 2021). Experiments show that the tweets containing certain surface markers, such as identity terms and expressions in African American English (AAE), are more likely to be classified as hate speech by the current TLD systems (Davidson et al., 2017; Xia et al., 2020), although some of them are not actually hateful. Such an issue is predominantly attributed to the biases in training datasets for the TLD models; when the models are trained on the biased datasets, these biases are inherited by the models and further exacerbated during the learning process (Zhou et al., 2021). The biases in TLD systems can make the opinions from the members of minority groups more likely to be removed by the online platform, which may significantly hinder their experience as well as exacerbate the discrimination against them in real life.

So far, many debiasing methods have been developed to mitigate biases in learned models, such as data re-balancing (Dixon et al., 2018), residual fitting (He et al., 2019; Clark et al., 2019), adversarial training (Xia et al., 2020) and data filtering approach (Bras et al., 2020; Zhou et al., 2021). While most of these works are successful on other natural language processing (NLP) tasks, their performance on debasing the TLD tasks are unsatisfactory (Zhou et al., 2021). A possible reason is that the toxicity of language is more subjective and nuanced than general NLP tasks that often have unequivocally correct labels (Zhou et al., 2021). As current debiasing techniques reduce the biased behaviors of models by correcting the training data or measuring the difficulty of modeling them, which prevents models from capturing spurious and non-linguistic correlation between input texts and labels, the nuance of toxicity annotation can make such techniques insufficient for the TLD task.

In this paper, we address the challenge by combining the TLD classifier with the selective rationalization method, which is widely used to inter-

* Work is not related to employment at Amazon.

[1]The source code is available at https://github.com/voidism/invrat_debias.

Proceedings of the Fifth Workshop on Online Abuse and Harms, pages 114–120
August 6, 2021.

pret the predictions of complex neural networks. Specifically, we use the framework of Invariant Rationalization (INVRAT) (Chang et al., 2020) to rule out the syntactic and semantic patterns in input texts that are highly but spuriously correlated with the toxicity label, and mask such parts during inference. Experimental results show that INVRAT successfully reduce the lexical and dialectal biases in the TLD model with little compromise on overall performance. Our method avoids superficial correlation at the level of syntax and semantics, and makes the toxicity detector learn to use generalizable features for prediction, thus effectively reducing the impact of dataset biases and yielding a fair TLD model.

2 Previous works

Debiasing the TLD Task Researchers have proposed a range of debiasing methods for the TLD task. Some of them try to mitigate the biases by processing the training dataset. For example, Dixon et al. (2018) add additional non-toxic examples containing the identity terms highly correlated to toxicity to balance their distribution in the training dataset. Park et al. (2018) use the combination of debiased *word2vec* and gender swap data augmentation to reduce the gender bias in TLD task. Badjatiya et al. (2019) apply the strategy of replacing the bias sensitive words (BSW) in training data based on multiple knowledge generalization.

Some researchers pay more attention to modifying the models and learning less biased features. Xia et al. (2020) use adversarial training to reduce the tendency of the TLD system to misclassify the AAE texts as toxic speech. Mozafari et al. (2020) propose a novel re-weighting mechanism to alleviate the racial bias in English tweets. Vaidya et al. (2020) implement a multi-task learning framework with an attention layer to prevent the model from picking up the spurious correlation between the certain trigger-words and toxicity labels.

Debiasing Other NLP Task There are many methods proposed to mitigate the biases in NLP tasks other than TLD. Clark et al. (2019) train a robust classifier in an ensemble with a bias-only model to learn the more generalizable patterns in training dataset, which are difficult to be learned by the naive bias-only model. Bras et al. (2020) develop AFLITE, an iterative greedy algorithm that can adversarially filter the biases from the training dataset, as well as the framework to support it. Utama et al. (2020) introduce a novel approach of regularizing the confidence of models on the biased examples, which successfully makes the models perform well on both in-distribution and out-of-distribution data.

3 Invariant Rationalization

3.1 Basic Formulation for Rationalization

We propose TLD debiasing based on INVRAT in this paper. The goal of rationalization is to find a subset of inputs that 1) suffices to yield the same outcome 2) is human interpretable. Normally, we would prefer to find rationale in unsupervised ways because the lack of such annotations in the data. A typical formulation to find rationale is as following: Given the input-output pairs $(\boldsymbol{X}, Y)$ from a text classification dataset, we use a classifier f to predict the labels $f(\boldsymbol{X})$. To extract the rationale here, an intermediate rationale generator g is introduced to find a rationale $\boldsymbol{Z} = g(\boldsymbol{X})$, a masked version of X that can be used to predict the output Y, i.e. maximize mutual information between $\boldsymbol{Z}$ and Y.[2]

$$\max_{\boldsymbol{m} \in \mathcal{S}} I(Y; \boldsymbol{Z}) \quad \text{s.t. } \boldsymbol{Z} = \boldsymbol{m} \odot \boldsymbol{X} \tag{1}$$

Regularization loss $\mathcal{L}_{\text{reg}}$ is often applied to keep the rationale sparse and contiguous:

$$\mathcal{L}_{\text{reg}} = \lambda_1 \left| \frac{1}{N} \mathbb{E}\left[\|\boldsymbol{m}\|_1\right] - \alpha \right| + \lambda_2 \mathbb{E}\left[\sum_{n=2}^{N} |m_n - m_{n-1}| \right] \tag{2}$$

3.2 The INVRAT Framework

INVRAT (Chang et al., 2020) introduces the idea of *environment* to rationalization. We assume that the data are collected from different environments with different prior distributions. Among these environments, the predictive power of spurious correlated features will be variant, while the genuine causal explanations always have invariant predictive power to Y. Thus, the desired rationale should satisfy the following invariant constraint:

$$H(Y|\boldsymbol{Z}, E) = H(Y|\boldsymbol{Z}), \tag{3}$$

where E is the given environment and H is the cross-entropy between the prediction and the ground truth Y. We can use a three-player framework to find the solution for the above equation: an environment-agnostic predictor $f_i(\boldsymbol{Z})$, an environment-aware predictor $f_e(\boldsymbol{Z}, E)$, and a rationale generator $g(\boldsymbol{X})$. The learning objective of the two predictors are:

[2] Real examples of $\boldsymbol{X}, \boldsymbol{Z}$ can be found in Table 2.

$$\mathcal{L}_i^* = \min_{f_i(\cdot)} \mathbb{E}\left[\mathcal{L}\left(Y; f_i(\boldsymbol{Z})\right)\right] \quad (4)$$

$$\mathcal{L}_e^* = \min_{f_e(\cdot,\cdot)} \mathbb{E}\left[\mathcal{L}\left(Y; f_e(\boldsymbol{Z}, E)\right)\right] \quad (5)$$

In addition to minimizing the invariant prediction loss $\mathcal{L}_i^*$ and the regularization loss $\mathcal{L}_{\text{reg}}$, the other objective of the rationale generator is to minimize the gap between $\mathcal{L}_i^*$ and $\mathcal{L}_e^*$, that is:

$$\min_{g(\cdot)} \mathcal{L}_i^* + \mathcal{L}_{\text{reg}} + \lambda_{\text{diff}} \cdot \text{ReLU}\left(\mathcal{L}_i^* - \mathcal{L}_e^*\right), \quad (6)$$

where ReLU is applied to prevent the penalty when $\mathcal{L}_i^*$ has been lower than $\mathcal{L}_e^*$.

4 INVRAT for TLD Debiasing

4.1 TLD Dataset and its Biases

We apply INVRAT to debiasing TLD task. For clarity, we seed our following description with a specific TLD dataset where we conducted experiment on, hate speech in Twitter created by Founta et al. (2018) and modified by Zhou et al. (2021), and we will show how to generalize our approach. The dataset contains 32K toxic and 54K non-toxic tweets. Following works done by Zhou et al. (2021), we focus on two types of biases in the dataset: lexical biases and dialectal biases. Lexical biases contain the spurious correlation of toxic language with attributes including Non-offensive minority identity (NOI), Offensive minority identity (OI), and Offensive non-identity (ONI); dialectal biases are relating African-American English (AAE) attribute directly to toxicity. All these attributes are tagged at the document level. We provide more details for the four attributes (NOI, OI, ONI, and AAE) in Appendix A.

4.2 Use INVRAT for Debiasing

We directly use the lexical and dialectal attributes as the environments in INVRAT for debiasing TLD[3]. Under these different environments, the predictive power of spurious correlation between original input texts $\boldsymbol{X}$ and output labels $\boldsymbol{Y}$ will change. Thus, in INVRAT, the rationale generator will learn to exclude the biased phrases that are spurious correlated to toxicity labels from the rationale $\boldsymbol{Z}$. On the other hand, the predictive power for the genuine linguistic clues will be generalizable across environments, so the rationale generator attempts to keep them in the rationale $\boldsymbol{Z}$.

[3]To generalize our method for any other attributes or datasets, one can simply map environments to the attributes in consideration for debiasing.

Since there is no human labeling for the attributes in the original dataset, we infer the labels following Zhou et al. (2021). We match $\boldsymbol{X}$ with TOXTRIG, a handcrafted word bank collected for NOI, OI, and ONI; for dialectal biases, we use the topic model from Blodgett et al. (2016) to classify $\boldsymbol{X}$ into four dialects: AAE, white-aligned English (WAE), Hispanic, and other.

We build two debiasing variants with the obtained attribute labels, INVRAT (lexical) and INVRAT (dialect). The former is learned with the compound loss function in Equation (6) and four lexical-related environment subsets (NOI, OI, ONI, and none of the above); we train the latter using the same loss function but along with four dialectal environments (AAE, WAE, Hispanic, and other). In both variants, the learned $f_i(\boldsymbol{Z})$ is our environment-agnostic TLD predictor that classifies toxic languages based on generalizable clues. Also, in the INVRAT framework, the environment-aware predictor $f_e(\boldsymbol{Z}, E)$ needs to access the environment information. We use an additional embedding layer Emb_{env} to embed the environment id e into a n-dimensional vector $\text{Emb}_{\text{env}}(e)$, where n is the input dimension of the pretrained language model. Word embeddings and $\text{Emb}_{\text{env}}(e)$ are summed to construct the input representation for f_e.

5 Experiment

5.1 Experiment Settings

We leverage RoBERTa-base (Liu et al., 2019) as the backbone of our TLD models in experiments. F_1 scores and false positive rate (FPR) when specific attributes exist in texts are used to quantify TLD and debiasing performance, respectively. The positive label is "toxic" and the negative label is "non-toxic" for computing F_1 scores. When evaluating models debiased by INVRAT, we use the following strategy to balance F_1 and FPR, and have a stable performance measurement. We first select all checkpoints with F_1 scores no less than the best TLD performance in dev set by 3%. Then, we pick the checkpoint with the lowest dev set FPR among these selected ones to evaluate on the test set. We describe more training details and used hyperparameters in Appendix B.

5.2 Quantitative Debiasing Results

In the left four columns of Table 1, we show the F_1 scores and FPR in the entire dataset and in the NOI, OI, and ONI attributes for measuring lexical

		Test	NOI		OI		ONI		AAE	
		$F_1 \uparrow$	$F_1 \uparrow$	FPR $\downarrow$	$F_1 \uparrow$	FPR $\downarrow$	$F_1 \uparrow$	FPR $\downarrow$	$F_1 \uparrow$	FPR $\downarrow$
	Vanilla	$92.3_{0.0}$	$89.8_{0.3}$	$10.2_{1.3}$	$98.8_{0.1}$	$85.7_{0.0}$	$97.3_{0.1}$	$64.7_{0.8}$	$92.3_{0.0}$	$16.8_{0.3}$
	LMIXIN-ONI	$85.6_{2.5}$	$87.0_{1.1}$	$14.0_{1.5}$	$98.9_{0.0}$	$85.7_{0.0}$	$87.9_{4.5}$	$\mathbf{43.7}_{3.1}$	-	-
	LMIXIN-TOXTRIG	$86.9_{1.1}$	$85.5_{0.3}$	$11.2_{1.7}$	$97.6_{0.3}$	$\mathbf{71.4}_{0.0}$	$90.4_{1.8}$	$44.5_{1.5}$	-	-
	LMIXIN-AAE	-	-	-	-	-	-	-	$92.3_{0.1}$	$16.1_{0.4}$
33% train	Random	$92.2_{0.1}$	$89.5_{0.4}$	$9.3_{0.7}$	$\mathbf{98.9}_{0.0}$	$\mathbf{83.3}_{3.4}$	$97.4_{0.1}$	$67.2_{0.6}$	$92.2_{0.1}$	$16.7_{0.6}$
33% train	AFLite	$91.9_{0.1}$	$\mathbf{90.2}_{0.4}$	$11.3_{1.1}$	$98.9_{0.0}$	$85.7_{0.0}$	$97.3_{0.1}$	$68.0_{3.4}$	$91.9_{0.1}$	$16.8_{0.8}$
33% train	DataMaps-Ambig.	$92.5_{0.1}$	$89.2_{0.7}$	$7.4_{1.0}$	$98.9_{0.0}$	$85.7_{0.0}$	$\mathbf{97.5}_{0.0}$	$64.4_{1.4}$	$92.5_{0.1}$	$16.0_{0.4}$
33% train	DataMaps-Hard	$\mathbf{92.6}_{0.1}$	$89.5_{0.4}$	$6.3_{0.9}$	$98.8_{0.0}$	$85.7_{0.0}$	$97.4_{0.0}$	$62.0_{1.1}$	$\mathbf{92.6}_{0.1}$	$\mathbf{13.7}_{0.2}$
33% train	DataMaps-Easy	$91.9_{0.2}$	$86.8_{0.6}$	$\mathbf{5.9}_{0.7}$	$98.9_{0.0}$	$\mathbf{83.3}_{3.4}$	$97.2_{0.1}$	$\mathbf{60.3}_{3.8}$	$91.9_{0.2}$	$19.5_{2.8}$
Ours (RoBERTa-base)										
	Vanilla	$\mathbf{91.7}_{0.1}$	$\mathbf{90.1}_{0.3}$	$8.4_{0.4}$	$\mathbf{98.6}_{0.0}$	$81.0_{3.4}$	$97.0_{0.0}$	$63.4_{1.4}$	$\mathbf{95.9}_{0.2}$	$16.9_{1.0}$
	lexical removal	$90.9_{0.0}$	$86.0_{0.7}$	$18.3_{1.5}$	$98.1_{0.1}$	$78.6_{0.0}$	$96.4_{0.0}$	$61.7_{0.2}$	$95.1_{0.1}$	$18.7_{0.6}$
	InvRat (lexical)	$91.0_{0.5}$	$85.5_{1.6}$	$\mathbf{3.4}_{0.6}$	$97.5_{1.0}$	$76.2_{3.4}$	$\mathbf{97.2}_{0.2}$	$61.1_{1.5}$	$95.0_{0.5}$	$19.6_{1.0}$
	InvRat (dialect)	$91.0_{0.1}$	$85.9_{0.7}$	$\mathbf{3.4}_{0.5}$	$97.6_{0.5}$	$\mathbf{71.4}_{5.8}$	$97.1_{0.1}$	$\mathbf{57.9}_{2.2}$	$93.1_{1.0}$	$\mathbf{14.0}_{1.2}$

Table 1: Evaluation of all debiasing methods on the Founta et al. (2018) test set. We show the mean and s.d. (subscript) of F_1 and FPR across 3 runs. The top two sections contain the scores reported in Zhou et al. (2021). The bottom section contains scores of our methods. When FPR is lower, the model is less biased by lexical associations for toxicity. We used RoBERTa-base, while RoBERTa-large is used in Zhou et al. (2021). Thus, our Vanilla F_1 score is slightly lower than that of Zhou et al. (2021) by 0.5%.

bias. In addition to Vanilla, we include *lexical removal*, a naive baseline that simply removes all words existing in TOXTRIG before training and testing.

For our INVRAT (lexical/dialect) model, we can see a significant reduction in the FPR of NOI, OI, and ONI over Vanilla (RoBERTa without debiasing). Our approach also yields consistent and usually more considerable bias reduction in all three attributes, compared to the ensemble and data filtering debiasing baselines discussed in Zhou et al. (2021), where no approach improves in more than two attributes (e.g., LMIXIN-ONI reduces bias in ONI but not the rest two; DataMaps-Easy improves in NOI and ONI but has similar FPR to Vanilla in OI). The result suggests that INVRAT can effectively remove the spurious correlation between mentioning words in three lexical attributes and toxicity. Moreover, our INVRAT debiasing sacrifices little TLD performance[4], which can sometimes be a concern for debiasing (e.g., the overall performance of LMIXIN). It is worth noting that the lexical removal baseline does not get as much bias reduction as our method, even inducing more bias in NOI. We surmise that the weak result arises from the limitation of TOXTRIG, since a word bank cannot enumerate all biased words, and there are always other terms that can carry the bias to the model.

We summarize the debiasing results for the dialectal attribute in the rightmost column of Table 1. Compared with the Vanilla model, our method effectively reduces the FPR of AAE, suggesting the consistent benefit of INVRAT in debiasing dialect biases. Although the results from data relabeling (Zhou et al., 2021) and some data filtering approaches are better than INVRAT, these approaches are complementary to INVRAT, and combining them presumably improves debiasing performance.

5.3 Qualitative Study

We demonstrate how INVRAT removes biases and keeps detectors focusing on genuine toxic clues by showing examples of generated rationales in Table 2. Part (a) of Table 2 shows two utterances where both the baseline and our INVRAT debiasing predict the correct labels. We can see that when toxic terms appear in the sentence, the rationale generator will capture them. In part (b), we show three examples where the baseline model incorrectly predicts the sentences as toxic, presumably due to some biased but not toxic words (depend on the context) like *#sexlife, Shits, bullshit*. However, our rationale generator rules out these words and allows the TLD model to focus on main verbs in the sentences like *keeps, blame, have*. In part (c), we show some examples that our INVRAT model

[4]There is some degradation in NOI, which may result from some performance fluctuation in the small dataset and the labeling issues mentioned in Zhou et al. (2021). We see the degradation as an opportunity for future dive deep rather than concerns.

		Gold	Vanilla	Ours
(a)	Oh my **god** there's a **f**king** STINKBUG and it's **in my ASS**	⚠	⚠	⚠
	@user yes I hear that it's **great** for a relationship to try and change your partner..	✌	✌	✌
(b)	Other than #kids, what **keeps** you from the #sexlife you want?	✌	⚠	✌
	Shits crazy but bet they'll **blame** us... wait for it	✌	⚠	✌
	@user @user You don't **have** to pay for their bullshit read your rights read the law I don't pay fo...	✌	⚠	✌
(c)	RT @user: my ex so ugly to me now like...i'll **beat** that hoe ass	⚠	⚠	✌
	@user **Stop** that, it's not your **fault** a scumbag decided to steal otems which were obviously meant for someone i...	⚠	⚠	✌
(d)	A shark washed up in the street after a cyclone in Australia	✌	✌	✌

Table 2: Examples from the test set with the predictions from vanilla and our models. ⚠ denotes toxic labels, and ✌ denotes non-toxic labels. The underlined words are selected as the rationale by our ratinoale generator.

fails to generate the true answer, while the baseline model can do it correctly. In these two examples, we observe that our rationale generator remove the offensive words, probably due to the small degree of toxicity, while the annotator marked them as toxic sentences. Part (d) of Table 2 shows another common case that when the sentence can be easily classified as non-toxic, the rationale generator tends not to output any words, and the TLD model will output non-toxic label. It is probably caused by the non-stable predictive power of these non-toxic words (they are *variant*), so the rationale generator choose to rule them out and keep rationale clean and invariant.

6 Conclusion

In this paper, we propose to use INVRAT to reduce the biases in the TLD models effectively. By separately using lexical and dialectal attributes as the environments in INVRAT framework, the rationale generator can learn to generate genuine linguistic clues and rule out spurious correlations. Experimental results show that our method can better mitigate both lexical and dialectal biases without sacrificing much overall accuracy. Furthermore, our method does not rely on complicated data filtering or relabeling process, so it can be applied to new datasets without much effort, showing the potential of being applied to practical scenarios.

References

Pinkesh Badjatiya, Manish Gupta, and Vasudeva Varma. 2019. Stereotypical bias removal for hate speech detection task using knowledge-based generalizations. In *The World Wide Web Conference*, pages 49–59.

Su Lin Blodgett, Lisa Green, and Brendan O'Connor. 2016. Demographic dialectal variation in social media: A case study of african-american english. In *Proceedings of the 2016 Conference on Empirical Methods in Natural Language Processing*, pages 1119–1130.

Michal Bojkovský and Matúš Pikuliak. 2019. Stufiit at semeval-2019 task 5: Multilingual hate speech detection on twitter with muse and elmo embeddings. In *Proceedings of the 13th International Workshop on Semantic Evaluation*, pages 464–468.

Ronan Le Bras, Swabha Swayamdipta, Chandra Bhagavatula, Rowan Zellers, Matthew E Peters, Ashish Sabharwal, and Yejin Choi. 2020. Adversarial filters of dataset biases. In *International Conference on Machine Learning*, pages 1078–1088. PMLR.

Shiyu Chang, Yang Zhang, Mo Yu, and Tommi Jaakkola. 2020. Invariant rationalization. In *International Conference on Machine Learning*, pages 1448–1458. PMLR.

Christopher Clark, Mark Yatskar, and Luke Zettlemoyer. 2019. Don't take the easy way out: Ensemble based methods for avoiding known dataset biases. In *Proceedings of the 2019 Conference on Empirical Methods in Natural Language Processing and the 9th International Joint Conference on Natural Language Processing (EMNLP-IJCNLP)*, pages 4060–4073.

Thomas Davidson, Dana Warmsley, Michael Macy, and Ingmar Weber. 2017. Automated hate speech detection and the problem of offensive language. In *Proceedings of the International AAAI Conference on Web and Social Media*, volume 11(1).

Lucas Dixon, John Li, Jeffrey Sorensen, Nithum Thain, and Lucy Vasserman. 2018. Measuring and mitigating unintended bias in text classification. In *Proceedings of the 2018 AAAI/ACM Conference on AI, Ethics, and Society*, pages 67–73.

Ashwin Geet d'Sa, Irina Illina, and Dominique Fohr. 2020. Bert and fasttext embeddings for automatic detection of toxic speech. In *2020 International Multi-Conference on:"Organization of Knowledge and Advanced Technologies"(OCTA)*, pages 1–5. IEEE.

Marta Dynel. 2012. Swearing methodologically: the (im) politeness of expletives in anonymous commentaries on youtube. *Journal of English studies*, 10:25–50.

Antigoni Founta, Constantinos Djouvas, Despoina Chatzakou, Ilias Leontiadis, Jeremy Blackburn, Gianluca Stringhini, Athena Vakali, Michael Sirivianos, and Nicolas Kourtellis. 2018. Large scale crowdsourcing and characterization of twitter abusive behavior. In *Proceedings of the International AAAI Conference on Web and Social Media*, volume 12(1).

Aditya Gaydhani, Vikrant Doma, Shrikant Kendre, and Laxmi Bhagwat. 2018. Detecting hate speech and offensive language on twitter using machine learning: An n-gram and tfidf based approach. *arXiv preprint arXiv:1809.08651*.

Lisa J Green. 2002. *African American English: a linguistic introduction*. Cambridge University Press.

He He, Sheng Zha, and Haohan Wang. 2019. Unlearn dataset bias in natural language inference by fitting the residual. *EMNLP-IJCNLP 2019*, page 132.

Yinhan Liu, Myle Ott, Naman Goyal, Jingfei Du, Mandar Joshi, Danqi Chen, Omer Levy, Mike Lewis, Luke Zettlemoyer, and Veselin Stoyanov. 2019. Roberta: A robustly optimized bert pretraining approach. *arXiv preprint arXiv:1907.11692*.

Marzieh Mozafari, Reza Farahbakhsh, and Noël Crespi. 2020. Hate speech detection and racial bias mitigation in social media based on bert model. *PloS one*, 15(8):e0237861.

Ji Ho Park, Jamin Shin, and Pascale Fung. 2018. Reducing gender bias in abusive language detection. In *Proceedings of the 2018 Conference on Empirical Methods in Natural Language Processing*, pages 2799–2804.

Maarten Sap, Dallas Card, Saadia Gabriel, Yejin Choi, and Noah A Smith. 2019. The risk of racial bias in hate speech detection. In *Proceedings of the 57th annual meeting of the association for computational linguistics*, pages 1668–1678.

Prasetya Ajie Utama, Nafise Sadat Moosavi, and Iryna Gurevych. 2020. Mind the trade-off: Debiasing nlu models without degrading the in-distribution performance. In *Proceedings of the 58th Annual Meeting of the Association for Computational Linguistics*, pages 8717–8729.

Ameya Vaidya, Feng Mai, and Yue Ning. 2020. Empirical analysis of multi-task learning for reducing identity bias in toxic comment detection. In *Proceedings of the International AAAI Conference on Web and Social Media*, volume 14, pages 683–693.

Mengzhou Xia, Anjalie Field, and Yulia Tsvetkov. 2020. Demoting racial bias in hate speech detection. In *Proceedings of the Eighth International Workshop on Natural Language Processing for Social Media*, pages 7–14.

Xuhui Zhou, Maarten Sap, Swabha Swayamdipta, Yejin Choi, and Noah A Smith. 2021. Challenges in automated debiasing for toxic language detection. In *Proceedings of the 16th Conference of the European Chapter of the Association for Computational Linguistics: Main Volume*, pages 3143–3155.

A Bias attributes

We follow Zhou et al. (2021) to define four attributes (NOI, OI, ONI, and AAE) that are often falsy related to toxic language. NOI is mention of minoritized identities (e.g., *gay, female, Muslim*); OI mentions offensive words about minorities (e.g., *queer, n*gga*); ONI is mention of swear words (e.g., *f*ck, sh*t*). NOI should not be correlated with toxic language but is often found in hateful speech towards minorities (Dixon et al., 2018). Although OI and ONI can be toxic sometimes, they are used to simply convey closeness or emphasize the emotion in specific contexts (Dynel, 2012). AAE contains dialectal markers that are commonly used among African Americans. Even though AAE simply signals a cultural identity in the US (Green, 2002), AAE markers are often falsy related to toxicity and cause content by Black authors to mean suppressed more often than non-Black authors (Sap et al., 2019).

B Training Details

We use a single NVIDIA TESLA V100 (32G) for each experiment. The average runtime of experiments for *Vanilla* model in Table 1 are 2 hours. The INVRAT model in Table 1 need about 9 hours for a single experiment.

The main hyperparameters are listed in Table 3. More details can be found in our released code. We did not conduct hyperparameter search, but follow all settings in the official implementation of Zhou et al. (2021) [5]. One difference is that because INVRAT framework needs three RoBERTa models to run at the same time, we choose to use RoBERTa-base, while Zhou et al. (2021) uses RoBERTa-large. As a result, our F_1 score for the Vanilla model is about 0.5 less than the score in Zhou et al. (2021).

hyperparameter	value
optimizer	AdamW
adam epsilon	1.0×10^{-8}
learning rate	1.0×10^{-5}
training epochs	10
batch size	8
max gradient norm	1.0
weight decay	0.0
sparsity percentage (α)	0.2
sparsity lambda (λ_1)	1.0
continuity lambda (λ_2)	5.0
diff lambda (λ_{diff})	10.0

Table 3: The main hyperparameters in the experiment. Sparsity percentage is the value of α in $\mathcal{L}_{reg}$ mentioned in equation 2; sparsity lambda and continuity lambda are λ_1 and λ_2 in equation 2; diff lambda is λ_{diff} in equation 6.

[5] https://github.com/XuhuiZhou/Toxic_Debias

Fine-grained Classification of Political Bias in German News: A Data Set and Initial Experiments

Dmitrii Aksenov, Peter Bourgonje, Karolina Zaczynska,
Malte Ostendorff, Julián Moreno-Schneider, Georg Rehm
DFKI GmbH, Berlin, Germany
firstname.lastname@dfki.de

Abstract

We[1] present a data set consisting of German news articles labeled for political bias on a five-point scale in a semi-supervised way. While earlier work on hyperpartisan news detection uses binary classification (i. e., hyperpartisan or not) and English data, we argue for a more fine-grained classification, covering the full political spectrum (i. e., far-left, left, centre, right, far-right) and for extending research to German data. Understanding political bias helps in accurately detecting hate speech and online abuse. We experiment with different classification methods for political bias detection. Their comparatively low performance (a macro-F_1 of 43 for our best setup, compared to a macro-F_1 of 79 for the binary classification task) underlines the need for more (balanced) data annotated in a fine-grained way.

1 Introduction

The social web and social media networks have received an ever-increasing amount of attention since their emergence 15-20 years ago. Their popularity among billions of users has had a significant effect on the way people consume information in general, and news in particular (Newman et al., 2016). This development is accompanied by a number of challenges, which resulted in various NLP tasks that deal with information quality (Derczynski and Bontcheva, 2014; Dale, 2017; Saquete et al., 2020). Due to the data-driven nature of these tasks, they are often evaluated under the umbrella of (un)shared tasks, on topics such as rumour detection or verification (Derczynski et al., 2017; Gorrell et al., 2019), offensive language and hate speech detection (Zampieri et al., 2019; Basile et al., 2019; Struß et al., 2019; Waseem et al., 2017; Fišer et al., 2018; Roberts et al., 2019; Akiwowo et al., 2020) or fake news and fact-checking (Hanselowski et al., 2018; Thorne et al., 2019; Mihaylova et al., 2019).

Several shared tasks concentrate on stance (Mohammad et al., 2016) and hyper-partisan news detection (Kiesel et al., 2019), which predict either the stance of the author towards the topic of a news piece, or whether or not they exhibit allegiance to a particular party or cause. We argue that transparency and de-centralisation (i. e., moving away from a single, objective "truth" and a single institution, organisation or algorithm that decides on this) are essential in the analysis and dissemination of online information (Rehm, 2018). The prediction of political bias was recently examined by the 2019 Hyperpartisan News Detection task (Kiesel et al., 2019) with 42 teams submitting valid runs, resulting in over 30 publications. This task's test/evaluation data comprised English news articles and used labels obtained by Vincent and Mestre (2018), but their five-point scale was binarised so the challenge was to label articles as being either *hyperpartisan* or *not hyperpartisan*.

We follow Wich et al. (2020) in claiming that, in order to better understand online abuse and hate speech, biases in data sets and trained classifiers should be made transparent, as what can be considered hateful or abusive depends on many factors (relating to both sender and recipient), including race (Vidgen et al., 2020; Davidson et al., 2019), gender (Brooke, 2019; Clarke and Grieve, 2017), and political orientation (Vidgen and Derczynski, 2021; Jiang et al., 2020). This paper contributes to the detection of online abuse by attempting to uncover political bias in content.

We describe the creation of a new data set of German news articles labeled for political bias. For annotation, we adopt the semi-supervised strategy of Kiesel et al. (2019) who label (English) articles

[1]This work was done while all co-authors were at DFKI. The new affiliations of the first two authors are ambeRoad Tech GmbH, Aachen, Germany (dmitrii@amberoad.de) and Morningsun Technology GmbH, Saarbrücken, Germany (peter.bourgonje@morningsun-technology.com).

Proceedings of the Fifth Workshop on Online Abuse and Harms, pages 121–131
August 6, 2021. ©2021 Association for Computational Linguistics

according to their publisher. In addition to opening up this line of research to a new language, we use a more fine-grained set of labels. We argue that, in addition to knowing whether content is hyperpartisan, the *direction* of bias (i. e., left-wing or right-wing) is important for end user transparency and overall credibility assessment. As our labels are not just about hyperpartisanism as a binary feature, we refer to this task as *political bias classification*. We apply and evaluate various classification models to the data set. We also provide suggestions for improving performance on this challenging task. The rest of this paper is structured as follows. Section 2 discusses related work on bias and hyperpartisanism. Section 3 describes the data set and provides basic statistics. Section 4 explains the methods we apply to the 2019 Hyperpartisan News Detection task data (for evaluation and benchmarking purposes) and to our own data set. Sections 5 and 6 evaluate and discuss the results. Section 7 sums up our main findings.

2 Related Work

2.1 Data sets

For benchmarking purposes, we run our system on the data from Kiesel et al. (2019). They introduce a small number of articles (1,273) manually labeled by content, and a large number of articles (754,000) labeled by publisher via distant supervision, using labels from BuzzFeed news[2] and Media Bias Fact Check[3]. Due to the lack of article-level labels for German media, we adopt the strategy of labeling articles by publisher.

Several studies use the data from *allsides.com*[4], which provides annotations on political ideology for individual articles in English. Using this data, Baly et al. (2020) introduce adversarial domain adaptation and triplet loss pre-training that prevents over-fitting to the style of a specific news medium, Kulkarni et al. (2018) demonstrate the importance of the article's title and link structure for bias prediction and Li and Goldwasser (2019) explore how social content can be used to improve bias prediction by leveraging Graph Convolutional Networks to encode a social network graph.

Zhou et al. (2021) analysed several unreliable news data sets and showed that heterogeneity of the news sources is crucial for the prevention of source-related bias. We adopt their strategy of splitting the sources into two disjoint sets used for building train and test data sets respectively.

Gangula et al. (2019) work on detecting bias in news articles in the Indian language Telugu. They annotate 1,329 articles concentrating on headlines, which they find to be indicative of political bias. In contrast to Kiesel et al. (2019), but similar to our approach, Gangula et al. (2019) treat bias detection as a multi-class classification problem. They use the five main political parties present in the Telugu-speaking region as their classification labels, but do not position these parties on the political spectrum.

Taking into account the political orientation of the author, SemEval 2016 Task 6 (Mohammad et al., 2016) worked on stance detection, where sub-task A comprised a set of tweets, the target entity or issue (e. g., "Hillary Clinton", or "Climate Change") and a label (one of *favour*, *against*, *neither*). The tweet-target-stance triples were split into training and test data. Sub-task B had a similar setup, but covered a target not included in the targets of task A, and presented the tweet-target-stance triples as test data only (i. e., without any training data for this target). While (political) stance of the author is at the core of this challenge, it differs from the problems we tackle in two important ways: 1) The task dealt with tweets, whereas we process news articles, which are considerably longer (on average 650 words per text for both corpora combined, see Section 3, compared to the 140-character limit[5] enforced by Twitter) and are written by professional authors and edited before posted. And 2) unlike the shared task setup, we have no target entity or issue and aim to predict the political stance, bias or orientation (in the context of this paper, we consider these three words synonymous and use the phrase *political bias* throughout the rest of this paper) from the text, irrespective of a particular topic, entity or issue.

One of the key challenges acknowledged in the literature is cross-target or cross-topic performance of stance detection systems (Küçük and Can, 2020). Trained for a specific target or topic (Sobhani et al., 2017), performance is considerably lower when these systems are applied to new targets. Vamvas and Sennrich (2020) address this issue by annotating and publishing a multilingual (standard Swiss

[2]https://github.com/BuzzFeedNews/2017-08-partisan-sites-and-facebook-pages

[3]https://mediabiasfactcheck.com

[4]https://www.allsides.com/media-bias

[5]The shared task took place before Twitter increased the character limit of one tweet from 140 to 280 in 2017.

German, French, Italian) stance detection corpus that covers a considerably higher number of targets (over 150, compared to six in Mohammad et al., 2016). Vamvas and Sennrich (2020) work with comments, which are longer than tweets (on average 26 words), but still shorter than our news articles. Similar to Mohammad et al. (2016) but unlike our approach, the data is annotated for stance toward a particular target.

Earlier work on political stance is represented by Thomas et al. (2006), who work on a corpus of US congressional debates, which is labeled for stance with regard to a particular issue (i. e., a proposed legislation) and which uses binary labels for supporting or opposing the proposed legislation. From this, political bias could potentially be deduced, if information on the party of the person that proposed the legislation is available. However, first of all this correlation is not necessarily present, and second, it results in a binary (republican vs. democratic) labeling scheme, whereas we use a larger set of labels covering the political spectrum from left-wing to right-wing (see Section 3).

A comprehensive review of media bias in news articles, especially attempting to cover insights from social sciences (representing a more theoretical, rational approach) and computer science (representing a more practical, empiricist approach), is provided by Hamborg et al. (2018). The authors observe a lack of inter-disciplinary work, and although our work is mainly empirical, we agree that using a more diverse range of corpora and languages is one way to move away from "too simplistic (models)" (Hamborg et al., 2018, p. 410) that are currently in use. In this respect, we would like to stress that, unlike Kulkarni et al. (2018); Baly et al. (2020); Li and Goldwasser (2019), who all either work on or contribute data sets (or both) to political bias classification in English, we strongly believe that a sub-discipline dealing with bias detection benefits especially from a wide range of different data sets, ideally from as many different languages and cultural backgrounds as possible. We contribute to this cause by publishing and working with a German data set.

2.2 Models

With regard to the system architecture, Bießmann (2016) use similar techniques as we do (bag-of-words and a Logistic Regression classifier, though we do not use these two in combination), but work on the domain of German parliament speeches, attempting to predict the speaker's affiliation based on their speech. Iyyer et al. (2014) use a bag-of-words and Logistic Regression system as well, but improve over this with a Recursive Neural Network setup, working on the Convote data set (Thomas et al., 2006) and the Ideological Book Corpus[6]. Hamborg et al. (2020) use BERT for sentiment analysis after finding Named Entities first, in order to find descriptions of entities that suggest either a left-wing or a right-wing bias (e. g., using either "freedom fighters" or "terrorists" to denote the same target entity or group). Salminen et al. (2020) work on hate speech classification. We adopt their idea of evaluating several methods (features and models, see Sections 4.1 and 4.2) on the same data and also adopt their strategy of integrating BERT representations with different classification algorithms.

3 Data Collection and Processing

We obtain our German data through two different crawling processes, described in Sections 3.1 and 3.2, which also explain how we assign labels that reflect the political bias of the crawled, German news articles. Since the 2019 shared task data which we use for benchmarking purposes is downloaded and used as is, we refer to Kiesel et al. (2019) for more information on this data set.

3.1 News-Streaming Data

This work on political bias classification is carried out in the context of a project on content curation (Rehm et al., 2020).[7] One of the project partners[8] provided us with access to a news streaming service that delivers a cleaned and augmented stream of content from a wide range of media outlets, containing the text of the web page (without advertisements, HTML elements or other non-informative pieces of text) and various metadata, such as publisher, publication date, recognised named entities and sentiment value. We collected German news articles published between February 2020 and August 2020. Filtering these for publishers for which we have a label (Section 3.4) resulted in 28,954 articles from 35 publishers. The average length of an article is 741 words, compared to 618 words for the 2019 Hyperpartisan News Detection shared task data (for the by-publisher data set).

[6] https://people.cs.umass.edu/~miyyer/ibc/index.html
[7] https://qurator.ai
[8] https://www.ubermetrics-technologies.com

Data set	Type	Far-left	Centre-left	Centre	Centre-right	Far-right	General	Regional	Overall
Training	Num. publishers	2	3	11	8	2	23	3	26
	Num. articles	1,146	11,958	11,714	15,624	1,772	41,175	1,039	42,214
Test	Num. publishers	1	3	3	2	1	8	2	10
	Num. articles	215	1,159	1,349	1,754	671	3,597	1,551	5,148

Table 1: Basic statistics of our data set.

3.2 Crawled Data

To further augment the data set described in Section 3.1, we used the open-source news crawler news-please[9]. Given a root URL, the crawler extracts text from a website, together with metadata such as author name, title and publication date.

We used the 40 German news outlets for which we have bias labels (Section 3.4) as root URLs to extract news articles. We applied regular expression patterns to skip sections of websites unlikely to contain indications of political bias[10]. This resulted in over 60,000 articles from 15 different publishers.

3.3 Data Cleaning

After collecting the data, we filtered and cleaned the two data sets. First, we removed duplicates in each collection. Because the two crawling methods start from different perspectives – with the first one collecting large volumes and filtering for particular publishers later, and the second one targeting these particular publishers right from the beginning – but overlap temporally, we also checked for duplicates in the two collections. While we found no exact duplicates (probably due to differences in the implementation of the crawlers), we checked articles with identical headlines and manually examined the text, to find irrelevant crawling output.

Second, we removed non-news articles (e. g., personal pages of authors, pages related to legal or contact information, or lists of headlines). This step was mostly based on article headlines and URLs. Because the vast majority of data collected was published after 2018, we filtered out all texts published earlier, fearing too severe data sparsity issues with the older articles. Due to the low number of articles, a model may associate particular events that happened before 2018 with a specific label only because this was the only available label for articles covering that specific event.

Finally, we inspected our collection trying to detect and delete pieces of texts that are not part of the articles (such as imprints, advertisements or subscription requests). This process was based on keyword search, after which particular articles or sections of articles were removed manually.

This procedure resulted in 26,235 articles from 34 publishers and 21,127 articles from 15 publishers[11] in our two collections respectively. We combined these collections, resulting in a set of 47,362 articles from 34 different publishers. For our experiments on this data, we created a 90-10 training-test data split. Because initial experiments showed that models quickly over-fit on publisher identity (through section names, stylistic features or other implicit identity-related information left after cleaning), we ensured that none of the publishers in the test set appear in the training data. Due to the low number of publishers for certain classes, this requirement could not be met in combination with 10-fold cross-validation, which is why we refrain from 10-fold cross-validation and use a single, static training and test data split (see Table 1).

3.4 Label Assignment

To assign political bias labels to our news articles, we follow the semi-supervised strategy of Kiesel et al. (2019), who use the identity of the publisher to label (the largest part of) their data set. The values for our labels are based on a survey carried out by Medienkompass.org, in which subjects were asked to rate 40 different German media outlets on a scale of partiality and quality. For partiality, a range from 1 to 7 was used with the following labels: *1 – left-wing extremism (fake news and conspiracy theories), 2 – left-wing mission (questionable journalistic values), 3 – tendentiously left, 4 – minimal partisan tendency, 5 – tendentiously right, 6 – right-wing mission (questionable journalistic values), 7 – right-wing extremism (fake news and conspiracy theories).* For quality, a range from 1 to

[9]https://github.com/fhamborg/news-please

[10]For some websites, the URL was indicative of the category, like domain.com/politics/ or domain.com/sports/. These are filtered out through regular expressions.

[11]For 25 out of the 40 root URLs, we have been unable to extract anything using the news-please crawler.

5 was used: *1 – click bait, 2 – basic information, 3 – meets high standards, 4 – analytical, 5 – complex.*

A total of 1,065 respondents positioned these 40 news outlets between (an averaged) 2.1 (indymedia) and 5.9 (Compact) for partiality, and between 1.3 (BILD) and 3.5 (Die Zeit, Deutschlandfunk) for quality. We used the result of this survey, available online[12], to filter and annotate our news articles for political bias based on their publisher. In this paper we use the bias labels for classification and leave quality classification for further research.

Because 60-way classification for partiality (1 to 7 with decimals coming from averaging respondents' answers) results in very sparsely populated (or even empty) classes for many labels, and even rounding off to the nearest natural number (i. e., 7-way classification) leads to some empty classes, we converted the 7-point scale to a 5-point scale, using the following boundaries: 1-2.5 – far-left, 2.5-3.5 – centre-left, 3.5-4.5 – centre, 4.5-5.5 – centre-right, 5.5-7 – far-right. We favoured this equal distribution over the scale of the survey over class size balance (there are more far-right articles than far-left articles, for example). The distribution of our data over this 5-point scale is shown in Table 1.

3.5 Topic Detection

To get an overview of the topics and domains covered in the data set, we applied a topic detection model, which was trained on a multilingual data set for stance detection (Vamvas and Sennrich, 2020) where, in addition to stance, items are classified as belonging to one of 12 different news topics. We trained a multinomial Naive Bayes model on the BOW representation of all German items (just under 50k in total) in this multilingual data set, achieving an accuracy of 79% and a macro-averaged F_1-score of 78. We applied this model to our own data set. The results are shown in Table 2. Note that this is just to provide an impression of the distribution and variance of topics. Vamvas and Sennrich (2020) work on question-answer/comment pairs, and the extent to which a topic detection model trained on such answers or comments is eligible for transfer to pure news articles is a question we leave for future work.

Since the majority of articles was published in 2020, a year massively impacted by the COVID-19 pandemic, we applied simple keyword-based heuristics, resulting in the estimate that approximately 40% of all articles are about COVID-19, as illustrated in the bottom rows of Table 2.

Topic	Training set	Test set
Digitisation	53	6
Economy	4,843	628
Education	1,379	126
Finances	1,309	79
Foreign Policy	8,638	969
Healthcare	925	79
Immigration	3,881	455
Infrastructure & Environment	3,132	473
Political System	5,087	563
Security	7,175	883
Society	4,077	709
Welfare	1,715	178
About COVID-19	16,994	2,414
Not about COVID-19	25,220	2,734

Table 2: Predicted topics of the articles

We publish the data set as a list of URLs and corresponding labels. Due to copyright issues, we are unable to make available the full texts.

4 Methodology

In this section we describe the different (feature) representations of the data we use to train different classification models on as well as our attempts to alleviate the class imbalance problem (Table 1).

4.1 Features

Bag-Of-Words Bag-of-Words (BOW) represents the text sequence as a vector of $|V|$ features with V being the vocabulary size. Each feature value contains the frequency of the word associated with the position in the vector in the input text. The vocabulary is based on the training data.

TF-IDF Term-Frequency times Inverse-Document-Frequency (TF-IDF) differs from BOW in that it takes into account the frequency of terms in the entire corpus (the training data, in our case). In addition to its popularity in all kinds of IR and NLP tasks, TF-IDF has recently been used in hate speech detection tasks (Salminen et al., 2019).

BERT Since its introduction, BERT (Devlin et al., 2019), has been used in many NLP tasks. We use the German BERT base model from the Hugging Face Transformers library[13]. We adopt the fine-tuning strategy from (Salminen et al., 2020): first, we fine-tune the BertForSequenceClassification model, consisting of BERT's model and a linear softmax activation layer. After training, we

[12]https://medienkompass.org/deutsche-medienlandschaft/

[13]https://huggingface.co/bert-base-german-cased

drop the softmax activation layer and use BERT's hidden state as the feature vector, which we then use as input for different classification algorithms.

4.2 Models

Logistic Regression We use logistic regression as our first and relatively straightforward method, motivated by its popularity for text classification. We add L2 regularization to the cross-Entropy loss and optimize it using Stochastic Average Gradient (SAGA) (Defazio et al., 2014).

Naive Bayes Equally popular in text classification, Naive Bayes is based on the conditional independence assumption. We model BOW and TF-IDF features as random variables distributed according to the multinomial distribution with Lidstone smoothing. BERT features are modeled as Gaussian random variables.

Random Forest Random Forest is an ensemble algorithm using decision tree models. The random selection of features and instances allows reduction of the model's variance and co-adaptation of the models. To handle class imbalance we use the Weighted Random Forest method (Chen and Breiman, 2004). This changes the weights assigned to each class when calculating the impurity score at the split point, penalises mis-classification of the minority classes and reduces the majority bias.

EasyEnsemble EasyEnsemble is another ensemble method targeting the class imbalance problem (Liu et al., 2009). It creates balanced training samples by taking all examples from the minority class and randomly selecting examples from the majority class, after which AdaBoost (Schapire, 1999) is applied to the re-sampled data.

5 Evaluation

5.1 Hyperpartisan News Detection Data

For benchmarking purposes, we first apply our models to the 2019 Hyperpartisan News Detection task. This data set uses binary labels as opposed to our 5-point scale. Since the 2019 shared task used TIRA (Potthast et al., 2019), the organisers requested submission of functioning code and ran the evaluation on a dedicated machine to which the shared task participants did not have access. The test set used in the shared task was *not* published and even after submission deadline has not been made publicly available. As a consequence, we use the validation set to produce our scores on the data. This renders a direct comparison impossible. To provide an estimate of our performance, we include Table 3, which lists the top 3 systems participating in the task. As illustrated by the row TF-IDF+Naive Bayes (our best-performing setup on this data set), we achieve a considerably lower accuracy score, but a comparable macro F_1-score. The performance of the other setups is shown in Table 3. BERT+Logistic Regression scored just slightly worse than TF-IDF+Naive Bayes, with a precision score that is one point lower.

5.2 German Data Set

We apply the models to our own data. The results are shown in Table 5 for accuracy and in Table 6 for macro-averaged F_1-score. The per-class performance is shown in Table 7, which, in addition, contains performance when binarising our labels (the last three rows) to compare this to the 2019 shared task data and to provide an idea of the difference in performance when using more fine-grained labels. We assume articles with the labels Far-left and Far-right to be hyperpartisan, and label all other articles as non-hyperpartisan. The accuracy for binary classification (not listed in Table 7) was 86%, compared to 43% (Naive Bayes+BOW in Table 5) for 5-class classification.

From the results we can conclude the following. First, class imbalance poses a serious problem, though some setups suffer from this more than others. Linear Regression, on all different features, performed poorly on the Far-left articles. We assume this is due to the small number of Far-left articles (215 in the test set, 1,146 in the training set) and publishers (one in the test set, two in the training set). Despite the high degree of class imbalance, the EasyEnsemble method, designed to target this problem particularly, does not outperform the others with any of the different feature sets. Second, BERT features scored surprisingly low with all classification models. Overall, we can conclude that the two best-performing setups that show both high accuracy and F_1-score are BOW+Naive Bayes and TF-IDF+Random Forest features. Table 7 includes the scores for TF-IDF+Random Forest, our best-performing setup.

6 Discussion

In many NLP tasks, the strategy of using BERT as a language model that is fine-tuned to a specific

Team	Rank	Accuracy	Precision	Recall	F_1
tintin	1	**0.70**	**0.74**	0.63	0.68
joseph-rouletabille	2	0.68	0.64	0.83	**0.72**
brenda-starr	3	0.66	0.63	0.81	0.71
TF-IDF + Naive Bayes (ours)	n. a.	0.58	0.55	**0.84**	0.67

Table 3: Our best performing setup (TF-IDF + Naive Bayes) on the 2019 Hyperpartisan News Detection validation set compared to the top 3 systems of the 2019 Hyperpartisan News Detection task on the by-publisher test set.

Model	Accuracy	Precision	Recall	F_1
BOW + Random Forest	0.51	0.51	0.59	0.55
BOW + Naive Bayes	0.57	0.54	0.81	0.65
TF-IDF + Random Forest	0.52	0.51	0.59	0.55
TF-IDF + Naive Bayes	0.58	0.55	0.85	0.67
BERT + Logistic Regression	0.58	0.55	0.84	0.66
BERT + Logistic Regression (10%)	0.56	0.54	0.85	0.66

Table 4: Results of our setups on the 2019 Hyperpartisan News Detection task (by-publisher validation set).

Model	BOW	TF-IDF	BERT
Logistic Regression	0.4289	**0.4472**	0.4202
Naive Bayes	**0.4304**	0.4021	0.4188
Random Forest	0.3980	0.4258	**0.4320**
EasyEnsemble	0.3811	0.3798	0.3646

Table 5: Accuracy for different features and classification methods

Model	BOW	TF-IDF	BERT
Logistic Regression	0.3132	0.2621	0.3389
Naive Bayes	**0.4243**	0.2234	0.3637
Random Forest	0.4007	**0.4303**	**0.3836**
EasyEnsemble	0.4197	0.4070	0.3432

Table 6: Macro-averaged F_1-measure for different features and classification methods

Class	Precision	Recall	F_1	Support
Far-left	0.59	0.40	0.48	215
Centre-left	0.34	0.38	0.36	1,159
Centre	0.31	0.23	0.27	1,349
Centre-right	0.51	0.55	0.53	1,754
Far-right	0.46	0.58	0.51	671
Total	**0.44**	**0.43**	**0.43**	**5,148**
Hyperpartisan	0.56	0.81	0.66	886
Non-hyperpartisan	0.96	0.87	0.87	4262
Total	**0.76**	**0.84**	**0.79**	**5,148**

Table 7: Experimental results for TF-IDF+Random Forest, per class for political bias and hyperpartisan classification.

task, has recently been shown to exhibit significant improvements over previously used methods and models, such as Naive Bayes and Random Forest. To determine why our BERT-based setups did not outperform the others, we investigated the impact of training data volume. We trained the BERT+Logistic Regression setup on only 10% of the original training data of the 2019 setup explained earlier and evaluated it on the same test setup (i. e., the validation set in the 2019 shared task). As illustrated by the last row in Table 4, the accuracy dropped by only 2% and F_1-score remained the same, suggesting that data volume has relatively little impact.

To further analyse our results, we examined the attention scores of the first BERT layer and selected the ten tokens BERT paid most attention to for every article. We then combined adjacent tokens and finished non-complete words (with their most likely candidate) to determine the key phrases of the text that the model used for classification. We repeated this procedure on all hyperpartisan articles (i. e., Far-left and Far-right) and derived a list of words and phrases that the model paid most attention to. The result is shown in Table 8.

The question whether or not attention can be used for explaining a model's prediction is still under discussion (Jain and Wallace, 2019; Wiegreffe and Pinter, 2019). Note that with Table 8, we attempt to gain insight into how words are used to construct BERT embeddings, and not necessarily which words are used for prediction.

The lists of words show that the majority of words for the Far-left classification are neither exclusively nor mainly used by left-wing news media in general, e. g., *wirkt* (works), *seither* (since) or *Geliebte* (beloved, lover). An exception is *antisemi-*

Far-left	Far-right
wirkt	Checklisten
neunziger	*Willkommenskultur*
Hungernden	*Wohlverhaltensvorschriften*
antisemitische	Alltagsgebrauch
Seither	*Tichys [Einblick]*
Geliebte	Witz
Plausch	*Islam*
biologistischen	*Gutmenschen*
Sahelzone	korrekte
undurchsichtige	*Diversity*

Table 8: The top ten words most indicative of Far-left or Far-right content according to BERT's attention scores.

tische (anti-semitic), with anti-semitism in society being a common topic in left-wing media. Other highlighted words are likely to be related to the topic of refugee migration and its causes, such as *Hungernden* (hungry people) and *Sahelzone* (Sahel), an area known for its conflicts and current societal challenges. In contrast to the words we identified for the Far-left, we found most of the words we identified for the Far-right to be more descriptive of this side of the political spectrum. Nearly all words listed under Far-right in Table 8 are typically either used sarcastically or in a highly critical manner in typical right-wing media outlets. For example, *Willkommenskultur* (welcoming culture) is a German compound describing a welcoming and positive attitude towards immigrants, which is often mocked and criticised by the far right. Another example is *Gutmensch* (of which *Gutmenschen* is the plural), a term mainly used by the right as an ironic or contemptuous denigration of individuals or groups that strive to be 'politically correct'. Another word in the right column of Table 8 is *Tichys*, referring to the blog and print magazine *Tichys Einblick*. This news magazine calls itself a platform for authors of the liberal and conservative spectrum but is considered by some observers to be a highly controversial right-wing magazine with neo-liberal tendencies.[14] Since we made sure that the training data publishers and test data publishers are disjoint sets, this cannot be a case of publisher identity still being present in the text and the model over-fitting to this. Upon closer investigation, we found[15] that indeed, many other publishers refer to *Tichy's Einblick*, and these were predominantly publishers with the Far-right label.

[14]https://www.politico.eu/article/new-conservative-magazine-takes-on-angela-merkel-and-the-media-roland-tichy-tichys-einblick/ (last visited: March 21, 2021).

[15]Through simple string search on "Tichy" in the articles.

Generally, entries in Table 8 (for both the Far-left and Far-right columns) in italics are those we consider indicative of their particular position on the political spectrum. Some words on the right side are in themselves neutral but often used by right-wing media with a negative connotation, which is why we italicised them, too (e. g., *Islam*, *Diversity*).

7 Conclusion and Future Work

We present a collection of German news articles labeled for political bias in a semi-supervised way, by exploiting the results of a survey on the political affiliation of a list of prominent German news outlets.[16] This data set extends on earlier work on political bias classification by including a more fine-grained set of labels, and by allowing for research on political bias in German articles. We propose various classification setups that we evaluate on existing data for benchmarking purposes, and then apply to our own data set. Our results show that political bias classification is very challenging, especially when assuming a non-binary set of labels. When using a more fine-grained label set, we demonstrate that performance drops by 36 points in accuracy, from 79 in the binary case to 43 in the more fine-grained setup.

Political orientation plays a role in the detection of hate speech and online abuse (along with other dimensions, such as gender and race). By making available more data sets, in different languages, and using as many different publishers as possible (our results validate earlier findings that models quickly over-fit to particular publisher identity features), we contribute to uncovering and making transparent political bias of online content, which in turn contributes to the cause of detecting hate speech and abusive language (Bourgonje et al., 2018).

While labeling articles by publisher has the obvious advantage of producing a larger number of labeled instances more quickly, critical investigation and large-scale labeling of individual articles must be an important direction of future work.

Acknowledgments

This work has received funding from the German Federal Ministry of Education and Research (BMBF) through the projects QURATOR (no. 03WKDA1A, https://qurator.ai) and PANQURA (no. 03COV03E).

[16]The URLs of the documents in our data set and the labels can be found at https://github.com/axenov/politik-news.

References

Seyi Akiwowo, Bertie Vidgen, Vinodkumar Prabhakaran, and Zeerak Waseem, editors. 2020. *Proceedings of the Fourth Workshop on Online Abuse and Harms*. Association for Computational Linguistics, Online.

Ramy Baly, Giovanni Da San Martino, James Glass, and Preslav Nakov. 2020. We can detect your bias: Predicting the political ideology of news articles. In *Proceedings of the 2020 Conference on Empirical Methods in Natural Language Processing (EMNLP)*, pages 4982–4991, Online. Association for Computational Linguistics.

Valerio Basile, Cristina Bosco, Elisabetta Fersini, Debora Nozza, Viviana Patti, Francisco Manuel Rangel Pardo, Paolo Rosso, and Manuela Sanguinetti. 2019. SemEval-2019 task 5: Multilingual detection of hate speech against immigrants and women in Twitter. In *Proceedings of the 13th International Workshop on Semantic Evaluation*, pages 54–63, Minneapolis, Minnesota, USA. Association for Computational Linguistics.

Felix Bießmann. 2016. Automating political bias prediction. *CoRR*, abs/1608.02195.

Peter Bourgonje, Julián Moreno Schneider, and Georg Rehm. 2018. Automatic Classification of Abusive Language and Personal Attacks in Various Forms of Online Communication. In *Language Technologies for the Challenges of the Digital Age: 27th International Conference, GSCL 2017, Berlin, Germany, September 13-14, 2017, Proceedings*, number 10713 in Lecture Notes in Artificial Intelligence (LNAI), pages 180–191, Cham, Switzerland. Gesellschaft für Sprachtechnologie und Computerlinguistik e.V., Springer. 13/14 September 2017.

Sian Brooke. 2019. "condescending, rude, assholes": Framing gender and hostility on Stack Overflow. In *Proceedings of the Third Workshop on Abusive Language Online*, pages 172–180, Florence, Italy. Association for Computational Linguistics.

Chao Chen and Leo Breiman. 2004. Using random forest to learn imbalanced data. *University of California, Berkeley*.

Isobelle Clarke and Jack Grieve. 2017. Dimensions of abusive language on Twitter. In *Proceedings of the First Workshop on Abusive Language Online*, pages 1–10, Vancouver, BC, Canada. Association for Computational Linguistics.

Robert Dale. 2017. NLP in a post-truth world. *Natural Language Engineering*, 23(2):319–324.

Thomas Davidson, Debasmita Bhattacharya, and Ingmar Weber. 2019. Racial bias in hate speech and abusive language detection datasets. In *Proceedings of the Third Workshop on Abusive Language Online*, pages 25–35, Florence, Italy. Association for Computational Linguistics.

Aaron Defazio, Francis Bach, and Simon Lacoste-Julien. 2014. Saga: A fast incremental gradient method with support for non-strongly convex composite objectives.

Leon Derczynski and Kalina Bontcheva. 2014. Pheme: Veracity in digital social networks. In *Posters, Demos, Late-breaking Results and Workshop Proceedings of the 22nd Conference on User Modeling, Adaptation, and Personalization co-located with the 22nd Conference on User Modeling, Adaptation, and Personalization (UMAP2014), Aalborg, Denmark, July 7-11, 2014*, volume 1181 of *CEUR Workshop Proceedings*. CEUR-WS.org.

Leon Derczynski, Kalina Bontcheva, Maria Liakata, Rob Procter, Geraldine Wong Sak Hoi, and Arkaitz Zubiaga. 2017. SemEval-2017 task 8: RumourEval: Determining rumour veracity and support for rumours. In *Proceedings of the 11th International Workshop on Semantic Evaluation (SemEval-2017)*, pages 69–76, Vancouver, Canada. Association for Computational Linguistics.

Jacob Devlin, Ming-Wei Chang, Kenton Lee, and Kristina Toutanova. 2019. BERT: Pre-training of deep bidirectional transformers for language understanding. In *Proceedings of the 2019 Conference of the North American Chapter of the Association for Computational Linguistics: Human Language Technologies, Volume 1 (Long and Short Papers)*, pages 4171–4186, Minneapolis, Minnesota. Association for Computational Linguistics.

Darja Fišer, Ruihong Huang, Vinodkumar Prabhakaran, Rob Voigt, Zeerak Waseem, and Jacqueline Wernimont, editors. 2018. *Proceedings of the 2nd Workshop on Abusive Language Online (ALW2)*. Association for Computational Linguistics, Brussels, Belgium.

Rama Rohit Reddy Gangula, Suma Reddy Duggenpudi, and Radhika Mamidi. 2019. Detecting political bias in news articles using headline attention. In *Proceedings of the 2019 ACL Workshop BlackboxNLP: Analyzing and Interpreting Neural Networks for NLP*, pages 77–84, Florence, Italy. Association for Computational Linguistics.

Genevieve Gorrell, Elena Kochkina, Maria Liakata, Ahmet Aker, Arkaitz Zubiaga, Kalina Bontcheva, and Leon Derczynski. 2019. SemEval-2019 task 7: RumourEval, determining rumour veracity and support for rumours. In *Proceedings of the 13th International Workshop on Semantic Evaluation*, pages 845–854, Minneapolis, Minnesota, USA. Association for Computational Linguistics.

Felix Hamborg, Karsten Donnay, and Bela Gipp. 2018. Automated identification of media bias in news articles: An interdisciplinary literature review. *International Journal on Digital Libraries (IJDL)*, pages 391–415.

Felix Hamborg, Anastasia Zhukova, Karsten Donnay, and Bela Gipp. 2020. Newsalyze: Enabling news consumers to understand media bias. In *Proceedings of the ACM/IEEE Joint Conference on Digital Libraries in 2020*, JCDL '20, page 455–456, New York, NY, USA. Association for Computing Machinery.

Andreas Hanselowski, Avinesh PVS, Benjamin Schiller, Felix Caspelherr, Debanjan Chaudhuri, Christian M. Meyer, and Iryna Gurevych. 2018. A retrospective analysis of the fake news challenge stance-detection task. In *Proceedings of the 27th International Conference on Computational Linguistics*, pages 1859–1874, Santa Fe, New Mexico, USA. Association for Computational Linguistics.

Mohit Iyyer, Peter Enns, Jordan Boyd-Graber, and Philip Resnik. 2014. Political ideology detection using recursive neural networks. In *Proceedings of the 52nd Annual Meeting of the Association for Computational Linguistics (Volume 1: Long Papers)*, pages 1113–1122, Baltimore, Maryland. Association for Computational Linguistics.

Sarthak Jain and Byron C. Wallace. 2019. Attention is not Explanation. In *Proceedings of the 2019 Conference of the North American Chapter of the Association for Computational Linguistics: Human Language Technologies, Volume 1 (Long and Short Papers)*, pages 3543–3556, Minneapolis, Minnesota. Association for Computational Linguistics.

Shan Jiang, Ronald E. Robertson, and Christo Wilson. 2020. Reasoning about political bias in content moderation. *Proceedings of the AAAI Conference on Artificial Intelligence*, 34(09):13669–13672.

Johannes Kiesel, Maria Mestre, Rishabh Shukla, Emmanuel Vincent, Payam Adineh, David Corney, Benno Stein, and Martin Potthast. 2019. SemEval-2019 task 4: Hyperpartisan news detection. In *Proceedings of the 13th International Workshop on Semantic Evaluation*, pages 829–839, Minneapolis, Minnesota, USA. Association for Computational Linguistics.

Dilek Küçük and Fazli Can. 2020. Stance detection: A survey. *ACM Computing Surveys*, 53(1).

Vivek Kulkarni, Junting Ye, Steve Skiena, and William Yang Wang. 2018. Multi-view models for political ideology detection of news articles. In *Proceedings of the 2018 Conference on Empirical Methods in Natural Language Processing*, pages 3518–3527, Brussels, Belgium. Association for Computational Linguistics.

Chang Li and Dan Goldwasser. 2019. Encoding social information with graph convolutional networks forPolitical perspective detection in news media. In *Proceedings of the 57th Annual Meeting of the Association for Computational Linguistics*, pages 2594–2604, Florence, Italy. Association for Computational Linguistics.

X. Liu, J. Wu, and Z. Zhou. 2009. Exploratory undersampling for class-imbalance learning. *IEEE Transactions on Systems, Man, and Cybernetics, Part B (Cybernetics)*, 39(2):539–550.

Tsvetomila Mihaylova, Georgi Karadzhov, Pepa Atanasova, Ramy Baly, Mitra Mohtarami, and Preslav Nakov. 2019. SemEval-2019 task 8: Fact checking in community question answering forums. In *Proceedings of the 13th International Workshop on Semantic Evaluation*, pages 860–869, Minneapolis, Minnesota, USA. Association for Computational Linguistics.

Saif Mohammad, Svetlana Kiritchenko, Parinaz Sobhani, Xiaodan Zhu, and Colin Cherry. 2016. SemEval-2016 task 6: Detecting stance in tweets. In *Proceedings of the 10th International Workshop on Semantic Evaluation (SemEval-2016)*, pages 31–41, San Diego, California. Association for Computational Linguistics.

Nic Newman, Richard Fletcher, David A. L. Levy, and Rasmus Kleis Nielsen. 2016. Reuters institute digital news report.

Martin Potthast, Tim Gollub, Matti Wiegmann, and Benno Stein. 2019. TIRA integrated research architecture. In Nicola Ferro and Carol Peters, editors, *Information Retrieval Evaluation in a Changing World - Lessons Learned from 20 Years of CLEF*, volume 41 of *The Information Retrieval Series*, pages 123–160. Springer.

Georg Rehm. 2018. An Infrastructure for Empowering Internet Users to handle Fake News and other Online Media Phenomena. In *Language Technologies for the Challenges of the Digital Age: 27th International Conference, GSCL 2017, Berlin, Germany, September 13-14, 2017, Proceedings*, number 10713 in Lecture Notes in Artificial Intelligence (LNAI), pages 216–231, Cham, Switzerland. Gesellschaft für Sprachtechnologie und Computerlinguistik e.V., Springer. 13/14 September 2017.

Georg Rehm, Peter Bourgonje, Stefanie Hegele, Florian Kintzel, Julián Moreno Schneider, Malte Ostendorff, Karolina Zaczynska, Armin Berger, Stefan Grill, Sören Räuchle, Jens Rauenbusch, Lisa Rutenburg, André Schmidt, Mikka Wild, Henry Hoffmann, Julian Fink, Sarah Schulz, Jurica Seva, Joachim Quantz, Joachim Böttger, Josefine Matthey, Rolf Fricke, Jan Thomsen, Adrian Paschke, Jamal Al Qundus, Thomas Hoppe, Naouel Karam, Frauke Weichhardt, Christian Fillies, Clemens Neudecker, Mike Gerber, Kai Labusch, Vahid Rezanezhad, Robin Schaefer, David Zellhöfer, Daniel Siewert, Patrick Bunk, Lydia Pintscher, Elena Aleynikova, and Franziska Heine. 2020. QURATOR: Innovative Technologies for Content and Data Curation. In *Proceedings of QURATOR 2020 – The conference for intelligent content solutions*, Berlin, Germany. CEUR Workshop Proceedings, Volume 2535. 20/21 January 2020.

Sarah T. Roberts, Joel Tetreault, Vinodkumar Prabhakaran, and Zeerak Waseem, editors. 2019. *Proceedings of the Third Workshop on Abusive Language Online*. Association for Computational Linguistics, Florence, Italy.

Joni Salminen, Hind Almerekhi, Milica Milenkovic, Soon-Gyo Jung, Jisun An, Haewoon Kwak, and Jim Jansen. 2019. Anatomy of online hate: Developing a taxonomy and machine learning models for identifying and classifying hate in online news media.

Joni Salminen, Maximilian Hopf, S. A. Chowdhury, Soon-Gyo Jung, H. Almerekhi, and Bernard J. Jansen. 2020. Developing an online hate classifier for multiple social media platforms. *Human-centric Computing and Information Sciences*, 10:1–34.

Estela Saquete, David Tomás, Paloma Moreda, Patricio Martínez-Barco, and Manuel Palomar. 2020. Fighting post-truth using natural language processing: A review and open challenges. *Expert Systems with Applications*, 141:112943.

Robert E. Schapire. 1999. A brief introduction to boosting. In *Proceedings of the 16th International Joint Conference on Artificial Intelligence - Volume 2*, IJCAI'99, page 1401–1406, San Francisco, CA, USA. Morgan Kaufmann Publishers Inc.

Parinaz Sobhani, Diana Inkpen, and Xiaodan Zhu. 2017. A dataset for multi-target stance detection. In *Proceedings of the 15th Conference of the European Chapter of the Association for Computational Linguistics: Volume 2, Short Papers*, pages 551–557, Valencia, Spain. Association for Computational Linguistics.

Julia Maria Struß, Melanie Siegel, Josef Ruppenhofer, Michael Wiegand, and Manfred Klenner. 2019. Overview of germeval task 2, 2019 shared task on the identification of offensive language. Preliminary proceedings of the 15th Conference on Natural Language Processing (KONVENS 2019), October 9 – 11, 2019 at Friedrich-Alexander-Universität Erlangen-Nürnberg, pages 352 – 363, München [u.a.]. German Society for Computational Linguistics & Language Technology und Friedrich-Alexander-Universität Erlangen-Nürnberg.

Matt Thomas, Bo Pang, and Lillian Lee. 2006. Get out the vote: Determining support or opposition from congressional floor-debate transcripts. In *Proceedings of the 2006 Conference on Empirical Methods in Natural Language Processing*, pages 327–335, Sydney, Australia. Association for Computational Linguistics.

James Thorne, Andreas Vlachos, Oana Cocarascu, Christos Christodoulopoulos, and Arpit Mittal. 2019. The FEVER2.0 shared task. In *Proceedings of the Second Workshop on Fact Extraction and VERification (FEVER)*, pages 1–6, Hong Kong, China. Association for Computational Linguistics.

Jannis Vamvas and Rico Sennrich. 2020. X-stance: A multilingual multi-target dataset for stance detection. *CoRR*, abs/2003.08385.

Bertie Vidgen and Leon Derczynski. 2021. Directions in abusive language training data, a systematic review: Garbage in, garbage out. *PLOS ONE*, 15(12):1–32.

Bertie Vidgen, Scott Hale, Ella Guest, Helen Margetts, David Broniatowski, Zeerak Waseem, Austin Botelho, Matthew Hall, and Rebekah Tromble. 2020. Detecting East Asian prejudice on social media. In *Proceedings of the Fourth Workshop on Online Abuse and Harms*, pages 162–172, Online. Association for Computational Linguistics.

Emmanuel Vincent and Maria Mestre. 2018. Crowdsourced measure of news articles bias: Assessing contributors' reliability. In *Proceedings of the 1st Workshop on Subjectivity, Ambiguity and Disagreement in Crowdsourcing, and Short Paper Proceedings of the 1st Workshop on Disentangling the Relation Between Crowdsourcing and Bias Management (SAD 2018 and CrowdBias 2018) co-located the 6th AAAI Conference on Human Computation and Crowdsourcing (HCOMP 2018), Zürich, Switzerland, July 5, 2018*, volume 2276 of *CEUR Workshop Proceedings*, pages 1–10. CEUR-WS.org.

Zeerak Waseem, Wendy Hui Kyong Chung, Dirk Hovy, and Joel Tetreault, editors. 2017. *Proceedings of the First Workshop on Abusive Language Online*. Association for Computational Linguistics, Vancouver, BC, Canada.

Maximilian Wich, Jan Bauer, and Georg Groh. 2020. Impact of politically biased data on hate speech classification. In *Proceedings of the Fourth Workshop on Online Abuse and Harms*, pages 54–64, Online. Association for Computational Linguistics.

Sarah Wiegreffe and Yuval Pinter. 2019. Attention is not not explanation. In *Proceedings of the 2019 Conference on Empirical Methods in Natural Language Processing and the 9th International Joint Conference on Natural Language Processing (EMNLP-IJCNLP)*, pages 11–20, Hong Kong, China. Association for Computational Linguistics.

Marcos Zampieri, Shervin Malmasi, Preslav Nakov, Sara Rosenthal, Noura Farra, and Ritesh Kumar. 2019. SemEval-2019 task 6: Identifying and categorizing offensive language in social media (OffensEval). In *Proceedings of the 13th International Workshop on Semantic Evaluation*, pages 75–86, Minneapolis, Minnesota, USA. Association for Computational Linguistics.

Xiang Zhou, Heba Elfardy, Christos Christodoulopoulos, Thomas Butler, and Mohit Bansal. 2021. Hidden biases in unreliable news detection datasets. In *Proceedings of the 16th Conference of the European Chapter of the Association for Computational Linguistics: Main Volume*, pages 2482–2492, Online. Association for Computational Linguistics.

Jibes & Delights: A Dataset of Targeted Insults and Compliments to Tackle Online Abuse

Ravsimar Sodhi and **Kartikey Pant** and **Radhika Mamidi**
International Institute of Information Technology
Hyderabad, Telangana, India
ravsimar.sodhi@research.iiit.ac.in
kartikey.pant@research.iiit.ac.in
radhika.mamidi@iiit.ac.in

Abstract

Online abuse and offensive language on social media have become widespread problems in today's digital age. In this paper, we contribute a Reddit-based dataset, consisting of 68,159 insults and 51,102 compliments targeted at individuals instead of targeting a particular community or race. Secondly, we benchmark multiple existing state-of-the-art models for both classification and unsupervised style transfer on the dataset. Finally, we analyse the experimental results and conclude that the transfer task is challenging, requiring the models to understand the high degree of creativity exhibited in the data.

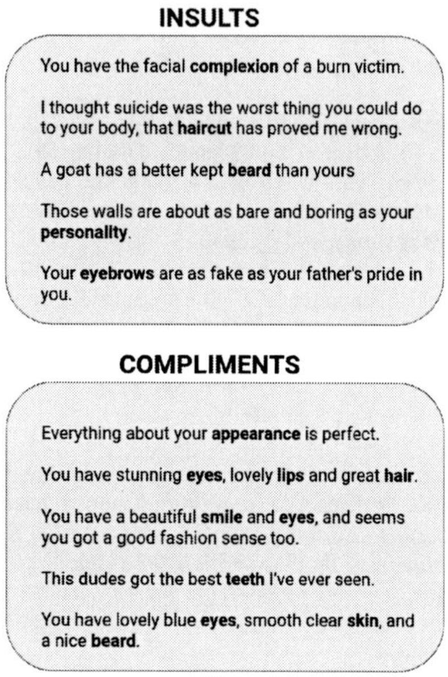

Figure 1: Examples of indirect insults and compliments with attributes highlighted in bold

1 Introduction

Online abuse and targeted negative comments on online social networks have become a prevalent phenomenon, especially impacting adolescents. Victims of prolonged and targeted online harassment can experience negative emotions leading to adverse consequences such as anxiety and isolation from the community, which can, in turn, lead to suicidal behaviour.[1] Various attempts have been made to detect such harassment (Dadvar et al., 2013; Chatzakou et al., 2019) and hate speech (Davidson et al., 2017; Badjatiya et al., 2017) in the past, but very few have attempted to transfer the negative aspect of such speech.

Recently, many new tasks have been introduced in the domain of text style transfer. However, since parallel corpora is usually not available, most style transfer approaches adopt an unsupervised manner (Li et al., 2018; Zhang et al., 2018; John et al., 2019; Wang et al., 2019) . We contribute a dataset of non-parallel sentences, each sentence being either an insult or a compliment, collected from Reddit, more specifically, from three subreddits r/RoastMe, r/ToastMe, and r/FreeCompliments. Some examples of such sentences can be seen in Figure 1.

With a diverse range of online communication platforms being introduced across the world, and existing platforms' user-bases growing at a fast pace, moderation of such negative comments and harassment becomes even more necessary. We hope that our work can enable and further research in this daunting task, for instance in building moderation systems which can detect such negative speech and nudge users to engage in more positive and non-toxic discourse.

Reddit is a popular social media website with forums known as subreddits where users can comment and vote on posts and other comments. It has been used as a source of data in wide variety of tasks. r/RoastMe can be described as a sub-

[1]Source: https://www.stopbullying.gov/resources/facts

Proceedings of the Fifth Workshop on Online Abuse and Harms, pages 132–139
August 6, 2021. ©2021 Association for Computational Linguistics

reddit consisting of "abrasive humor" and consists of "creative" insults where users can voluntarily submit their picture to be "roasted." r/ToastMe and r/FreeCompliments are similar in principle but have the opposite purpose. A more detailed description of the data source and preparation can be found in Section 3. Since "creativity" is encouraged in r/RoastMe, this makes our dataset consist of indirect insults that do not necessarily use any profanity or curse words and may slip past most existing toxic speech filters.

In this work, we release the JDC (**J**ibe and **D**elight **C**orpus), a dataset of $\sim 120,000$ Reddit comments tagged as insults or compliments which are targeted towards particular attributes of an individual including their *face*, *hair*, and *eyes*[2]. We also propose to use classification models to detect and style transfer models to convert such targeted negative comments, often associated with online harassment, in which menacing or insulting messages are sent by direct messages or posted on social media. We also perform benchmarking experiments using existing state-of-the-art models on both fronts and analyse its results.

2 Related Work

Existing work primarily focuses on the *detection* of offensive language or hate speech on social media using classification models (Davidson et al., 2017; Badjatiya et al., 2017; Dadu and Pant, 2020), and not on *transferring* the negative aspect of such speech into a positive counterpart. Detection usually involves either lexical or rule-based approach (Pérez et al., 2012; Serra and Venter, 2011), or more recently, a supervised learning approach (Yin et al., 2009; Dinakar et al., 2011). Many attempts on detection of specific types of toxic speech have also been attempted (Basile et al., 2019; Zampieri et al., 2020). Previous work on text style transfer has largely focused on transferring attributes of sentiment in reviews (Li et al., 2018; Hu et al., 2017; Pant et al., 2020) or converting factual captions to humorous or romantic ones (Li et al., 2018). Other tasks include transferring formality (Xu et al., 2019) or gender or political style (Reddy and Knight, 2016). Recently, transferring politeness has also been proposed by Madaan et al. (2020).

Most approaches use unsupervised methods since parallel data is usually not available. These approaches can be broadly divided into three groups: 1) *Explicit disentanglement* (Li et al., 2018; Sudhakar et al., 2019) which separates content from style attributes in an explicit manner and then combines the separated content with the target attribute and pass it through a generator. 2) *Disentanglement in latent space* (John et al., 2019) which tries to separate style from content within the embedding space by using suitable objective functions. 3) *Adversarial or reinforcement learning based* (Luo et al., 2019) approaches in which disentanglement may not be even required.

Reddit has been widely used in multiple natural language processing tasks as a data source. While Khodak et al. (2018) use Reddit to create a large corpus for sarcasm, Nogueira dos Santos et al. (2018) source their data from r/Politics on Reddit along with Twitter. Many controversial subreddits such r/The_Donald have been used for detection of hate speech in the past (Qian et al., 2019).

Although Nogueira dos Santos et al. (2018) proposed the task of translating offensive sentences to non-offensive ones using style transfer, in our work, we go one step further and propose to convert offensive sentences into positive compliments. Prior work on r/RoastMe has mostly been on a socio-pragmatic perspective (Dynel and Poppi, 2019; Kasunic and Kaufman, 2018). However, there is no previous work that uses r/RoastMe as a data source in a style transfer task to the best of our knowledge.

3 The JDC Dataset

We contribute the Jibe and Delight Corpus (JDC), a new non-parallel style transfer dataset consisting of $\sim 120,000$ comments tagged as insults or compliments, and perform experiments and analysis on the same.

3.1 Data Collection

We use Pushshift (Baumgartner et al., 2020) to extract Reddit posts and comments.While r/RoastMe is often characterized as a humourous subreddit, where users can voluntarily submit pictures of themselves to be "roasted" or insulted, internet users who are not familiar with the community can associate r/RoastMe with malicious activities including cyberbullying (Jenaro et al., 2018). r/RoastMe has even been described as "a new cy-

[2]Made available at https://github.com/ravsimar-sodhi/jibes-and-delights

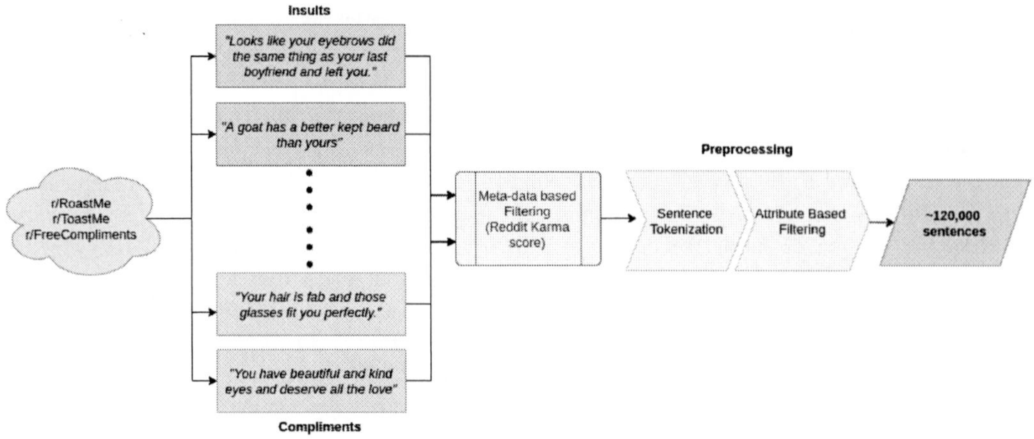

Figure 2: Dataset Creation Pipeline

berbullying trend" by news media[3]. The "roasters" will come up with comments that insult or demean the poster of the picture while trying to be as "creative" as possible. r/ToastMe and r/FreeCompliments work similarly, but with the opposite intent. These communities are much smaller and less popular than r/RoastMe, and hence, the number of insults in our dataset is greater than the number of compliments.

It is essential to distinguish between insults and slurs since the two are frequently clubbed together. A slur is a taboo remark that is usually used to deprecate, disparage or derogate a targeted member of a select category, such as ethnicity, race, or sexual orientation. Insults can consist of slurs, but they are much broader, and a more diversified phenomenon (Dynel and Poppi, 2019). While slurs are common in hate speech datasets, it is interesting to observe that slurs are comparatively rare in posts from r/RoastMe. This characteristic makes our dataset unique concerning other offensive speech datasets. Figure 2 illustrates our pipeline for the creation of the JDC.

3.2 Data Preparation

Since Reddit is a conversational social media platform, we limit the JDC to comments having the following characteristics:

- *They are top-level comments.* While nested comments may also sometimes contain relevant data, they often diverge from the topic and begin a conversation with the parent comment, which may add noise to our dataset.

- *They have a Reddit karma score of at least 3.* Reddit karma score is defined to be the number of upvotes minus the number of downvotes. This filtering helps in weeding out spam or irrelevant comments which are not relevant to the topic. Generally, users downvote comments which they find unfunny or off-topic. Thus, we utilize crowdsourced user scores to ensure quality sentences.

This filtering yields a corpus of roughly $300,000$ insult comments and $100,000$ compliment comments. However, due to users' wide variety of insults and creativity, we utilize several other filters to limit our dataset to a particular type of insult or compliment. We manually create an attribute list[4] consisting of words which correspond to a physical attribute (for example, *hair*, *skin*, *complexion*, *teeth*, and *eyes*) or a trait (for example, *personality*, *kindness*, and *appearance*) and keep our insults containing keywords for such attributes. We use the NLTK (Bird et al., 2009) and spaCy (Honnibal and Montani, 2017) libraries for preprocessing and filtering. We tokenize each comment into sentences, and check if the lemma of any word in a sentence matches a word in our attribute list. This process helps us keep relevant sentences, especially from longer comments, which would be otherwise discarded. We also filter out very short sentences (containing only one or two words). We obtain

[3] Source:https://abcnews.go.com/Lifestyle/parents-roasting-cyberbullying-trend/story?id=49407671

[4] https://github.com/ravsimar-sodhi/jibes-and-delight/blob/main/attr-list.txt

Input	Your teeth are more stained than my toilet
StyleEmb	Your hair is beautiful than your face.
RetrieveOnly	Beautiful smile - your teeth are remarkably straight
DeleteRetrieve	Your hair is beautiful and your teeth are more stained than my
LingST	Your teeth are so beautiful
Tag&Gen	Your teeth are more stained than my heart
Input	The only thing lazier than your eye is God when he designed your busted face
StyleEmb	Keep your hair and I love your hair and you look like the kind of person who look like a
RetrieveOnly	Your hair is fantastic and your face is absolutely adorable.
DeleteRetrieve	And your eye expressive is God wonderful lips designed especially your face
LingST	The only thing more crooked than your face is the absolute cutest thing i
Tag&Gen	Love the only thing lazier than your eye is god when he designed your busted face

Table 1: Examples of Style Transfer model outputs

a corpus of around 68, 159 *insult* sentences and 51, 102 *compliment* sentences. Finally, we take 1, 000 instances each from both categories for evaluation purposes.

4 Experiments & Results

We perform experiments using both classification and style transfer models and evaluate the performance of five models for each task from works on the JDC. We also discuss about the challenges faced and the metrics used for evaluation.

4.1 Models

For classification experiments, we experiment using the following models:

1. **Logistic Regression**: One of the most common classification algorithms used, Logistic Regression (*LR*) uses the logistic (sigmoid) function to return a probability value that can be further mapped to multiple classes.

2. **SVM**: Support Vector Machines (*SVM*) use an objective function that finds a hyperplane in an N dimensional space, where N is the number of features, which distinctly separates the data points into classes.

3. **BERT** (Devlin et al., 2019): Bidirectional Encoder Representations from Transformers or *BERT* is a relatively recent transformer-based model, which leverages transfer learning. At the time of release, *BERT* outperformed several other models in language modeling tasks.

4. **RoBERTa** (Liu et al., 2019): *RoBERTa* improves on *BERT* by modifying several hyperparameters and performs pretraining on larger amounts of data for a longer amount of time.

5. **XLNet** (Yang et al., 2019): While *BERT* and *RoBERTa* are categorized as autoencoder language models, *XLNet* is a generalized autoregressive pretraining method. Instead of using Masked Language modeling like *BERT*, it proposed a new objective called Permuation Language Modeling, and its results improved upon *BERT* in many tasks.

We fine-tune the models for classification in case of **BERT**, **RoBERTa**, and **XLNet**, and use the Hugging Face's transformers library (Wolf et al., 2020) for our experiments.

For style transfer experiments, we use the following models:

1. **StyleEmb** (Shen et al., 2017): This model uses a cross-aligned auto-encoder, aligning representations in latent space to perform style transfer.

2. **RetrieveOnly** and **DeleteRetrieve** (Li et al., 2018): While *RetrieveOnly* only returns a sentence from the target style without any changes, *DeleteRetrieve* returns the *best match* according to the attribute markers from the source sentences. Both models use explicit disentanglement to separate content from style along with a decoder and are often used as baselines in multiple works in style transfer.

3. **LingST** (John et al., 2019): This model uses a variational auto-encoder and utilizes multiple adversarial objectives for both style and content preservation.

4. **Tag&Gen** (Madaan et al., 2020): This model uses an encoder-decoder approach where both encoder and decoder are transformer-based.

Model	Acc.	Prec.	Recall	F1
LR	0.875	0.980	0.897	0.883
SVM	0.801	0.979	0.851	0.818
BERT	0.977	0.967	**0.974**	0.970
RoBERTa	0.977	**0.971**	0.973	0.971
XLNet	**0.978**	0.970	0.973	**0.972**

Table 2: Automatic Evaluation Results of Classification models on the dataset

This has recently been utilized for the politeness transfer task.

4.2 Evaluation

For the classification experiments, we evaluate using the well-known metrics of Accuracy, Precision, Recall and F1-Score.

For the style transfer experiments, we evaluate the performance on three different aspects, following previous works:

1. **Style Transfer Intensity**: We train a separate fastText model (Joulin et al., 2017) on the training data and evaluate the different model outputs to determine the accuracy of style transfer.
2. **Content Preservation**: We use BLEU as an evaluation metric and utilize the *SacreBLEU* (Post, 2018) implementation.
3. **Fluency**: We calculate fluency using a language model from the *KenLM* library for our experiments. (Heafield, 2011) after training the language model on the target domain (*compliment*). A lower perplexity indicates a more fluent sentence and vice-versa.

Apart from automatic evaluation, we also do human evaluation on 280 sentences randomly selected from the test set. The evaluators were asked to rank sentences on basis of their fluency and degree of being a compliment (DOC) on a scale of 1 to 5. Two annotators were shown a list of sentences, with no indication of the source of the sentence. The Cohen's Kappa metric (Cohen, 1960) was used to measure the agreement between the two annotators. The value of kappa for DOC and fluency come out to be 0.69 and 0.65 respectively.

4.3 Results

Table 2 shows that most of the models perform very well in classifying insults and compliments into different categories. Even ML-based models like *LR* and *SVM* perform adequately on the task, but the more state-of-the-art BERT-based models perform excellently, having high F1-scores above 0.9. *XLNet* shows the highest F1-score, with *BERT* and *RoBERTa* only marginally lower.

Model	Acc(%)	BLEU	PPL
StyleEmb	87.41	2.27	615.59
RetrieveOnly	**97.77**	3.83	241.04
DeleteRetrieve	81.35	23.81	857.19
LingST	93.00	3.16	**63.03**
Tag&Gen	30.17	**85.40**	637.39

Table 3: Automatic Evaluation results of Style Transfer models on the dataset

Model	DOC	Fluency
Input	1.116	**4.648**
StyleEmb	1.904	1.786
RetrieveOnly	**4.170**	4.468
DeleteRetrieve	2.595	2.051
LingST	3.851	3.414
Tag&Gen	1.382	3.819

Table 4: Human Evaluation results of Style Transfer models on the dataset. DOC is the "Degree of Compliment" and Fluency is the naturalness of the sentence, both being rated on a scale of 1 to 5

From Table 3, we observe that *RetrieveOnly*, *StyleEmb*, and *LingST* show high accuracy in transfer but do not perform well in content preservation. *Tag&Gen* performs very well on content preservation but fails to transfer the style adequately. *DeleteRetrieve* obtains a better balance in accuracy and BLEU, but it loses out on fluency, producing the least fluent sentences among all models. This implies that although the relevant words from style and content are transferred, the output may not be grammatical or natural.

Human evaluation results in Table 4 also show that the input sentence is judged as more fluent rather than the model outputs. We see that *RetrieveOnly* and *LingST* outputs are more likely to be judged as compliments. However, *StyleEmb* is judged to be as poor in both DOC and Fluency.

4.4 Discussion

Even though the insults are "creative", we find that the classification models perform excellently in differentiating insults and compliments into two separate categories. This shows that both insults

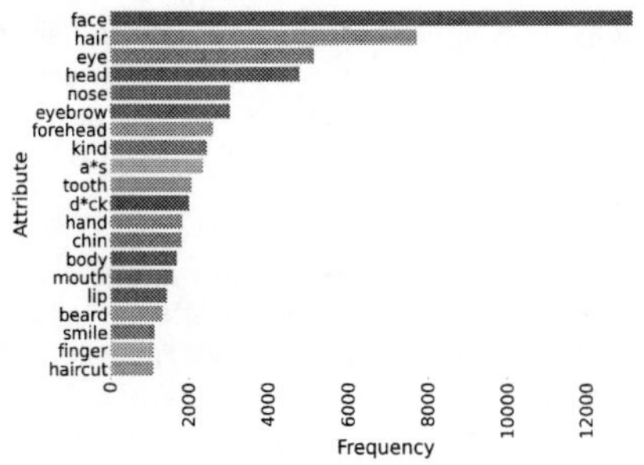

Figure 3: Insult distribution by top 20 attributes

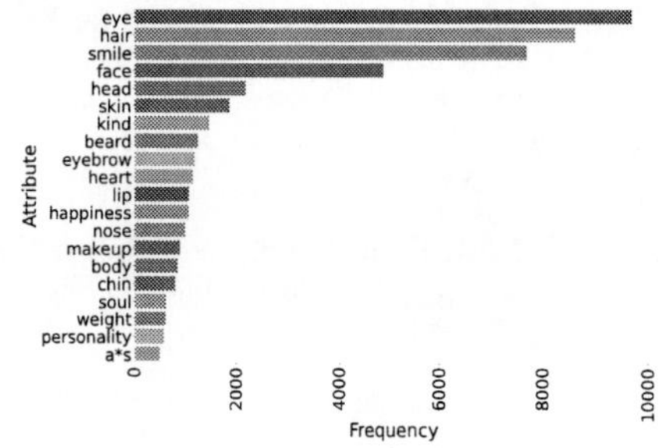

Figure 4: Compliment distribution by top 20 attributes

and compliments, even though they may target the same physical attributes, have different styles and models can be trained to detect and classify them with good results.

However, performance of the style transfer models is lacking. We observe that there are different shortcomings in each model. Table 1 shows sample outputs produced by the models. *RetrieveOnly* fetches a sentence from the target style using specific attributes from the input sentence, often leading to invalid outputs if a corresponding positive sentence does not exist in the data. In the second example in Table 1, *DeleteRetrieve* gives a nonsensical output. Other models have similarly tried to transfer the intent by introducing words like "kind","wonderful" and "cute", but there is still a significant gap between the generated outputs and genuine compliments. We observe that *LingST* has the lowest perplexity while still having high accuracy. This ensures that generated outputs are positive and are also grammatically fluent. Compared to sentiment transfer, converting an insult to a compliment usually involves multi-word modifications, explaining the poor content preservation across most of the models.

We observe that style transfer models have an easier time handling more direct insults ("You look very ugly"), rather than handling more complex and creative insults ("How many concrete walls did you have to run into to achieve that nose?"). Besides the more direct and creative the insults, there are some samples which need more context to understand and may seem out of place compared to the rest. However, most of these are filtered out with the help of the attribute list described in Section 3. The distribution of the data according to the top attributes can be seen in Figure 3 and Figure 4 for insults and compliments respectively. While a lot of creativity is exhibited in the insults, we find that compliments are usually of a direct form, and thus are simpler and easier to understand. This is desirable since some convoluted compliments may come across as patronizing, which is counterproductive to our goal.

5 Conclusion

In this work, we introduced a Reddit-based dataset consisting of indirect insults that favor creativity and rarely use slurs. We benchmarked classification models for detection and exploited unsupervised text style transfer to convert insults into compliments. We evaluated the performance of different state-of-the-art models on the dataset, observing that while detection is easier, transfer of the negative attribute is a challenging task. Future work may include enhancing methodologies for unsupervised text style transfer that capture the intricacies in the proposed dataset and building moderation systems for online platforms.

References

Pinkesh Badjatiya, Shashank Gupta, Manish Gupta, and Vasudeva Varma. 2017. Deep Learning for Hate Speech Detection in Tweets. In *Proceedings of the 26th International Conference on World Wide Web Companion*, WWW '17 Companion, pages 759–760, Republic and Canton of Geneva, CHE. International World Wide Web Conferences Steering Committee.

Valerio Basile, Cristina Bosco, Elisabetta Fersini, Debora Nozza, Viviana Patti, Francisco Manuel Rangel Pardo, Paolo Rosso, and Manuela Sanguinetti. 2019. SemEval-2019 Task 5: Multilingual Detection of Hate Speech Against Immigrants and Women in Twitter. In *Proceedings of the 13th International Workshop on Semantic Evaluation*, pages 54–63, Minneapolis, Minnesota, USA. Association for Computational Linguistics.

Jason Baumgartner, Savvas Zannettou, Brian Keegan, Megan Squire, and Jeremy Blackburn. 2020. The Pushshift Reddit Dataset. *Proceedings of the International AAAI Conference on Web and Social Media*, 14:830–839.

Steven Bird, Ewan Klein, and Edward Loper. 2009. *Natural Language Processing with Python*, 1st edition. O'Reilly Media, Inc.

Despoina Chatzakou, Ilias Leontiadis, Jeremy Blackburn, Emiliano De Cristofaro, Gianluca Stringhini, Athena Vakali, and Nicolas Kourtellis. 2019. Detecting Cyberbullying and Cyberaggression in Social Media. *ACM Transactions on the Web*, 13(3):17:1–17:51.

Jacob Cohen. 1960. A Coefficient of Agreement for Nominal Scales. *Educational and Psychological Measurement*, 20(1):37–46.

Tanvi Dadu and Kartikey Pant. 2020. Team rouges at SemEval-2020 task 12: Cross-lingual inductive transfer to detect offensive language. In *Proceedings of the Fourteenth Workshop on Semantic Evaluation*, pages 2183–2189, Barcelona (online). International Committee for Computational Linguistics.

Maral Dadvar, Dolf Trieschnigg, Roeland Ordelman, and Franciska de Jong. 2013. Improving Cyberbullying Detection with User Context. In *Advances in Information Retrieval*, Lecture Notes in Computer Science, pages 693–696, Berlin, Heidelberg. Springer.

Thomas Davidson, Dana Warmsley, M. Macy, and Ingmar Weber. 2017. Automated Hate Speech Detection and the Problem of Offensive Language. In *ICWSM*.

J. Devlin, Ming-Wei Chang, Kenton Lee, and Kristina Toutanova. 2019. BERT: Pre-training of Deep Bidirectional Transformers for Language Understanding. In *NAACL-HLT*.

K. Dinakar, Roi Reichart, and H. Lieberman. 2011. Modeling the Detection of Textual Cyberbullying. In *The Social Mobile Web*.

Marta Dynel and Fabio I. M. Poppi. 2019. Risum teneatis, amici?: The socio-pragmatics of RoastMe humour. *Journal of Pragmatics*, 139:1–21.

Kenneth Heafield. 2011. KenLM: Faster and smaller language model queries. In *Proceedings of the Sixth Workshop on Statistical Machine Translation*, WMT '11, pages 187–197, USA. Association for Computational Linguistics.

Matthew Honnibal and Ines Montani. 2017. spaCy 2: Natural language understanding with Bloom embeddings, convolutional neural networks and incremental parsing.

Zhiting Hu, Zichao Yang, Xiaodan Liang, R. Salakhutdinov, and E. Xing. 2017. Toward Controlled Generation of Text. In *ICML*.

Cristina Jenaro, Noelia Flores, and Cinthia Patricia Frías. 2018. Systematic review of empirical studies on cyberbullying in adults: What we know and what we should investigate. *Aggression and Violent Behavior*, 38:113–122.

Vineet John, Lili Mou, Hareesh Bahuleyan, and Olga Vechtomova. 2019. Disentangled Representation Learning for Non-Parallel Text Style Transfer. In *Proceedings of the 57th Annual Meeting of the Association for Computational Linguistics*, pages 424–434, Florence, Italy. Association for Computational Linguistics.

Armand Joulin, E. Grave, P. Bojanowski, and Tomas Mikolov. 2017. Bag of Tricks for Efficient Text Classification. In *EACL*.

Anna Kasunic and Geoff Kaufman. 2018. "At Least the Pizzas You Make Are Hot": Norms, Values, and Abrasive Humor on the Subreddit r/RoastMe. *Proceedings of the International AAAI Conference on Web and Social Media*, 12(1).

M. Khodak, Nikunj Saunshi, and Kiran Vodrahalli. 2018. A Large Self-Annotated Corpus for Sarcasm. *LREC*.

Juncen Li, Robin Jia, He He, and Percy Liang. 2018. Delete, Retrieve, Generate: A Simple Approach to Sentiment and Style Transfer. *NAACL-HLT*.

Y. Liu, Myle Ott, Naman Goyal, Jingfei Du, Mandar Joshi, Danqi Chen, Omer Levy, M. Lewis, Luke Zettlemoyer, and Veselin Stoyanov. 2019. RoBERTa: A Robustly Optimized BERT Pretraining Approach. *ArXiv*.

Fuli Luo, Peng Li, J. Zhou, Pengcheng Yang, Baobao Chang, Zhifang Sui, and X. Sun. 2019. A Dual Reinforcement Learning Framework for Unsupervised Text Style Transfer. *IJCAI*.

Aman Madaan, Amrith Rajagopal Setlur, Tanmay Parekh, B. Póczos, Graham Neubig, Yiming Yang, R. Salakhutdinov, A. Black, and Shrimai Prabhumoye. 2020. Politeness Transfer: A Tag and Generate Approach. In *ACL*.

Cicero Nogueira dos Santos, Igor Melnyk, and Inkit Padhi. 2018. Fighting Offensive Language on Social Media with Unsupervised Text Style Transfer. In *Proceedings of the 56th Annual Meeting of the Association for Computational Linguistics (Volume 2: Short Papers)*, pages 189–194, Melbourne, Australia. Association for Computational Linguistics.

Kartikey Pant, Yash Verma, and Radhika Mamidi. 2020. SentiInc: Incorporating Sentiment Information into Sentiment Transfer Without Parallel Data. In Joemon M. Jose, Emine Yilmaz, João Magalhães, Pablo Castells, Nicola Ferro, Mário J. Silva, and Flávio Martins, editors, *Advances in Information Retrieval*, volume 12036, pages 312–319. Springer International Publishing, Cham.

Perla Janeth Castro Pérez, Christian Javier Lucero Valdez, María De Guadalupe Cota Ortiz, Juan Pablo Soto Barrera, and Pedro Flores Pérez. 2012. MISAAC: Instant messaging tool for ciberbullying detection. In *Proceedings of the 2012 International Conference on Artificial Intelligence, ICAI 2012*, Proceedings of the 2012 International Conference on Artificial Intelligence, ICAI 2012, pages 1049–1052.

Matt Post. 2018. A call for clarity in reporting BLEU scores. In *Proceedings of the Third Conference on Machine Translation: Research Papers*, pages 186–191, Belgium, Brussels. Association for Computational Linguistics.

Jing Qian, Anna Bethke, Yinyin Liu, Elizabeth M. Belding-Royer, and William Yang Wang. 2019. A Benchmark Dataset for Learning to Intervene in Online Hate Speech. In *EMNLP/IJCNLP*.

S. Reddy and K. Knight. 2016. Obfuscating Gender in Social Media Writing. In *NLP+CSS@EMNLP*.

S. M. Serra and H. S. Venter. 2011. Mobile cyberbullying: A proposal for a pre-emptive approach to risk mitigation by employing digital forensic readiness. In *2011 Information Security for South Africa*, pages 1–5.

T. Shen, Tao Lei, R. Barzilay, and T. Jaakkola. 2017. Style Transfer from Non-Parallel Text by Cross-Alignment. In *NIPS*.

A. Sudhakar, Bhargav Upadhyay, and A. Maheswaran. 2019. Transforming Delete, Retrieve, Generate Approach for Controlled Text Style Transfer. *EMNLP/IJCNLP*.

Ke Wang, Hang Hua, and Xiaojun Wan. 2019. Controllable Unsupervised Text Attribute Transfer via Editing Entangled Latent Representation. In *NeurIPS*.

Thomas Wolf, Lysandre Debut, Victor Sanh, Julien Chaumond, Clement Delangue, Anthony Moi, Pierric Cistac, Tim Rault, Rémi Louf, Morgan Funtowicz, Joe Davison, Sam Shleifer, Patrick von Platen, Clara Ma, Yacine Jernite, Julien Plu, Canwen Xu, Teven Le Scao, Sylvain Gugger, Mariama Drame, Quentin Lhoest, and Alexander M. Rush. 2020. Transformers: State-of-the-art natural language processing. In *Proceedings of the 2020 Conference on Empirical Methods in Natural Language Processing: System Demonstrations*, pages 38–45, Online. Association for Computational Linguistics.

Ruochen Xu, Tao Ge, and Furu Wei. 2019. Formality Style Transfer with Hybrid Textual Annotations. *ArXiv*.

Z. Yang, Zihang Dai, Yiming Yang, J. Carbonell, R. Salakhutdinov, and Quoc V. Le. 2019. XLNet: Generalized Autoregressive Pretraining for Language Understanding. In *NeurIPS*.

Dawei Yin, Zhenzhen Xue, Liangjie Hong, Brian Davison, April Edwards, and Lynne Edwards. 2009. Detection of harassment on Web 2.0.

Marcos Zampieri, Preslav Nakov, Sara Rosenthal, Pepa Atanasova, Georgi Karadzhov, Hamdy Mubarak, Leon Derczynski, Zeses Pitenis, and Çağrı Çöltekin. 2020. SemEval-2020 Task 12: Multilingual Offensive Language Identification in Social Media (OffensEval 2020). In *Proceedings of the Fourteenth Workshop on Semantic Evaluation*, pages 1425–1447, Barcelona (online). International Committee for Computational Linguistics.

Zhirui Zhang, Shuo Ren, Shujie Liu, Jianyong Wang, Peng Chen, Mu Li, M. Zhou, and E. Chen. 2018. Style Transfer as Unsupervised Machine Translation. *ArXiv*.

Context Sensitivity Estimation in Toxicity Detection

Alexandros Xenos[♣], **John Pavlopoulos**[♠♣*], **Ion Androutsopoulos**[♣]
[♣]Department of Informatics, Athens University of Economics and Business, Greece
[♠]Department of Computer and Systems Sciences, Stockholm University, Sweden
{a.xenos20,annis,ion}@aueb.gr

Abstract

User posts whose perceived toxicity depends on the conversational context are rare in current toxicity detection datasets. Hence, toxicity detectors trained on current datasets will also disregard context, making the detection of context-sensitive toxicity a lot harder when it occurs. We constructed and publicly release a dataset of 10k posts with two kinds of toxicity labels per post, obtained from annotators who considered (i) both the current post and the previous one as context, or (ii) only the current post. We introduce a new task, *context sensitivity estimation*, which aims to identify posts whose perceived toxicity changes if the context (previous post) is also considered. Using the new dataset, we show that systems can be developed for this task. Such systems could be used to enhance toxicity detection datasets with more context-dependent posts, or to suggest when moderators should consider the parent posts, which may not always be necessary and may introduce an additional cost.

1 Introduction

Online fora are used to facilitate discussions, but hateful, insulting, identity-attacking, profane, or otherwise abusive posts may also occur. These posts are called toxic (Borkan et al., 2019) or abusive (Thylstrup and Waseem, 2020), and systems detecting them (Waseem and Hovy, 2016; Pavlopoulos et al., 2017b; Badjatiya et al., 2017) are called toxicity (or abusive language) detection systems. What most of these systems have in common, besides aiming to promote healthy discussions online (Zhang et al., 2018), is that they disregard the conversational context (e.g., the parent post in the discussion), making the detection of context-sensitive toxicity a lot harder. For instance, the post "Keep the hell out" may be considered as toxic by a moderator, if the previous (parent) post "What was the title of that 'hell out' movie?" is ignored. Although toxicity datasets that include conversational context have recently started to appear, in previous work we showed that context-sensitive posts are still too few in those datasets (Pavlopoulos et al., 2020), which does not allow models to learn to detect context-dependent toxicity. In this work, we focus on this problem. We constructed and publicly release a context-aware dataset of 10k posts, each of which was annotated by raters who (i) considered the previous (parent) post as context, apart from the post being annotated (the target post), and by raters who (ii) were given only the target post, without context.[1]

As a first step towards studying context-dependent toxicity, we limit the conversational context to the previous (parent) post of the thread, as in our previous work (Pavlopoulos et al., 2020). We use the new dataset to study the nature of context sensitivity in toxicity detection, and we introduce a new task, *context sensitivity estimation*, which aims to identify posts whose perceived toxicity changes if the context (previous post) is also considered. Using the dataset, we also show that systems can be developed for the new task. Such systems could be used to enhance toxicity detection datasets with more context-dependent posts, or to suggest when moderators should consider the parent posts; the latter may not always be necessary and may also introduce additional cost.

2 The dataset

To build the dataset of this work, we used the also publicly available Civil Comments (CC) dataset (Borkan et al., 2019). CC was originally annotated by ten annotators per post, but the parent post

*Corresponding author.

[1]The dataset is released under a CC0 licence. See `http://nlp.cs.aueb.gr/publications.html` for the link to download it.

Proceedings of the Fifth Workshop on Online Abuse and Harms, pages 140–145
August 6, 2021. ©2021 Association for Computational Linguistics

(the previous post in the thread) was not shown to the annotators. We randomly sampled 10,000 CC posts and gave both the target and the parent post to the annotators. We call this new dataset Civil Comments in Context (CCC). Each CCC post was rated either as NON-TOXIC, UNSURE, TOXIC, or VERY TOXIC, as in the original CC dataset. We unified the latter two labels in both CC and CCC annotations to simplify the problem. To obtain the new in-context labels of CCC, we used the APPEN platform and five high accuracy annotators per post (annotators from zone 3, allowing adult and warned for explicit content), selected from 7 English speaking countries, namely: UK, Ireland, USA, Canada, New Zealand, South Africa, and Australia.[2]

The free-marginal kappa (Randolph, 2010) of the CCC annotations is 83.93%, while the average (mean pairwise) percentage agreement is 92%. In only 71 posts (0.07%) an annotator said UNSURE, i.e., annotators were confident in their decisions most of the time. We exclude these 71 posts from our study, as they are too few. The average length of target posts in CCC is only slightly lower than that of parent posts. Fig. 1 shows this counting the length in characters, but the same holds when counting words (56.5 vs. 68.8 words on average). To obtain a single toxicity score per post, we calculated the percentage of the annotators who found the post to be insulting, profane, identity-attack, hateful, or toxic in another way (i.e., all toxicity sub-types provided by the annotators were collapsed to a single toxicity label). This is similar to arrangements in the work of Wulczyn et al. (2017), who also found that training using the empirical distribution (over annotators) of the toxic labels (a continuous score per post) leads to better toxicity detection performance, compared to using labels reflecting the majority opinion of the raters (a binary label per post). See also Fornaciari et al. (2021).

Combined with the original (out of context) annotations of the 10k posts from CC, the new dataset (CCC) contains 10k posts for which both in-context (IC) and out-of-context (OC) labels are available. Figure 2 shows the number of posts (Y axis) per ground truth toxicity score (X axis). Orange represents the ground truth obtained by annotators who were provided with the parent post when rating (IC), while blue is for annotators who rated the post without context (OC). The vast majority of the

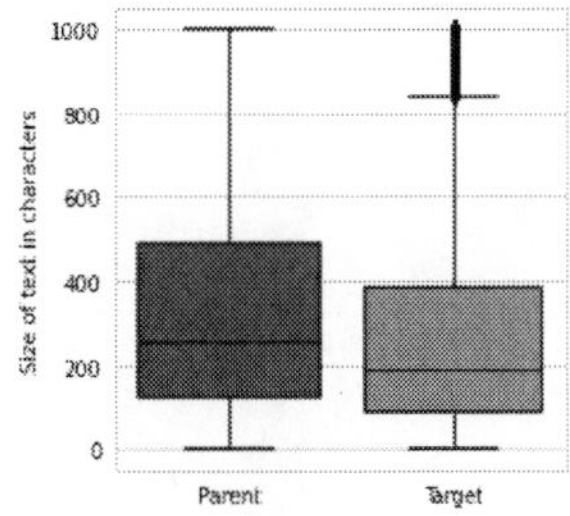

Figure 1: Length of parent/target posts in characters.

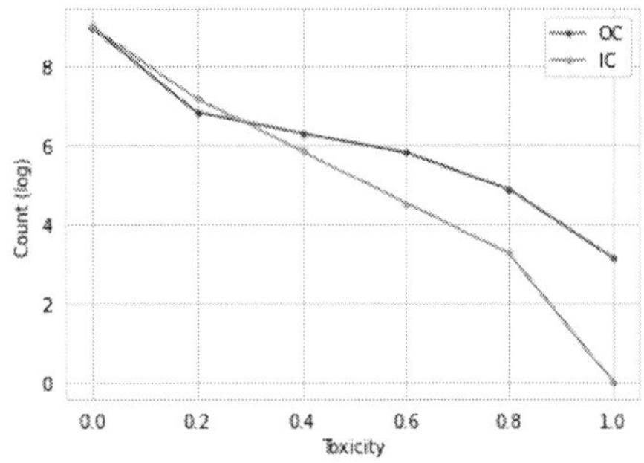

Figure 2: Histogram (converted to curve) of average toxicity according to annotators who were (IC) or were not (OC) given the parent post when annotating.

posts were unanimously perceived as NON-TOXIC (0.0 toxicity), both by the OC and the IC coders. However, IC coders found fewer posts with toxicity greater than 0.2, compared to OC coders. This is consistent with the findings of our previous work (Pavlopoulos et al., 2020), where we observed that when the parent post is provided, the majority of the annotators perceive fewer posts as toxic, compared to showing no context to the annotators. To study this further, in this work we compared the two scores (IC, OC) per post, as discussed below.

For each post p, we define $s^{ic}(p)$ to be the toxicity (fraction of coders who perceived the post as toxic) derived from the IC coders and $s^{oc}(p)$ to be the toxicity derived from the OC coders. Then, their difference is $\delta(p) = s^{oc}(p) - s^{ic}(p)$. A positive δ means that raters who were not given the parent post perceived the target post as toxic more often than raters who were given the parent post. A negative δ means the opposite. Fig. 3 shows that δ is most often zero, but when the toxicity score changes, δ is most often positive, i.e., showing the context to the annotators reduces the perceived toxicity in most cases. In numbers, in 66.1% of the posts the toxicity score remained unchanged while out of the remaining 33.9%, in 9.6% it increased

[2]We focused on known English-speaking countries. The most common country of origin was USA.

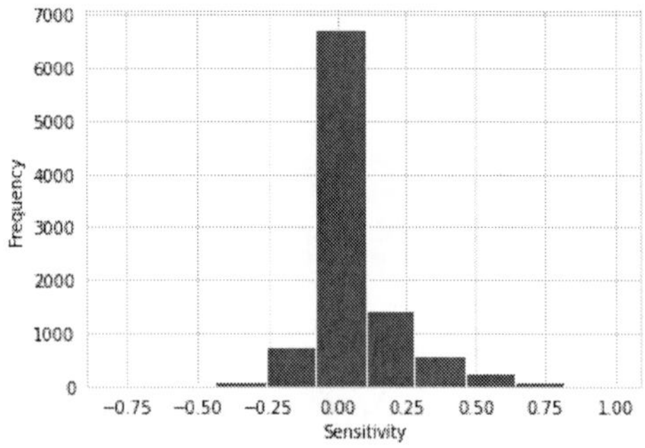

Figure 3: Histogram of context sensitivity. Negative (positive) sensitivity means the toxicity increased (decreased) when context was shown to the annotators.

(960 posts) and in 24.2% it decreased (2,408) when context was provided. If we binarize the ground truth we get a similar trend, but with the toxicity of more posts remaining unchanged (i.e., 94.7%).

When counting the number of posts for which $|\delta|$ exceeds a threshold t, called *context-sensitive posts* in Fig. 4, we observe that as t increases, the number of context sensitive posts decreases. This means that clearly context sensitive posts (e.g., in an edge case, ones that all OC coders found as toxic while all IC coders found as non toxic) are rare. Some examples of target posts, along with their parent posts and δ, are shown in Table 1.

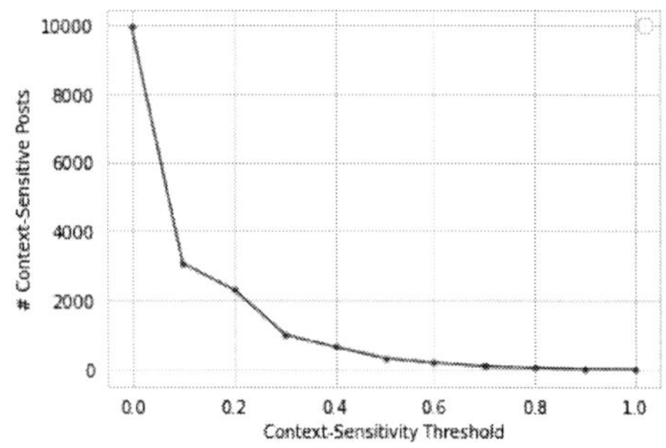

Figure 4: Number of context-sensitive posts ($|\delta| \geq t$), when varying the context-sensitivity threshold t.

3 Experimental Study

Initially, we used our dataset to experiment with existing toxicity detection systems, aiming to investigate if context-sensitive posts are more difficult to automatically classify correctly as toxic or non-toxic. Then, we trained new systems to solve a different task, that of estimating how sensitive the toxicity score of each post is to its parent post, i.e., to estimate the *context sensitivity* of a target post.

3.1 Toxicity Detection

We employed the Perspective API toxicity detection system to classify CCC posts as toxic or not.[3] We either concatenate the parent post to the target one to allow the model to "see" the parent, or not.[4] Figure 5 shows the Mean Absolute Error (MAE) of Perspective, with and without the parent post concatenated, when evaluating on all the CCC posts ($t = 0$) and when evaluating on smaller subsets with increasingly context-sensitive posts ($t > 0$). In all cases, we use the in-context (IC) gold labels as the ground truth. The greater the sensitivity threshold t, the smaller the sample (Fig. 4).

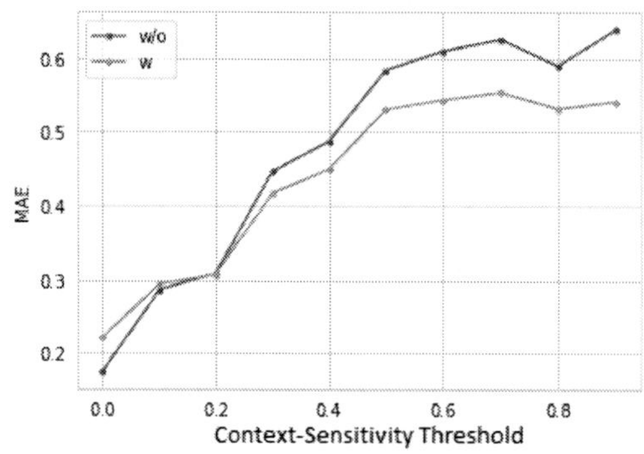

Figure 5: Mean Absolute Error (Y-axis) when *predicting toxicity* for different context-sensitivity thresholds (t; X-axis). We applied Perspective to target posts alone (w/o) or concatenating the parent posts (w).

Figure 5 shows that when we concatenate the parent to the target post (w), MAE is clearly smaller, provided that $t \geq 0.2$. Hence, the benefits of integrating context in toxicity detection systems may be visible only in sufficiently context-sensitive subsets, like the ones we would obtain by evaluating (and training) on posts with $t \geq 0.2$. By contrast, if no context-sensitivity threshold is imposed ($t = 0$) when constructing a dataset, the non-context sensitive posts ($|\delta| = 0$) dominate (Fig. 4), hence adding context mechanisms to toxicity detectors has no visible effect in test scores. This explains related observations in our previous work (Pavlopoulos et al., 2020), where we found that context-sensitive posts are too rare and, thus, context-aware models do not perform better on existing toxicity datasets.

It is worth observing that the more we move to the right of Fig. 5, the higher the error for both Per-

[3] `https://www.perspectiveapi.com`

[4] We are investigating better context-aware models.

PARENT OF POST p	POST p	$s^{OC}(p)$	$s^{IC}(p)$	δ
Oh Don..... you are soooo predictable.	oh Chuckie you are such a tattle tale.	36.6%	80%	-43.4%
Oh Why would you wish them well? They've destroyed the environment in their country and now they are coming here to do the same.	"They"? Who is they? Do all Chinese look alike to you? Or are you just revealing your innate bigotry and racism?	70%	0%	70%

Table 1: Examples of context-sensitive posts in CCC. Here $s^{\text{OC}}(p)$ and $s^{\text{IC}}(p)$ are the fractions of out-of-context or in-context annotators, respectively, who found the target post p to be toxic; and $\delta = s^{\text{OC}}(p) - s^{\text{IC}}(p)$.

spective variants (with, without context). This is probably due to the fact that Perspective is trained on posts that have been rated by annotators who were not provided with the parent post (out of context; OC), whereas here we use the in-context (IC) annotations as ground truth. The greater the t in Fig. 5, the larger the difference between the toxicity scores of OC and IC annotators, hence the larger the difference between the (OC) ground truth that Perspective saw and the ground truth that we use here (IC). Experimenting with artificial parent posts (long or short, toxic or not) confirmed that the error increases for context-sensitive posts.

The solution to the problem of increasing error as context sensitivity increases (Fig. 5) would be to train toxicity detectors on datasets that are richer in context-sensitive posts. However, such posts are rare (Fig. 4) and thus, they are hard to collect and annotate. This observation motivated the experiments of the next section, where we train ***context-sensitivity*** detectors, which allow us to collect posts that are likely to be context-sensitive. These posts can then be used to train toxicity detectors on datasets richer in context-sensitive posts.

3.2 Context Sensitivity Estimation

We trained and assessed four regressors on the new CCC dataset, to predict the context-sensitivity δ. We used Linear Regression, Support Vector Regression, a Random Forest regressor, and a BERT-based (Devlin et al., 2019) regression model (BERTr). The first three regressors use TF-IDF features. In the case of BERTr, we add a feed-forward neural network (FFNN) on top of the top-level embedding of the [CLS] token. The FFNN consists of a dense layer (128 neurons) and a tanh activation function, followed by another dense layer. The last dense layer has a single output neuron, with no activation function, that produces the context sensitivity score. Preliminary experiments showed that adding simplistic context-mechanisms (e.g., concatenating the parent post) to the context sensitivity regressors does not lead to improvements. This may be due to the fact that it is often possible to decide if a post is *context-sensitive* or not (we do not score the toxicity of posts in this section) by considering only the target post without its parent (e.g., in responses like "NO!!"). Future work will investigate this hypothesis further by experimenting with more elaborate context-mechanisms. If the hypothesis is verified, manually annotating context-sensitivity (not toxicity) may also require only the target post.

	MSE ↓	MAE ↓	AUPR ↑	AUC ↑
B1	2.3 (0.1)	11.56 (0.2)	12.69 (0.7)	50.00 (0.0)
B2	4.6 (0.0)	13.22 (0.1)	13.39 (0.8)	50.01 (1.6)
LR	2.1 (0.1)	11.0 (0.3)	30.11 (1.2)	71.67 (0.8)
SVR	2.3 (0.1)	12.8 (0.1)	28.66 (1.7)	71.56 (1.0)
RFs	2.2 (0.1)	11.2 (0.2)	21.57 (1.0)	59.67 (0.3)
BERTR	**1.8 (0.1)**	**9.2 (0.3)**	**42.01 (4.3)**	**80.46 (1.3)**

Table 2: Mean Squared Error (MSE), Mean Absolute Error (MAE), Area Under Precision-Recall curve (AUPR), and ROC AUC of all *context sensitivity estimation* models. An average (B1) and a random (B2) baseline have been included. All results averaged over three random splits, standard error of mean in brackets.

We used a train/validation/test split of 80/10/10, respectively, and we performed Monte Carlo 3-fold Cross Validation. We used mean square error (MSE) as our loss function and early stopping with patience of 5 epochs. Table 2 presents the MSE and the mean absolute error (MAE) of all the models on the test set. Unsurprisingly, BERTr outperforms the rest of the models in MSE and MAE. Previous work (Wulczyn et al., 2017) reported that training toxicity regressors (based on the empirical distribution of codes) instead of classifiers (based on the majority of the codes) leads to improved classification results too, so we also computed classification results. For the latter results, we turned the ground truth probabilities of the test instances to binary labels by setting a threshold t (Section 2) and assigning the label 1 if $\delta > t$ and 0 otherwise. In this experiment, t was set to the sum of the standard error of mean (SEM) of the OC and IC raters for that specific post: $t(p) = \text{SEM}^{oc}(p) + \text{SEM}^{ic}(p)$. By using this binary ground truth, AUPR and AUC verified that BERTr outperforms the rest of the models, even when the models are used as classifiers.

4 Related Work

Following the work of Borkan et al. (2019), this work uses toxicity as an umbrella term for hateful, identity-attack, insulting, profane or posts that are toxic in another way. Toxicity detection is a popular task that has been addressed by machine learning approaches (Davidson et al., 2017; Waseem and Hovy, 2016; Djuric et al., 2015), including deep learning approaches (Park and Fung, 2017; Pavlopoulos et al., 2017b,c; Chakrabarty et al., 2019; Badjatiya et al., 2017; Haddad et al., 2020; Ozler et al., 2020). Despite the plethora of computational approaches, what most of these have in common is that they disregard context, such as the parent post in discussions. The reason for this weakness is that datasets are developed while annotators ignore the context (Nobata et al., 2016; Wulczyn et al., 2017; Waseem and Hovy, 2016). Most of the datasets in the field are in English, but datasets in other languages have the same weakness (Pavlopoulos et al., 2017a; Mubarak et al., 2017; Chiril et al., 2020; Ibrohim and Budi, 2018; Ross et al., 2016; Wiegand et al., 2018). We started to investigate context-sensitivity in toxicity detection in our previous work (Pavlopoulos et al., 2020) using existing toxicity detection datasets and a much smaller dataset (250 posts) we constructed with both IC and OC labels. Comparing to our previous work, here we constructed and released a much larger dataset (10k posts) with IC and OC labels, we introduced the new task of context-sensitivity estimation, and we reported experimental results indicating that the new task is feasible.

5 Conclusions and Future Work

We introduced the task of estimating the context-sensitivity of posts in toxicity detection, i.e., estimating the extent to which the perceived toxicity of a post depends on the conversational context. We constructed, presented, and release a new dataset that can be used to train and evaluate systems for the new task, where context is the previous post. Context-sensitivity estimation systems can be used to collect larger samples of context-sensitive posts, which is a prerequisite to train toxicity detectors to better handle context-sensitive posts. Context-sensitivity estimators can also be used to suggest when moderators should consider the context of a post, which is more costly and may not always be necessary. In future work, we hope to incorporate context mechanisms in toxicity detectors and train (and evaluate) them on datasets sufficiently rich in context-sensitive posts.

Acknowledgement

We thank L. Dixon and J. Sorensen for their continuous assistance and advice. This research was funded in part by a Google Research Award.

References

Pinkesh Badjatiya, Shashank Gupta, Manish Gupta, and Vasudeva Varma. 2017. Deep learning for hate speech detection in tweets. *Proceedings of the 26th International Conference on World Wide Web Companion - WWW '17 Companion.*

Daniel Borkan, Lucas Dixon, Jeffrey Sorensen, Nithum Thain, and Lucy Vasserman. 2019. Nuanced metrics for measuring unintended bias with real data for text classification. In *WWW*, pages 491–500, San Francisco, USA.

Tuhin Chakrabarty, Kilol Gupta, and Smaranda Muresan. 2019. Pay "attention" to your context when classifying abusive language. In *Proceedings of the Third Workshop on Abusive Language Online*, pages 70–79, Florence, Italy. Association for Computational Linguistics.

Patricia Chiril, Véronique Moriceau, Farah Benamara, Alda Mari, Gloria Origgi, and Marlène Coulomb-Gully. 2020. An annotated corpus for sexism detection in French tweets. In *Proceedings of the 12th Language Resources and Evaluation Conference*, pages 1397–1403, Marseille, France. European Language Resources Association.

Thomas Davidson, Dana Warmsley, Michael Macy, and Ingmar Weber. 2017. Automated hate speech detection and the problem of offensive language. *Proceedings of the International AAAI Conference on Web and Social Media*, 11(1).

Jacob Devlin, Ming-Wei Chang, Kenton Lee, and Kristina Toutanova. 2019. BERT: Pre-training of deep bidirectional transformers for language understanding. In *Proceedings of the 2019 Conference of the North American Chapter of the Association for Computational Linguistics: Human Language Technologies, Volume 1 (Long and Short Papers)*, pages 4171–4186, Minneapolis, Minnesota. Association for Computational Linguistics.

Nemanja Djuric, Jing Zhou, Robin Morris, Mihajlo Grbovic, Vladan Radosavljevic, and Narayan Bhamidipati. 2015. Hate speech detection with comment embeddings. In *Proceedings of the 24th International*

Conference on World Wide Web, WWW '15 Companion, page 29–30, New York, NY, USA. Association for Computing Machinery.

Tommaso Fornaciari, Alexandra Uma, Silviu Paun, Barbara Plank, Dirk Hovy, and Massimo Poesio. 2021. Beyond black & white: Leveraging annotator disagreement via soft-label multi-task learning. In *Proceedings of the 2021 Conference of the North American Chapter of the Association for Computational Linguistics: Human Language Technologies*, pages 2591–2597, Online. Association for Computational Linguistics.

Bushr Haddad, Zoher Orabe, Anas Al-Abood, and Nada Ghneim. 2020. Arabic offensive language detection with attention-based deep neural networks. In *Proceedings of the 4th Workshop on Open-Source Arabic Corpora and Processing Tools, with a Shared Task on Offensive Language Detection*, pages 76–81, Marseille, France. European Language Resource Association.

Muhammad Okky Ibrohim and Indra Budi. 2018. A dataset and preliminaries study for abusive language detection in indonesian social media. *Procedia Computer Science*, 135:222–229. The 3rd International Conference on Computer Science and Computational Intelligence (ICCSCI 2018) : Empowering Smart Technology in Digital Era for a Better Life.

Hamdy Mubarak, Kareem Darwish, and Walid Magdy. 2017. Abusive language detection on Arabic social media. In *Proceedings of the First Workshop on Abusive Language Online*, pages 52–56, Vancouver, BC, Canada. Association for Computational Linguistics.

Chikashi Nobata, Joel Tetreault, Achint Thomas, Yashar Mehdad, and Yi Chang. 2016. Abusive language detection in online user content. In *Proceedings of the 25th International Conference on World Wide Web*, WWW '16, page 145–153, Republic and Canton of Geneva, CHE. International World Wide Web Conferences Steering Committee.

Kadir Bulut Ozler, Kate Kenski, Steve Rains, Yotam Shmargad, Kevin Coe, and Steven Bethard. 2020. Fine-tuning for multi-domain and multi-label uncivil language detection. In *Proceedings of the Fourth Workshop on Online Abuse and Harms*, pages 28–33, Online. Association for Computational Linguistics.

Ji Ho Park and Pascale Fung. 2017. One-step and two-step classification for abusive language detection on Twitter. In *Proceedings of the First Workshop on Abusive Language Online*, pages 41–45, Vancouver, BC, Canada. Association for Computational Linguistics.

John Pavlopoulos, Prodromos Malakasiotis, and Ion Androutsopoulos. 2017a. Deep learning for user comment moderation. In *Proceedings of the First Workshop on Abusive Language Online*, pages 25–35, Vancouver, BC, Canada. Association for Computational Linguistics.

John Pavlopoulos, Prodromos Malakasiotis, and Ion Androutsopoulos. 2017b. Deeper attention to abusive user content moderation. In *Proceedings of the 2017 Conference on Empirical Methods in Natural Language Processing*, pages 1125–1135, Copenhagen, Denmark. Association for Computational Linguistics.

John Pavlopoulos, Prodromos Malakasiotis, Juli Bakagianni, and Ion Androutsopoulos. 2017c. Improved abusive comment moderation with user embeddings. In *Proceedings of the 2017 EMNLP Workshop: Natural Language Processing meets Journalism*, pages 51–55, Copenhagen, Denmark. Association for Computational Linguistics.

John Pavlopoulos, Jeffrey Sorensen, Lucas Dixon, Nithum Thain, and Ion Androutsopoulos. 2020. Toxicity detection: Does context really matter?

Justus Randolph. 2010. Free-marginal multirater kappa (multirater ϰfree): An alternative to fleiss fixed-marginal multirater kappa. volume 4.

Björn Ross, Michael Rist, Guillermo Carbonell, Ben Cabrera, Nils Kurowsky, and Michael Wojatzki. 2016. Measuring the Reliability of Hate Speech Annotations: The Case of the European Refugee Crisis. In *Proceedings of NLP4CMC III: 3rd Workshop on Natural Language Processing for Computer-Mediated Communication*, pages 6–9.

Nanna Thylstrup and Zeerak Waseem. 2020. Detecting 'dirt' and 'toxicity': Rethinking content moderation as pollution behaviour.

Zeerak Waseem and Dirk Hovy. 2016. Hateful symbols or hateful people? predictive features for hate speech detection on Twitter. In *Proceedings of the NAACL Student Research Workshop*, pages 88–93, San Diego, California. Association for Computational Linguistics.

Michael Wiegand, Melanie Siegel, and Josef Ruppenhofer. 2018. Overview of the germeval 2018 shared task on the identification of offensive language. In *Proceedings of GermEval 2018, 14th Conference on Natural Language Processing (KONVENS 2018), Vienna, Austria – September 21, 2018.*

Ellery Wulczyn, Nithum Thain, and Lucas Dixon. 2017. Ex machina: Personal attacks seen at scale. In *Proceedings of the 26th International Conference on World Wide Web*, WWW '17, page 1391–1399, Republic and Canton of Geneva, CHE. International World Wide Web Conferences Steering Committee.

Justine Zhang, Jonathan Chang, Cristian Danescu-Niculescu-Mizil, Lucas Dixon, Yiqing Hua, Dario Taraborelli, and Nithum Thain. 2018. Conversations gone awry: Detecting early signs of conversational failure. In *Proceedings of the 56th Annual Meeting of the Association for Computational Linguistics (Volume 1: Long Papers)*, pages 1350–1361, Melbourne, Australia. Association for Computational Linguistics.

A Large-Scale English Multi-Label Twitter Dataset for Online Abuse Detection

Semiu Salawu
Aston University
Birmingham B4 7ET
salawusd@aston.ac.uk

Prof. Jo Lumsden
Aston University
Birmingham B4 7ET
j.lumsden@aston.ac.uk

Prof. Yulan He
The University of Warwick
Coventry CV4 7AL
Yulan.He@warwick.ac.uk

Abstract

In this paper, we introduce a new English Twitter-based dataset for online abuse and cyberbullying detection. Comprising 62,587 tweets, this dataset was sourced from Twitter using specific query terms designed to retrieve tweets with high probabilities of various forms of bullying and offensive content, including insult, profanity, sarcasm, threat, porn and exclusion. Analysis performed on the dataset confirmed common cyberbullying themes reported by other studies and revealed interesting relationships between the classes. The dataset was used to train a number of transformer-based deep learning models returning impressive results.

1 Introduction

Cyberbullying has been defined as an aggressive and intentional act repeatedly carried out using electronic means against a victim that cannot easily defend him or herself (Smith et al., 2008). Online abuse by contrast can refer to a wide range of behaviours that may be considered offensive by the parties to which it is directed to (Sambaraju and McVittie, 2020). This includes trolling, cyberbullying, sexual exploitation such as grooming and sexting and revenge porn (i.e., the sharing of inappropriate images of former romantic partners). A distinguishing feature of cyberbullying within the wider realm of online abuse is that it is a repeated act and its prevalence on social media (along with other forms of online abuse) has generated significant interest in its automated detection. This has lead to an increase in research efforts utilising supervised machine learning methods to achieve this automated detection. Training data plays a significant role in the detection of cyberbullying and online abuse. The domain-bias, composition and taxonomy of a dataset can impact the suitability of models trained on it for abuse detection purposes, and therefore the choice of training data plays a significant role in the performance of these tasks.

While profanity and online aggression are often associated with online abuse, the subjective nature of cyberbullying means that accurate detection extends beyond the mere identification of swear words. Indeed, some of the most potent abuse witnessed online has been committed without profane or aggressive language. This complexity often requires labelling schemes that are more advanced than the binary annotation schemes used on many existing labelled datasets. This, therefore, influenced our approach in creating the dataset. After extracting data from Twitter using targeted queries, we created a taxonomy for various forms of online abuse and bullying (including subtle and indirect forms of bullying) and identified instances of these and other inappropriate content (e.g., pornography and spam) present within the tweets using a fine-grained annotation scheme. The result is a large labelled dataset with a majority composition of offensive content.

This paper is organised as follows. In Section 2, we present an overview of existing online abuse-related datasets. Section 3 discusses the collection method, composition, annotation process and usage implications for our dataset. Results of the experiments performed using the dataset are discussed in Section 4. Finally, conclusion and future research are described in section 5.

2 Related Work

Social media has become the new playground and, much like physical recreation areas, bullies inhabit facets of this virtual world. The continually evolving nature of social media introduces a need for datasets to evolve in tandem to maintain relevance. Datasets such as the Barcelona Media dataset used in studies such as those by Dadvar and Jong (2012),

Proceedings of the Fifth Workshop on Online Abuse and Harms, pages 146–156
August 6, 2021.

Nahar et al. (2014), Huang et al. (2014), Nandhini and Sheeba (2015) was created over ten years ago and, while representative of social media usage at the time, social networks such as Myspace, Slashdot, Kongregate and Formspring from which some of the data was sourced are no longer widely used. The consequence of this is that such datasets are no longer representative of current social media usage. Twitter is one of the most widely used social media platforms globally; as such, it is no surprise that it is frequently used to source cyberbullying and online abuse data.

Bretschneider et al. (2014) annotated 5,362 tweets, 220 of which were found to contain online harassment; the low proportion of offensive tweets present within the dataset (less than 0.05%), however, limits its efficacy for classifier training. More recently, studies such as those by Rajadesingan et al. (2015), Waseem and Hovy (2016), Davidson et al. (2017), Chatzakou et al. (2017), Hee et al. (2018), Founta et al. (2018), Ousidhoum et al. (2019) have produced datasets with higher positive samples of cyberbullying and online abuse.

Rajadesingan et al. (2015) labelled 91,040 tweets for sarcasm. This is noteworthy because while sarcasm can be used to perpetrate online bullying, it is rarely featured in existing cyberbullying datasets' taxonomies. However, as the dataset was created for sarcasm detection only, this is the only context that can be learned from the dataset. As such, any model trained with this dataset will be unable to identify other forms of online abuse, thus limiting its usefulness. Waseem and Hovy (2016) annotated 17,000 tweets using labels like racism and sexism, and Davidson et al. (2017) labelled over 25,000 tweets based on the presence of offensive and hate speech. Chatzakou et al. (2017) extracted features to identify cyberbullies by clustering 9,484 tweets attributed to 303 unique Twitter users. In creating their bi-lingual dataset sourced from ASKfm, Hee et al. (2018) used a detailed labelling scheme that acknowledges the different types of cyberbullying discovered in the retrieved post types. The dataset's effectiveness in training classifiers may, however, be affected by the low percentage of abusive documents present. This dataset was subsequently re-annotated by Rathnayake et al. (2020) to identify which of the four roles of 'harasser', 'victim', 'bystander defender' and 'bystander assistant' was played by the authors of the posts contained in the dataset. Similarly, Sprugnoli et al. (2018) used the same four roles to annotate a dataset created from simulated cyberbullying episodes using the instant messaging tool; WhatsApp, along with the labels created by Hee et al. (2018)

Zampieri et al. (2019) used a hierarchical annotation scheme that, in addition to identifying offensive tweets, also identifies if such tweets are targeted at specific individuals or groups and what type of target it is (i.e., individual - *@username* or group – '*... all you republicans*'). Hierarchical annotation schemes have indeed shown promise as observed in their use in recent offensive language detection competitions like hatEval[1] and OffensEval[2]; that said, however, a hierarchical scheme could inadvertently filter out relevant labels depending on the first-level annotation scheme used.

Ousidhoum et al. (2019) used one of the most comprehensive annotation schemes encountered in an existing dataset and additionally included a very high percentage of positive cyberbullying samples in their dataset but, regrettably, the number of English documents included in the dataset is small in comparison to other datasets. Founta et al. (2018) annotated about 10,000 tweets using labels like abusive, hateful, spam and normal, while Bruwaene et al. (2020) experimented with a multi-platform dataset comprising of 14,900 English documents sourced from Instagram, Twitter, Facebook, Pinterest, Tumblr, YouTube and Gmail. Other notable publicly available datasets include the Kaggle Insult (Kaggle, 2012) and Kaggle Toxic Comments (Kaggle, 2018) datasets. A comprehensive review of publicly available datasets created to facilitate the detection of online abuse in different languages is presented in Vidgen and Derczynski (2020).

3 Data

In this section, we introduce our dataset and how it addresses some of the limitations of existing datasets used in cyberbullying and online abuse detection research.

3.1 Objective

In reviewing samples of offensive tweets from Twitter and existing datasets, we discovered that a single tweet could simultaneously contain elements of abuse, bullying, hate speech, spam and many other forms of content associated with cyberbullying. As such, attributing a single label to a tweet ignores

[1] competitions.codalab.org/competitions/19935
[2] sites.google.com/site/offensevalsharedtask

Label	Description	Example
Bullying	Tweets directed at a person(s) intended to provoke and cause offence. The target of the abuse must be from the tweet either via mentions or names.	@username You are actually disgusting in these slutty pictures Your parents are probably embarrassed...
Insult	Tweets containing insults typically directed at or referencing specific individual(s).	@username It's because you're a c*nt isn't it? Go on you are aren't you?
Profanity	This label is assigned to any tweets containing profane words.	@username please dont become that lowkey hating ass f**king friend please dont
Sarcasm	Sarcastic tweets aimed to ridicule. These tweets may be in the form of statements, observations and declarations.	@username Trump is the most innocent man wrongly accused since O.J. Simpson. #Sarcasm
Threat	Tweets threatening violence and aggression towards individuals.	@username Let me at him. I will f*ck him up and let my cat scratch the f*ck out of him.
Exclusion	Tweets designed to cause emotional distress via social exclusion.	@username @username You must be gay huh ? Why you here ? Fag !! And I got 2 TANK YA !
Porn	Tweets that contain or advertise pornographic content	CLICK TO WATCH [link] Tinder Sl*t Heather Gets her A*s Spanks and Spreads her C*nt
Spam	Unsolicited tweets containing and advertising irrelevant content. They typically include links to other web pages	HAPPY #NationalMasturbationDay #c*m and watch me celebrate Subscribe TODAY for a free #p*ssy play video of me [link]

Table 1: Annotation scheme with examples.

other salient labels that can be ascribed to the tweet. We propose a multi-label annotation scheme that identifies the many elements of abusive and offensive content that may be present in a single tweet. As existing cyberbullying datasets often contain a small percentage of bullying samples, we want our dataset to contain a sizeable portion of bullying and offensive content and so devised querying strategies to achieve this. Twitter, being one of the largest online social networks with a user base in excess of 260 million (Statista, 2019) and highly representative of current social media usage, was used to source the data.

3.2 Labels

Berger (2007) (as cited in Abeele and Cock 2013, p.95) distinguishes two types of cyberbullying, namely direct and indirect/relational cyberbullying. Direct cyberbullying is when the bully directly targets the victim (typified by sending explicit offensive and aggressive content to and about the victim) while indirect cyberbullying involves subtler forms of abuse such as social exclusion and the use of sarcasm to ridicule. As both forms of cyberbullying exist on Twitter, our annotation scheme (see Table 1) was designed to capture the presence of both forms of bullying within tweets.

3.3 Collection Methods

Offensive and cyberbullying samples are often minority classes within a cyberbullying dataset; as such, one of our key objectives was ensuring the inclusion of a significant portion of offensive and cyberbullying samples within the dataset to facilitate training without the need for oversampling. Rather than indiscriminately mining Twitter feeds, we executed a series of searches formulated to return tweets with a high probability of containing the various types of offensive content of interest. For insulting and profane tweets, we queried Twitter using the 15 most frequently used profane terms on Twitter as identified by Wang et al. (2014). These are: f*ck, sh*t, a*s, bi*ch, ni**a, hell, wh*re, d*ck, p*ss, pu**y, sl*t, p*ta, t*t, damn, f*g, c*nt, c*m, c*ck, bl*wj*b, retard. To retrieve tweets containing sarcasm, we used a strategy based on the work of Rajadesingan et al. (2015) which discovered that sarcastic tweets often include *#sarcasm* and *#not* hashtags to make it evident that sarcasm was the intention. For our purposes, we found *#sarcasm* more relevant and therefore queried Twitter using this hashtag.

To discover prospective query terms for threatening tweets, we reviewed a random sample of 5000 tweets retrieved via Twitter's Streaming API and identified the following hashtags as potential query terms: *#die*; *#killyou*; *#rape*; *#chink*, *#muslim*, *#FightAfterTheFight* and *#cops*. These hashtags were then used as the initial seed in a snowballing technique to discover other relevant hashtags. This was done by querying Twitter using the hashtags and inspecting the returned tweets for violence-related hashtags. The following additional hashtags were subsequently discovered through this process: *#killallblacks*; *#killallcrackers*; *#blm*; *#blacklivesmatter*; *#alllivesmatter*; *#bluelivesmatter*; *#killchinese*; *#bustyourhead*; *#f*ckyouup*; *#killallwhites*; *#maga*; *#killallniggas*; and *#nigger*.

Formulating a search to retrieve tweets relating to social exclusion was challenging as typical examples were rare. From the 5000 tweets seed sample, we classified six tweets as relating to social exclusion and from them identified the following hashtags for use as query terms: *#alone*, *#idontlikeyou* and *#stayinyourlane*. Due to the low number of tweets returned for these hashtags, we also extracted the replies associated with the returned tweets and discovered the following additional hashtags *#notinvited*, *#dontcometomyparty*, and *#thereisareasonwhy* which were all subsequently used as additional query terms. Rather than excluding re-tweets when querying as is common practice amongst researchers, our process initially extracted original tweets and retweets and then selected only one of a tweet and its retweets if they were all present in the results. This ensured relevant content was not discarded in situations where the original tweet was not included in the results returned, but retweets were. Our final dataset contained 62,587 tweets published in late 2019.

3.4 Annotation Process

Language use on social media platforms like Twitter is often colloquial; this, therefore, influenced the desired annotator profile as that of an active social media user that understands the nuances of Twitter's colloquial language use. While there is no universal definition of what constitutes an active user on an online social network, Facebook defined an active user as someone who has logged into the site and completed an action such as liking, sharing and posting within the previous 30 days (Cohen, 2015). With one in every five minutes spent online involving social media usage and an average of 39 minutes spent daily on social media (Ofcom Research, 2019), this definition is inadequate in view of the increased users' activities on social media. An active user was therefore redefined as one that has accessed any of the major social networks (e.g., Twitter, Instagram, Facebook, Snapchat) at least twice a week and made a post/comment, like/dislike or tweet/retweet at least once in the preceding two weeks. This new definition is more in keeping with typical social media usage.

Using personal contacts, we recruited a pool of 17 annotators. Our annotators are from different ethnic/racial backgrounds (i.e., Caucasian, African, Asian, Arabian) and reside in different countries (i.e., US, UK, Canada, Australia, Saudi Arabia, India, Pakistan, Nigeria and Ghana). Additionally, their self-reported online social networking habits met our definition of an active social media user. All annotators were provided with preliminary information about cyberbullying including news articles and video reports, documentaries and YouTube videos as well as detailed information about the labelling task. Due to the offensive nature of the tweets and the need to protect young people from such content while maintaining an annotator profile close to the typical age of the senders and recipients of the tweets, our annotators were aged 18 - 35 years.

Since the presence of many profane words can be automatically detected, a program was written to label the tweets for profane terms based on the 15 profane words used as query terms and the Google swear words list[3]. The profanity-labelled tweets were then provided to the annotators to alleviate this aspect of the labelling task. Each tweet was labelled by three different annotators from different ethnic/racial backgrounds, gender and countries of residence. This was done to control for annotators' cultural and gender bias.

An interesting observation of the annotation process was the influence of the annotators' culture on how labels are assigned. For example, we discovered that annotators from Asian, African and Arabian countries were less likely to assign the 'bullying', 'insult' and 'sarcasm' labels to tweets compared to annotators from the UK, Canada, US

[3] code.google.com/archive/p/badwordslist/downloads

and Australia. A possible explanation for this could be that the context of the abuse apparent to the annotators from the Caucasian countries may not translate well to other cultures. While no other substantial trend were noticed for the other labels, this, however, highlighted the impact of an annotator's personal views and culture on the labelling task and the labels' composition of our dataset could have been different if we had sourced annotators from different cultures. As identified by Bender and Friedman (2018), researchers should therefore be mindful of potential annotators' biases when creating online abuse datasets.

Inter-rater agreement was measured via Krippendorff's Alpha (α) and the majority of annotators' agreement was required for each label. The Krippendorff python library[4] was used to compute the value which was found to be 0.67 which can be interpreted as 'moderate agreement'. We believe that the culturally heterogeneous nature of our annotators pool could have 'diluted' the agreement amongst annotators and contributed to the final value achieved.

3.5 Analysis

The number of tweets each label was assigned to is presented in Table 2 with 'Profanity' emerging as the dominant label and 'Exclusion' the least assigned label. It can also be seen that about a sixth of the tweets were not assigned any labels.

Label	Profanity	Porn	Insult
Count	51,014	16,690	15,201
Label	Spam	Bullying	Sarcasm
Count	14,827	3,254	117
Label	Threat	Exclusion	None
Count	79	10	10,768

Table 2: Number of tweets each label was assigned to.

Before preprocessing, the maximum document length for the dataset was 167 characters with an average document length of 91. Following preprocessing, the maximum document length reduced to 143 characters (equating to 26 words) with an average document length of 67 characters. The removal of mentions (i.e., including a username with the @ symbol inside a tweet), URLs and non-ASCII characters were found to be the biggest contributor to document length reduction. There are 37,453 unique tokens in the dataset. Figure 1 illustrates the number of tweets assigned to multiple labels. Single label tweets make up more than a third of the dataset, which can be mostly attributed to the large number of tweets singly labelled as 'Profanity'.

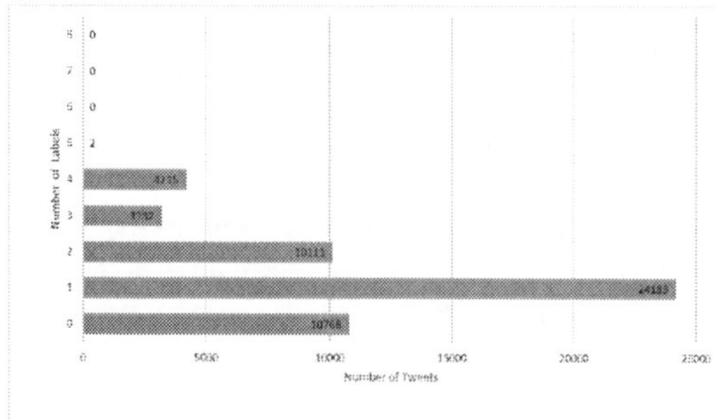

Figure 1: Distribution of tweet counts and number of labels assigned.

A significant number of tweets were also jointly labelled as 'Profanity' and 'Insult' or 'Insult' and 'Cyberbullying', and this contributed to double-labelled tweets being the second-largest proportion of the dataset. Interestingly, there were more tweets with quadruple labels than there were with triple and this was discovered to be due to the high positive correlation between 'Porn'/'Spam' and 'Profanity'/'Insult.'

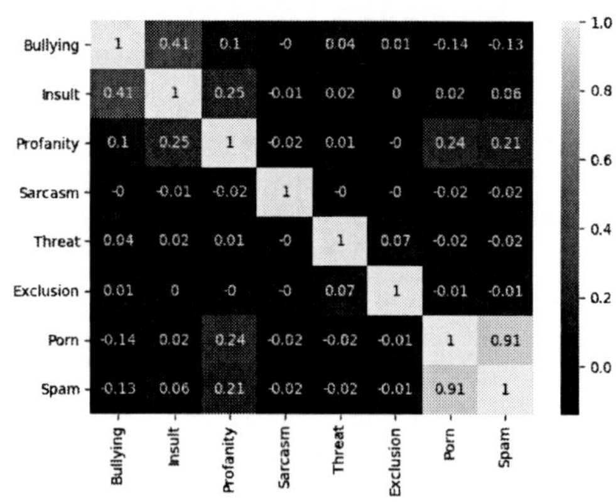

Figure 2: Correlation matrix for dataset's labels.

The correlation matrix for the classes in the dataset is illustrated in Figure 2. The closer the correlation value is to 1, the higher the positive correlation between the two classes. The highest positive correlation is shown to be between 'Porn' and 'Spam' (0.91) followed by 'Insult' and 'Bullying' (0.41) and 'Insult' and 'Profanity' (0.25). 'Porn' and 'Spam' also demonstrated a positive correlation between them and 'Profanity' which can be

[4]pypi.org/project/krippendorff

attributed to the high proportion of profane terms in pornographic content and spam; we found that many pornographic tweets are essentially profanity-laden spam. 'Insult' also exhibited a positive correlation with 'Bullying' and 'Profanity', a fact that can be attributed to the frequent use of profanity in insulting tweets as well as the use of insults to perpetrate bullying. The key negative correlations identified by the chart includes those between 'Bullying', and 'Porn' and 'Spam'. This can be attributed to bullying tweets often being personal attacks directed at specific individuals and typified by the use of usernames, person names or personal pronouns, all of which are rare in pornographic and spam tweets. The minority classes 'Sarcasm', 'Threat' and 'Exclusion' exhibited a minimal correlation with the other classes.

3.6 Bias Implication

Most datasets carry a risk of demographic bias (Hovy and Spruit, 2016) and this risk can be higher for datasets created using manually-defined query terms. Researchers, therefore, need to be aware of potential biases in datasets and address them where possible. Gender and ethnicity are common demographic biases that can be (often inadvertently) introduced into a dataset. To this end, we wanted to explore (as far as possible), whether our dataset had acquired gender bias. To do this we attempted to infer the gender of the users incorporated in our dataset. Since Twitter does not record users' gender information, we adopted an approach that uses the Gender API [5] to deduce the gender of users based on whether the users' first names are traditionally male or female: we assumed that as an accessible and feasible measure of users' gender identity. We were able to process the authorship of 13,641 tweets (21.8% of the dataset) in this way and inferred that 31.4% of the authors of these tweets identified as female and 68.6% male (at least in so far as was apparent from their Twitter account). This suggests a male-bias in the authorship of the tweets in the dataset. We, however, recognise the limitation of this approach as the names provided by users cannot always be regarded as truthful and as gender extends beyond the traditional binary types, a names-based approach such as this cannot be used to deduce all gender identities. A more empathetic and effective means to identify gender in Twitter users would be an interesting facet of future work.

With regards racial and ethnic bias, we mitigate potential bias by including generalised variants of any ethnicity-specific keyword used as a query term as well as including variants for different ethnicities. It should, however, be noted that the popularity and topicality of certain keywords may still introduce an unintended bias. For example, #blacklivematters returns several more tweets than #asianlivematters.

While the collection strategy used to create our dataset ensured a high concentration of offensive tweets, a potential consequence of the imbalanced distribution of the classes is that it may reinforce the unintentional bias of associating minority classes to specific hateful and offensive content. Dixon et al. (2018) defined unintended bias as when a model performs better for comments containing specific terms over others. For example, the phrase 'stay in your lane' was found in 4 of the 10 tweets identified as 'Exclusion' (due to the use of the hashtag #stayinyourlane as a query term), this can cause a model trained on the dataset to overgeneralised the phrase's association with the 'Exclusion' label, thus introducing a false positive bias in the model. Introducing more examples of the minority classes using a variety of query terms is a potential strategy for mitigating such unintended bias and is discussed further under future work.

3.7 Practical Use

Ultimately the aim of a dataset such as this is to train machine learning models that can subsequently be used in abuse detection systems. It is, therefore, crucial to understand how any bias in the dataset is manifested in the trained model and the impact of such bias in practical applications. A National Institute of Science and Technology (NIST) study (Grother et al., 2019) discovered that, for example, many US-developed facial recognition algorithms generated significantly higher false positives for Asian and African-American faces compared to Caucasian faces while similar algorithms developed in Asian countries did not show any such dramatic differences in false positive rates between Asian, African-American and Caucasian faces. The study concluded that the use of diverse training data is critical to the reduction of bias in such AI-based applications.

Our dataset has been used to train the classifier used in an online abuse prevention app (called

[5] https://gender-api.com

BullStop) which is available to the public via the Google play store. The app detects offensive messages sent to the user and automatically deletes them. It, however, acknowledges the possibility of both false positive and negative predictions, and thus allows the user to review and re-classify deleted messages and uses such corrections to re-train the system. This is especially important for a subjective field such as online abuse detection.

4 Experiments

4.1 Setup

Models for comparison We experimented with both traditional classifiers (Multinomial Naive Bayes, Linear SVC, Logistic Regression) and deep learning-based models (BERT, Roberta, XLNet, DistilBERT) to perform multi-label classification on the dataset. BERT (Bidirectional Encoder Representations from Transformers) is a language representation model designed to pre-train deep bi-directional representations from unlabeled text (Devlin et al., 2019). RoBERTa (Robustly Optimized BERT Pretraining Approach) is an optimised BERT-based model (Liu et al., 2019), and DistilBERT (Distilled BERT) is a compacted BERT-based model (Sanh et al., 2019) that requires fewer computing resources and training time than BERT (due to using about 40% fewer parameters) while preserving most of BERT performance gains. XL-Net (Yang et al., 2019) is an autoregressive language model designed to overcome some of the limitations of BERT. BERT, RoBERTa, XLNet, and DistilBERT are available as pre-trained models but can also be fine-tuned by first performing language modelling on a dataset.

Evaluation Each model's performance was evaluated using macro ROC-AUC (Area Under ROC Curve), Accuracy, Hamming Loss, Macro and Micro F_1 Score, which are typically used in imbalanced classification tasks.

4.2 Preprocessing

The primary objective of our preprocessing phase was the reduction of irrelevant and noisy data that may hamper classifier training. As is standard for many NLP tasks, punctuation, symbols and non-ASCII characters were removed. This was followed by the removal of mentions and URLs. We also discovered many made-up words created by combining multiple words (e.g. goaway, itdoesntwork, gokillyourself) in the tweets. These are due to hashtags, typos and attempts by users to mitigate the characters limit imposed by Twitter. The wordsegment python library was used to separate these into individual words. The library contains an extensive list of English words and is based on Google's 1T (1 Trillion) Web corpus.[6] Lastly, the text was converted to lower case.

4.3 Results

We provide the stratified 10-fold cross-validation results of the experiments in Table 3. The best macro ROC-AUC score was achieved by the pre-trained RoBERTa model, while the best macro and micro F_1 scores were attained using the pre-trained BERT and RoBERTa models, respectively. The best overall accuracy was returned by the fine-tuned DistilBERT model. As expected, the deep learning models outperformed the baseline classifiers with Multinomial Naive Bayes providing the worst results across the experiments and the BERT-like models achieving the best results for each metric. Interestingly, the pre-trained models were marginally better than the equivalent fine-tuned models implying that fine-tuning the models on the dataset degrades rather than improves performance.

As would be expected, the models performed better at predicting labels with higher distributions. For the minority classes like Sarcasm, Threat and Exclusion, RoBERTA and XLNet performed better. All the models performed well in predicting the none class, i.e. tweets with no applicable labels.

The resulting dataset from our collection methods is imbalanced with a high percentage of cyberbullying tweets. In reality, such a concentration of cyberbullying and offensive tweets is highly unusual and at odds with other cyberbullying datasets. To evaluate the generalisability of models trained on our dataset, we performed further experiments to evaluate how the models perform on other unseen datasets. We used our best performing model; RoBERTa (pre-trained), to perform prediction on samples extracted from two other datasets and compared the results against that achieved on our dataset by RoBERTa models trained on the other datasets.

The dataset created by Davidson et al. (2017) and the Kaggle Toxic Comments dataset (Kaggle, 2018) were selected for the experiments. We re-

[6] https://catalog.ldc.upenn.edu/LDC2006T13.

Model	Macro ROC-AUC(↑)	Accuracy (↑)	Hamming Loss (↓)	Macro F_1(↑)	Micro F_1(↑)
Multinomial Naive Bayes	0.8030	0.4568	0.1014	0.2618	0.7200
Linear SVC	0.8353	0.5702	0.0866	0.3811	0.7674
Logistic Regression	0.8354	0.5743	0.0836	0.3587	0.7725
BERT (pre-trained)	0.9657	0.5817	0.0736	**0.6318**	0.7998
DistilBERT (pre-trained)	0.9675	0.5802	0.0764	0.5202	0.7855
RoBERTa (pre-trained)	**0.9695**	0.5785	**0.0722**	0.5437	**0.8081**
XLNet(pre-trained)	0.9679	0.5806	0.0738	0.5441	0.8029
BERT (fine-tuned)	0.9651	0.5822	0.0725	0.5300	0.8022
DistilBERT (fine-tuned)	0.9633	**0.5834**	0.0753	0.5040	0.7872
RoBERTa (fine-tuned)	0.9670	0.5794	0.0724	0.5329	0.8044
XLNet(fine-tuned)	0.9654	0.5819	0.0741	0.5308	0.8037

Table 3: Results of classification. (↑: higher the better; ↓: lower the better)

Model	Macro ROC-AUC(↑)	Accuracy (↑)	Hamming Loss (↓)	Macro F_1(↑)	Micro F_1(↑)
RoBERTa$_{C\rightarrow D}$	**0.9923**	0.8809	**0.0288**	**0.8802**	**0.8810**
RoBERTa$_{D\rightarrow C}$	0.9681	0.5831	0.0708	0.5330	0.8076
RoBERTa$_{D\rightarrow D}$	0.9905	**0.8814**	0.0300	0.8427	0.8758
RoBERTa$_{C\rightarrow K}$	**0.9916**	0.5924	**0.0123**	**0.5670**	0.7436
RoBERTa$_{K\rightarrow C}$	0.9651	0.5811	0.0727	0.5352	**0.8054**
RoBERTa$_{K\rightarrow K}$	0.9733	**0.8449**	0.0174	0.5026	0.6354

Table 4: Results of cross-domain experiments. (↑: higher the better; ↓: lower the better)

ferred to these as the Davidson (D) and the Kaggle (K) datasets and our dataset as the Cyberbullying (C) dataset. The Davidson dataset is a multi-class-labelled dataset sourced from Twitter where each tweet is labelled as one of 'hate_speech', 'offensive' and 'neither'. In contrast, the Kaggle datasets contained Wikipedia documents labelled using a multi-label annotation scheme with each document associated with any number of classes from 'toxic','severe_toxic', 'obscene', 'threat', 'insult' and 'identity_hate'. Due to the difference in the number of labels for each dataset (our dataset contained 8 labels while the Davidson and Kaggle datasets used 3 and 6 labels respectively), it was necessary to amend the input and output layers of the RoBERTa model to allow it to predict the relevant labels for the Davidson and Kaggle datasets

We evaluated our model on the Davidson and Kaggle datasets and for the reverse experiments, evaluated new instances of RoBERTa trained on the other datasets on samples of the Cyberbullying dataset. As control experiments, RoBERTa models were trained and evaluated on the other datasets. The results of our experiments are presented in Table 4.

Overall, models trained on our dataset (RoBERTa$_{C\rightarrow D}$ and RoBERTa$_{C\rightarrow K}$) perform better on the other two datasets than the models trained on the other datasets and tested on the Cyberbullying dataset (RoBERTa$_{D\rightarrow C}$, RoBERTa$_{K\rightarrow C}$). Interestingly, models trained on our dataset achieved better ROC-AUC, Macro and Micro F_1 values on both the Davidson (D) and the Kaggle (K) datasets compared to in-domain results on those datasets (i.e., models trained and evaluated on the same datasets - RoBERTa$_{D\rightarrow D}$ and RoBERTa$_{K\rightarrow K}$). The results indicate that our dataset sufficiently captures enough context for classifiers to distinguish between both cyberbullying and non-cyberbullying text across different social media platforms.

4.4 Discussion and Future Work

Our collection strategy for creating the dataset was designed to target cyberbullying and offensive tweets and ensure that these types of tweets constitute the majority class. This differs from the collection strategies used in other datasets such as those by Dadvar et al. (2013), Kontostathis et al. (2013) and Hosseinmardi et al. (2015) which are designed to simulate a more realistic distribution of cyberbullying. As the occurrence of cyberbullying documents is naturally low, classifiers trained on our dataset can benefit from a high concentration of cyberbullying and offensive documents without the need for oversampling techniques.

When cross-domain evaluation was performed using our best performing classifier on two other datasets (Davidson et al., 2017; Kaggle, 2018), the model trained on our dataset performed better than those trained on the other datasets. It is also worth noting that the composition and annotation of these other datasets is entirely different from ours, and one was sourced from a different platform (Wikipedia). Our results demonstrated that deep learning models could learn sufficiently from an imbalanced dataset and generalise well on different data types.

We discovered a slight performance degradation for the deep learning-based models after fine-tuning. As recently shown in (Radiya-Dixit and Wang, 2020), fine-tuned networks do not deviate substantially from pre-trained ones and large pre-trained language models have high generalisation performance. We will explore in future work, more effective ways for producing fine-tuned networks such as learning to sparsify pre-trained parameters and optimising the most sensitive task-specific layers.

The distribution of 'Sarcasm', 'Exclusion' and 'Threat' labels is low within the dataset. Consequently, the models' ability to predict these classes is not comparable to that of the majority classes. Increasing the distribution of these labels within the dataset will improve the models training and mitigate unintended bias that may have been introduced by the minority classes; we therefore plan to supplement the dataset with more positive samples of these classes by exploring other querying strategies as well as incorporating samples from existing datasets such as Rajadesingan et al. (2015) and Hee et al. (2018).

5 Conclusion

In this paper, we presented a new cyberbullying dataset and demonstrated the use of transformer-based deep learning models to perform fine-grained detection of online abuse and cyberbullying with very encouraging results. To our knowledge, this is the first attempt to create a cyberbullying dataset with such a high concentration (82%) of cyberbullying and offensive content in this manner and using it to successfully evaluate a model trained with the dataset on a different domain. The dataset is available at https://bitbucket.org/ssalawu/cyberbullying-twitter for the use of other researchers.

References

Mariek Vanden Abeele and Rozane De Cock. 2013. Cyberbullying by mobile phone among adolescents: The role of gender and peer group status. *Communications*, 38:107–118.

Emily M Bender and Batya Friedman. 2018. Data statements for natural language processing: Toward mitigating system bias and enabling better science. *Transactions of the Association for Computational Linguistics*, 6:587–604.

Uwe Bretschneider, Thomas Wöhner, and Ralf Peters. 2014. Detecting online harassment in social networks.

David Van Bruwaene, Qianjia Huang, and Diana Inkpen. 2020. A multi-platform dataset for detecting cyberbullying in social media. *Language Resources and Evaluation*, pages 1–24.

Despoina Chatzakou, Nicolas Kourtellis, Jeremy Blackburn, Emiliano De Cristofaro, Gianluca Stringhini, and Athena Vakali. 2017. Mean birds: Detecting aggression and bullying on twitter. pages 13–22. Association for Computing Machinery, Inc.

David Cohen. 2015. Facebook changes definition of monthly active users.

Maral Dadvar and Franciska De Jong. 2012. Cyberbullying detection: A step toward a safer internet yard. pages 121–125.

Maral Dadvar, Dolf Trieschnigg, and Franciska De Jong. 2013. Expert knowledge for automatic detection of bullies in social networks. pages 57–64.

Thomas Davidson, Dana Warmsley, Michael Macy, and Ingmar Weber. 2017. Automated hate speech detection and the problem of offensive language.

Jacob Devlin, Ming-Wei Chang, Kenton Lee, and Kristina Toutanova. 2019. BERT: Pre-training of deep bidirectional transformers for language understanding. In *Proceedings of the 2019 Conference of the North American Chapter of the Association for Computational Linguistics: Human Language Technologies, Volume 1 (Long and Short Papers)*, pages 4171–4186, Minneapolis, Minnesota. Association for Computational Linguistics.

Lucas Dixon, John Li, Jeffrey Sorensen, Nithum Thain, and Lucy Vasserman. 2018. Measuring and mitigating unintended bias in text classification. volume 7, pages 67–73. Association for Computing Machinery, Inc.

Antigoni-Maria Founta, Constantinos Djouvas, Despoina Chatzakou, Ilias Leontiadis, Jeremy Blackburn, Gianluca Stringhini, Athena Vakali, Michael Sirivianos, and Nicolas Kourtellis. 2018. Large scale crowdsourcing and characterization of twitter abusive behavior.

Patrick J Grother, Mei L Ngan, and Kayee K Hanaoka. 2019. Face recognition vendor test (frvt) part 3: Demographic effects.

Cynthia Van Hee, Gilles Jacobs, Chris Emmery, Bart Desmet, Els Lefever, Ben Verhoeven, Guy De Pauw, Walter Daelemans, and Véronique Hoste. 2018. Automatic detection of cyberbullying in social media text. *PLOS ONE*, 13:e0203794.

Homa Hosseinmardi, Sabrina Arredondo Mattson, Rahat Ibn Rafiq, Richard Han, Qin Lv, and Shivakant Mishra. 2015. Poster: Detection of cyberbullying in a mobile social network: Systems issues. page 481. Association for Computing Machinery, Inc.

Dirk Hovy and Shannon L Spruit. 2016. The social impact of natural language processing. pages 591–598.

Qianjia Huang, Vivek Kumar Singh, and Pradeep Kumar Atrey. 2014. Cyber bullying detection using social and textual analysis. pages 3–6. ACM.

Kaggle. 2012. Detecting insults in social commentary.

Kaggle. 2018. Toxic comment classification challenge.

April Kontostathis, Kelly Reynolds, Andy Garron, and Lynne Edwards. 2013. Detecting cyberbullying: Query terms and techniques. volume volume, pages 195–204. Association for Computing Machinery.

Yinhan Liu, Myle Ott, Naman Goyal, Jingfei Du, Mandar Joshi, Danqi Chen, Omer Levy, Mike Lewis, Luke Zettlemoyer, and Veselin Stoyanov. 2019. Roberta: A robustly optimized bert pretraining approach. *Computing Research Repository*, arXiv:1907.11692.

Vinita Nahar, Sanad Al-Maskari, Xue Li, and Chaoyi Pang. 2014. Semi-supervised learning for cyberbullying detection in social networks. volume 8506 LNCS, pages 160–171. Springer Verlag.

B. Sri Nandhini and J. I. Sheeba. 2015. Online social network bullying detection using intelligence techniques. volume 45, pages 485–492. Elsevier B.V.

Ofcom Research. 2019. Online nation. *Ofcom Research.*

Nedjma Ousidhoum, Zizheng Lin, Hongming Zhang, Yangqiu Song, and Dit-Yan Yeung. 2019. Multilingual and multi-aspect hate speech analysis. *arXiv preprint arXiv:1908.11049.*

Evani Radiya-Dixit and Xin Wang. 2020. How fine can fine-tuning be? learning efficient language models.

Ashwin Rajadesingan, Reza Zafarani, and Huan Liu. 2015. Sarcasm detection on twitter:a behavioral modeling approach. pages 97–106. Association for Computing Machinery, Inc.

Gathika Rathnayake, Thushari Atapattu, Mahen Herath, Georgia Zhang, and Katrina Falkner. 2020. Enhancing the identification of cyberbullying through participant roles. In *Proceedings of the Fourth Workshop on Online Abuse and Harms*, pages 89–94, Online. Association for Computational Linguistics.

Rahul Sambaraju and Chris McVittie. 2020. Examining abuse in online media. *Social and personality psychology compass*, 14(3):e12521.

Victor Sanh, Lysandre Debut, Julien Chaumond, and Thomas Wolf. 2019. Distilbert, a distilled version of bert: smaller, faster, cheaper and lighter. *Computing Research Repository*, arXiv:1910.01108.

Peter K. Smith, Jess Mahdavi, Manuel Carvalho, Sonja Fisher, Shanette Russell, and Neil Tippett. 2008. Cyberbullying: Its nature and impact in secondary school pupils. *Journal of Child Psychology and Psychiatry and Allied Disciplines*, 49:376–385.

Rachele Sprugnoli, Stefano Menini, Sara Tonelli, Filippo Oncini, and Enrico Piras. 2018. Creating a WhatsApp dataset to study pre-teen cyberbullying. In *Proceedings of the 2nd Workshop on Abusive Language Online (ALW2)*, pages 51–59, Brussels, Belgium. Association for Computational Linguistics.

Statista. 2019. Global mobile social penetration rate 2019, by region.

Bertie Vidgen and Leon Derczynski. 2020. Directions in abusive language training data, a systematic review: Garbage in, garbage out. *Plos one*, 15(12):e0243300.

Wenbo Wang, Lu Chen, Krishnaprasad Thirunarayan, and Amit P Sheth. 2014. Cursing in english on twitter. pages 415–425.

Zeerak Waseem and Dirk Hovy. 2016. Hateful symbols or hateful people? predictive features for hate speech detection on twitter. pages 88–93.

Zhilin Yang, Zihang Dai, Yiming Yang, Jaime Carbonell, Ruslan Salakhutdinov, and Quoc V. Le. 2019. Xlnet: Generalized autoregressive pretraining for language understanding. *Computing Research Repository*, arXiv:1906.08237.

Marcos Zampieri, Shervin Malmasi, Preslav Nakov, Sara Rosenthal, Noura Farra, and Ritesh Kumar. 2019. Predicting the type and target of offensive posts in social media. volume 1, pages 1415–1420. Association for Computational Linguistics (ACL).

Data Integration for Toxic Comment Classification: Making More Than 40 Datasets Easily Accessible in One Unified Format

Julian Risch and **Philipp Schmidt** and **Ralf Krestel**
Hasso Plattner Institute, University of Potsdam
julian.risch@hpi.de, philipp.schmidt@student.hpi.de
ralf.krestel@hpi.de

Abstract

With the rise of research on toxic comment classification, more and more annotated datasets have been released. The wide variety of the task (different languages, different labeling processes and schemes) has led to a large amount of heterogeneous datasets that can be used for training and testing very specific settings. Despite recent efforts to create web pages that provide an overview, most publications still use only a single dataset. They are not stored in one central database, they come in many different data formats and it is difficult to interpret their class labels and how to reuse these labels in other projects.

To overcome these issues, we present a collection of more than forty datasets in the form of a software tool that automatizes downloading and processing of the data and presents them in a unified data format that also offers a mapping of compatible class labels. Another advantage of that tool is that it gives an overview of properties of available datasets, such as different languages, platforms, and class labels to make it easier to select suitable training and test data.

1 Toxic Comment Datasets

Supervised machine learning and more specifically supervised deep learning is the current state-of-the-art for text classification in general and for toxic comment classification in particular (van Aken et al., 2018). The performance of these classifiers depends heavily on the size and quality of available training data, which is mostly used for fine-tuning general language models. The rather small sizes of annotated toxic comment datasets dates from the high costs for obtaining high-quality labels and the high variety of the task itself. For each language and each specific set of labels (racism, attack, hate, abuse, offense, etc.) new training and test datasets are needed. To circumvent this need, transfer learning can be adapted up to a certain degree (Bigoulaeva et al., 2021; Risch and Krestel, 2018). As a result, many researchers have created their own training and test datasets customized to their specific use cases. Three recent surveys compare and discuss datasets used in the literature for hate speech and abusive language detection (Madukwe et al., 2020; Poletto et al., 2020; Vidgen and Derczynski, 2020). These overviews help to assess the dataset landscape but stop short of doing the next step: integrating and unifying the various datasets and making them easily accessible.

In this paper, we present a software tool that provides easy access to many individual toxic comment datasets using a simple API. The datasets are in a unified data format and can be filtered based on metadata. The collection currently contains datasets in thirteen different languages: Arabic, Danish, English, French, German, Greek, Hindi, Indonesian, Italian, Marathi, Portuguese, Slovenian, and Turkish. Further, it covers a wide range of labels of different kinds of toxicity, e.g., sexism, aggression, and hate. The code is available in a GitHub repository[1] and also as a PyPI package[2] so that users can easily install it via the command *pip install toxic-comment-collection* and import datasets from the collection within python.

With our tool, researchers can combine different datasets for customized training and testing. Further, it fosters research on toxic comments and the development of robust systems for practical application. Important research and practical questions that can be investigated with our provided tool are:

1. How well do hate speech, toxicity, abusive and offensive language classification models *generalize across datasets*?

[1] https://github.com/julian-risch/toxic-comment-collection

[2] https://pypi.org/project/toxic-comment-collection

Proceedings of the Fifth Workshop on Online Abuse and Harms, pages 157–163
August 6, 2021. ©2021 Association for Computational Linguistics

2. What are the effects of different fine-tuning methods and *transfer learning*?

3. What is the relation of *different labeling schemes* and their effect on training?

4. Does toxic content look different on *different platforms* (Twitter, Wikipedia, Facebook, news comments)

5. How do *different language* influence classifier performance?

2 Unified Toxic Comment Collection

Creating a unified collection of toxic comment datasets comes with several challenges. First, the datasets are stored on various platforms and need to be retrieved. Second, different file formats of the datasets complicate data integration, and third, the different sets of class labels need to be mapped to a common namespace. This section describes how the creation of our collection addresses these two challenges and presents statistics of the collection.

2.1 Collection Creation

We consider all publicly accessible comment datasets for the collection that contain labels that are subclasses of toxicity, such as offensive language, abusive language, and aggression. The broad definition of toxicity as a higher-level concept builds a bridge between the different lower-level concepts. The term denotes comments that contain toxic language and was made popular by the Kaggle Challenge on Toxic Comment Classification in 2018, which defined toxic comments as comments that are likely to make a reader leave a discussion.[3] We exclude datasets that consider users instead of comments as the level of annotation (Chatzakou et al., 2017; Ribeiro et al., 2018) or study a different type of conversation, e.g., WhatsApp chats, where the participants presumably know each other in person (Sprugnoli et al., 2018).

The datasets that we collected come from various sources, such as GitHub repositories, web pages of universities, or google drive and other file storage platforms. Even more diverse than the different source platforms are the file formats of the datasets. From csv files with different column separators and quoting characters, over excel sheets, sql dumps, to txt files with single records spanning multiple rows, optionally compressed as zip or tar files — converting all these formats into the same standardized csv format of our collection is the second step of the data integration after the datasets are retrieved.

The third step focuses on the class labels. These labels are encoded in different ways. In the simplest format, there is a single column that contains one string per row, which is the class label. In some datasets, the class labels are encoded with integers, presumably to reduce file size. For multi-label classification datasets, the column might contain a list of strings or lists of integers. We unify the format of the labels to lists of strings.

More importantly, we create a mapping of class labels so that labels with the same meaning but different names are replaced with the same label. This mapping is stored in a configuration file and can be customized by users. Different use cases require different mappings. For example, one mapping can be used to map all datasets in the collection to a binary classification task of toxic and non-toxic comments. The next section describes the effect of this mapping on the toxic comment collection and other statistics of collection in the next section.

2.2 Collection Statistics

The collection contains comments in thirteen different languages, from twelve platforms, and with 162 distinct class labels (before mapping them to a smaller set of class labels). There is a large set of labels that occurs only in one dataset, with each label referring to a particular subclass of toxicity and target, e.g., female football players as in the dataset by Fortuna et al. (2019).

After combining similar names through our mapping strategy, 126 class labels remain, with 57 of them occurring in more than 100 samples. The total number of samples is currently 812,993. We are constantly adding more datasets.

As described in the previous section, a mapping can also be used to create a binary view on the collection with only two class labels: toxic and non-toxic. To this end, the class labels *none* (471,871 comments), *normal* (37,922 comments), *other* (2,248 comments), *positive* (4,038 comments), and *appropriate* (2,997 comments) are mapped to *non-toxic* (519,076 comments). The labels *idk/skip* (73 comments) are discarded and all other labels are mapped to *toxic* (293,844 comments).

Table 1 gives an overview of the collection by listing all datasets currently included in the collec-

[3] `https://kaggle.com/c/jigsaw-toxic-comment-classification-challenge`

tion together with their number of samples, source platform, language, and class labels. The table reveals that Twitter is the primary data source and that there is no common set of class labels. As per Twitter's content redistribution policy,[4] the tweets themselves were (in almost all cases) not released by the researchers but only the tweet ids. These ids allow re-collecting the dataset via the Twitter API. Our tool automatizes this process, which is also called re-hydration.

A challenge that is not visible in Table 1 is the inherent class imbalance of many datasets. For example, the class distribution of the dataset of attacking comments by Wulczyn et al. (2017) exhibits a bias towards "clean" comments (201,081 clean; 21,384 attack), whereas the dataset by Davidson et al. (2017) exhibits a bias towards "offensive" comments (19,190 offensive; 4,163 clean). The latter class distribution is not representative of the underlying data in general. It is due to biased sampling, similar to the issues that apply to the dataset by Zhang et al. (2018). Zhang et al. (2018) collected their dataset via the Twitter API by filtering for a list of keywords, e.g., *muslim, refugee, terrorist,* and *attack* or hashtags, such as *#banislam, #refugeesnotwelcome,* and *#DeportallMuslims.* This step introduces a strong bias because all hateful tweets in the created dataset contain at least one of the keywords or hashtags. Thus, the data is not a representative sample of all hateful tweets on Twitter, and models trained on that data might overfit to the list of keywords and hashtags. However, the advantage of this step is that it reduces the annotation effort: fewer annotations are required to create a larger set of hateful tweets. In fact, most comment platforms contain only a tiny percentage of toxic comments. Since research datasets are collected with a focus on toxic comments, they can be biased in a significant way. This focused data collection creates non-realistic evaluation scenarios and needs to be taken into account when deploying models trained on these datasets in real-world scenarios.

Figure 1 visualizes the overlap of the set of class labels used in the different datasets contained in the toxic comment collection. On the one hand, there are rarely any pairs of datasets with the exact same set of labels (yellow cells). Exceptions are datasets by the same authors. On the other hand, there are also only a few pairs of datasets with no common class label at all.

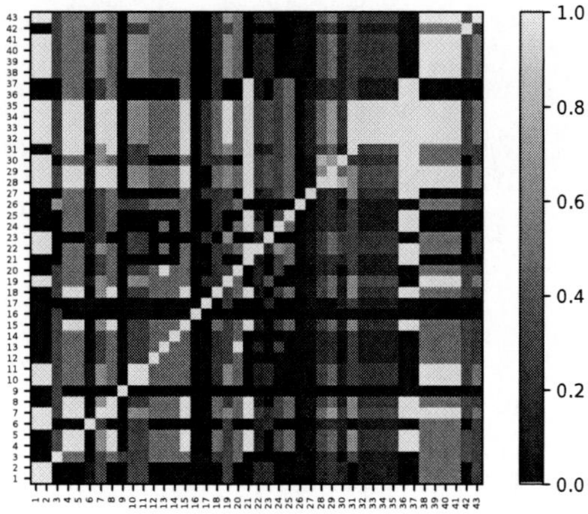

Figure 1: Heatmap of the pair-wise overlap of dataset class labels. Yellow cell color means that all class labels contained in the dataset of that row are also contained in the dataset of that column. See IDs in Table 1 for dataset names.

3 Conclusions and Future Work

In this paper, we addressed three challenges that hinder accessibility of research datasets of toxic comments: retrieving the datasets, unifying their file formats, and mapping their class labels to a common subset. To overcome these challenges, we present the toxic comment collection, which does not contain the datasets themselves, but code that automatically fetches these datasets from their source and transforms them into a unified format. Its advantages are the easy access to a large number of datasets and the option to filter by language, platform, and class label.

With the toxic comment collection, we aim to foster repeatability and reproducibility of research on toxic comments and to allow research on multilingual toxic comment classification by combining multiple datasets. We are continuously adding more datasets to the collection with routines to download them and to standardize their format automatically, e.g., we plan to integrate the datasets by Kumar et al. (2018) and Zampieri et al. (2019) next. We also plan to add contact information and instructions for datasets that are not publicly accessible but available only on request, such as the datasets by Golbeck et al. (2017), Rezvan et al. (2018), and Tulkens et al. (2016).

[4] `https://developer.twitter.com/en/developer-terms/agreement-and-policy`

Table 1: Datasets currently included in the toxic comment collection (sorted by year of publication). For this tabular presentation, we combined labels, e.g., *target* represents several different labels of targets.

ID	Study	Size	Source	Lang.	Classes
1	Bretschneider and Peters (2016)	1.8k	Forum	en	offense
2	Bretschneider and Peters (2016)	1.2k	Forum	en	offense
3	Waseem and Hovy (2016)	16.9k	Twitter	en	racism,sexism
4	Alfina et al. (2017)	0.7k	Twitter	id	hate
5	Ross et al. (2016)	0.5k	Twitter	de	hate
6	Bretschneider and Peters (2017)	5.8k	Facebook	de	strong/weak offense,target
7	Davidson et al. (2017)	25.0k	Twitter	en	hate,offense
8	Gao and Huang (2017)	1.5k	news	en	hate
9	Jha and Mamidi (2017)	10.0k	Twitter	en	benevolent/hostile sexism
10	Mubarak et al. (2017)	31.7k	news	ar	obscene,offensive
11	Mubarak et al. (2017)	1.1k	Twitter	ar	obscene,offensive
12	Wulczyn et al. (2017)	115.9k	Wikipedia	en	attack
13	Wulczyn et al. (2017)	115.9k	Wikipedia	en	aggressive
14	Wulczyn et al. (2017)	160.0k	Wikipedia	en	toxic
15	Albadi et al. (2018)	6.1k	Twitter	ar	hate
16	ElSherief et al. (2018)	28.0k	Twitter	en	hate,target
17	Founta et al. (2018)	80.0k	Twitter	en	six classes[d]
18	de Gibert et al. (2018)	10.6k	Forum	en	hate
19	Ibrohim and Budi (2018)	2.0k	Twitter	id	abuse,offense
20	Kumar et al. (2018)	11.6k	Facebook	hing	aggressive
21	Mathur et al. (2018)	3.2k	Twitter	en,hi	abuse,hate
22	Sanguinetti et al. (2018)	6.9k	Twitter	it	five classes[b]
23	Wiegand et al. (2018)	8.5k	Twitter	de	abuse,insult,profanity
24	Basile et al. (2019)	19.6k	Twitter	en,es	aggression,hate,target
25	Chung et al. (2019)	15.0k	misc	en,fr,it	hate,counter-narrative
26	Fortuna et al. (2019)	5.7k	Twitter	pt	hate,target
27	Ibrohim and Budi (2019)	13.2k	Twitter	id	abuse,strong/weak hate,target
28	Mandl et al. (2019)	6.0k	Twitter	hi	hate,offense,profanity,target
29	Mandl et al. (2019)	4.7k	Twitter	de	hate,offense,profanity,target
30	Mandl et al. (2019)	7.0k	Twitter	en	hate,offense,profanity,target
31	Mulki et al. (2019)	5.8k	Twitter	ar	abuse,hate
32	Ousidhoum et al. (2019)	5.6k	Twitter	fr	abuse,hate,offense,target
33	Ousidhoum et al. (2019)	5.6k	Twitter	en	abuse,hate,offense,target
34	Ousidhoum et al. (2019)	4.0k	Twitter	en	abuse,hate,offense,target
35	Ousidhoum et al. (2019)	3.3k	Twitter	ar	abuse,hate,offense,target
36	Qian et al. (2019)	22.3k	Forum	en	hate
37	Qian et al. (2019)	33.8k	Forum	en	hate
38	Zampieri et al. (2019)	13.2k	Twitter	en	offense
39	Çöltekin (2020)	36.0k	Twitter	tr	offense,target
40	Pitenis et al. (2020)	4.8k	Twitter	el	offense
41	Sigurbergsson and Derczynski (2020)	3.6k	misc	da	offense,target
42	Kulkarni et al. (2021)	15.9k	Twitter	mr	negative
43	Kralj Novak et al. (2021)	60.0k	Twitter	sl	offense,profanity,target,violent

[a] argument,discrimination,feedback,inappropriate,sentiment,personal,off-topic

[b] aggression,hate,irony,offense,stereotype

[c] derailment,discredit,harassment,misogyny,stereotype,target

[d] abuse,aggression,cyberbullying,hate,offense,spam

References

Nuha Albadi, Maram Kurdi, and Shivakant Mishra. 2018. Are they our brothers? analysis and detection of religious hate speech in the arabic twittersphere. In *Proceedings of the International Conference on Advances in Social Networks Analysis and Mining (ASONAM)*, pages 69–76. ACM.

Ika Alfina, Rio Mulia, Mohamad Ivan Fanany, and Yudo Ekanata. 2017. Hate speech detection in the indonesian language: A dataset and preliminary study. In *International Conference on Advanced Computer Science and Information Systems (ICACSIS)*, pages 233–238. IEEE.

Valerio Basile, Cristina Bosco, Elisabetta Fersini, Debora Nozza, Viviana Patti, Francisco Manuel Rangel Pardo, Paolo Rosso, and Manuela Sanguinetti. 2019. Semeval-2019 task 5: Multilingual detection of hate speech against immigrants and women in twitter. In *Proceedings of the International Workshop on Semantic Evaluation (SemEval@NAACL)*, pages 54–63. ACL.

Irina Bigoulaeva, Viktor Hangya, and Alexander Fraser. 2021. Cross-lingual transfer learning for hate speech detection. In *Proceedings of the Workshop on Language Technology for Equality, Diversity and Inclusion*, pages 15–25. ACL.

Uwe Bretschneider and Ralf Peters. 2016. Detecting cyberbullying in online communities. In *Proceedings of the European Conference on Information Systems (ECIS)*, pages 1–14.

Uwe Bretschneider and Ralf Peters. 2017. Detecting offensive statements towards foreigners in social media. In *Proceedings of the Hawaii International Conference on System Sciences*, pages 2213–2222.

Despoina Chatzakou, Nicolas Kourtellis, Jeremy Blackburn, Emiliano De Cristofaro, Gianluca Stringhini, and Athena Vakali. 2017. Mean birds: Detecting aggression and bullying on twitter. In *Proceedings of the International Web Science Conference (WebSci)*, page 13–22. ACM.

Yi-Ling Chung, Elizaveta Kuzmenko, Serra Sinem Tekiroglu, and Marco Guerini. 2019. CONAN - COunter NArratives through nichesourcing: a multilingual dataset of responses to fight online hate speech. In *Proceedings of the Annual Meeting of the Association for Computational Linguistics (ACL)*, pages 2819–2829. ACL.

Çağrı Çöltekin. 2020. A corpus of Turkish offensive language on social media. In *Proceedings of the Language Resources and Evaluation Conference (LREC)*, pages 6174–6184. ELRA.

Thomas Davidson, Dana Warmsley, Michael Macy, and Ingmar Weber. 2017. Automated Hate Speech Detection and the Problem of Offensive Language. In *Proceedings of the International Conference on Web and Social Media (ICWSM)*, pages 512–515. AAAI Press.

Ona de Gibert, Naiara Perez, Aitor García-Pablos, and Montse Cuadros. 2018. Hate Speech Dataset from a White Supremacy Forum. In *Proceedings of the Workshop on Abusive Language Online (ALW@EMNLP)*, pages 11–20. ACL.

Mai ElSherief, Vivek Kulkarni, Dana Nguyen, William Yang Wang, and Elizabeth Belding. 2018. Hate lingo: A target-based linguistic analysis of hate speech in social media. In *Proceedings of the International Conference on Web and Social Media (ICWSM)*, pages 42–51. AAAI Press.

Paula Fortuna, João Rocha da Silva, Juan Soler-Company, Leo Wanner, and Sérgio Nunes. 2019. A hierarchically-labeled Portuguese hate speech dataset. In *Proceedings of the Workshop on Abusive Language Online (ALW@ACL)*, pages 94–104. ACL.

Antigoni-Maria Founta, Constantinos Djouvas, Despoina Chatzakou, Ilias Leontiadis, Jeremy Blackburn, Gianluca Stringhini, Athena Vakali, Michael Sirivianos, and Nicolas Kourtellis. 2018. Large Scale Crowdsourcing and Characterization of Twitter Abusive Behavior. In *Proceedings of the International Conference on Web and Social Media (ICWSM)*, pages 491–500. AAAI Press.

Lei Gao and Ruihong Huang. 2017. Detecting online hate speech using context aware models. In *Proceedings of the International Conference Recent Advances in Natural Language Processing (RANLP)*, pages 260–266. INCOMA Ltd.

Jennifer Golbeck, Zahra Ashktorab, Rashad O. Banjo, Alexandra Berlinger, Siddharth Bhagwan, Cody Buntain, Paul Cheakalos, Alicia A. Geller, Quint Gergory, Rajesh Kumar Gnanasekaran, Raja Rajan Gunasekaran, Kelly M. Hoffman, Jenny Hottle, Vichita Jienjitlert, Shivika Khare, Ryan Lau, Marianna J. Martindale, Shalmali Naik, Heather L. Nixon, Piyush Ramachandran, Kristine M. Rogers, Lisa Rogers, Meghna Sardana Sarin, Gaurav Shahane, Jayanee Thanki, Priyanka Vengataraman, Zijian Wan, and Derek Michael Wu. 2017. A large labeled corpus for online harassment research. In *Proceedings of the International Web Science Conference (WebSci)*, pages 229–233. ACM.

Muhammad Okky Ibrohim and Indra Budi. 2018. A dataset and preliminaries study for abusive language detection in indonesian social media. *Procedia Computer Science*, 135:222–229.

Muhammad Okky Ibrohim and Indra Budi. 2019. Multi-label hate speech and abusive language detection in Indonesian Twitter. In *Proceedings of the Workshop on Abusive Language Online (ALW@ACL)*, pages 46–57. ACL.

Akshita Jha and Radhika Mamidi. 2017. When does a compliment become sexist? analysis and classification of ambivalent sexism using twitter data.

In *Proceedings of the Workshop on Natural Language Processing and Computational Social Science (NLP+CSS@ACL)*, pages 7–16. ACL.

Petra Kralj Novak, Igor Mozetič, and Nikola Ljubešić. 2021. Slovenian twitter hate speech dataset IMSyPP-sl. Slovenian language resource repository CLARIN.SI.

Atharva Kulkarni, Meet Mandhane, Manali Likhitkar, Gayatri Kshirsagar, and Raviraj Joshi. 2021. L3cubemahasent: A marathi tweet-based sentiment analysis dataset. *arXiv preprint arXiv:2103.11408*.

Ritesh Kumar, Aishwarya N. Reganti, Akshit Bhatia, and Tushar Maheshwari. 2018. Aggression-annotated Corpus of Hindi-English Code-mixed Data. In *Proceedings of the Language Resources and Evaluation Conference (LREC)*, pages 1425–1431. ELRA.

Kosisochukwu Madukwe, Xiaoying Gao, and Bing Xue. 2020. In data we trust: A critical analysis of hate speech detection datasets. In *Proceedings of the Workshop on Abusive Language Online (ALW@EMNLP)*, pages 150–161. ACL.

Thomas Mandl, Sandip Modha, Prasenjit Majumder, Daksh Patel, Mohana Dave, Chintak Mandlia, and Aditya Patel. 2019. Overview of the hasoc track at fire 2019: Hate speech and offensive content identification in indo-european languages. In *Proceedings of the Forum for Information Retrieval Evaluation*, page 14–17. ACM.

Puneet Mathur, Ramit Sawhney, Meghna Ayyar, and Rajiv Shah. 2018. Did you offend me? classification of offensive tweets in hinglish language. In *Proceedings of the Workshop on Abusive Language Online (ALW@EMNLP)*, pages 138–148. ACL.

Hamdy Mubarak, Darwish Kareem, and Magdy Walid. 2017. Abusive Language Detection on Arabic Social Media. In *Proceedings of the Workshop on Abusive Language Online (ALW@ACL)*, pages 52–56. ACL.

Hala Mulki, Hatem Haddad, Chedi Bechikh Ali, and Halima Alshabani. 2019. L-HSAB: A Levantine Twitter dataset for hate speech and abusive language. In *Proceedings of the Workshop on Abusive Language Online (ALW@ACL)*, pages 111–118. ACL.

Nedjma Ousidhoum, Zizheng Lin, Hongming Zhang, Yangqiu Song, and Dit-Yan Yeung. 2019. Multilingual and multi-aspect hate speech analysis. In *Proceedings of the Conference on Empirical Methods in Natural Language Processing and the International Joint Conference on Natural Language Processing (EMNLP-IJCNLP)*, pages 4675–4684. ACL.

Zesis Pitenis, Marcos Zampieri, and Tharindu Ranasinghe. 2020. Offensive language identification in Greek. In *Proceedings of the Language Resources and Evaluation Conference (LREC)*, pages 5113–5119. ELRA.

Fabio Poletto, Valerio Basile, Manuela Sanguinetti, Cristina Bosco, and Viviana Patti. 2020. Resources and benchmark corpora for hate speech detection: a systematic review. *Language Resources and Evaluation*, pages 1–47.

Jing Qian, Anna Bethke, Yinyin Liu, Elizabeth Belding, and William Yang Wang. 2019. A benchmark dataset for learning to intervene in online hate speech. In *Proceedings of the Conference on Empirical Methods in Natural Language Processing and the International Joint Conference on Natural Language Processing (EMNLP-IJCNLP)*, pages 4755–4764. ACL.

Mohammadreza Rezvan, Saeedeh Shekarpour, Lakshika Balasuriya, Krishnaprasad Thirunarayan, Valerie L. Shalin, and Amit Sheth. 2018. A quality type-aware annotated corpus and lexicon for harassment research. In *Proceedings of the International Web Science Conference (WebSci)*, page 33–36. ACM.

Manoel Horta Ribeiro, Pedro H. Calais, Yuri A. Santos, Virgılio A. F. Almeida, and Wagner Meira Jr. 2018. Characterizing and detecting hateful users on twitter. In *Proceedings of the International Conference on Web and Social Media (ICWSM)*, pages 676–679. AAAI Press.

Julian Risch and Ralf Krestel. 2018. Aggression identification using deep learning and data augmentation. In *Proceedings of the Workshop on Trolling, Aggression and Cyberbullying (TRAC@COLING)*, pages 150–158. ACL.

Björn Ross, Michael Rist, Guillermo Carbonell, Benjamin Cabrera, Nils Kurowsky, and Michael Wojatzki. 2016. Measuring the reliability of hate speech annotations: The case of the european refugee crisis. In *Proceedings of the Workshop on Natural Language Processing for Computer-Mediated Communication (NLP4CMC@KONVENS)*, pages 6–9. University Frankfurt.

Manuela Sanguinetti, Fabio Poletto, Cristina Bosco, Viviana Patti, and Marco Stranisci. 2018. An Italian Twitter corpus of hate speech against immigrants. In *Proceedings of the Language Resources and Evaluation Conference (LREC)*, pages 2798–2805. ELRA.

Gudbjartur Ingi Sigurbergsson and Leon Derczynski. 2020. Offensive language and hate speech detection for Danish. In *Proceedings of the Language Resources and Evaluation Conference (LREC)*, pages 3498–3508. ELRA.

Rachele Sprugnoli, Stefano Menini, Sara Tonelli, Filippo Oncini, and Enrico Piras. 2018. Creating a WhatsApp dataset to study pre-teen cyberbullying. In *Proceedings of the Workshop on Abusive Language Online (ALW@EMNLP)*, pages 51–59. ACL.

Stéphan Tulkens, Lisa Hilte, Elise Lodewyckx, Ben Verhoeven, and Walter Daelemans. 2016. The automated detection of racist discourse in dutch social media. *Computational Linguistics in the Netherlands Journal*, 6:3–20.

Betty van Aken, Julian Risch, Ralf Krestel, and Alexander Löser. 2018. Challenges for toxic comment classification: An in-depth error analysis. In *Proceedings of the Workshop on Abusive Language Online (ALW@EMNLP)*, pages 33–42. ACL.

Bertie Vidgen and Leon Derczynski. 2020. Directions in abusive language training data, a systematic review: Garbage in, garbage out. *PloS one*, 15(12):1–32.

Zeerak Waseem and Dirk Hovy. 2016. Hateful symbols or hateful people? predictive features for hate speech detection on twitter. In *Proceedings of the Student Research Workshop@NAACL*, pages 88–93. ACL.

Michael Wiegand, Melanie Siegel, and Josef Ruppenhofer. 2018. Overview of the GermEval 2018 shared task on the identification of offensive language. In *Proceedings of the Conference on Natural Language Processing (KONVENS)*, pages 1–10. Austrian Academy of Sciences.

Ellery Wulczyn, Nithum Thain, and Lucas Dixon. 2017. Ex machina: Personal attacks seen at scale. In *Proceedings of the International Conference on World Wide Web (WWW)*, pages 1391–1399. ACM.

Marcos Zampieri, Shervin Malmasi, Preslav Nakov, Sara Rosenthal, Noura Farra, and Ritesh Kumar. 2019. Predicting the type and target of offensive posts in social media. In *Proceedings of the North American Chapter of the Association for Computational Linguistics (NAACL)*, pages 1415–1420. ACL.

Ziqi Zhang, David Robinson, and Jonathan A. Tepper. 2018. Detecting hate speech on twitter using a convolution-gru based deep neural network. In *Proceedings of the Extended Semantic Web Conference (ESWC)*, pages 745–760. Springer.

When the Echo Chamber Shatters: Examining the Use of Community-Specific Language Post-Subreddit Ban

Milo Z. Trujillo
University of Vermont
milo.trujillo@uvm.edu

Samuel F. Rosenblatt
University of Vermont
samuel.f.rosenblatt@uvm.edu

Guillermo de Anda Jáuregui
National Institute of Genomic Medicine (INMEGEN)
Programa de Cátedras CONACYT para Jóvenes Investigadores
Universidad Nacional Autónoma de México
gdeanda@inmegen.edu.mx

Emily Moog
University of Illinois at Urbana-Champaign
emoog2@illinois.edu

Briane Paul V. Samson
De La Salle University
briane.samson@dlsu.edu.ph

Laurent Hébert-Dufresne
University of Vermont
laurent.hebert-dufresne@uvm.edu

Allison M. Roth
University of Florida
amr2264@columbia.edu

Abstract

Community-level bans are a common tool against groups that enable online harassment and harmful speech. Unfortunately, the efficacy of community bans has only been partially studied and with mixed results. Here, we provide a flexible unsupervised methodology to identify in-group language and track user activity on Reddit both before and after the ban of a community (subreddit). We use a simple word frequency divergence to identify uncommon words overrepresented in a given community, not as a proxy for harmful speech but as a linguistic signature of the community. We apply our method to 15 banned subreddits, and find that community response is heterogeneous between subreddits and between users of a subreddit. Top users were more likely to become less active overall, while random users often reduced use of in-group language without decreasing activity. Finally, we find some evidence that the effectiveness of bans aligns with the content of a community. Users of dark humor communities were largely unaffected by bans while users of communities organized around white supremacy and fascism were the most affected. Altogether, our results show that bans do not affect all groups or users equally, and pave the way to understanding the effect of bans across communities.

1 Introduction

Online spaces often contain toxic behaviors such as abuse or harmful speech (Blackwell et al., 2017; Saleem et al., 2017; Jhaver et al., 2018; Saleem and Ruths, 2018; Habib et al., 2019; Ribeiro et al., 2020a; de Gibert et al., 2018a; Sprugnoli et al., 2018; Park and Fung, 2017; Singh et al., 2018; Lee et al., 2018). Such toxicity may result in platform-wide decreases in user participation and engagement which, combined with external pressure (e.g., bad press), may motivate platform managers to moderate harmful behavior (Saleem and Ruths, 2018; Habib et al., 2019). Moreover, the radicalization of individuals through their engagement with toxic online spaces may have real-world consequences, making toxic online communities a cause for broader concern (Ohlheiser, 2016; Habib et al., 2019; Ribeiro et al., 2020a,b).

Reddit is a social media platform that consists of an ecosystem of different online spaces. As of January 2020, Reddit had over 52 million daily active users organized in over 100,000 communities, known as "subreddits", where people gather to discuss common interests or share subject- or format-specific creative content and news (Reddit, 2021). Every post made on Reddit is placed in one distinct subreddit, and every comment on Reddit is associated with an individual post and therefore

Proceedings of the Fifth Workshop on Online Abuse and Harms, pages 164–178
August 6, 2021.

also associated with a single subreddit. As Reddit continues to gain popularity, moderation of content is becoming increasingly necessary. Content may be moderated in several ways, including: (1) by community voting that results in increased or decreased visibility of specific posts, (2) by subreddit-specific volunteer moderators who may delete posts or ban users that violate the subreddit guidelines, and (3) by platform-wide administrators that may remove posts, users, or entire communities which violate broader site policies. The removal of an entire subreddit is known as a "subreddit ban," and does not typically indicate that the users active in the subreddit have been banned.

Given that the ostensible purpose of subreddit bans is to remove subreddits that are in habitual noncompliance with Reddit's Terms of Service, it is important to understand whether such bans are successful in reducing the offending content. This is especially of interest when the offending content is related to harmful language. Though limited, there is some evidence to suggest that subreddit bans may be effective by certain metrics. Past work has demonstrated that these bans can have both user- and community-level effects (Hazel Kwon and Shao, 2020; Chandrasekharan et al., 2017; Saleem and Ruths, 2018; Ribeiro et al., 2020a; Thomas et al., 2021; Habib et al., 2019). Several of these studies have suggested that (1) subreddit bans may lead a significant number of users to completely stop using the site, and that (2) following a ban, users that remain on the platform appear to decrease their levels of harmful speech on Reddit (Saleem and Ruths, 2018; Thomas et al., 2021; Habib et al., 2019). Chandrasekharan et al. (2017) also illustrated that postban migrations of users to different subreddits did not result in naive users adopting offensive language related to the banned communities. More work is required to better understand changes in the language of individual users after such bans.

2 Previous work

Previous research provides a foundation for investigating the effects of subreddit bans on harmful language and user activity. Detection of offensive content typically takes the form of automated classification. Different machine learning approaches have been applied with varied success, including but not limited to support vector machines and random forests to convolutional and recurrent neural networks (Zhang and Luo, 2019; Bosco et al., 2018; de Gibert et al., 2018b; Kshirsagar et al., 2018; Malmasi and Zampieri, 2018; Pitsilis et al., 2018; Al-Hassan and Al-Dossari, 2019; Vidgen and Yasseri, 2020; Zimmerman et al., 2018). More recently, Garland et al. (2020) used an ensemble learning algorithm to classify both hate speech and counter speech in a curated collection of German messages on Twitter. Unfortunately, these approaches require labeled sets of speech to train classifiers and therefore risk not transferring from one type of harmful speech (e.g. misogyny) to another (e.g. racism). We therefore aim for a more flexible approach that does not attempt to classify speech directly, but rather identifies language over-represented in harmful groups; i.e., their in-group language. That language is not a signal of, for example, hate speech per se. In fact, any group is likely to have significant in-group language (e.g. hockey communities are more likely to use the word "slapshot"). However, detection of in-group language can be fully automated in an unsupervised fashion and is tractable.

The majority of past work on bans of harmful communities on Reddit only examined one or two subreddits, often chosen due to notoriety (Hazel Kwon and Shao, 2020; Chandrasekharan et al., 2017; Saleem and Ruths, 2018; Ribeiro et al., 2020a; Habib et al., 2019; Thomas et al., 2021). Many of these studies focused on the average change in behavior across users and did not consider the factors which may drive inter-individual differences in behavior following a ban (Chandrasekharan et al., 2017; Saleem and Ruths, 2018; Habib et al., 2019). Different users may respond differently to subreddit bans based on their level of overall activity or community engagement. For example, Ribeiro et al. (2020a) found that users that were more active on Reddit prior to a subreddit ban were more likely to migrate to a different platform following a ban. A user's activity levels prior to a ban also impacted whether activity levels increased or decreased upon migrating to a different platform (Ribeiro et al., 2020a). Similarly, Thomas et al. (2021) demonstrated that users who were more active in a subreddit prior to a ban were more likely to change their behavior following the banning of that subreddit, but the authors did not investigate the ways in which users changed their behavior. Lastly, Hazel Kwon and Shao (2020) found that a user's pre-ban activity level within r/alphabaymarket influenced post-ban shifts in communicative activity.

While we are interested in the effects of moderation on any online community, we study Reddit because the platform is strongly partitioned into sub-communities, and historical data on both subreddits and users are readily available (Baumgartner et al., 2020). Reddit users are regularly active in multiple subreddits concurrently, and unlike other sub-community partitioned platforms like Discord, Slack, or Telegram, we can easily retrieve a user's activity on *all* sub-communities. This provides an opportunity to understand how the members of a community change their behavior after that community is banned. Furthermore, knowledge of the drivers of inter-individual behavioral differences may permit moderators to monitor the post-ban activity of certain subsets of users more closely than others, which may lead to an increase in the efficacy of platform-wide moderation.

3 Methodology

As part of investigating whether different communities respond differently to a subreddit ban, we examine whether top users differ from random users in their change in activity and in-group language usage following community-level interventions. Specifically, we utilize natural language processing to track community activity after a subreddit ban, across 15 subreddits that were banned during the so-called "Great Ban" of 2020. We first identified words that had a higher prevalence in these subreddits than on Reddit as a whole prior to a ban. These words do not necessarily correspond to harmful speech but provide a linguistic signature of the community. The strengths and drawbacks of this approach are discussed in the discussion and appendix. We then compared the frequency of use of community-specific language, as well as the overall activity level of a user (i.e., the number of total comments), 60 days pre- and post-ban for (1) the 100 users that were most active in the banned subreddit 6 months prior to the ban and (2) 1000 randomly sampled non-top users. We predicted that top and random users that remained on the site following a subreddit ban would react differently to the ban, and we anticipated that there would be variation in how different communities responded to a ban.

3.1 Data Selection

We selected 15 subreddits banned in June 2020, after Reddit changed their content policies regarding communities that "incite violence or that promote hate based on identity or vulnerability" and subsequently banned approximately 2000 subreddits (i.e., "the Great Ban"). Based on a list of subreddits banned in the Great Ban [1] and an obscured list of subreddits ordered by daily active users [2], we examined the subreddits with more than 2000 active daily users and which had not previously become private subreddits. These most-visited subreddits were "obscured" by representing all letters except the first two as asterisks, but were de-anonymized as described in the appendix (Section 9.1). By selecting highly active subreddits from the Great Ban we can compare many subreddits banned on the same date, and the differences in how their users responded. The list of subreddits we examined is included in Table 1.

3.2 Data Collection

For each chosen subreddit, we collected all the submissions and comments made during the 182 days before it was banned. This is possible through the Pushshift API[3], which archives Reddit regularly, but may miss a minority of comments if they are deleted (by the author or by moderators) very shortly after they are posted (Baumgartner et al., 2020). We use this sample of the banned subreddits to identify users from the community and specific language used by the community. To accomplish the former, we examine the "author" field of each comment to get a list of users and how many comments they made on the subreddit during the time frame prior to the ban.

To automatically determine in-group vocabulary words for a subreddit, we create a corpus of all text from the comments in a banned subreddit and compare it the baseline corpus to a corpus of 70 million non-bot comments from across all of Reddit during the same time frame. Bot detection is described in Section 3.4. We can gather this cross-site sample by using comment IDs: every Reddit comment has a unique increasing numeric ID. By taking the

[1] https://www.reddit.com/r/reclassified/comments/fg3608/updated_list_of_all_known_banned_subreddits/

[2] https://www.redditstatic.com/banned-subreddits-june-2020.txt

[3] https://psaw.readthedocs.io/en/latest/

comment ID of the first and last comments from our banned sample, and then uniformly sampling all comment IDs between that range and retrieving the associated comments, we can uniformly sample from Reddit as a whole over arbitrary time ranges.

We used this baseline corpus instead of a more standard English corpus because many such standard corpora rely on books, often in the public domain, whose language may be dated and more formal than Reddit comments. These corpora often also lack terms from current events such as sports team names or political figures, which occur frequently across large parts of Reddit.

3.3 Determining In-Group Vocabulary

We compare word frequencies between the two corpora to identify language that is more prominent in the banned subreddit than in the general sample. Since the two samples are from the same date range on the same platform, this methodology filters out current events and Reddit-specific vocabulary more than we would achieve by comparing to a general English-language corpus like LIWC (Tausczik and Pennebaker, 2010). Rather than comparing relative word occurrence frequency directly, which has pitfalls regarding low-frequency words that may only occur in one corpus, we apply Jensen-Shannon Divergence (JSD) which compares the word frequencies in the two corpora against a mixture text. JSD scores words highly if they appear disproportionately frequently in one corpus, even if they are common in both. For example, JSD identifies "female" as a top word in gender-discussion subreddits. Treating "female" as in-group vocabulary is undesirable for our specific use-case, where we would prefer to find language specific to the subreddit that is uncommon elsewhere. Therefore, we remove the top 10,000 most common words in the general corpus from both the general corpus and the subreddit corpus before processing. JSD functionality is provided by the Shifterator software package (Gallagher et al., 2021). Based on the resulting JSD scores, we then select the top 100 words in the banned subreddit corpus, and treat this as our final list of in-group vocabulary. We used the top 100 words to maintain consistency with the distinctive vocabulary size used by Chandrasekharan et al. (2017). In the appendix, our approach is compared to the Sparse Additive Generative model (SAGE) of Chandrasekharan et al. (2017) to show the additional flexibility of JSD as well as similarity of the results (see Section 9.2).

3.4 Examining User Behavior

With a list of users from the banned community ranked by comment count and a list of in-group vocabulary, we are able to measure user behavior after the subreddit ban. Since larger subreddits can have tens of thousands to millions of users, we limit ourselves to examining two groups: (1) the 100 most active accounts from a banned subreddit, known as the "top users", and (2) a random sample of 1000 non-top users from the subreddit. In forming these lists of top and random users, we skip over accounts from a pre-defined list of automated Reddit bots as well as users that have deleted their accounts and cannot have their post histories retrieved. Additionally, as our focus for this study is users who used in-group language and who continue to use the platform, we omit users that have never used in-group vocabulary pre- or post-ban or who have zero comments post-ban. All forms of user-filtering are discussed further in the appendix (Section 9.4).

For each user, we download all the comments they made in the 60 days before and after the subreddit ban. We compare the number of comments made before and after the ban to establish a change of activity, on a scale from -1 to 1, with -1 indicating "100% of the user's comments were made prior to the ban", 0 indicating "an equal number of comments were made before and after the ban", and 1 indicating that all of their comments on Reddit were made after the ban. We can similarly track the user's use of in-group vocabulary on a scale from -1 to 1, for "100% of their in-group vocabulary usage was before the ban" to "all uses of in-group vocabulary were post-ban". This is calculated as the fraction of posted words that were in-group vocabulary after the ban, minus the fraction of posted words that we in-group vocabulary before the ban, divided by the sum of the fractions.

$$\frac{r_a - r_b}{r_a + r_b}$$

Examples of results for individual subreddits are shown in Fig.1.

3.5 Statistical Methods

We do not necessarily expect all subreddits to respond to a ban in the same way. From the user data for the 60 days before and after the subreddit's

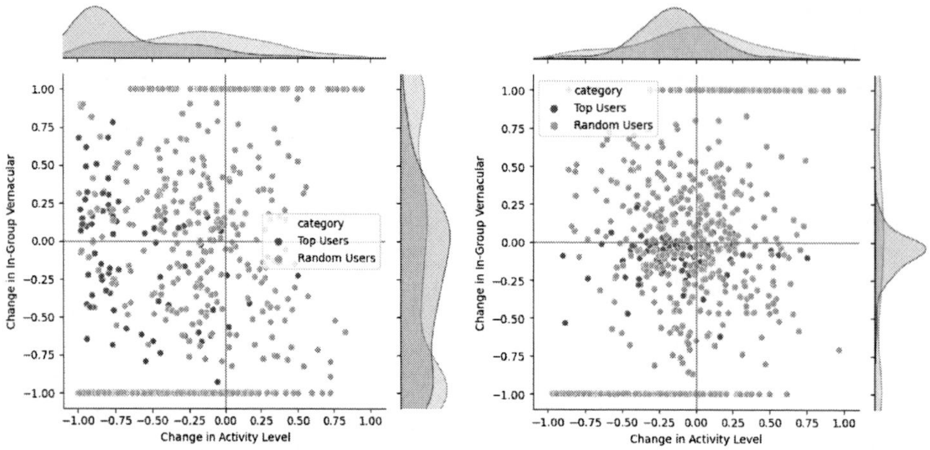

(a) Ban effect on *r/gendercritical* users

(b) Ban effect on *r/the_donald* users

Figure 1: Example plots comparing user behavior after a subreddit ban. Users from the top 100 and random samples are displayed in terms of their relative change in activity and change in in-group vocabulary usage. Distributions are displayed along each axis for convenience.

Category	**Subreddits**
Dark Jokes	darkjokecentral, darkhumorandmemes, imgoingtohellforthis2
Anti-Political	consumeproduct, soyboys, wojak
Mainstream Right Wing	the_donald, thenewright, hatecrimehoaxes
Extreme Right Wing	debatealtright, shitneoconssay
Uncategorized	ccj2, chapotraphouse, gendercritical, oandaexclusiveforum

Table 1: Subreddit categorization by qualitative assessment of content

banning, we examined whether there was any difference between subreddits for (1) the proportion of a user's total posts that occurred postban vs preban and (2) the proportion of a user's total in-group vocabulary that occurred postban vs preban. We also explored whether a user's engagement in a subreddit (i.e., whether they were a top or random user) influenced either measure. To examine the predictors of the proportion of a user's total posts that occurred postban vs preban, we ran a generalized linear mixed model with a binomial error distribution. This model included the ratio of a user's posts after the ban to their posts before the ban as the predictor, and subreddit identity and user engagement (i.e., top or random) as fixed effects. To examine the predictors of pre-ban vs post-ban total in-group vocabulary, we ran a second generalized linear mixed model with a binomial error distribution. Its predictor was the ratio of the number of in-group vocabulary words a user used after the ban to the number of in-group vocabulary words that they used before the ban. Subreddit identity and user engagement (i.e., top or random) were fixed effects. For both models, we included user identity (i.e. top or random) as a random effect, since some users were active in more than one of the studied subreddits. Additionally, we used a likelihood ratio test (LRT) to explore whether there was an overall effect of subreddit identity on the proportion of a user's total posts that occurred postban vs preban, and the proportion of a user's total in-group vocabulary that occurred postban vs preban. In the LRT, we compared each described model to a model without subreddit identity. We also used LRTs to compare models with and without user engagement to assess whether there was an overall effect of user engagement on either measure.

We performed statistical comparisons in order to understand whether users' vocabulary and activity differed before and after the ban, as well as whether top and random users of a given subreddit experienced similar shifts.

To confirm the shifts displayed in Fig. 2a are meaningful we performed Wilcoxon Signed-Rank tests ($\alpha = FDR = 0.05$) on the normalized vocabulary ratios and normalized activity ratios before

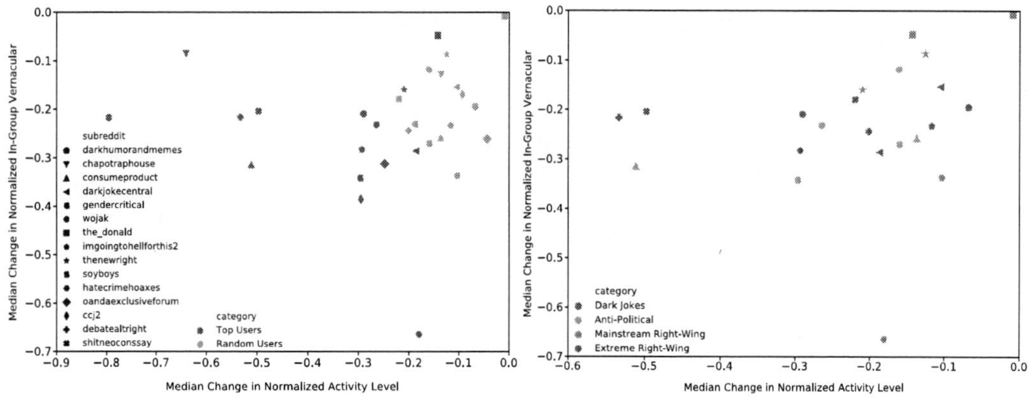

(a) Comparison of top/random users in all 15 subreddits

(b) Comparison of top/random users across by categories

Figure 2: Comparison of top and random user behavior changes across fifteen subreddits banned after a change in Reddit content policy in January, 2020. (a) Top users show more significant drop-offs in posting activity after a ban, but have around the same change in in-group vocabulary usage as a uniform sampling of subreddit participants. (b) Ban impact on eleven subreddits categorized by content. Each subreddit appears twice, representing top and random users. Four uncategorized subreddits are excluded from the plot. Trends are summarized in Table 2.

and after the ban. Except for users of the_donald (both user types) and the top users of chapotraphouse, these tests decreases in-group vocabulary usage in all subreddit/user-type pairs. The same tests showed the ban had a significant effect on all subreddit/user-type pairs in terms of activity level except for the random users of the_donald, though these effects were not all decreases.

We used the Wilcoxon rank sum test to compare the previously defined metrics for vocabulary shift and activity shift between the top and random users within each subreddit. The p-values for each individual comparison at the subreddit level were corrected using false discovery rate (FDR), and are illustrated in Fig. 3.

3.6 Subreddit Categorization

To better understand our results, we categorized each banned subreddit as "dark jokes", "anti-political", "mainstream right wing", and "extreme right wing", as shown in Table 1. These categories encompass eleven of our fifteen subreddits, leaving four that are significantly distinct from their peers. Note that the "uncategorized" subreddits are not necessarily difficult to classify (for example, r/gendercritical is a trans-exclusionary radical feminist subreddit), but without similar banned subreddits of comparable size we cannot suggest that results for these subreddits are generalizable. While these categories were chosen based on qualitative assessment of each subreddit's content, they are verified by a quantitative comparison of the unique vocabulary of each subreddit available in the appendix.

4 Results

By comparing the median change in activity and vocabulary usage among top and random users, we found a consistent pattern: Top users, for every subreddit studied, decrease their activity more than their peers. This result is important to keep in mind when a uniform sampling of subreddit users post-ban may indicate that a community ban was ineffective. We do not find as consistent a difference between top and random user when looking at vocabulary change; suggesting that while bans may drive harmful users to inactivity, they are less clearly effectual at reforming user behavior. These results are summarized in Fig. 2a.

To confirm our findings, we tested the statistical significance of differences between top and random distributions for each subreddit, illustrated in Fig. 3. In all subreddits, there was a significant difference between top and random user changes in either activity shifts, vocabulary shifts, or both. Considering a significance threshold on the false discovery rate, FDR < 0.05, we found two subreddits (r/ccj2 and r/hatecrimehoaxes) that show significant differences in both shifts. The subreddit r/darkjokecentral shows significant differences between top and random users in vocabulary shift, but not activity; whereas the rest of the subreddits show differences in activity but not vocabulary shift

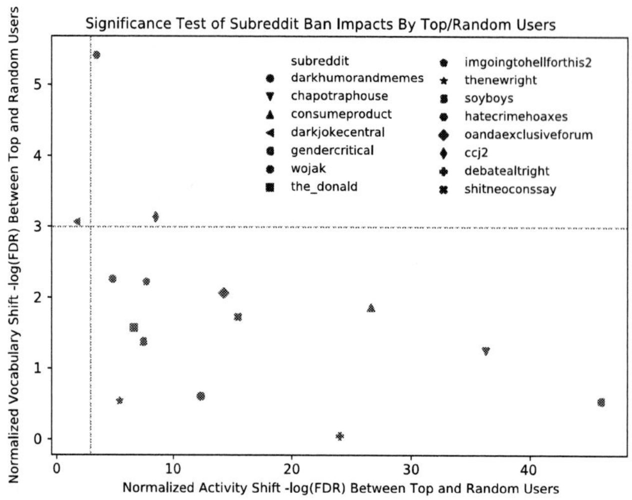

Figure 3: Scatterplot showing differences in activity and vocabulary shifts between top and random users of each subreddit. Each axis shows the statistical significance, expressed as -log(FDR), of either activity (x-axis) or vocabulary (y-axis) shift. Dashed lines indicate significance at a threshold of 0.05, such that subreddits with greater values show significant differences between top and random users.

between top and random users.

We found that, controlling for user engagement (i.e., whether a user was a top or random user), there was a significant overall effect of subreddit identity on both the proportion of a user's total posts that occurred postban vs preban (LRT, Chi-squared = 133.730, $p < 0.001$) and the proportion of a user's total in-group vocabulary that occurred postban vs preban (LRT, Chi-squared = 239.680, $p < 0.001$). Controlling for subreddit identity, there was also a significant overall effect of user engagement on the proportion of a user's total posts that occurred postban vs preban (LRT, Chi-squared = 23.452, $p < 0.001$) and the proportion of a user's total in-group vocabulary that occurred postban (LRT, Chi-squared = 220.020, $p < 0.001$). Postban posts made up a lower proportion of a user's total posts and postban use of in-group vocabulary made up a lower portion of a user's total in-group vocabulary use for top users compared to random users (Fig. 4). There were a few subreddits that were significantly different from most or all of the other subreddits. For example, in r/the_donald, postban posts comprised a higher proportion of a user's total posts, compared to all other subreddits (Fig. 4a), and postban use of in-group vocabulary comprised a higher portion of a user's total in-group vocabulary use, compared to all other subreddits (Fig. 4b). Postban posts also comprised a higher proportion of a user's total posts in r/oandaexclusiveforum, compared to most other subreddits, while postban posts comprised a lower proportion of a user's total posts in r/soyboys, compared to most other subreddits (Fig. 4a). The proportion of a user's total in-group vocabulary that occurred postban was lower for both r/gendercritical and r/hatecrimehoaxes, compared to most other subreddits (Fig. 4b).

5 Discussion

Past work has been quick to conclude that subreddit bans either are (Chandrasekharan et al., 2017; Saleem and Ruths, 2018; Thomas et al., 2021) or are not (Habib et al., 2019) effective at changing user behavior. We have found that results differ between subreddits and between more and less active users within a subreddit. Since many prior studies on banning efficacy focus on one to two subreddit case studies, these distinctions may not have been apparent in some previous datasets.

To automatically study a larger number of communities, we tackle the simpler problem of tracking user activity and use of in-group language rather than more subjective harmful language. This approach has strengths and drawbacks. On the one hand, in-group language is easier to automatically identify with little expert knowledge or human intervention, while also including lesser known slang terms or dog whistles that could be harmful. On the other hand, our approach requires a large reference corpus that controls for relevant features of the

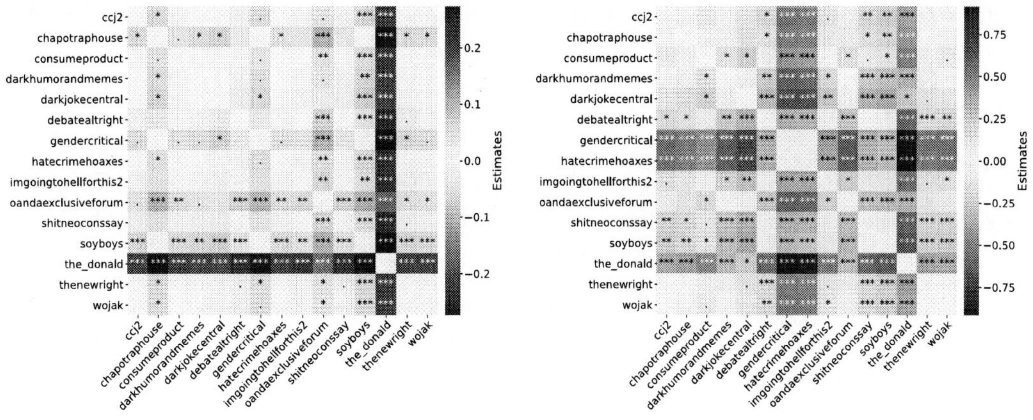

(a) Proportion of Total Posts Post/Pre-ban

(b) Proportion of Total In-Group Vocabulary Post/Pre-ban

Figure 4: Visualization of GLMM results showing differences between subreddits in postban behavior. For each row, blue cells indicate that the subreddit in a given column had a lower proportion of postban activity/ingroup vocabulary use than the subreddit in that row, while red cells indicate that the subreddit in a given column had a higher proportion of postban activity/ingroup vocabulary use than the subreddit in that row. · indicates $p < 0.10$. * indicates $p < 0.05$. ** indicates $p < 0.01$. *** indicates $p < 0.001$.

Category	Activity Impact	Vocabulary Impact
Dark Jokes	Minimal	Minimal
Anti-Political	Top users less active	Decrease among top users
Mainstream Right Wing	Minimal	Inconsistent
Extreme Right Wing	All users decrease, especially top users	Minimal

Table 2: The impact of subreddit bans within each category.

studied corpus to produce meaningful results. For Reddit, using non-banned subreddits as a baseline corpus allows us to automatically study changes in activity and language around community bans while requiring little expert knowledge on these communities. However, choosing a reference corpus may be more challenging on other platforms without a broader "mainstream" population (such as alt-tech platforms), with small populations, or without a clear means of sampling the overall population (such as Slack, Discord, and Telegram).

Our study examines 15 subreddits with over 5000 daily users that were banned simultaneously after a change in Reddit content policy, and our results suggest that subreddit bans impact top and random users differently (in agreement with prior studies such as Hazel Kwon and Shao (2020); Ribeiro et al. (2020a); Thomas et al. (2021)) and that community-level banning has a heterogeneous impact across subreddits.

Additionally, we see patterns in subreddit responses to bans that loosely correlate with the type of content the community focused on, summarized in Table 2 and illustrated in Fig. 2b. Dark joke subreddits were banned for casual racism, sexism, or other bigotry, do not have as clearly defined in-group language, and were largely unaffected by bans. Users are not more or less active, and use similar language pre and post-ban. Anti-political subreddits, who ridicule most activism and view social progressiveness as performative, were moderately impacted by bans. Top users from these communities became less active after the ban, and randomly sampled users commented using less in-group language. Mainstream right-wing communities show the least consistency in ban response. The most impacted subreddits were extreme political communities that blatantly advocated for white supremacy, anti-multiculturalism, and fascism. These communities saw median top user activity drop to under a third of pre-ban levels, followed by a significant decrease in random user activity, and a modest decrease in in-group vocabulary usage (about -0.2 to -0.3 for all user groups). Since our sample includes only two to four subreddits per category, these trends are not robust but suggest that some pattern might exist within the heterogeneous responses to community-level bans. These results could guide future moderation of online spaces and therefore merit further investigation.

6 Conclusion

We have provided a broad investigation of the impact of banning online communities on the activity and in-group vocabulary of the users therein. Our work expands the scope of other studies on this subject, both in terms of the number and types of communities examined. Through this more comprehensive analysis, we have demonstrated heterogeneity in the impact of bans, depending on the type of subreddit and the level of user engagement. We found that top users generally showed greater reductions in activity and in-group vocabulary usage, compared to random users. We also found that the efficacy of banning differs across subreddits, with subreddit content potentially underlying these differences. However, while we provide strong evidence of heterogeneity in ban efficacy, even more comprehensive research must be conducted on a larger group of subreddits in order to fully understand the dynamics behind this heterogeneity.

7 Future Work

This study finds heterogeneity in the outcomes of the largest online communities banned on Reddit at the community level and at the individual level. Though we find a clear trend relating outcomes to pre-ban activity level between the top and random users, there are likely other factors at play. Future work could investigate which factors correlate with individual user responses to subreddit bans, including: user demographics (both those directly measurable, such as age of account, and those like gender or country of residence ascertained via tools such as machine learning classifiers), more complex activity metrics (e.g. position of users in interaction networks within the community), and activity in other communities (as measured by number and label of other communities engaged with and level and response of engagement within those communities).

While we find evidence that community-level responses to bans loosely correlate with the content of the subreddit, our limited sample size of 15 subreddits precludes any thorough quantitative comparisons. Unfortunately, including subreddits with fewer users than the 15 we selected would make community-level statistics less consistent. Were a future study to include large banned subreddits from before or after the "great ban", identifying the factors and mechanisms that contribute to the differences in subreddit responses would be an important contribution. Potential such factors include: the demographic makeup of the communities, interaction types within the community (potentially measured via network analysis of the comment interaction network of the community), and position in a subreddit-subreddit network of shared users. Studies examining longer-term impacts of community bans would also benefit from considering when some communities attempt to "rebuild" in a new subreddit, versus integrate into existing subreddits, or rebuild off Reddit entirely.

However, we believe the most valuable insights may come from embracing more holistic, qualitative methodologies to characterize these banned communities and their responses to moderation. While quantitative metrics indicate heterogeneous community responses, researchers from anthropology and sociology, as well as communications and media studies, may find additional depth in community and user response to censorship. Computational linguists may be able to refine techniques for detecting in-group vocabulary, while linguists and cultural evolution specialists may be best equipped to determine how these vocabularies drift over time. Finally, social computing experts may be in the best position to adapt these multidisciplinary findings to improve platform moderation tools and policies.

8 Acknowledgements

The authors wish to thank the Complex Networks Winter Workshop (CNWW) where the project started, CNWW mentors Daniel B. Larremore, Peter S. Dodds, and Brooke Foucault Welles, as well as Upasana Dutta and Achille Brighton who participated in an early iteration of this work.

M.Z.T. and L.H.-D. were supported by Google Open Source under the Open-Source Complex Ecosystems And Networks (OCEAN) project. S.F.R. is supported as a Fellow of the National Science Foundation under NRT award DGE-1735316. Any opinions, findings, and conclusions or recommendations expressed in this material are those of the authors and do not necessarily reflect the views of the funders.

References

Areej Al-Hassan and Hmood Al-Dossari. 2019. Detection of hate speech in social networks: a survey on multilingual corpus. In *6th International Conference on Computer Science and Information Technology*.

Jason Baumgartner, Savvas Zannettou, Brian Keegan, Megan Squire, and Jeremy Blackburn. 2020. The pushshift Reddit dataset. In *Proceedings of the International AAAI Conference on Web and Social Media*, volume 14, pages 830–839.

Lindsay Blackwell, Jill Dimond, Sarita Schoenebeck, and Cliff Lampe. 2017. Classification and its consequences for online harassment: Design insights from heartmob. *Proceedings of the ACM on Human-Computer Interaction*, 1(CSCW):1–19.

Cristina Bosco, Dell'Orletta Felice, Fabio Poletto, Manuela Sanguinetti, and Tesconi Maurizio. 2018. Overview of the EVALITA 2018 hate speech detection task. In *EVALITA 2018-Sixth Evaluation Campaign of Natural Language Processing and Speech Tools for Italian*, volume 2263. CEUR.

Eshwar Chandrasekharan, Umashanthi Pavalanathan, Anirudh Srinivasan, Adam Glynn, Jacob Eisenstein, and Eric Gilbert. 2017. You can't stay here: The efficacy of Reddit's 2015 ban examined through hate speech. *Proceedings of the ACM on Human-Computer Interaction*, 1(CSCW):1–22.

Ryan J Gallagher, Morgan R Frank, Lewis Mitchell, Aaron J Schwartz, Andrew J Reagan, Christopher M Danforth, and Peter Sheridan Dodds. 2021. Generalized word shift graphs: a method for visualizing and explaining pairwise comparisons between texts. *EPJ Data Science*, 10(1):4.

Joshua Garland, Keyan Ghazi-Zahedi, Jean-Gabriel Young, Laurent Hébert-Dufresne, and Mirta Galesic. 2020. Countering hate on social media: Large scale classification of hate and counter speech. *ACL Workshop on Online Abuse and Harms*, pages 102–112.

Ona de Gibert, Naiara Perez, Aitor García-Pablos, and Montse Cuadros. 2018a. Hate speech dataset from a white supremacy forum. In *Proceedings of the 2nd Workshop on Abusive Language Online (ALW2)*, pages 11–20.

Ona de Gibert, Naiara Perez, Aitor García-Pablos, and Montse Cuadros. 2018b. Hate speech dataset from a white supremacy forum. In *Proceedings of the 2nd Workshop on Abusive Language Online (ALW2)*, pages 11–20. Association for Computational Linguistics.

Hussam Habib, Maaz Bin Musa, Fareed Zaffar, and Rishab Nithyanand. 2019. To act or react: Investigating proactive strategies for online community moderation. *arXiv preprint arXiv:1906.11932*.

K Hazel Kwon and Chun Shao. 2020. Communicative constitution of illicit online trade collectives: An exploration of darkweb market subreddits. In *International Conference on Social Media and Society*, pages 65–72.

Shagun Jhaver, Sucheta Ghoshal, Amy Bruckman, and Eric Gilbert. 2018. Online harassment and content moderation: The case of blocklists. *ACM Transactions on Computer-Human Interaction (TOCHI)*, 25(2):1–33.

Rohan Kshirsagar, Tyus Cukuvac, Kathleen McKeown, and Susan McGregor. 2018. Predictive embeddings for hate speech detection on Twitter. In *Proceedings of the 2nd Workshop on Abusive Language Online (ALW2)*, pages 26–32. Association for Computational Linguistics.

Younghun Lee, Seunghyun Yoon, and Kyomin Jung. 2018. Comparative studies of detecting abusive language on twitter. In *Proceedings of the 2nd Workshop on Abusive Language Online (ALW2)*, pages 101–106.

Shervin Malmasi and Marcos Zampieri. 2018. Challenges in discriminating profanity from hate speech. *J. Exp. Theor. Artif. Intell.*, 30(2):187–202.

Abby Ohlheiser. 2016. Fearing yet another witch hunt, reddit bans 'pizzagate'. *The Washington Post*.

Ji Ho Park and Pascale Fung. 2017. One-step and two-step classification for abusive language detection on twitter. In *Proceedings of the First Workshop on Abusive Language Online*, pages 41–45.

Georgios K Pitsilis, Heri Ramampiaro, and Helge Langseth. 2018. Effective hate-speech detection in Twitter data using recurrent neural networks. *Appl. Intell.*, 48(12):4730–4742.

Reddit. 2021. Homepage, reddit inc.

Manoel Horta Ribeiro, Shagun Jhaver, Savvas Zannettou, Jeremy Blackburn, Emiliano De Cristofaro, Gianluca Stringhini, and Robert West. 2020a. Does platform migration compromise content moderation? Evidence from r/The_Donald and r/Incels. *arXiv preprint arXiv:2010.10397*.

Manoel Horta Ribeiro, Raphael Ottoni, Robert West, Virgílio AF Almeida, and Wagner Meira Jr. 2020b. Auditing radicalization pathways on YouTube. In *Proceedings of the 2020 conference on fairness, accountability, and transparency*, pages 131–141.

Haji Mohammad Saleem, Kelly P Dillon, Susan Benesch, and Derek Ruths. 2017. A web of hate: Tackling hateful speech in online social spaces. *arXiv preprint arXiv:1709.10159*.

Haji Mohammad Saleem and Derek Ruths. 2018. The aftermath of disbanding an online hateful community. *arXiv preprint arXiv:1804.07354*.

Vinay Singh, Aman Varshney, Syed Sarfaraz Akhtar, Deepanshu Vijay, and Manish Shrivastava. 2018. Aggression detection on social media text using deep neural networks. In *Proceedings of the 2nd Workshop on Abusive Language Online (ALW2)*, pages 43–50.

Rachele Sprugnoli, Stefano Menini, Sara Tonelli, Filippo Oncini, and Enrico Piras. 2018. Creating a whatsapp dataset to study pre-teen cyberbullying. In *Proceedings of the 2nd Workshop on Abusive Language Online (ALW2)*, pages 51–59.

Yla R Tausczik and James W Pennebaker. 2010. The psychological meaning of words: Liwc and computerized text analysis methods. *Journal of language and social psychology*, 29(1):24–54.

Pamela Bilo Thomas, Daniel Riehm, Maria Glenski, and Tim Weninger. 2021. Behavior change in response to subreddit bans and external events. *arXiv preprint arXiv:2101.01793*.

Bertie Vidgen and Taha Yasseri. 2020. Detecting weak and strong islamophobic hate speech on social media. *J. Inf. Technol. Politics*, 17(1):66–78.

Ziqi Zhang and Lei Luo. 2019. Hate speech detection: A solved problem? the challenging case of long tail on Twitter. *Semantic Web*, 10(5):925–945.

Steven Zimmerman, Udo Kruschwitz, and Chris Fox. 2018. Improving hate speech detection with deep learning ensembles. In *Proceedings of the Eleventh International Conference on Language Resources and Evaluation (LREC 2018)*.

9 Appendix

9.1 Banned Subreddit De-Obfuscation Process

We used a report of the subreddits banned in the "Great Ban" ranked by daily average users (DAU) [4]. The top 20 subreddits with the highest DAU were reported with their names in clear text. The rest of the subreddits had their names obscured, showing only the first two letters and the remaining characters replaced by asterisks.

To de-obfuscate these, we used the subreddit *r/reclassified* [5], in which users report banned and quarantined subreddits. We used the Pushshift API to recover posts for the week after the "Great Ban", and selected those that had been flagged with the flair *BANNED*.

We then used the following routine to identify the obfuscated banned subreddits from the first list:

For a given sequence of two initial letters and a given subreddit name length, let N be the number of obscured subreddits with this sequence and name length. Let M be the number of purged subreddits with this initial sequence of letters and length. The M purged subreddits are therefore candidates for the N obscured subreddits.

If $N \geq M$, disambiguate the N obscured subreddits as the M purged subreddits. Any unmatched obscured subreddits are omitted from our analysis.

If $N < M$, manually select the N most-populous subreddits from the M candidate subreddits. Number of commenters was manually researched in the `https://reddit.guide/` page for the candidate subreddits.

9.2 Comparison of Keyword-Selection Methods

The identification of community specific keywords or the identification of hateful speech is an essential part of the pipeline for any kind of analysis on the effect of interventions on online speech. Just as there are numerous methods for the identification of hateful speech (de Gibert et al., 2018a; Park and Fung, 2017; Singh et al., 2018; Lee et al., 2018), there are numerous related methods for the identification of community-specific keywords. Chandrasekharan et al. (2017) used a topic modelling framework to identify keywords for their study called the Sparse Additive Generative model (SAGE) which compares "... the parameters of two logistically-parameterized multinomial models, using a self-tuned regularization parameter to control the tradeoff between frequent and rare terms." The core of this method, the parameter comparison of two logistically-parameterized multinomial models, performs a similar task as our ranking of the contributions of each term to the overall Jensen Shannon Divergence (JSD), and the regularization parameter performs a similar task as our explicit removal of the most common terms in our baseline corpus. As both our methodology and that of Chandrasekharan et al. (2017) perform comparable steps to achieve a comparable outcome, one would expect comparable results. This is somewhat the case when the results are defined for both methods as we can see in the table 4 below by considering the intersection of terms. However, an important feature of Jensen Shannon Divergence is how it addresses the "out-of-vocabulary problem" where an instance of a term of any frequency in one corpus has infinitely higher relative frequency than in a compared corpus if that compared corpus does not contain that term. Simplistically, JSD addresses this issue by comparing both corpora to a reference corpus made up of an amalgamation of the two. The SAGE methodology on the other hand, does not have an answer to this problem laid out and so without additional modifications, the SAGE coefficients for such terms that appear in a subreddit of interest but not in a baseline corpus are undefined, and a list of keywords is methodologically impossible to ascertain. As such, we argue that using our JSD-based methodology is more robust to this out-of-vocabulary problem and thus more widely applicable in a variety of settings. Additionally, we view the explicitness of our keyword selection methodology as an advantage compared to the relative "black box" nature of SAGE.

However, despite the fact that the SAGE-based keyword selection methodology yielded undefined values for a number of the subreddits we studied, given the importance of Chandrasekharan et al. (2017) as foundational to our work, we developed a small extension to the SAGE-based methodology which provides estimates of what the SAGE coefficients would be with a baseline corpus of the entire population of Reddit comments rather than only a

[4] `https://www.redditstatic.com/banned-subreddits-june-2020.txt`

[5] `https://www.reddit.com/r/reclassified/`

sample (note that such a baseline corpus would no longer face this out-of-vocabulary problem as all terms in the subreddit of interest would appear in the population since the subreddit of interest is part of the population). The way these estimates were reached was to use additional known metadata to estimate the counts of all the terms in the baseline corpus as well as the terms in the subreddit of interest which did not appear in the baseline. This was achieved as follows: First, take the frequency counts of each word in the baseline corpus and normalize them to calculate the empirically estimated probability mass function for words in the population of all comments on Reddit for our 6 month timeframe. Second, estimate the number of words on Reddit during this timeframe by taking the exact number of comments on Reddit during this timeframe (calculated by subtracting the first comment ID from this timeframe from the last comment ID from this timeframe) and multiplying this number by the mean number of words per comment in the baseline corpus of 70 million random comments. Third, multiply this estimated number of words on Reddit by the estimated probability mass function for each word to calculate the estimated count of each word in the population rather than the sample. Fourth, add the counts of the out-of-vocabulary terms to these estimated population-sized counts. In the event that those terms appeared only in the subreddit of interest and nowhere else on Reddit during the timeframe examined, this count will be the exact count for that term in the population and it will be at the approximate relative scale when compared to the estimated counts of the other terms in this new estimated population corpus. Using this newly estimated "population" baseline corpus, we follow the SAGE-based methodology as in Chandrasekharan et al. (2017) to determine the set of keywords identified by this methodology. Note that in the event that there are no out-of-vocabulary terms, this method simply scales up the frequencies by a constant amount for each term and as a result, reduces exactly to if this extra step had not been performed, but for cases where the out-of-vocabulary problem presents itself, this allows us to gather a list of terms comparable to that methodology.

Examining figure 5, we first notice that for the most part, most subreddit/user-type pairs are in relatively similar positions under the SAGE methodology as under the JSD-based keyword selection, especially when compared relative to each other.

Subreddit	Intersection
ccj2	20
chapotraphouse	51
consumeproduct	61
darkhumorandmemes	46
darkjokecentral	17
debatealtright	35
gendercritical	53
hatecrimehoaxes	33
imgoingtohellforthis2	36
oandaexclusiveforum	9
shitneoconssay	31
soyboys	51
the_donald	56
thenewright	57
wojak	34
MEAN	**39.65**

Table 3: Number of shared vocabulary words between our JSD-based keyword selection methodology and the SAGE-based methodology

Chandrasekharan et al. (2017) found strong negative shifts in in-group vocabulary usage after bans. Upon reproduction of their methodology, we also find stronger negative shifts, including several subreddit/user-type pairs which exhibit a median value of the maximum possible negative vocabulary shift (-1). I.e. the majority of users in these subreddits used at least one SAGE-selected keyword prior to the ban and none thereafter. Examining the data directly, we find that among the subreddit/user-type pairs where this occurred, all five had over half of their users use a SAGE-identified in-group vocabulary word between one and three times only prior to the ban. Additionally, three out of five had a majority use a SAGE-identified in-group vocabulary word one to three times prior to the ban and then zero times after the ban. Under the JSD-based methodology, no subreddit/user-type exhibited behavior where the majority of the users ceased all vocabulary usage after the ban.

The implication that the words chosen by SAGE are not used frequently by a majority of the users of subreddits they are selected from, and are thus not ideally representative, is further supported by the fact that a much larger portion users initially collected had to be omitted due to having zero vocabulary word usage before or after the ban. For the JSD-based methodology, an average of 263 of the initially collected 1000 users were omitted for having never used a single JSD-selected keyword at any time. Under the SAGE-based methodology, this number was 158 users higher on average. I.e. there was a substantially greater portion of users who used no SAGE identified vocabulary words either before or after the ban than users who used no JSD-identified vocabulary words.

The omissions mentioned above are the only cause of differences in activity shift between the the two methodologies. Apart from which users were omitted, the users studied under each methodology were identical and thus had identical activity shifts.

9.3 Validation of Subreddit Categories by Vocabulary Overlap

We initially classified each subreddit by a qualitative assessment of community content. However, we can hypothesize that subreddits with similar focuses are more likely to share in-group vocabulary terms, or conversely, that unrelated subreddits with divergent content are unlikely to share in-group vocabulary. Therefore, if our categorization is accurate, subreddits in each category should share more in-group vocabulary with one another than with other subreddits. This is easily tested, and the results are shown in Table 4.

9.4 Accounts Omitted from Analysis

In order to limit the analysis to human users and exclude any unobservable or misleading data, we excluded from all parts of the pipeline of this research (from keyword identification to vocabulary shift analysis) any comment which was made by a username in an amassed list of non-human 'bot' users. Additionally, we excluded any comment which was made by a user who deleted their account between the time of posting and the time of data ingestion by PushShift, as comments made by these users all present with the indistinguishable username "[deleted]." We used a list of bots curated by `botrank.pastimes.eu`, which itself uses its own Reddit bot to scrape comments searching for replies to accounts indicating that the replying user considers the account to be a bot. These comments are a common practice on Reddit and take the form of users indicating their approval or disapproval of an account they perceive to be a bot via the phrases "Good bot/good bot" and "Bad bot/bad bot" respectively. The system that populates `botrank.pastimes.eu` scrapes from all comments on Reddit at intervals and compiles a list of accounts who have had either "good bot" or "bad bot" replied to them, as well as the number of times this has been done for each such account. The higher the sum of the counts of "good bot" and "bad bot" replies, the more users who have identified the given account as a bot (and are expressing their approval or disapproval of this account). Thus, accounts which have high counts of these replies can be considered as very likely to be bots. As such, we assembled the majority of the list of accounts we excluded from our analysis via identifying each such account in the above mentioned compilation which had over 300 occurrences of users reply either "good bot" or "bad bot" to them. This contributed 263 accounts we excluded. Additionally, we manually identified two other accounts below this threshold of 300 occurrences as bots by combing through the data ('darkrepostbot', and 'tweettranscriberbot'). With the addition of the '[deleted]' accounts, this resulted in a total of 266 usernames for which comments were excluded from our analysis, which are included in supplementary material.

Because the focus of our study was users who continued to use the platform and who used in-group language, we omitted users who had zero comments after the ban and users who had zero instances of in-group vocabulary usage before or after the ban. No top users fell into either of these categories as they all used in group language either before or after the ban and all made at least one comment after the ban. The breakdown of how many users this final sequence of omissions results in amongst the random users, broken down as subreddit:(number users omitted for having zero postban comments, number users omitted for having no in-group vocabulary usage), is as follows: oandaexclusiveforum: (171, 239); ccj2: (174, 264); darkjokecentral: (132, 468); darkhumorandmemes: (146, 477); shitneoconssay:(223, 119) ; imgoingtohellforthis2:(141, 358); consumeproduct:(147, 292); the_donald:(94, 332); debatealtright:(257, 118); gendercritical: (207, 278); chapotraphouse:(108, 222); soyboys:(203 , 214); hatecrimehoaxes:(141, 113); thenewright:(128, 190); wojak:(137, 257).

9.5 Software and Data

Software is available for review through anonymous figshare[6], to be published via GitHub. Analysis data included in supplementary material.

[6] `https://figshare.com/s/a8f250ed3edfecaa5de3`

Subreddit	1st Match	2nd Match	3rd Match
ccj2	imgoingtohellforthis2 (4)	darkhumorandmemes (3)	chapotraphouse (2)
chapotraphouse	shitneoconssay (8)	consumeproduct (7)	thenewright (5)
consumeproduct	wojak (37)	soyboys (37)	shitneoconssay (19)
darkhumorandmemes	imgoingtohellforthis2 (22)	darkjokecentral (18)	wojak (11)
darkjokecentral	darkhumorandmemes (18)	imgoingtohellforthis2 (7)	wojak (4)
debatealtright	shitneoconssay (49)	thenewright (30)	consumeproduct (14)
gendercritical	darkhumorandmemes (5)	consumeproduct (3)	soyboys (2)
hatecrimehoaxes	imgoingtohellforthis2 (14)	thenewright (6)	debatealtright (5)
imgoingtohellforthis2	darkhumorandmemes (22)	thenewright (16)	soyboys (14)
oandaexclusiveforum	darkhumorandmemes (4)	wojak (4)	imgoingtohellforthis2 (3)
shitneoconssay	debatealtright (49)	thenewright (29)	consumeproduct (19)
soyboys	consumeproduct (37)	wojak (26)	imgoingtohellforthis2 (14)
the_donald	thenewright (15)	shitneoconssay (11)	consumeproduct (7)
thenewright	debatealtright (30)	shitneoconssay (29)	imgoingtohellforthis2 (16)
wojak	consumeproduct (37)	soyboys (26)	imgoingtohellforthis2 (13)

Table 4: Comparison of subreddits based on number of shared terms in their respective top 100 in-group vocabulary. These number of shared terms, shown in parenthesis, reinforce qualitative categorization in Table 1

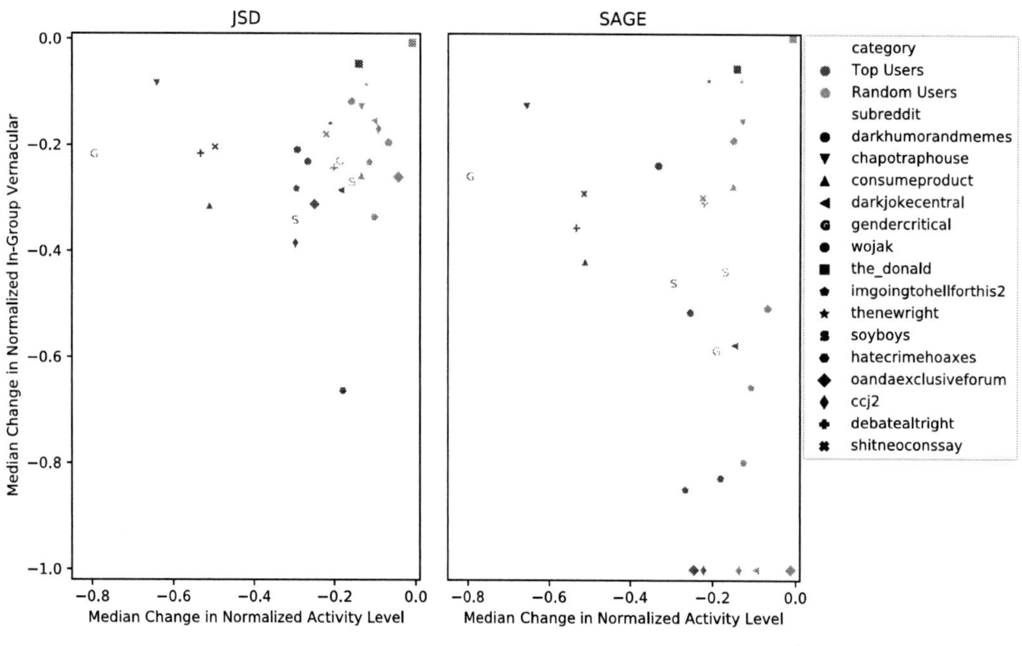

Figure 5: Comparison of top and random user behavior changes under different keyword selection methodology. The subplot on the left corresponds to 2a in the main text. The differences in activity shift between the two plots are minute and only due to omission of slightly different users for having no in-group vocabulary usage before or after the ban. The relative positions on the vocabulary shift axis remain largely the same except for a wider distribution and several subreddit user-type pairs exhibiting the maximum possible negative shift as the median.

Targets and Aspects in Social Media Hate Speech

Alexander Shvets[1], Paula Fortuna[1], Juan Soler-Company[1], Leo Wanner[2.1]

[1]NLP Group, Pompeu Fabra University, Barcelona, Spain
[2]Catalan Institute for Research and Advanced Studies
alexander.shvets|paula.fortuna|juan.soler|leo.wanner@upf.edu

Abstract

Mainstream research on hate speech focused so far predominantly on the task of classifying mainly social media posts with respect to predefined typologies of rather coarse-grained hate speech categories. This may be sufficient if the goal is to detect and delete abusive language posts. However, removal is not always possible due to the legislation of a country. Also, there is evidence that hate speech cannot be successfully combated by merely removing hate speech posts; they should be countered by education and counter-narratives. For this purpose, we need to identify (i) who is the target in a given hate speech post, and (ii) what aspects (or characteristics) of the target are attributed to the target in the post. As the first approximation, we propose to adapt a generic state-of-the-art concept extraction model to the hate speech domain. The outcome of the experiments is promising and can serve as inspiration for further work on the task.

1 Introduction

Online hate speech and, in particular, hate speech in social media, is the cause for growing concern. Already six years ago, 73% of adult internet users have seen someone harassed online, and 40% have personally experienced it (Duggan, 2014). Therefore, research on hate speech identification is of increasing importance. A significant body of work has been conducted over the last decade; cf., e.g., (Waseem and Hovy, 2016a; Schmidt and Wiegand, 2017; Davidson et al., 2017a; Fortuna and Nunes, 2018; Kennedy et al., 2020). Most of this work focused on the task of classifying, for instance, social media posts, with respect to predefined typologies of rather coarse-grained hate speech categories, such as 'hate speech', 'racism', 'sexism', 'offense', etc. This may be sufficient if the task is to detect and remove abusive language posts. However, for instance, in the US, hate speech has been repeatedly judged as being covered by the First Amendment.[1] Furthermore, a number of studies suggest that hate speech cannot be successfully combated by merely removing identified hate speech posts[2] and should be countered by education and counter-narratives (Tekiroğlu et al., 2020; Mathew et al., 2019). But to provide a basis for education and counter-narratives, we need a more detailed analysis of hate speech. In particular, we need to identify (i) who is the **target** in the identified hate speech post, and (ii) what **aspects** of the target are referred to or what aspects are attributed to the target in the post. For instance, we need to be able to determine that post (1) below targets Muslims of Palestine and that it attributes to them to be terrorists. Similarly, for post (2), we need to determine that it targets female sports reporters and that they "should come to an end" (i.e., that they should be removed from their jobs).[3] The analogy to aspect-oriented sentiment analysis (Schouten and Frasincar, 2016) is evident.

(1) *I'm standing outside and looking in and there isn't a shadow of doubt that the Muslims of Palestine are the terrorists.*

(2) *I'm not sexist but female sports reporters need to come to an end.*

Some recent works on hate speech go beyond the mere classification task and, actually, some of them also use the term *aspect*, but, again, with a

[1]See, among others, Brandenburg vs. Ohio (1969), Snyder vs. Phelps (2011), Matal vs. Tam (2017), etc.; https://en.wikipedia.org/wiki/Hate_speech_in_the_United_States provides further details and references.

[2]See, e.g., https://unesdoc.unesco.org/ark:/48223/pf0000233231.

[3]Both posts are from the (Waseem and Hovy, 2016a) dataset.

Proceedings of the Fifth Workshop on Online Abuse and Harms, pages 179–190
August 6, 2021. ©2021 Association for Computational Linguistics

different interpretation. In this paper, we present an approach that is different from these works and that aims to identify (i) the entity (most often, a group of individuals or an individual) who is *targeted* in the post, without drawing upon a predefined range of categories (which will necessarily be always limited and coarse-grained and will not cover new or intersecting categories, like 'black women'), (ii) the *aspect* (or *characteristics*) assigned to the targeted entity. We use an open-domain neural network-based concept extraction model for the identification of target and aspect candidates in each post. The obtained candidates are then further processed taking into account the idiosyncrasies of the codification of both targets and aspects in the domain.

The remainder of the paper is structured as follows. In the next section, we introduce the notions of *target* and *aspect* we are working with. Section 3 summarizes the work that is related to ours, including aspect-oriented sentiment analysis, to which our proposal shows some clear analogies. Section 4 outlines the generic concept extraction model from which we start and presents its adaptation to the problem of target and aspect extraction from hate speech data, while Section 5 describes the experiments we carried out and discusses their outcome. Section 6, finally, draws some conclusions and outlines several lines of research that we aim to address in the future.

2 Targets and Aspects

Let us define more precisely what we mean by'target' and 'aspect' in the context of our work.

Definition 1 (Target). A **target** is the entity that is in the focus of a hate post, i.e., the entity that incurs the hate of the author.

Very often, the target is an individual or a group of individuals, e.g., women, people of color, refugees, Muslims, Jews, etc.:

(3) *Bruh im tired of* ***niggas*** *retweetin Miley Cyrus naked that bitch aint no types of bad.*

However, the target can also be a specific political conviction, a religion, an object related to an individual or a group of individuals, etc.; see, e.g., *feminist novels* in (4):[4]

(4) *I'm not sexist, but nothing bores me more than* ***feminist novels***.

Definition 2 (Aspect). Aspect is a characteristic, attitude, or behavior or the lack of it (as a rule, with a pejorative connotation) that the author attributes to the target.

The aspect is often expressed as a modifier(e.g., *boring*, *stupid*, *lazy*, *not funny*, etc.) of the target in the focus of the author, as in:

(5) *I'm not sexist, but female comedians just* ***aren't funny***

(6) *I'm not sexist but *most girls are* ***fucking stupid***.

where *not funny* is the aspect of *female comedians* (5) and *fucking stupid* of (*most*) *girls* (6). It can also be a verbal group, as *can't cook* in (7):

(7) *Scoring like a Cunt because you* ***can't cook*** *for shit isn't fighting hard Kat.*

In some posts, no targets and/or aspects can be identified; see, e.g., (8).

(8) *I asked that question recently and actually got an answer http://t.co/oD98sptcGT.*

We discard such posts in our current experiments.

3 Related Work

As mentioned in Section 1, most of the works on online hate speech focused on the task of classifying social media posts with respect to predefined typologies of rather coarse-grained hate speech categories, such as 'hate speech', 'racism', 'sexism', 'offense', etc. (Schmidt and Wiegand, 2017; Davidson et al., 2017a; Fortuna and Nunes, 2018; Swamy et al., 2019; Arango et al., 2019; Salminen et al., 2020; Kennedy et al., 2020; Rajamanickam et al., 2020).[5] Vidgen and Derczynski (2020) distinguish between binary classification (as in (Alfina et al., 2017; Ross et al., 2017)), multi-class classification into several hate speech categories (e.g., 'racism', 'sexism', and 'none' in (Waseem and Hovy, 2016b)), different strengths of abuse classification (e.g., 'hateful', 'offensive' and 'neutral' contents as in (Davidson et al., 2017b)), classification into different types of statements (e.g., 'denouncing', 'facts', 'humor', 'hypocrisy' and others) and themes (e.g., 'crimes', 'culture', 'islamization',

[4]In (4), *feminist* is a classifying attribute of *novels* (see also Section 4) and should thus be part of the target.

[5]Cf. (Fortuna et al., 2020) for a list of categories used in the most common hate speech datasets.

'rapism' and others) as in (Chung et al., 2019)), and classification of different focuses of abuse (e.g., 'stereotype & objectification', 'dominance', 'derailing', 'sexual harassment', 'threats of violence', and 'discredit' as in (Fersini et al., 2018)). All these works do not aim to identify the specific targeted group of individuals or the individual and neither do they aim to identify characteristics of the targets that provoked hate. Rather, they identify posts related to hate speech in general or to one of its more specific categories – which is a step prior to detection of targets and aspects, where we start.

Some previous works use a similar terminology as we do, but with a different meaning. For instance, Zainuddin et al. (2017, 2018, 2019) aim to identify the sentiment (positive or negative) of the author of a given post towards a range of specific hate speech categories (e.g., 'race' and 'gender'), which they call "aspect". In (Gautam et al., 2020), tweets related to the MeToo movement are annotated manually with respect to five different linguistic "aspects": relevance, stance, hate speech, sarcasm, and dialogue acts. In this case, too, the interpretation of the notion of *aspect* is different from ours. Ousidhoum et al. (2019) define five different "aspects" that include specific targets, among others: (i) whether the text is direct or indirect; (ii) whether it is offensive, disrespectful, hateful, fearful out of ignorance, abusive, or normal; (iii) whether it is against an individual or a group of people; (iv) the name of the targeted group (16 common target groups are identified); and (v) the annotators' sentiment. Fersini et al. (2018) are also concerned with target detection in that they determine whether the messages were purposely sent to a specific target or to many potential receivers (e.g., groups of women). In (Silva et al., 2016), targets are identified using a short list of offensive words built drawing upon Hatebase[6] and a single template "<one word> people" to capture "black people", "stupid people", "rude people", etc.

Our work also aligns with Mathew et al. (2020) and Sap et al. (2020) in the sense that Mathew et al. (2020) annotate a hate speech dataset at the word and phrase level, capturing human rationales for the labelling (which is similar to the target–aspect labelling), while Sap et al. (2020) propose to understand and fight hate speech prejudices with accurate underlying explanations. However, Mathew et al. (2020) take into account only three labels ('hate', 'offensive', and 'normal') and ten target communities performing supervised classification, while we aim at retrieving and distinguishing open-class targets and aspects in a semi-supervised manner. Sap et al. (2020) perform supervised training of a conditional language generation model that often results in generic stereotypes about the targeted groups rather than in implications meant in the post, while we use a language generation model only to produce candidates and further expand, rank, and select them such that a connection of a target and an aspect to the text is guaranteed.

To summarize, although the identification of the targets and characteristics of hate speech in the above works are significant advancements compared to the more traditional hate speech classification, all of these works still assume predefined target categories and do not identify which characteristics of the targets are concerned. In contrast, open-class target and aspect extraction may allow for modeling of the particular forms of discrimination and hate experienced by individuals or groups of individuals covered or not covered by previously identified target categories.

As already mentioned in Section 1, our work is also related to aspect-oriented sentiment analysis, in which "targets" are specific entities (e.g., products, sights, celebrities) and "aspects" are characteristics or components of a given entity (Kobayashi et al., 2007; Nikolić et al., 2020). For each identified aspect, the "sentiment value" aligned with it is extracted; see, e.g., (Nazir et al., 2020) for a recent comprehensive survey of aspect-oriented sentiment analysis. In some (more traditional) works, aspects and their values are identified in separate stages (Hu and Liu, 2004; Hai et al., 2011). In more recent works, both tasks are addressed by one model, with aspects being partially identified by attention mechanisms realized, e.g., in an LSTM (Wang et al., 2016), CNN (Liu and Shen, 2020) or an alternative common deep NN model. The targets are, as a rule, predefined, such that the challenge consists in analysing the sentiment of tweets towards these predefined targets; cf., e.g., (Tang et al., 2016; Dong et al., 2014). The problem of open-class target identification has not been broadly investigated and sometimes solved simply as a named entity recognition problem due to the nature of the data in wihch the targets are often represented by proper names (Mitchell et al., 2013; Ma et al., 2018). However, targets in hate speech texts go far beyond named

[6]http://www.hatebase.org/

entities, and the overall task is inverse to target-oriented sentiment classification: given a known category (hate speech of negative sentiment as a rule), we have to identify the hate target and its corresponding "opinioned" aspect. Still, our proposal is similar to the modern approaches to aspect-oriented sentiment analysis in the sense that we also use an NN model (in our case, LSTM-based encoder) with attention mechanisms for initial hate speech target and aspect candidates identification, before a domain-adaptation post-processing stage.

4 Outline of the Model

The study of social media hate speech posts reveals that targets are entities that are, as a rule, verbalized in terms of *classifying nominal groups* (Halliday, 2013). Aspects may also be expressed by classifying nominal groups, but adjectival (attributive) and participle groups (actions) are also common. In other words, overall, targets can be considered *concepts* (Waldis et al., 2018). Therefore, we envision the detection of surface forms of targets in the posts primarily as a concept extraction (CE) task. For aspects, it is often not sufficient to apply concept extraction if we want to also capture the adjectival and verbal group aspects.

Given that hate speech datasets are, in general, too small to serve for training neural networks for reliable concept extraction, we opt for applying an open-domain-oriented concept extraction model with a follow-up algorithmic domain adaptation.

4.1 Generic Concept Extraction

As an open-domain concept extraction model, we use an open-source state-of-the-art model that comprises two pointer-generator networks pretrained on different concept-annotated datasets within distant supervision (Shvets and Wanner, 2020). Given a sentence, each network generates a list of concepts which are then merged and aligned with the sequence of tokens of a sentence. In case of ambiguity due to the overlap of surface forms of concepts, the first detected and the longest spans are selected as the resulting positions; see the implementation in the original publicly available code published along with the released models.[7]

The model is a sequence-to-sequence model; cf. Figure 1. The *pointer* mechanism makes it possible to copy out-of-vocabulary words directly to the outcome, which is especially relevant to our work, as the hate speech dataset includes specific words unseen during generic training, such as proper names, hashtags, and Twitter names. The *generator* implies the ability to adjust internal vocabulary distribution for selecting the next word (which might be a termination token "*") based on weights of global attention a^t (Luong et al., 2015), which are updated at each generation step t. The probability of generating the next word instead of copying one is defined as follows:

$$p_{gen} = \sigma(w_{h*}^T h_t^* + w_x^T x_t + w_s^T s_t + b_{ptr}) \quad (1)$$

where h_t^* is the sum of the hidden states of the encoder weighted with the attention distribution a^t, x_t is the decoder input, s_t is the decoder state, w_{h*}, w_x, w_s, b_{ptr} are learnable parameters, and σ is the sigmoid function. The encoder is a stacked bidirectional LSTM, while the decoder is a stacked unidirectional LSTM (Hochreiter and Schmidhuber, 1997).

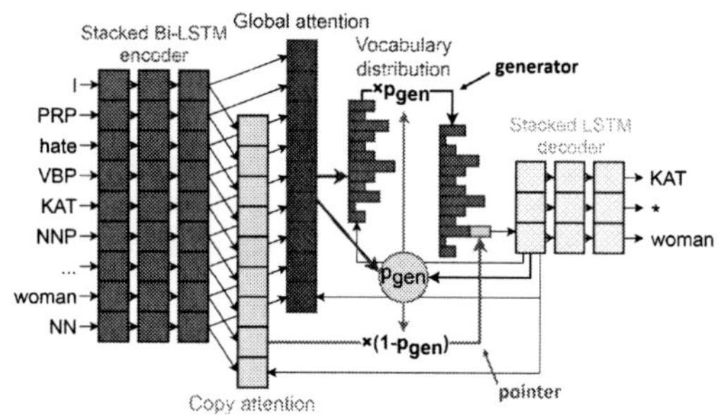

Figure 1: The neural architecture for generic concept extraction

4.2 Domain Adaptation

The goal of the domain adaptation with respect to target and aspect determination in hate speech posts is to take into account the most relevant idiosyncrasies of the genre into account. In the case of targets, the following observations can be made with respect to such idiosyncrasies:

(i) While in generic discourse, targets can be assumed to be classifying nominal groups (see above), in hate speech, we observe also adjectival and participle targets that need to be captured.

(ii) Some targets form part of compounds and would thus be skipped by Shvets and Wanner (2020)'s generic concept extraction algorithm since it was trained to generate tokens from the input sentence without compound decomposition; cf.,

[7] `https://github.com/TalnUPF/ConceptExtraction/`

e.g., *Daeshbags* ≡ *Daesh+bags*. The consideration of "subwords" instead of entire words has already proved to be beneficial for many NLP applications, including, e.g., machine translation (Sennrich et al., 2016). We thus consider also subwords of tokens. **(iii)** As a rule, a single post contains one target only; multiple targets are very seldom in short posts.[8] This means that all target candidates in a post must be ranked in terms of their probability to be a target. A high term frequency of a candidate across the posts implies a higher probability that this candidate is a common target, such that we favour candidates with a higher term frequency in a reference corpus. However, this is not the only criterion as this would introduce a strong bias towards frequent terms and contradict the idea of having unseen open-class targets. If no nominal candidates have been identified, we favour the adjectival/participle candidate with the highest *tf*idf*, with the term frequency (tf) being calculated over a reference corpus and the inverse document frequency (idf) being calculated over the English Gigaword v.5 corpus (Parker et al., 2011). The same idea applies to aspects: aspect candidates should be ranked with respect to their likeliness to be a real aspect. To determine aspect candidates, we take into account the PoS and their position with respect to the previously determined target. Candidate aspects are: **(i)** concepts, which are detected by Shvets and Wanner (2020)'s generic concept extraction algorithm and which precede or follow the target; **(ii)** adjectival or participle modifiers either preceding or following the target.

Similarly to non-nominal target candidates, we favour aspect candidates with the highest *tf*idf*, but regardless of their PoS. In addition to frequency terms, we chose several variables that give priority to different target and aspect candidates, depending on the weight assigned to them. They are listed in Table 1. Learning the weights within the domain adaptation stage using target-aspect expert annotated posts results in ranking criteria that are further used for the selection of target and aspect candidates in other (unseen) posts.

Three algorithms carry out the target and aspect identification. Algorithm 1 fine-tunes the weight variables from Table 1 for domain-specific target–aspect identification. An exhaustive weight variable fine-tuning procedure is run over all variable weight combinations. Algorithm 1 takes as input a domain reference dataset from which nominal concepts are extracted using the generic concept extraction model (reference target candidates T_{ref}), and a development dataset from which new domain-specific targets and aspects are extracted (not necessarily nominal) using Algorithms 2 and 3. Expert annotation of the development dataset TA_d^{TRUE} serves as a reference during the weight variable tuning procedure.

Algorithm 2 outputs the target–aspect pair of a given post, extracted using the weight variables. It calls Algorithm 3 for the first stage target identification by a ranking based on variables a_1–a_5, then refines the delivered target and identifies the aspect by a ranking based on variables v_1–v_5.

Var	Weight of
a_1	nominal target candidate
a_2	proper name target candidate
a_3	target candidate comprises entire words
a_4	position of the candidate in p
a_5	expansion of the detected target
v_1	temporal expansion of the detected target within aspect detection
v_2	expansion of the detected aspect
v_3	nominal concept aspect candidate located in a span following the target
v_4	adjectival/participle aspect candidates regardless of their location in a post
v_5	nominal concept aspect candidate located in a span prior to the target

Table 1: Weight variables used in Algorithms 2 and 3

5 Experiments

5.1 Data

For our experiments, we use the 'sexism' and 'racism' partitions of the (Waseem and Hovy, 2016a) dataset, with 5,355 positive instances in total. The 5,355 instances are split into disjoint reference (90% of the 5,355 instances), development (2%) and test (8%) datasets. The reference dataset is used for the identification of domain-specific nominal group target candidates. The development set serves for fine-tuning the discrete variables used in Algorithms 2 and 3.

The development set (of 100 posts) and test set (of 440 posts) are annotated in terms of targets and aspects by three annotators. For this purpose, the annotators were provided with the definitions of the notions of 'target' and 'aspect' (see Section 2) and the instruction to first identify the target (which

[8] Only about 2% of the posts in our dataset contain two targets. In order to expand the coverage of our algorithm, we plan to consider in our future work also datasets with longer texts; see the discussion of Figure 2 for details.

Algorithm 1: *GetSettings*: Domain adaptation

Input: S_{ref}: reference set, S_{dev}: development set, TA_d^{TRUE}: expert annotation of S_{dev},
$a_1, \ldots, a_5, v_1, \ldots, v_5$: sets of possible discrete values for the weight variables
Output: $(T_{ref}, \vec{a}_{best}, \vec{v}_{best})$
Dependencies: $GetTA\_Pair$ // Algorithm 2;
$C_{ref} \leftarrow ExtractConcepts(S_{ref})$ // Apply concept extraction to S_{ref};
$T_{ref} \leftarrow DetectSubjects(S_{ref}, C_{ref})$ // Detect target candidates as concepts in the grammatical subject position;
$TA_d \leftarrow \emptyset$;
$R^* \leftarrow \emptyset$;
foreach $(\vec{a} \in \{a_1 \times a_2 \times a_3 \times a_4 \times a_5\}, \vec{v} \in \{v_1 \times v_2 \times v_3 \times v_4 \times v_5\})$ **do**
  // Select discrete values for components of $\vec{a}$ and $\vec{v}$ iteratively on a grid to extract target-aspect pairs from S_{dev};
  foreach p_d : *post* $\in S_{dev}$ **do**
    $TA_d \leftarrow TA_d \cup GetTA\_Pair(p_d, T_{ref}, \vec{a}, \vec{v})$ // Get target–aspect pairs using Algorithm 2: *GetTA_Pair*;
  end
  $r_{av} \leftarrow Score(TA_d, TA_d^{TRUE})$ // Score resulting pairs TA_d;
  $R^* \leftarrow R^* \cup (\vec{a}, \vec{v}, r_{av})$
end
$(\vec{a}_{d_{best}}, \vec{v}_{d_{best}}) \leftarrow (\vec{a}, \vec{v}) \in R^* \mid max(r_{av_{best}})$ // variable values that give the best targets and aspects on dev set;
$(T_{ref}, \vec{a}_{best}, \vec{v}_{best}) \leftarrow (T_{ref}, \vec{a}_{d_{best}}, \vec{v}_{d_{best}})$ // Output tuned settings for Algorithm 2: *GetTA_Pair* for using them at all subsequent extractions (including extractions on test set)

Algorithm 2: *GetTA_Pair*: Target and aspect extraction

Input: p: *post*, T_{ref}: *target candidates in reference data*, $\vec{a}, \vec{v}$: *fine-tuned weight variables*
Output: (t_{out}, a_{out})
Dependencies: $GetTarget$ // Algorithm 3;
$C \leftarrow ExtractConcepts(p)$ // Apply concept extraction to p;
$APM \leftarrow AdjectivalMod(p) \cup ParticipleMod(p)$ // Obtain the adjectival and participle modifiers in p;
$t_{in} \leftarrow GetTarget(p, T_{ref}, C, APM, \vec{a})$ // Apply Algorithm 3: *GetTarget*;
$t_{in} \leftarrow SelectIF(t_{in}, Expand(t_{in}), \vec{v})$ // Select t_{in} or t_{in} expanded to a complete group depending on $\vec{v}$;
if $t_{in} \equiv$ *modifier* $\in APM$ + *concept* **then**
  $t_{in} \leftarrow$ *concept*; $a_{best} \leftarrow$ *modifier* // Select concept in t_{in} as updated target t_{in} and its modifier as a_{best};
else
  $A_c \leftarrow \{c \mid \forall c_s : c_s \text{ IS } subword(c), c \in C \text{ OR } c \in APM \land \nexists t_s : t_s \text{ IS } subword(t_{in}) \land c_s = t_s\}$;
  // Identify concepts and modifiers in p which do not have common subwords with the extracted target t_{in};
  $A^* \leftarrow Order(Weight(A_c, \vec{v}))$;
  // Weight concepts and modifiers in p according to $\vec{v}$ and order them in descending weight order
  $a_{best} \leftarrow FirstElement(A^*)$ // the top-ranked aspect candidate;
$t_{out} \leftarrow t_{in}$;
$a_{out} \leftarrow SelectIF(a_{best}, Expand(a_{best}), \vec{v})$ // Output a_{best} or a_{best} expanded to a complete group depending on $\vec{v}$.

Algorithm 3: *GetTarget*: Target determination

Input: p: *post*, T_{ref}: *target candidates in reference data*, C: *concepts in p*, APM: *adj/participle modifiers in p*,
$\vec{a}$: *fine-tuned weight variables*
Output: t_{out}: identified target
$T_p \leftarrow \{t \mid t \in C \land t \in T_{ref}\}$ // Identify concepts in p already seen as target candidates in the reference data;
$T_c \leftarrow \{c \mid (c \in C \land \nexists t_p \in T_p : t_p = c)\}$ // Identify other concepts in p;
$T_{sub} \leftarrow SubwordConcepts(C) \cup SubwordConcepts(APM)$;
  // Identify concepts in p which are subwords in nominal compounds or adjectival/participle modifiers;
$T_{overlap} \leftarrow \{c \mid c \in T_{sub} \land c \in T_{ref}\}$;
  // Collect subword concepts in p that overlap with the target candidates seen in the reference data;
$T_{disj} \leftarrow \{c \mid c \in T_{sub} \land c \notin T_{ref}\}$;
  // Collect subword concepts in p that do not overlap with the target candidates seen in the reference data;
$T_1^* \leftarrow Order(Weight(T_p \cup T_{overlap}, \vec{a}))$;
  // Weight concepts + subword concepts in p seen as target candidates in the reference data according to $\vec{a}$ and order
  // them in descending weight order
$T_2^* \leftarrow Order(Weight(T_c \cup T_{disj} \cup APM, \vec{a}))$;
  // Weight other concepts + subword concepts in p according to $\vec{a}$ and order them in descending weight order
$T^* \leftarrow APPEND(T_1^*, T_2^*)$;
$t_{best} \leftarrow FirstElement(T^*)$ // the top-ranked target candidate;
$t_{out} \leftarrow SelectIF(t_{best}, Expand(t_{best}), \vec{a})$ // Output t_{best} or t_{best} expanded to a complete group depending on $\vec{a}$.

Sexism	Racism
women (143), girls (102), woman (43), men (35), kat (33), feminists (23), people (20), girl (14), andre (13), man (12), females (11), nikki (8), guy (8), bitches (7), annie (6), feminism (5), bitch (5), producers (4), football (4), female comedians (4), guys (4), gender (4)	islam (97), muslims (89), mohammed (84), isis (34), prophet (22), quran (20), people (19), jews (15), muslim (14), religion (12), women (11), world (10), hamas (10), salon (9), jesus (9), hadith (8), woman (7), prophet mohammed (7), men (6), christians (6)

Table 2: Concepts with the highest TF over the reference set, which appear in the grammatical subject position in the reference set

should be explicitly mentioned in the text and not inferred) and then the (potentially multiple) aspects, keeping in mind that the target and the aspect can be the same. The annotation was carried out in several iterations. After each iteration, a consensus among the annotators with respect to the annotation of each post was reached, such that the annotated 540 posts can be considered a solid ground truth.[9]

5.2 Experiments and Their Results

5.2.1 Domain adaptation

Our domain adaptation consists in applying Algorithms 1–3 to the reference dataset (S_{ref}) of 5205 posts and the development set ($S_{develop}$) of 100 posts from 'racism' and 'sexism' categories of (Waseem and Hovy, 2016a). Shvets and Wanner (2020)'s concept extraction detects in S_{ref} about 7K concepts in the 'sexism' subset (e.g., 'dinner', 'iq', 'wings', 'abortion', 'female commentator', 'women', 'girls', etc.), and about 4K concepts in the 'racism' subset (e.g., 'hypocrite', 'armies', 'death cult', 'countries', 'honor killings'). Already at the first glance, we reckon that not all of them can be targets in the sense defined in Section 2. This shows the importance of the proposed domain adaptation. The concepts with the highest *tf* in the S_{ref} (and thus the candidates to be targets) are shown in Table 2. Note that for the *tf* figures, we used only concepts from the S_{ref} that appear in the subject position in S_{ref}, as we observed that 94% of the targets in $S_{develop}$ are subjects in S_{ref}. It is also worth noting that this list of generic targets provides only candidates that are further dynamically extended by other concepts for each new post, such that generic candidates may appear in a compound target or can even be dropped altogether.

The fine-tuning procedure of Algorithm 1 provides $a_1 = 10^6 \gg a_2 = 10^3 \gg max(tf_{T_{ref}}) > min(tf_{T_{ref}}) \gg a_3 = 10^{-3} \gg a_4 = 10^{-6} \neq 0; a_5 = 0$, and $v_1 = 1, v_2 = 1; v_3 = 10^9 \gg v_4 = 10^6 \gg v_5 = 10^3 \gg Length(p)$ (p being the post under consideration). Thus, the importance of variables for target detection is the following: nominal target candidate > proper name target candidate > target candidate comprises entire words > position of the candidate in p. For aspects, this procedure results in: nominal concept candidate following target > adjectival/participle candidate > nominal concept candidate preceding the target.

5.2.2 Target and Aspect Extraction

After the adaptation, we identify the targets and aspects using the fine-tuned weight variables $\vec{a}_{best}$ and $\vec{v}_{best}$ (specified in Section 4.2) in the test set (S_{test}) of 440 posts. Consider a few examples, with the identified targets and aspects marked in bold.

(9) *The* ***Muslims*** (Target) ***conquered 2/3 of the Christian world*** (Aspect) *before it attacked back. So again, what are you crying about.*

(10) *There's something wrong when a* ***girl*** (Target) ***wins Wayne Rooney street striker*** (Aspect) #NotSexist.

(11) ***Feminism*** (Target) *is a* ***snoring issue*** (Aspect).

(12) *But why propagandize your bigotry when* ***Pakistani Muslims*** (Target) *are* ***murdering Christians and Hindus for blasphemy*** (Aspect)?

(13) *Why haven't you stopped the sick* ***Muslims*** (Target) *from* ***trying to exterminate Israel*** (Aspect)?

(14) ***Kat*** (Target) *is a* ***sociopath*** (Aspect) #mkr

We can observe that the identified targets are nominal entities, while the aspects are mainly verbal groups that have been obtained by the expansion of an initial nominal aspect candidate (*Christian world, women*, etc.) to a full verbal group. However, as (11) and (14) show, we cannot reduce aspect identification to verbal group extraction: an aspect can readily be also a nominal group.

We evaluated the performance of the proposed model along with several baselines for target identification on $S_{develop}$ (dev) and S_{test} (test) with respect to accuracy in terms of the Jaccard index, partial and exact match and with respect to precision, recall and F1 for ROUGE-L (Lin, 2004); cf. Table 3. The first baseline takes the first noun as a target. This baseline already provides many correct matches due to the reduced lengths of the posts in our dataset. The second baseline identifies a noun

[9] This makes the calculation of the inter-annotator agreement obsolete; it will, obviously, become of relevance in the case of the annotation of larger datasets.

	Accuracy			ROUGE-L		
Algorithm	Jaccard index	Partial match	Exact match	P	R	F_1
Targets (dev)						
Baseline 1 - first noun as a target	0.1	0.08	0.08	0.11	0.1	0.10
Baseline 2 - noun with a hypernym "person" / "group"	0.28	0.34	0.24	0.34	0.29	0.3
$GetTA\_Pair(T_{ref}, p, \vec{a}_{best}, \vec{v}_{best})$	**0.68**	**0.79**	**0.65**	**0.74**	**0.7**	**0.7**
Targets (test)						
BERT - fine-tuned on the dev set	0.58	0.76	0.45	0.65	0.67	0.63
$GetTA\_Pair(T_{ref}, p, \vec{a}_{best}, \vec{v}_{best})$	0.63	0.74	**0.57**	**0.7**	0.66	0.66
$GetTA\_Pair(T_{ref}, p, \vec{a}_{best}, \vec{v}_{best})$ $+BERT$	**0.63**	**0.82**	0.49	0.69	**0.74**	**0.68**
Aspects (dev)						
$GetTA\_Pair(T_{ref}, p, \vec{a}_{best}, \vec{v}_{best})$	0.39	0.64	0.18	0.51	0.54	0.45
Aspects (test)						
BERT - fine-tuned on the dev set	0.34	0.67	0.11	**0.5**	0.45	0.42
$GetTA\_Pair(T_{ref}, p, \vec{a}_{best}, \vec{v}_{best})$	0.29	0.62	0.11	0.44	0.41	0.36
$GetTA\_Pair(T_{ref}, p, \vec{a}_{best}, \vec{v}_{best})$ $+BERT$	**0.36**	**0.74**	**0.12**	0.48	**0.55**	**0.45**

Table 3: Evaluation of the quality of the detected targets and aspects on the development and test set

	Accuracy			ROUGE-L		
Algorithm setup	Jaccard index	Partial match	Exact match	P	R	F_1
w/o learning targets with reference set and w/o tf*idf for nominals and α_1=0	0.16	0.21	0.14	0.18	0.16	0.16
w/o learning targets with reference set and w/o tf*idf for adjectival / past participle groups	0.38	0.49	0.36	0.43	0.39	0.39
w/o learning targets with reference set	0.38	0.49	0.36	0.44	0.39	0.4
w/o using subject position in reference set for tf	0.55	0.67	0.53	0.61	0.57	0.57
w/ target expanding (α_5=1) and w/o tf and α_2=0	0.59	0.76	0.52	0.64	0.69	0.63
w/ target expanding (α_5=1) and w/o tf and α_4=0	0.6	0.76	0.53	0.65	0.69	0.64
w/ target expanding (α_5=1) and w/o tf and α_3=0	0.61	0.75	0.55	0.65	0.69	0.64
w/o all subwords	0.63	0.73	0.6	0.69	0.64	0.64
w/o nominal subwords	0.63	0.74	0.61	0.7	0.65	0.65
w/ target expanding (α_5=1) and w/o tf	0.63	**0.79**	0.57	0.68	0.71	0.66
w/ target expanding (α_5=1)	0.63	**0.79**	0.56	0.68	**0.73**	0.67
$GetTA\_Pair(T_{ref}, p, \vec{a}_{best}, \vec{v}_{best})$	**0.68**	**0.79**	**0.65**	**0.74**	0.7	**0.7**

Table 4: Evaluation of the quality of the detected targets during fine-tuning on the development set

with a hypernym *person* or *group* that is a relevant candidate entity according to the definition of a target. We also fine-tuned a BERT model (Devlin et al., 2019) on the development set for target recognition in order to compare our pointer-generator-based model to transformer-based models.

We can observe that target identification as invoked by the *GetTA_Pair* (Algorithm 2) achieves a rather good performance. Thus, the accuracy for the exact match between the ground truth targets and predicted targets is 0.65 for the development set and 0.57 for the test set. With BERT, we achieve somewhat lower accuracy. It is interesting to observe that combining *GetTA_Pair* with BERT results in lower accuracy for the exact match, but in considerably higher accuracy (of 0.82) for a partial match, i.e., the match between the semantic head of the predicted target and the semantic head of the ground truth target. This is likely due to the limited amount of material in the development set, which seems to be sufficient to learn the essence of what an aspect is, but is not sufficient to learn well the composition of the aspect in terms of lexico-syntactic patterns.[10] The performance for aspect recognition is, in general, lower, which can be explained by the higher complexity of the task. However, for the partial aspect match, the accuracy is still 0.74, and the ROUGE-L F1 score is 0.45.

Table 4 shows the performance of our target detection algorithm with different variable settings. As can be observed, just the use of the *tf*idf* feature already improves the performance considerably. When only concepts in the subject position are taken into account as target candidates, the Jaccard index improves significantly; the best performance is achieved when all variables are set as indicated in the description of the Algorithms 2 and 3.

In addition, we assessed the performance of the model when Algorithm 3 is applied successively several times, excluding targets predicted at previous steps from consideration. Similarly, for each detected target we ran several times Algorithm 2. The improvement in ROUGE-L score with each run is shown in Figure 2, when the best of the predicted top n targets and the best corresponding top n aspects are scored. Figures provided for aspects correspond to the second run of the Algorithm 3, but this does not distort the overall picture since they are at the same scale for any number of predicted targets. We can observe a steady increase in performance already for small values of n, which shows the potential of our model. This strategy of selecting top n targets can also be used for detecting multiple targets in longer texts.

To verify that the proposed fine-tuning procedure of the weight variables is not dataset-specific, we ran it also on the negative sentiment subset of (Dong et al., 2014) as T_{ref}, with the targets originally obtained through dictionary search as test set targets.[11] To avoid a bias in the evaluation by "seen" targets, we ensured that 50% of the targets in

[10] Pretraining BERT on concept annotated datasets may improve the figures for the exact match. If this proves to be the case, transformer-based models are likely to outperform other models on the overall target identification task.

[11] Recall that no aspects in our sense are annotated in this sentiment dataset.

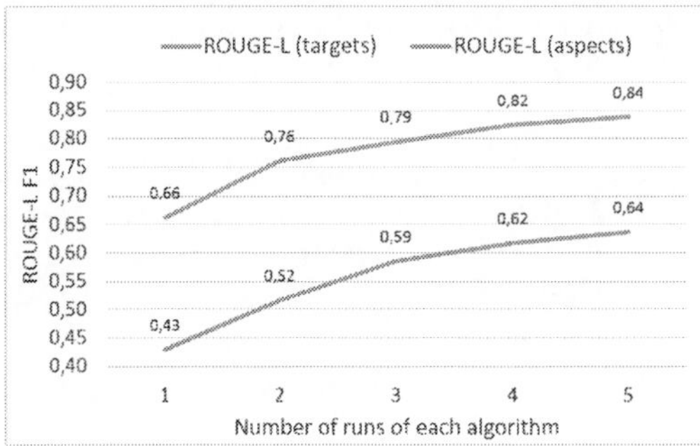

Figure 2: Mean ROUGE values over the test set for different number of algorithm runs

		Accuracy		ROUGE-L		
Part of the test set	Jaccard index	Partial match	Exact match	P	R	F_1
Only posts with targets from T_{ref}	0.88	0.92	0.85	0.88	0.91	0.89
Only posts with unseen targets	0.53	0.57	0.51	0.54	0.55	0.54
All posts	0.73	0.77	0.71	0.73	0.76	0.74

Table 5: Evaluation of target detection on Dong et al. (2014)'s negative sentiment sub-dataset

the test set are unseen by removing a number of examples with targets appearing in both the reference set and the test set from the reference set. Table 5 shows the scores obtained in this experiment for targets. We can observe that the evaluation figures are even considerably higher than those in Tables 3 and 4. This is likely because of the high percentage of named entities in this dataset, which facilitates an accurate detection of concepts.

6 Conclusions and Future Work

Classification of hate speech in terms of broad categories is not sufficient; in order to effectively combat hate speech, a detailed target–aspect analysis is necessary. We presented a model that adapts a generic concept extraction model and showed that it is able to reach a reasonable quality for target and aspect identification in the 'sexism' and 'racism' categories of the (Waseem and Hovy, 2016a) hate speech dataset. The model is semi-supervised and works already with a small annotated dataset. This is an advantage in view of the absence of large hate speech datasets annotated with the target–aspect information.

Despite the promising figures, our model still has some limitations. Thus, aspect identification quality should be further improved. Furthermore, we plan to use distance learning in order to make the model language-independent, which will be an advantage compared to the presented implementation, which is to a certain extent language-specific. In addition, experiments on other hate speech datasets should be carried out in order to demonstrate that the proposed variable tuning and implemented syntactic target and aspect patterns generalize well across datasets. Finally, although the vast majority of posts indeed contains just one target, to capture multiple targets would be desirable.

The annotated development and test sets and the code are available in the following GitHub repository: `https://github.com/TalnUPF/HateSpeechTargetsAspects/`.

Acknowledgements

We would like to thank the three anonymous reviewers for their insightful comments, which helped to improve the final version of the paper considerably.

Paula Fortuna is supported by the research grant SFRH/BD/143623/2019, provided by the Portuguese national funding agency for science, research and technology, Fundação para a Ciência e a Tecnologia (FCT), within the scope of the Operational Program *Human Capital* (POCH), supported by the European Social Fund and by national funds from MCTES. The work of Alexander Shvets, Juan Soler-Company, and Leo Wanner has been supported by the European Commission in the context of the H2020 Research Program under the contract numbers 700024, 786731, and 825079.

References

Ika Alfina, Rio Mulia, Mohamad Ivan Fanany, and Yudo Ekanata. 2017. Hate speech detection in the indonesian language: A dataset and preliminary study. In *2017 International Conference on Advanced Computer Science and Information Systems (ICACSIS)*, pages 233–238. IEEE.

Aymé Arango, Jorge Pérez, and Barbara Poblete. 2019. Hate speech detection is not as easy as you may think: A closer look at model validation. In *Proceedings of the 42nd International ACM SIGIR Conference on Research and Development in Information Retrieval*, SIGIR'19, page 45–54, New York, NY, USA. Association for Computing Machinery.

Yi-Ling Chung, Elizaveta Kuzmenko, Serra Sinem Tekiroglu, and Marco Guerini. 2019. CONAN - counter narratives through nichesourcing: a multilingual dataset of responses to fight online hate speech. In *Proceedings of the 57th Conference of the Association for Computational Linguistics, ACL 2019, Florence, Italy, July 28- August 2, 2019, Volume 1: Long Papers*, pages 2819–2829. Association for Computational Linguistics.

Thomas Davidson, Dana Warmsley, Michael W. Macy, and Ingmar Weber. 2017a. Automated hate speech detection and the problem of offensive language. In *Proceedings of the Eleventh International Conference on Web and Social Media, ICWSM 2017, Montréal, Québec, Canada, May 15-18, 2017*, pages 512–515. AAAI Press.

Thomas Davidson, Dana Warmsley, Michael W. Macy, and Ingmar Weber. 2017b. Automated hate speech detection and the problem of offensive language. In *Proceedings of the Eleventh International Conference on Web and Social Media, ICWSM 2017, Montréal, Québec, Canada, May 15-18, 2017*, pages 512–515. AAAI Press.

Jacob Devlin, Ming-Wei Chang, Kenton Lee, and Kristina Toutanova. 2019. Bert: Pre-training of deep bidirectional transformers for language understanding. In *Proceedings of the 2019 Conference of the North American Chapter of the Association for Computational Linguistics: Human Language Technologies, Volume 1 (Long and Short Papers)*, pages 4171–4186.

Li Dong, Furu Wei, Chuanqi Tan, Duyu Tang, Ming Zhou, and Ke Xu. 2014. Adaptive recursive neural network for target-dependent twitter sentiment classification. In *Proceedings of the 52nd Annual Meeting of the Association for Computational Linguistics, ACL 2014, June 22-27, 2014, Baltimore, MD, USA, Volume 2: Short Papers*, pages 49–54. The Association for Computer Linguistics.

Maeve Duggan. 2014. Online harassment. Technical report, Pew Research Center, Washington, USA. Available at `https://radimrehurek.com/gensim/summarization/keywords.html`.

Elisabetta Fersini, Debora Nozza, and Paolo Rosso. 2018. Overview of the evalita 2018 task on automatic misogyny identification (ami). In *EVALITA@ CLiC-it*.

Paula Fortuna and Sérgio Nunes. 2018. A survey on automatic detection of hate speech in text. *ACM Computer Surveys*, 51(4):85:1–85:30.

Paula Fortuna, Juan Soler Company, and Leo Wanner. 2020. Toxic, hateful, offensive or abusive? what are we really classifying? an empirical analysis of hate speech datasets. In *Proceedings of The 12th Language Resources and Evaluation Conference, LREC 2020, Marseille, France, May 11-16, 2020*, pages 6786–6794. European Language Resources Association.

Akash Kumar Gautam, Puneet Mathur, Rakesh Gosangi, Debanjan Mahata, Ramit Sawhney, and Rajiv Ratn Shah. 2020. #metooma: Multi-aspect annotations of tweets related to the metoo movement. In *Proceedings of the Fourteenth International AAAI Conference on Web and Social Media, ICWSM 2020, Held Virtually, Original Venue: Atlanta, Georgia, USA, June 8-11, 2020*, pages 209–216. AAAI Press.

Zhen Hai, Kuiyu Chang, and Jung-jae Kim. 2011. Implicit feature identification via co-occurrence association rule mining. In *Computational Linguistics and Intelligent Text Processing - 12th International Conference, CICLing 2011, Tokyo, Japan, February 20-26, 2011. Proceedings, Part I*, volume 6608 of *Lecture Notes in Computer Science*, pages 393–404. Springer.

M.A.K. Halliday. 2013. *Halliday's Introduction to Functional Grammar*. Routledge, London & New York.

Sepp Hochreiter and Jürgen Schmidhuber. 1997. Long short-term memory. *Neural computation*, 9(8):1735–1780.

Minqing Hu and Bing Liu. 2004. Mining and summarizing customer reviews. In *Proceedings of the Tenth ACM SIGKDD International Conference on Knowledge Discovery and Data Mining, Seattle, Washington, USA, August 22-25, 2004*, pages 168–177. ACM.

Brendan Kennedy, Xisen Jin, Aida Mostafazadeh Davani, Morteza Dehghani, and Xiang Ren. 2020. Contextualizing hate speech classifiers with post-hoc explanation. In *Proceedings of the 58th Annual Meeting of the Association for Computational Linguistics*, pages 5435–5442, Online. Association for Computational Linguistics.

Nozomi Kobayashi, Kentaro Inui, and Yuji Matsumoto. 2007. Extracting aspect-evaluation and aspect-of relations in opinion mining. In *Proceedings of the 2007 Joint Conference on Empirical Methods in Natural Language Processing and Computational Natural Language Learning (EMNLP-CoNLL)*, pages 1065–1074.

Chin-Yew Lin. 2004. Rouge: A package for automatic evaluation of summaries. In *Text summarization branches out*, pages 74–81.

Ning Liu and Bo Shen. 2020. Aspect-based sentiment analysis with gated alternate neural network. *Knowl. Based Syst.*, 188.

T. Luong, H. Pham, and C.D. Manning. 2015. Effective approaches to attention-based neural machine translation. In *Proc. of the EMNLP*, pages 1412–1421.

Dehong Ma, Sujian Li, and Houfeng Wang. 2018. Joint learning for targeted sentiment analysis. In *Proceedings of the 2018 Conference on Empirical Methods in Natural Language Processing*, pages 4737–4742.

Binny Mathew, Punyajoy Saha, Hardik Tharad, Subham Rajgaria, Prajwal Singhania, Suman Kalyan Maity, Pawan Goyal, and Animesh Mukherjee. 2019. Thou shalt not hate: Countering online hate speech. In *Proceedings of the Thirteenth International Conference on Web and Social Media, ICWSM 2019, Munich, Germany, June 11-14, 2019*, pages 369–380. AAAI Press.

Binny Mathew, Punyajoy Saha, Seid Muhie Yimam, Chris Biemann, Pawan Goyal, and Animesh Mukherjee. 2020. Hatexplain: A benchmark dataset for explainable hate speech detection. *CoRR*, abs/2012.10289.

Margaret Mitchell, Jacqui Aguilar, Theresa Wilson, and Benjamin Van Durme. 2013. Open domain targeted sentiment. In *Proceedings of the 2013 Conference on Empirical Methods in Natural Language Processing*, pages 1643–1654.

A. Nazir, Y. Rao, L. Wu, and L. Sun. 2020. Issues and challenges of aspect-based sentiment analysis: A comprehensive survey. *IEEE Transactions on Affective Computing; doi: 10.1109/TAFFC.2020.2970399*.

N. Nikolić, O. Grljević, and A. Kovačević. 2020. Aspect-based sentiment analysis of reviews in the domain of higher education. *The Electronic Library*, 38(1):44–64.

Nedjma Ousidhoum, Zizheng Lin, Hongming Zhang, Yangqiu Song, and Dit-Yan Yeung. 2019. Multilingual and multi-aspect hate speech analysis. In *Proceedings of the 2019 Conference on Empirical Methods in Natural Language Processing and the 9th International Joint Conference on Natural Language Processing (EMNLP-IJCNLP)*, pages 4675–4684, Hong Kong, China. Association for Computational Linguistics.

Robert Parker, David Graff, Junbo Kong, Ke Chen, and Kazuaki Maeda. 2011. English gigaword fifth edition ldc2011t07, 2011. *URL https://catalog. ldc. upenn. edu/LDC2011T07.[Online]*.

Santhosh Rajamanickam, Pushkar Mishra, Helen Yannakoudakis, and Ekaterina Shutova. 2020. Joint modelling of emotion and abusive language detection. In *Proceedings of the 58th Annual Meeting of the Association for Computational Linguistics*, pages 4270–4279, Online. Association for Computational Linguistics.

Björn Ross, Michael Rist, Guillermo Carbonell, Benjamin Cabrera, Nils Kurowsky, and Michael Wojatzki. 2017. Measuring the reliability of hate speech annotations: The case of the european refugee crisis. *CoRR*, abs/1701.08118.

Joni Salminen, Maximilian Hopf, Shammur A. Chowdhury, Soon-gyo Jung, Hind Almerekhi, and Bernard J. Jansen. 2020. Developing an online hate classifier for multiple social media platforms. *Human-centric Computing and Information Sciences*, 10(1):1.

Maarten Sap, Saadia Gabriel, Lianhui Qin, Dan Jurafsky, Noah A. Smith, and Yejin Choi. 2020. Social bias frames: Reasoning about social and power implications of language. In *Proceedings of the 58th Annual Meeting of the Association for Computational Linguistics, ACL 2020, Online, July 5-10, 2020*, pages 5477–5490. Association for Computational Linguistics.

Anna Schmidt and Michael Wiegand. 2017. A survey on hate speech detection using natural language processing. In *Proceedings of the Fifth International Workshop on Natural Language Processing for Social Media*, pages 1–10, Valencia, Spain. Association for Computational Linguistics.

Kim Schouten and Flavius Frasincar. 2016. Survey on aspect-level sentiment analysis. *IEEE Trans. Knowl. Data Eng.*, 28(3):813–830.

Rico Sennrich, Barry Haddow, and Alexandra Birch. 2016. Neural machine translation of rare words with subword units. In *Proceedings of the 54th Annual Meeting of the Association for Computational Linguistics (Volume 1: Long Papers)*, pages 1715–1725, Berlin, Germany. Association for Computational Linguistics.

Alexander V. Shvets and Leo Wanner. 2020. Concept extraction using pointer-generator networks and distant supervision for data augmentation. In *Knowledge Engineering and Knowledge Management - 22nd International Conference, EKAW 2020, Bolzano, Italy, September 16-20, 2020, Proceedings*, volume 12387 of *Lecture Notes in Computer Science*, pages 120–135. Springer.

Leandro Araújo Silva, Mainack Mondal, Denzil Correa, Fabrício Benevenuto, and Ingmar Weber. 2016. Analyzing the targets of hate in online social media. In *Proceedings of the Tenth International Conference on Web and Social Media, Cologne, Germany, May 17-20, 2016*, pages 687–690. AAAI Press.

Steve Durairaj Swamy, Anupam Jamatia, and Björn Gambäck. 2019. Studying generalisability across abusive language detection datasets. In *Proceedings of the 23rd Conference on Computational Natural Language Learning (CoNLL)*, pages 940–950, Hong Kong, China. Association for Computational Linguistics.

Duyu Tang, Bing Qin, Xiaocheng Feng, and Ting Liu. 2016. Effective lstms for target-dependent sentiment classification. In *COLING 2016, 26th International Conference on Computational Linguistics, Proceedings of the Conference: Technical Papers, December 11-16, 2016, Osaka, Japan*, pages 3298–3307. ACL.

Serra Sinem Tekiroğlu, Yi-Ling Chung, and Marco Guerini. 2020. Generating counter narratives against online hate speech: Data and strategies. In *Proceedings of the 58th Annual Meeting of the Association for Computational Linguistics*, pages 1177–1190, Online. Association for Computational Linguistics.

Bertie Vidgen and Leon Derczynski. 2020. Directions in abusive language training data, a systematic review: Garbage in, garbage out. *Plos one*, 15(12):e0243300.

A. Waldis, L. Mazzola, and M.A. Kaufmann. 2018. Concept extraction with convolutional neural networks. In *Proceedings of the 7th International Conference on Data Science, Technology and Applications (DATA 2018)*, Porto, Portugal.

Yequan Wang, Minlie Huang, Xiaoyan Zhu, and Li Zhao. 2016. Attention-based LSTM for aspect-level sentiment classification. In *Proceedings of the 2016 Conference on Empirical Methods in Natural Language Processing, EMNLP 2016, Austin, Texas, USA, November 1-4, 2016*, pages 606–615. The Association for Computational Linguistics.

Zeerak Waseem and Dirk Hovy. 2016a. Hateful symbols or hateful people? predictive features for hate speech detection on Twitter. In *Proceedings of the NAACL Student Research Workshop*, pages 88–93, San Diego, California. Association for Computational Linguistics.

Zeerak Waseem and Dirk Hovy. 2016b. Hateful symbols or hateful people? predictive features for hate speech detection on twitter. In *Proceedings of the Student Research Workshop, SRW@HLT-NAACL 2016, The 2016 Conference of the North American Chapter of the Association for Computational Linguistics: Human Language Technologies, San Diego California, USA, June 12-17, 2016*, pages 88–93. The Association for Computational Linguistics.

Nurulhuda Zainuddin, Ali Selamat, and Roliana Ibrahim. 2017. Twitter hate aspect extraction using association analysis and dictionary-based approach. In *New Trends in Intelligent Software Methodologies, Tools and Techniques - Proceedings of the 16th International Conference, SoMeT_17, Kitakyushu City, Japan, September 26-28, 2017*, volume 297 of *Frontiers in Artificial Intelligence and Applications*, pages 641–651. IOS Press.

Nurulhuda Zainuddin, Ali Selamat, and Roliana Ibrahim. 2018. Evaluating aspect-based sentiment classification on twitter hate speech using neural networks and word embedding features. In *New Trends in Intelligent Software Methodologies, Tools and Techniques - Proceedings of the 17th International Conference SoMeT_18, Granada, Spain, 26-28 September 2018*, volume 303 of *Frontiers in Artificial Intelligence and Applications*, pages 723–734. IOS Press.

Nurulhuda Zainuddin, Ali Selamat, and Roliana Ibrahim. 2019. Hate crime on twitter: Aspect-based sentiment analysis approach. In *Advancing Technology Industrialization Through Intelligent Software Methodologies, Tools and Techniques - Proceedings of the 18th International Conference on New Trends in Intelligent Software Methodologies, Tools and Techniques (SoMeT_19), Kuching, Malaysia, 23-25 September 2019*, volume 318 of *Frontiers in Artificial Intelligence and Applications*, pages 284–297. IOS Press.

Abusive Language on Social Media Through the Legal Looking Glass

Thales Bertaglia[1,3], Andreea Grigoriu[2], Michel Dumontier [1], and Gijs van Dijck [2]

{t.costabertaglia, a.grigoriu, michel.dumontier, gijs.vandijck}@maastrichtuniversity.nl

[1]Institute of Data Science, Maastricht, The Netherlands

[2]Maastricht Law and Tech Lab, Maastricht, The Netherlands

[3]Studio Europa, Maastricht, The Netherlands

Abstract

Abusive language is a growing phenomenon on social media platforms. Its effects can reach beyond the online context, contributing to mental or emotional stress on users. Automatic tools for detecting abuse can alleviate the issue. In practice, developing automated methods to detect abusive language relies on good quality data. However, there is currently a lack of standards for creating datasets in the field. These standards include definitions of what is considered abusive language, annotation guidelines and reporting on the process. This paper introduces an annotation framework inspired by legal concepts to define abusive language in the context of online harassment. The framework uses a 7-point Likert scale for labelling instead of class labels. We also present ALYT – a dataset of **A**busive **L**anguage on **Y**ou**T**ube. ALYT includes YouTube comments in English extracted from videos on different controversial topics and labelled by Law students. The comments were sampled from the actual collected data, without artificial methods for increasing the abusive content. The paper describes the annotation process thoroughly, including all its guidelines and training steps.

1 Introduction

The increased use of social media can worsen the issue of online harassment. Nowadays, more than half of online harassment cases happen on social media platforms (Center, 2017). A specific popular form of online harassment is the use of abusive language. One abusive or toxic statement is being sent every 30 seconds across the globe[1]. The use of abusive language on social media contributes to mental or emotional stress, with one in ten people developing such issues (Center, 2017).

Automatic detection tools for detecting abusive language are used for combating online harassment. These tools are mainly based on machine learning algorithms that rely on training data. Therefore, there is a need for good quality datasets to create high performing algorithms to alleviate online harassment. There are various datasets in the field of online harassment research. However, there is a lack of standards for developing these resources. These standards include the definitions used to determine what content is abusive and the steps of the annotation process (including the annotators). The lack of standards leads to conflicting definitions, which ultimately results in disagreement within the field regarding which tasks to solve, creating annotation guidelines, and terminology.

Our Contribution In this project, we introduce ALYT – a dataset of 20k YouTube comments in English labelled for abusive language. The dataset and its data statement are available online[2]. We manually selected videos focusing on a range of controversial topics and included different video types. Rather than artificially balancing the data for abusive content, we randomly sampled the collected data. We developed an annotation framework inspired by legal definitions by analysing various European provisions and case law ranging from insults, defamation and incitement to hatred. Instead of class labels, we use a 7-point Likert scale to encapsulate the complexity of the labelling decisions. We analyse the n-grams in our corpus to characterise its content and understand the abusive language's nature. The results show that the dataset contains diverse topics, targets, and expressions of abuse.

2 Related Work

Creating dataset for online harassment research, including abusive language, has been a challeng-

[1] https://decoders.amnesty.org/projects/troll-patrol/findings. For all links, the content refers to the page version last accessed on 8 June 2021.

[2] https://github.com/thalesbertaglia/ALYT

Proceedings of the Fifth Workshop on Online Abuse and Harms, pages 191–200
August 6, 2021.

ing task. Vidgen and Derczynski (2020) review a wide range of datasets – and their creation process – within the field and identify many issues. Various approaches have been explored over the years, including different data collection strategies, labelling methodologies and employing different views and definitions of online harassment.

In terms of annotation methods, crowdsourcing is a popular option for labelling abusive language data (Burnap and Williams, 2015; Zhong et al., 2016; Chatzakou et al., 2017; Ribeiro et al., 2017; Zampieri et al., 2019). However, in some instances, a small group of non-experts in harassment research (Bretschneider et al., 2014; Mathew et al., 2018; van Rosendaal et al., 2020) or domain experts annotate the data (Golbeck et al., 2017; Waseem and Hovy, 2016). The definitions used to label the data can vary as well. At times, definitions are derived from literature (Chatzakou et al., 2017) on the topic, or existing social media platform's guidelines (Ribeiro et al., 2017). In other instances, annotators decide by themselves when abuse is present in the text (Walker et al., 2012).

A recent direction in the field has been applying legal provisions to decide whether content should be removed, given criminal law provisions on hate speech or incitement to hatred. These approaches represent legal provisions as decision trees that guide the annotation process. Zufall et al. (2020) apply this methodology focusing on the German provision related to incitement to hatred. Two non-expert annotators label the data, guided by the created decision tree. The experiments show that there was little difference between using expert and non-expert annotators in this case.

3 Data Collection

We aimed to include a representative sample of abusive language on social media in our dataset. Therefore, we did not search directly for abusive content. Instead, we chose topics likely to contain abusive comments. We chose three different topics before the video selection: Gender Identity (GI), Veganism (VG), and Workplace Diversity (WD). The topics generate controversial videos on YouTube while not being limited to one type of controversy (e.g. gender identity, diet choices, socio-economical issues). The videos in GI focus on the disclosure of transgender identity and the impact of transgender people in sports. The videos in the VG category concentrate on describing the vegan movement and influencers deciding to become vegan. In WD, the videos illustrate the gender wage gap and its implications.

We searched for content in one language; therefore, the videos and majority of the comments are in English. We manually searched for videos using the topics as keywords. We selected popular videos (considering the number of views) made by well-known influencers posting controversial content. We included three types of videos: personal videos (posted by influencers on the topic), reaction videos (videos in which the author reacts to another video) and official videos (posted by news and media channels).

To create our dataset, we retrieved all comments from the selected videos, excluding replies. We removed comments containing URLs because these are often spam or make reference to external content. We also removed comments with fewer than three tokens. In total, we obtained 879,000 comments after these steps. Out of this sample, we selected 20,215 to annotate. We randomly sampled comments from the total distribution, not attempting to balance the data according to content. We aimed to balance video topics and types equally, but as the total number of comments was not even per video category, the final sample was not perfectly balanced. Table 1 shows the distribution per video category of the comments included in the dataset.

Category	%	#
VG	34.75	6967
GI	34.46	7024
WD	30.79	6224
Official	50.31	10171
Personal	31.38	6343
Reaction	18.31	3701

Table 1: Distribution of comments per video category

Collecting Abusive Content

Searching for keywords related to harassment is a common approach to increase the amount of abusive content in datasets. We do not employ any method to balance the data artificially – i.e., we do not try to search for abusive content directly. Instead, we randomly select comments from the total distribution of comments, resulting in a realistic data sample, similar to what is available on the platform. To compare our sampling approach to keyword search, we conduct two experiments comparing our dataset to others. First, we compare the final distribution of abusive content. Then, we compare the prevalence of hateful keywords. We use Hatebase[3] as a source of keywords, limiting it to the 500 most frequent terms (by the number of sightings).

We compare our dataset to three others, all containing tweets: Davidson et al. (2017) (HSOL), Waseem and Hovy (2016) (HSHP), and Zampieri et al. (2019) (OLID). Twitter is the most popular social media platform for online harassment research, so most datasets contain tweets. HSHP is distributed as tweet ids, so all experiments refer to the distribution of the tweets we were able to retrieve in April 2021. These datasets use different definitions of abusive content. To harmonise the definitions and compare the data distributions, we consider that the following classes match our definition of *abuse*: tweets labelled as *hateful* on HSOL; *sexist* or *racist* on HSHP; and *offensive* **and** *targeted* on OLID. Table 2 presents the distribution of abusive content on each dataset.

Dataset	%	#
ALYT	11.42	2274
HSOL	5.77	1430
HSHP	25.78	2715
OLID	29.00	4089

Table 2: Distribution of abusive content in each dataset

The datasets that use hateful keyword search have a higher prevalence of hate. ALYT has a lower, but comparable, proportion of abusive content. Considering that we do not explicitly try to balance the data, our approach leads to a more representative sample of the actual scenario of social media while still having a significant amount of abusive comments. HSOL uses keywords from Hatebase to search for tweets. Davidson et al. (2017) conclude that Hatebase is imprecise and leads to a small amount of actual hate speech; therefore, this sampling approach is inefficient. HSHP and OLID use a few hateful keywords and others associated with abusive tweets, such as messages directed to political accounts and hashtags about tv shows. This approach allows increasing the amount of abusive content without biasing it to specific keywords. However, the content may still correlate to the hashtags or accounts being used to search for tweets. Our approach is similar in the sense that the video topics delimit the scope of the comments, but the comments are not filtered; thus, they provide a representative sample of the entire data. To further investigate the prevalence of hateful keywords on the datasets, we analyse the proportion of content that contains at least one term from Hatebase. Table 3 presents the results.

Dataset	%	#
ALYT	8.81	246
HSOL	87.55	1252
HSHP	7.51	204
OLID	6.43	263

Table 3: Distribution of comments containing at least one term from Hatebase

ALYT has a low prevalence of Hatebase keywords, with a distribution similar to HSHP and OLID. This result shows that the abusive content in our dataset is not limited to frequent hateful words. Therefore, not searching for specific keywords leads to higher lexical diversity. The distribution of HSOL further confirms this observation: abusive content from the dataset predominantly contains terms from Hatebase. Although this experiment is limited to a single lexicon, it provides evidence that our sampling approach does not result in abusive content defined by specific keywords. section 6 will discuss the content of the dataset in details.

4 Annotation Framework

Datasets presented in state-of-the-art research mainly use several definitions for abusive language or focus on specific phenomena – such as hate speech, racism, and sexism. What constitutes *abusive content* is often not precisely defined. Dataset creators – in an attempt to make these concepts clear – rely on various definitions, ranging from platform guidelines to dictionary entries. Our goal is to develop an annotation framework inspired by legal definitions and to define abusive content concretely in light of these concepts. Using legal definitions as inspiration can provide a consistent and stable background for deciding which content is abusive, since most occurrences of abusive language are already covered in legal systems.

[3] https://hatebase.org/

Definitions

We collected legislative resources (provisions and case law) in the context of abusive language expressed online. We focused on the European landscape by studying four countries: The Netherlands, France, Germany and the UK. These countries include both civil and common law, providing a comprehensive sample of legal traditions. The legislative sources focus both on offensive language towards an individual and towards a specific group/minority. In this project, we also focus on both types of offences.

For Germany, we selected the following provisions using the Criminal Code[4]: incitement to hatred (Article 130); insulting (Section 185); malicious gossip defined as "degrading that person or negatively affecting public opinion about that person" (Section 186); and defamation (Section 187). Similarly, for the Netherlands, using the Criminal Code[5], we included: Article 137, which focuses on incitement to hatred and general defamation (Section 261), slander (Section 262), and insults (Section 266). For France, we used the Press Freedom Act of 29 July 1881[6], focusing on actions such as discrimination, hate, violence (Article 24), defamation (Article 32) and insult (Article 33). In the UK, the Public Order Act 1986[7] defines offensive messages and threats, specifically in Part 3 (focusing on racial grounds) and 3A (religious and sexual orientation grounds). After selecting the sources, we harmonised the elements present in the provisions such as the targets of the attack, protected attributes (grounds on which the targets are attacked such as race, religion etc) and the harmful acts specified to be performed (such as insult, defamation). Even though the countries might have elements in common which can be easy to harmonise, we also found elements specific to some countries only (for example specifically mentioning the effect caused by the attack to the victim in the UK, such as distress and anxiety). The analysis resulted in three main abstract categories found in provisions: incitement of hatred towards specific protected groups, acts which cause distress and anxiety and acts involving public opinion such as degradement or belittlement.

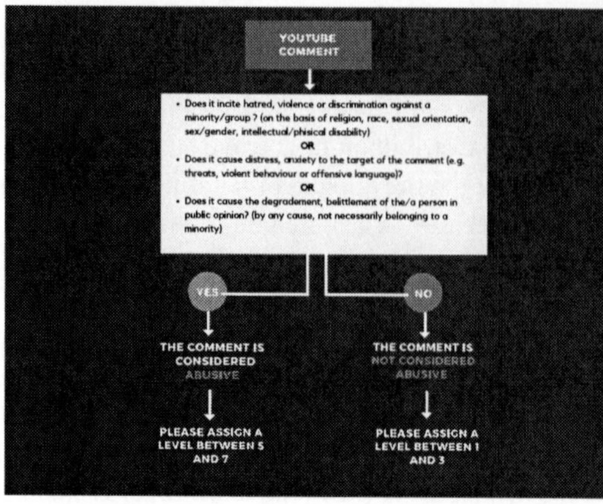

Figure 1: Annotation process diagram

We developed three questions comprising elements found in all the mentioned provisions to define *abusive language*:

- Does it incite hatred, violence or discrimination against a minority/group (on the basis of religion, race, sexual orientation, sex/gender, intellectual/physical disability)?
- Does it cause distress, anxiety to the target of the comment (e.g. threats, violent behaviour or offensive language)?
- Does it cause the degradement, belittlement of the/a person in public opinion? (by any cause, not necessarily belonging to a minority)

The annotators used these questions to determine whether a comment is abusive, as described in Figure 1. The full version of the annotation manual included examples and is available online[8].

Annotation Scale

For labelling, we used a 7-point Likert scale (Joshi et al., 2015) instead of class labels. The scale represents a mix of two features: the intensity of the abuse present in the comment and how confident the annotator is about the labelling decision. Specifically, numbers from 1 to 3 represent non-abusive content, with 1 describing comments with no abusive content at all. Comments labelled with 2 or 3 might contain sarcasm or jokes that could be considered abusive. Number 4 indicates comments that fall between abusive and non-abusive – so it also

[4]https://www.gesetze-im-internet.de/stgb/

[5]https://www.legislationline.org/documents/section/criminal-codes/country/12/Netherlands/show

[6]https://www.legifrance.gouv.fr/loda/id/JORFTEXT000000877119/

[7]https://www.legislation.gov.uk/ukpga/1986/64

[8]http://bit.ly/alyt-manual

encodes labelling uncertainty. Numbers between 5 and 7 represent abusive comments, with 7 describing clearly abusive comments. Comments labelled with 5 or 6 might contain less obvious abuse.

5 Annotation Process

Throughout the data annotation process, annotators encode our framework and apply it to label the data. A proper annotation methodology, therefore, is fundamental to ensure data quality. Yet, most works presenting abusive language datasets fail to report this process in details. We follow the corpus annotation pipeline proposed by Hovy and Lavid (2010) and thoroughly describe how we conducted its main steps when creating ALYT. To measure the reliability of the annotation, we use Krippendorf's alpha (α) with ordinal level of measurement (Krippendorff, 2011) and majority agreement to calculate the overall inter-annotator agreement. Antoine et al. (2014) highlight that α is a reliable metric for ordinal annotations, such as the 7-point scale from our framework.

Training

A team of six Law students enrolled in an European university labelled ALYT. Before the main annotation stage, we conducted a careful training phase, actively engaging in discussions with the annotators to improve the annotation framework and manual. We instructed the team to watch the videos included in the dataset before labelling the comments. We organised three training meetings with the annotators. Also, we evaluated their performance by giving an assignment sample of comments after each meeting. We annotated 50 comments together during the first meeting, aiming to familiarise the team with the task and annotation platform. The inter-annotator agreement for the first round of training was $\alpha = 45.0$.

For the second meeting, we created a sample of the comments that had the most disagreements in the previous assignment. Then, we asked the annotators to specify which questions (from our annotation framework) they used to decide whether a comment was abusive. For the second assignment sample, we also required the team to mention the questions used for each comment. This round had $\alpha = 51.2$.

In the third meeting, we decided to change the labelling process. We used a shared document for annotation, in which each annotator added their label for the comments. Then, we discussed the examples that had disagreements with the whole group. This discussion allowed us to answer a variety of questions and incorporate feedback into the annotation manual. This round achieved $\alpha = 65.8$. After this meeting, we reached a satisfactory agreement and also noticed less confusion in the annotations.

The training phase showed that the interaction with annotators is fundamental to improve the annotation process. We received feedback about the framework, improved the manual, and clarified concepts related to the labelling decisions. The improvement in inter-annotator agreement allied to our empirical observations showed that the training phase led to higher data quality.

Main Annotation Phase

After the training phase, we proceeded to label the entire dataset. We randomly split the dataset into six samples, one for each annotator. A single annotator labelled each comment. Given the extensive training process, we consider that each annotator is qualified to apply the framework properly; thus, we opt not to have multiple annotations on the same comment to allow a more significant number of labelled samples in total. The annotation interface displayed the text of each comment (including emojis and special symbols) and the video id; therefore, annotators could check the video to understand the context. We sorted comments by their video ids, displaying comments belonging to the same videos in sequence to reduce context-switching during labelling. Annotators could also access a summary of the annotation framework within the platform.

We randomly selected 300 comments to be labelled by all annotators; we used this sample to calculate the inter-annotator agreement. In addition to α and majority agreement, we also compute the majority agreement for the class labels (i.e., the scale numbers grouped into three classes). This metric is relevant to verify whether annotators agree on the polarity of a comment – represented by the extremes of the scale. It also illustrates the annotation reliability for applications that would use class labels instead of the full scale. Table 4 presents the inter-annotator agreement metrics for the whole dataset and per video category. # indicates the number of comments in a given category; *Majority* shows the percentage of comments with at least four matching annotations (out of a total of six); *Grouped* refers to majority agreement over class labels.

Topic	#	α	Majority	Grouped
All	300	73.8	64.3%	92.3%
VG	134	64.9	88.1%	98.5%
GI	135	55.2	44.4%	84.4%
WD	31	24.0	48.4%	100%
Official	76	60.0	50.0%	90.8%
Personal	179	77.9	76.5%	95.0%
Reaction	45	47.3	40.0%	84.4%

Table 4: Inter-annotator agreement metrics per category

The overall value of alpha indicates substantial agreement. The majority agreement was lower, which is expected given the 7-point scale. The grouped majority shows a high agreement about the polarity of comments, confirming that annotators agree whether a comment is abusive. There are significant differences between video categories. Disparities in sample size can lead to the difference in metrics: WD, for instance, had only 31 comments. For categories with similar size, a lower agreement can be attributed to controversial topics, confusing comments, or conflicting views. section 6 further investigates the content of each category and analyses how abuse is expressed in each one. In general, the annotation achieved significant inter-annotator agreement – which indicates that the annotation process was consistent and the dataset is reliable.

6 Dataset

The labelled dataset includes 19,915 comments, excluding the comments used in the training phase and the sample used for calculating the inter-annotator agreement. Each comment has a label ranging from 1 to 7, corresponding to the scale used in the annotation framework. We also aggregate the labels into classes: values from 1 to 3 correspond to *non-abusive* content; 5 to 7, *abusive*; and 4, *uncertain*. In this section, we analyse the aggregated labels. Table 5 presents the class distribution per category of the dataset. The percentage refers to the distribution over the specific category (video topic or type).

The annotators labelled 2274 comments as *Abusive*. This number represents 11.42% of the total distribution, showing a low prevalence of abusive content. Considering that we selected random samples and did not balance the data according to content, these comments potentially represent the actual distribution. However, since we balanced the number of comments per category, the dataset might misrepresent some video topics and types. The distribution of abusive content per category shows evidence of this imbalance. Videos about gender identity include 76.17% of the total amount of *abusive* comments and videos from an official source, 67.81%. To investigate the difference in content between categories, we analyse the lexical distribution within each topic and type.

Category	Abusive	Non-Abusive	Uncertain
Total	11.42%	85.98%	2.61%
VG	9.19%	38.02%	22.16%
GI	76.17%	28.55%	51.83%
WD	14.64%	33.44%	26.01%
Official	67.81%	47.99%	64.74%
Personal	17.46%	33.03%	21.39%
Reaction	14.73%	18.98%	13.87%

Table 5: Distribution of classes in the dataset per category

Lexical Analysis

We preprocess the comments by removing stopwords, punctuation marks, and character repetitions over three. First, we analyse the average length (in number of tokens) of comments in each class. *Abusive* comments have on average 31.67 tokens; *non-abusive*, 31.23; and *uncertain*, 41.25. Comments labelled as *uncertain* tend to be 30% longer than the other classes. However, sequences of short tokens, such as emojis, may impact the mean length. To avoid this issue, we also compute the average number of characters per comment, subtracting whitespaces. *Abusive* comments have on average 137.18 characters; *non-abusive*, 132.36; and *uncertain*, 179.02. Again, the *uncertain* class contains longer comments. These comments might be less readable and confusing, leading annotators to choose to label them as *uncertain*.

To analyse the content of the comments in depth, we identify the most frequent unigrams in the *abusive* class for each video category. Table 6 presents the ten most frequent unigrams.

In general, slurs and hateful terms are not prevalent among the most frequent unigrams. Each topic contains words related to videos from that cate-

VG	GI	WD	Official	Personal	Reaction
vegan	girls	women	women	trans	trisha
freelee	like	men	men	like	like
meat	men	gap	girls	f*cking	trans
like	trans	work	boys	b*tch	people
eating	women	wage	like	f*ck	think
b*tch	people	less	compete	people	needs
video	boys	make	people	video	i'm
go	compete	feminists	unfair	get	b*tch
eat	transgender	get	male	trisha	video
fat	male	pay	get	i'm	even

Table 6: Ten most frequent unigrams on abusive comments per category

gory, but there is some lexical overlap. *Veganism* includes neutral terms (meat, eat, vegan) and some derogatory words (fat, b*itch). The second most common unigram, Freelee, refers to a popular YouTuber – which shows that the *abusive* comments may target a specific person. *Gender Identity* and *Workplace Diversity* contain many gender-related words, which potentially occur in sexist comments.

For video types, *Personal* and *Reaction* have similar distributions. Personal has a higher prevalence of offensive words, and both include "Trisha" (a YouTuber) – indicating targeted comments. The dataset has both a video by Trisha and a reaction video to it, so mentions about the YouTuber are expected. Unigrams from *Official* videos are primarily about the video topics, following a pattern analogous to the topics of GI and WD.

Unigram distributions enable the identification of potentially relevant keywords related to abusive content. Understanding how abusive comments are expressed, however, requires more context. Therefore, we also identify the most frequent trigrams for each class to examine larger language constructs. We exclude trigrams consisting entirely of sequences of symbols or emojis. Many trigrams had the same frequency, so we highlight a sample of the total for each category. For the topic of *Veganism*, frequent trigrams include "*freele shut f*ck*", "*b*tch going vegan*", and "*vegans hate asians*". The first two phrases confirm that some abusive comments target content creators. *Gender Identity* contains "*boys competing girls*", "*make trans league*", and "*natural born gender*". The video with the most comments on this topic is about transgender athletes in sports – and these trigrams expose the prevalence of discriminatory comments against them. *Workplace Diversity* includes "*gender wage gap*", "*work long hours*", and "*take care children*". Interestingly, "*work less hours*" is also among the most frequent phrases, which indicates that the topic is controversial. Trigrams such as "*take care children*" show that comments about WD often express sexism.

Official videos, in general, combine trigrams from GI and WD. "*compelling argument sides*" and "*men better women*" are among the most frequent phrases; the former shows that comments contain civilised discussion; the latter, however, indicates the predominance of sexism. While the unigram distributions of *Personal* and *Reaction* videos are similar, their trigram frequencies exhibit different patterns. *Personal* includes "*identify natural born*", "*b*tch going vegan*", and "*whole trans community*", showing a combination of comments about GI and VG. *Reaction* displays a high prevalence of targeted comments with phrases such as "*trisha looks like*", "*trisha mentally ill*", and "*needs mental help*". Although these trigrams are the most frequent, their absolute number of occurrences is low. Therefore, lexical analysis indicates general trends about the content of comments but does not represent the entirety of abusive content in the dataset.

Classification Experiments

We perform classification experiments to explore ALYT as a source of training data for abusive language detection models. We frame the task as binary classification, using the grouped class labels *Abusive* and *Not Abusive*. We experiment with two models: logistic regression and a BERT-based classifier (Devlin et al., 2019).

The first baseline is a logistic regression clas-

Model	Class	P	R	F1
	NOT	$.914 \pm .014$	$.976 \pm .019$	$.944 \pm .003$
LogReg	ABU	$.678 \pm .081$	$.307 \pm .132$	$.395 \pm .102$
	AVG	$.796 \pm .034$	$.641 \pm .057$	$.670 \pm .050$
	NOT	$.944 \pm .002$	$.952 \pm .004$	$.948 \pm .001$
BERT	ABU	$.588 \pm .013$	$.546 \pm .017$	$.566 \pm .006$
	AVG	$.766 \pm .006$	$.749 \pm .007$	**.757** $\pm .003$

Table 7: Results for abusive language detection

sifier trained on word n-grams ranging from 1 to 3. We preprocessed all comments using the steps described in section 6. We used the implementation from scikit-learn with default hyperparameters (Pedregosa et al., 2011). We trained the model using 5-fold cross-validation and report the metrics averaged over the folds, along with standard deviation.

The second baseline is a BERT model pre-trained on English tweets (BERTweet) (Nguyen et al., 2020). In a preliminary experiment, BERTweet outperformed BERT-base by 3 points of macro F1. In addition to this result, we chose to use BERTweet because its vocabulary is more similar to ALYT's than BERT-base. We tokenised comments using TweetTokenizer from NLTK and translated emojis into strings using the emoji[9] package. We fine-tuned BERTweet for classification by training it with ALYT. We used a learning rate of 2^{-5}, a batch size of 32, and trained the model for a single epoch to avoid overfitting. We trained the model using a 80/20 train and test split; the results are averaged over five runs.

Table 7 presents the classification results. We report Precision (P), Recall (R), and F1 for each model on all classes (Not Abusive (NOT) and Abusive (ABU)) and macro averages (AVG). Values after $\pm$ represent the standard deviation.

The BERT-based model outperformed logistic regression by 8.6 points in macro F1 on average; the difference in the *Abusive* class was 17 points. Both models perform considerably worse when predicting abusive comments – which is expected given the data imbalance. Interestingly, logistic regression achieved higher precision but much lower recall than BERT. This result indicates that the classifier is making safe predictions based on surface-level patterns. To further investigate this effect, we compute the ten most relevant n-grams for the logistic regression (based on the model coefficients summed over all folds) and analyse their distribution over both classes. The top ten n-grams are *b*tch*, *dudes*, *femin*zis*, *d*ck*, *f*ck*, *idiot*, *drugs*, *f*cking*, *fair*, and *insane*. We then identify all comments that contain at least one of these terms and check their class distribution. 50.89% belong to *Not-Abusive* and 49.11% to *Abusive*. Although this percentage shows that these n-grams discriminate abusive comments above their actual distribution (11.42%), they are still frequent in non-abusive contexts. Therefore, the logistic regression classifier relies on lexical clues and fails to capture context. In conclusion, the higher recall that BERT achieves shows it can capture higher-level features.

7 Conclusion

This paper presented a dataset of YouTube comments in English, labelled as abusive by law students, using a 7-point Likert scale. The comments were collected from videos on three controversial topics: *Gender Identity*, *Veganism*, and *Workplace Diversity*. The dataset includes a sample of the actual amount of extracted comments, without any artificial balancing of the abusive content distribution.

We developed an annotation framework that includes legally inspired labelling rules based on European provisions and case law. Our annotation process includes developing and refining guidelines through various training sessions with active discussions. Our data sampling analysis shows that not purposefully searching for abusive content still leads to a considerable amount of abusive comments, while maintaining the characteristics of the social media platform's data distribution.

The content analyses show that ALYT contains various expressions of abuse, ranging from different topics and targets. The abusive content is not limited to specific keywords or slurs associated

[9] `https://pypi.org/project/emoji/`

with hateful content. Using a scale to label the content has the potential to capture multiple nuances of abusive language. However, we did not explore the implications of using a scale versus binary labels in this paper. This comparison might be a relevant research direction for future work.

We believe ALYT can be a valuable resource for training machine learning algorithms for abusive language detection and understanding online abuse on social media. Our annotation framework is a significant contribution toward the standardisation of practices in the field.

References

Jean-Yves Antoine, Jeanne Villaneau, and Anaïs Lefeuvre. 2014. Weighted krippendorff's alpha is a more reliable metrics for multi-coders ordinal annotations: experimental studies on emotion, opinion and coreference annotation. In *Proceedings of the 14th Conference of the European Chapter of the Association for Computational Linguistics*, pages 550–559.

Uwe Bretschneider, Thomas Wöhner, and Ralf Peters. 2014. Detecting online harassment in social networks. In *Proceedings of the ICIS 2014 conference*.

Pete Burnap and Matthew L Williams. 2015. Cyber hate speech on twitter: An application of machine classification and statistical modeling for policy and decision making. *Policy & Internet*, 7(2):223–242.

Pew Research Center. 2017. Online harassment 2017.

Despoina Chatzakou, Nicolas Kourtellis, Jeremy Blackburn, Emiliano De Cristofaro, Gianluca Stringhini, and Athena Vakali. 2017. Mean birds: Detecting aggression and bullying on twitter. In *Proceedings of the 2017 ACM on web science conference*, pages 13–22.

Thomas Davidson, Dana Warmsley, Michael Macy, and Ingmar Weber. 2017. Automated hate speech detection and the problem of offensive language. In *Eleventh international aaai conference on web and social media*.

Jacob Devlin, Ming-Wei Chang, Kenton Lee, and Kristina Toutanova. 2019. BERT: Pre-training of deep bidirectional transformers for language understanding. In *Proceedings of the 2019 Conference of the North American Chapter of the Association for Computational Linguistics: Human Language Technologies, Volume 1 (Long and Short Papers)*, pages 4171–4186, Minneapolis, Minnesota. Association for Computational Linguistics.

Jennifer Golbeck, Zahra Ashktorab, Rashad O Banjo, Alexandra Berlinger, Siddharth Bhagwan, Cody Buntain, Paul Cheakalos, Alicia A Geller, Rajesh Kumar Gnanasekaran, Raja Rajan Gunasekaran, et al. 2017. A large labeled corpus for online harassment research. In *Proceedings of the 2017 ACM on web science conference*, pages 229–233.

Eduard Hovy and Julia Lavid. 2010. Towards a 'science'of corpus annotation: a new methodological challenge for corpus linguistics. *International journal of translation*, 22(1):13–36.

Ankur Joshi, Saket Kale, Satish Chandel, and D Kumar Pal. 2015. Likert scale: Explored and explained. *Current Journal of Applied Science and Technology*, pages 396–403.

Klaus Krippendorff. 2011. Computing krippendorff's alpha-reliability. 2011. *Annenberg School for Communication Departmental Papers: Philadelphia*.

Binny Mathew, Navish Kumar, Pawan Goyal, Animesh Mukherjee, et al. 2018. Analyzing the hate and counter speech accounts on twitter. *arXiv preprint arXiv:1812.02712*.

Dat Quoc Nguyen, Thanh Vu, and Anh Tuan Nguyen. 2020. BERTweet: A pre-trained language model for English tweets. In *Proceedings of the 2020 Conference on Empirical Methods in Natural Language Processing: System Demonstrations*, pages 9–14, Online. Association for Computational Linguistics.

F. Pedregosa, G. Varoquaux, A. Gramfort, V. Michel, B. Thirion, O. Grisel, M. Blondel, P. Prettenhofer, R. Weiss, V. Dubourg, J. Vanderplas, A. Passos, D. Cournapeau, M. Brucher, M. Perrot, and E. Duchesnay. 2011. Scikit-learn: Machine learning in Python. *Journal of Machine Learning Research*, 12:2825–2830.

Manoel Horta Ribeiro, Pedro H Calais, Yuri A Santos, Virgílio AF Almeida, and Wagner Meira Jr. 2017. " like sheep among wolves": Characterizing hateful users on twitter. *arXiv preprint arXiv:1801.00317*.

Juliet van Rosendaal, Tommaso Caselli, and Malvina Nissim. 2020. Lower bias, higher density abusive language datasets: A recipe. In *Proceedings of the Workshop on Resources and Techniques for User and Author Profiling in Abusive Language*, pages 14–19.

Bertie Vidgen and Leon Derczynski. 2020. Directions in abusive language training data, a systematic review: Garbage in, garbage out. *Plos one*, 15(12):e0243300.

Marilyn A Walker, Jean E Fox Tree, Pranav Anand, Rob Abbott, and Joseph King. 2012. A corpus for research on deliberation and debate. In *LREC*, volume 812, page 817. Istanbul.

Zeerak Waseem and Dirk Hovy. 2016. Hateful symbols or hateful people? predictive features for hate speech detection on twitter. In *Proceedings of the NAACL student research workshop*, pages 88–93.

Marcos Zampieri, Shervin Malmasi, Preslav Nakov, Sara Rosenthal, Noura Farra, and Ritesh Kumar. 2019. Predicting the type and target of offensive posts in social media. In *Proceedings of the 2019 Conference of the North American Chapter of the Association for Computational Linguistics: Human Language Technologies, Volume 1 (Long and Short Papers)*, pages 1415–1420.

Haoti Zhong, Hao Li, Anna Cinzia Squicciarini, Sarah Michele Rajtmajer, Christopher Griffin, David J Miller, and Cornelia Caragea. 2016. Content-driven detection of cyberbullying on the instagram social network. In *IJCAI*, pages 3952–3958.

Frederike Zufall, Huangpan Zhang, Katharina Kloppenborg, and Torsten Zesch. 2020. Operationalizing the legal concept of'incitement to hatred'as an nlp task. *arXiv preprint arXiv:2004.03422*.

Findings of the WOAH 5 Shared Task on Fine Grained Hateful Memes Detection

Lambert Mathias[†], **Shaoliang Nie**[†], **Aida Davani**[‡],

Douwe Kiela[†], **Vinodkumar Prabhakaran**[⋆] **Bertie Vidgen**[§], **Zeerak Waseem**[¶]

[†]Facebook AI Research; [‡]University of Southern California; [⋆]Google AI
[§]The Alan Turing Institute; [¶]University of Sheffield
mathiasl@fb.com

1 Abstract

We present the results and main findings of the shared task at WOAH 5 on hateful memes detection. The task include two subtasks relating to distinct challenges in the fine-grained detection of hateful memes: (1) the protected category attacked by the meme and (2) the attack type. 3 teams submitted system description papers. This shared task builds on the hateful memes detection task created by Facebook AI Research in 2020.

2 Introduction

The spread and impact of online hate is a growing concern across societies, and increasingly there is consensus that social media companies must do more to counter such content (League, 2020; Vidgen et al., 2021). At the same time, any interventions must be balanced with protecting people's freedom of expression and ability to engage in open discussions. Ensuring that online spaces are both open and safe requires being able to reliably and accurately find, rate and remove harmful content such as hate. Scalable machine learning based solutions offer a powerful way of solving this problem, reducing the burden on human moderators.

To date, detecting online hate has proven remarkably difficult and concerns have been raised about the performance, robustness, generalizability and fairness of even state-of-the-art models (Waseem et al., 2018; Vidgen et al., 2019; Caselli et al., 2020b; Mishra et al., 2019; Davidson et al., 2019). To advance the field, and develop models which can be used in real-world settings, research needs to go beyond simple binary classifications of textual content. To this end, we have used trained professional moderators to re-annotate the hateful memes dataset from (Kiela et al., 2020)[1]. It contains two sets of labels, which correspond to our two sub-tasks: the protected category that has been attacked (e.g., women, black people, immigrants) as well as the type of attack (e.g., inciting violence, dehumanizing, mocking the group).

Detecting hateful memes is a particularly challenging task because the content is multi-modal rather than uni-modal, such as text or images alone. When humans look at memes they do not think about the words and photos independently but, instead, combine the two together. In contrast, most AI detection systems analyze text and image separately and do not learn a joint representation. This is inefficient and limits the performance of systems. They are likely to fail when an image that by itself is non-hateful is combined with non-hateful text to produce content that expresses hate through the *interaction* of the image and text. For AI to detect hate communicated through multiple modalities, it must learn to understand content the way that people do: holistically. In this paper we present the results of the WOAH 5 shared task on fine-grained hateful memes detection.

3 Dataset

3.1 Dataset Size

The dataset we present for the shared task is from phase 1 of the hateful memes challenge Kiela et al. (2020)[2]. Table 1 shows the distribution and data splits associated with the released dataset. We reannotated the hateful memes for the two fine-grained categories (Protected category and Attack type). For the non-hateful memes we assigned a label of 'none' for both categories.

[1]Dataset is available at https://github.com/facebookresearch/fine_grained_hateful_memes

[2]Dataset is available at https://hatefulmemeschallenge.com/

Proceedings of the Fifth Workshop on Online Abuse and Harms, pages 201–206
August 6, 2021.

label	train	dev_seen	dev_unseen	test_seen
not_hateful	5493	254	341	520
hateful	3007	246	199	480
Total	8500	500	540	1000

Table 1: Hateful Memes Dataset Statistics

3.2 Dataset Labels

Each meme was originally labelled as 'Hateful' or 'Not Hateful' by Kiela et al. (2020). Hate is a contested concept and there is no generally agreed upon definition or taxonomy in the field (Caselli et al., 2020a; Waseem et al., 2017; Zampieri et al., 2019). For the purposes of this work, hate is defined as a direct attack against people based on 'protected characteristics'[3]. Protected characteristics are core aspects of a person's social identity which are generally fixed or immutable. Table 2 provides the set of fine-grained labels for protected classes and attack types.

3.3 Annotations

Each hateful meme was annotated by three annotators for the protected characteristic and the attack type (from the set defined in Table 2). If no clear protected group or attack type could be identified the annotator could select "not sure". Annotators were allowed to select multiple labels for both the protected characteristic and attack type.

Since our annotation is multi-label, we computed Krippendorff's α, which supports multiple annotators as well as multi-label agreement computation (Krippendorff, 2018). We obtain Krippendorff's $\alpha = 0.77$ for the protected categories, and $\alpha = 0.66$ for attack types, indicating that while there is some uncertainty, it is within usable range i.e $\alpha \geq 0.66$ (Krippendorff, 2004). This indicates 'moderate' to 'strong' agreement (Mchugh, 2012) and compares favourably with other abusive content datasets (Gomez et al., 2020; Fortuna and Nunes, 2018; Wulczyn et al., 2017), especially given that our labels contain five and seven levels respectively. We used a majority voting scheme to decide the final labels from the annotations.

[3]This aligns with the definition described in `https://www.facebook.com/communitystandards/hate_speech`

4 Shared Task Results & Analysis

4.1 Shared Task Setup

For WOAH 5, collocated with ACL, we introduced two hateful meme detection tasks:

Task A: Protected Category For each meme, detect the protected category. The protected categories recorded in the dataset are: race, disability, religion, nationality, sex.[4] If the meme is not hateful the protected category is recorded as "pc_empty".

Task B: Attack Type For each meme, detect the attack type. The attack types recorded in the dataset are: contempt, mocking, inferiority, slurs, exclusion, dehumanizing, inciting violence. If the meme is not hateful the attack type is recorded as "attack_empty".

Tasks A and B are multi-label because each meme can contain attacks against multiple protected categories and can involve multiple attack types. For evaluating performance on both tasks we use the standard ROC_AUC metric for multi-label classification (Pedregosa et al., 2011).[5].

We used the same splits from the original dataset as described in Table 1. Participants had access to the train, dev_seen and dev_unseen splits for developing and tuning their models. The final evaluation was done on the test_seen split. The ground truth labels were not provided at time of submission and each participant was expected to submit their predictions with model scores. Each participant was limited to a maximum of 2 submissions per task.

4.2 System Descriptions

Majority Baseline A simple majority decision-rule, applied over the entire dataset. We predict the majority class for all instances, i.e. "pc_empty" for Task A and "attack_empty" for Task B.

VisualBERT Baseline A VisualBERT multimodal model (Li et al., 2019) that has been pre-trained on the MS COCO

[4]Note that the characterisation and definition of some protected categories, such as race, is highly contested. For further analysis of the concept of 'race' see Omi and Winant (2005)

[5]The evaluation script and fine-grained labels are available at `https://github.com/facebookresearch/fine_grained_hateful_memes`

Protected Category	Definition
Religion	A group defined by a shared belief system
Race	A group defined by similar, distinct racialised physical characteristics
Sex	A group defined by their physical sexual attributes or sexual identifications
Nationality	A group defined by the country/region they belong to
Disability	A group defined by conditions that generally lead to permanent dependencies (on people, medical treatments or equipment)
Attack Type	**Definition**
Dehumanizing	Explicitly or implicitly describing or presenting a group as subhuman
Inferiority	Claiming that a group is inferior, less worthy or less important than either society in general or another group
Inciting violence	Explicitly or implicitly calling for harm to be inflicted on a group, including physical attacks
Mocking	Making jokes about, undermining, belittling, or disparaging a group
Contempt	Expressing intensely negative feelings or emotions about a group
Slurs	Using prejudicial terms to refer to, describe or characterise a group
Exclusion	Advocating, planning or justifying the exclusion or segregation of a group from all of society or certain parts

Table 2: Protected Category and Attack Type definitions used for fine-grained annotations.

Fine-grained attributes		train	dev_unseen	dev_seen	test_seen
Attack type	dehumanizing	1318	104	121	209
	inferiority	658	35	49	102
	inciting_violence	407	23	26	68
	mocking	378	29	35	84
	contempt	235	6	10	21
	slurs	205	4	6	10
	exclusion	114	8	13	12
Protected category	religion	1078	77	95	166
	race	1008	63	78	169
	sex	746	46	56	82
	nationality	325	20	26	42
	disability	255	17	22	63

Table 3: Distribution of attack types and protected characteristics on the "hateful" subset of the hateful memes dataset in Table 1

System	Task A - protected category	Task B - attack type
Majority Baseline	0.70	0.72
VisualBERT Baseline	0.864	0.873
LTL-UDE1	0.912	-
LTL-UDE2	**0.914**	-
QMUL	0.901	**0.913**
SU1	0.876	0.881
SU2	0.865	0.89

Table 4: Overall results from the shared task submissions on the blind test set partition

dataset (Lin et al., 2014). We use the setup in MMF (Singh et al., 2020) to pre-train the models. Each task is trained and evaluated independently.[6] VisualBERT was also used in the original hateful memes paper by Kiela et al. (2020), although here we set it up for multilabel detection.

Duisburg-Essen System 1 (LTL-UDE1) The solution builds on the multimodal approach used for the winning entry in the hateful memes challenge (Zhu, 2020) - a VLBERT multimodal model with image specific metadata. It was fine-tuned on the fine-grained data. The system was only submitted for Task A.

Duisburg-Essen System 2 (LTL-UDE2) An additional emotion tags are added to DE1 which are extracted from the facial expressions of persons objects available in the meme image. The system was only submitted for Task A.

Queen Mary University London (QMUL) The submitted system is a multimodal model that uses CLIP (Radford et al., 2021) image encoder to embed the meme images, and CLIP text encoder, LASER (Artetxe and Schwenk, 2019) & LaBSE (Feng et al., 2020) to embed the meme text. All the representations are concatenated, and a multi-label logistic regression classifier is trained, one for each task, to predict the labels.

Stockholm University System 1 (SU1) A BERT-base based model that only uses the text of the meme as input. The BERT model was fine-tuned independently for each task.

Stockholm University System 2 (SU2) A multimodal model (ImgBERT) which combines SU1 with image embeddings. The image embeddings were extracted using DenseNet-121 convolutional neural networks(CNNs), pretrained on ImageNet (Deng et al., 2009). The input to the multi-label classification layer is the concatenation of the text representation from the [CLS] token of SU1, and the image embedding. The final classifier is an ensemble between the ImgBERT model and the text-only model from SU1. The scores provided by each of the labels were averaged to decide the final label.

4.3 Analysis

Table 4 shows the performance on the 2 tasks across all the participants. All the systems used some variant of pre-trained multimodal representations fine-tuned on the shared task datasets. None of the submissions exploited the correlation across all the tasks, and instead trained the systems independently on each of the tasks. The systems from LTL-DE1 and LTL-DE2 were the only ones to exploit image level metadata as an additional signal that was not part of the provided training data that showed best performance on Task A. Moreover, the LTL-DE1 and LTL-DE2 submissions were the only ones to leverage state of the art multimodal representations from VLBERT (Su et al., 2019), while all other submissions encoded the image and text channel independently. Interestingly, SU1, which is a text BERT system finetuned on the tasks performed remarkably strongly, even outperforming their multimodal system and the provided baselines. It is unclear if the model is picking up some unintended biases in the data, considering the relatively small size of the datasets provided for the shared task. QMUL system encoded the text representation using multiple different pre-trained representations concatenated with the image representation, further supporting the evidence that potentially stronger encoding of text might be sufficient to achieve strong performance on this dataset.

5 Conclusion

Detecting hate remains technically difficult, with many unaddressed or unsolved challenges and frontiers. Hateful memes are one issue that has received little attention, despite the ubiquity of such media online. The shared task at WOAH 5, with two subtasks for fine-grained detection of the protected category and the attack type, is another step forward in this still-nascent research area.

For future work, we hope to scale the fine-grained annotations to other hate speech datasets, as we think it is important toi develop classifiers that can detect the nuances of hate speech. Meanwhile, the annotated datasets are publicly available and we welcome researchers to make use of them.

[6]See `https://github.com/facebookresearch/mmf/tree/master/projects/hateful_memes/fine_grained` for training configuration

References

Mikel Artetxe and Holger Schwenk. 2019. Massively multilingual sentence embeddings for zero-shot cross-lingual transfer and beyond. *Transactions of the Association for Computational Linguistics*, 7:597–610.

Tommaso Caselli, Valerio Basile, Jelena Mitrović, Inga Kartoziya, and Michael Granitzer. 2020a. I Feel Offended, Don't Be Abusive! Implicit/Explicit Messages in Offensive and Abusive Language. In *Proceedings of the 12th Conference on Language Resources and Evaluation (LREC)*, pages 6193–6202.

Tommaso Caselli, Valerio Basile, Jelena Mitrović, Inga Kartoziya, and Michael Granitzer. 2020b. I feel offended, don't be abusive! implicit/explicit messages in offensive and abusive language. In *Proceedings of the 12th language resources and evaluation conference*, pages 6193–6202.

Thomas Davidson, Debasmita Bhattacharya, and Ingmar Weber. 2019. Racial bias in hate speech and abusive language detection datasets. In *Proceedings of the Third Workshop on Abusive Language Online*, pages 25–35, Florence, Italy. Association for Computational Linguistics.

Jia Deng, Wei Dong, Richard Socher, Li-Jia Li, Kai Li, and Li Fei-Fei. 2009. Imagenet: A large-scale hierarchical image database. In *2009 IEEE conference on computer vision and pattern recognition*, pages 248–255. Ieee.

Fangxiaoyu Feng, Yinfei Yang, Daniel Cer, Naveen Arivazhagan, and Wei Wang. 2020. Language-agnostic bert sentence embedding. *arXiv preprint arXiv:2007.01852*.

Paula Fortuna and Sérgio Nunes. 2018. A survey on automatic detection of hate speech in text. *ACM Comput. Surv.*, 51(4).

Raul Gomez, Jaume Gibert, Lluis Gomez, and Dimosthenis Karatzas. 2020. Exploring Hate Speech Detection in Multimodal Publications. In *Proceedings of the Winter Conference on Applications of Computer Vision*, pages 1–8.

Douwe Kiela, Hamed Firooz, Aravind Mohan, Vedanuj Goswami, Amanpreet Singh, Pratik Ringshia, and Davide Testuggine. 2020. The hateful memes challenge: Detecting hate speech in multimodal memes. *Advances in Neural Information Processing Systems*, 33.

Klaus Krippendorff. 2004. Reliability in content analysis: Some common misconceptions and recommendations. *Human communication research*, 30(3):411–433.

Klaus Krippendorff. 2018. *Content analysis: An introduction to its methodology*. Sage publications.

Anti-Defamation League. 2020. Online hate and harassment. the american experience 2021. *Center for Technology and Society. Retrieved from www. adl. org/media/14643/download.*

Liunian Harold Li, Mark Yatskar, Da Yin, Cho-Jui Hsieh, and Kai-Wei Chang. 2019. Visualbert: Asimple and performant baseline for vision and language. *arXiv preprint arXiv:1908.03557*.

Tsung-Yi Lin, Michael Maire, Serge Belongie, James Hays, Pietro Perona, Deva Ramanan, Piotr Dollár, and C Lawrence Zitnick. 2014. Microsoft coco: Common objects in context. In *European conference on computer vision*, pages 740–755. Springer.

Mary L Mchugh. 2012. Interrater reliability: the Kappa statistic. *Biochemia Medica*, 22(3):276–282.

Pushkar Mishra, Helen Yannakoudakis, and Ekaterina Shutova. 2019. Tackling online abuse: A survey of automated abuse detection methods. *arXiv preprint arXiv:1908.06024*.

Michael Omi and Howard Winant. 2005. The Theoretical Status of the Concept of Race. In Cameron McCarthy, Warren Crichlow, Greg Dimitriadis, and Nadine Dolby, editors, *Race, Identity and Representation in Education*. Routledge, London.

Fabian Pedregosa, Gaël Varoquaux, Alexandre Gramfort, Vincent Michel, Bertrand Thirion, Olivier Grisel, Mathieu Blondel, Peter Prettenhofer, Ron Weiss, Vincent Dubourg, et al. 2011. Scikit-learn: Machine learning in python. *the Journal of machine Learning research*, 12:2825–2830.

Alec Radford, Jong Wook Kim, Chris Hallacy, Aditya Ramesh, Gabriel Goh, Sandhini Agarwal, Girish Sastry, Amanda Askell, Pamela Mishkin, Jack Clark, et al. 2021. Learning transferable visual models from natural language supervision. *arXiv preprint arXiv:2103.00020*.

Amanpreet Singh, Vedanuj Goswami, Vivek Natarajan, Yu Jiang, Xinlei Chen, Meet Shah, Marcus Rohrbach, Dhruv Batra, and Devi Parikh. 2020. Mmf: A multimodal framework for vision and language research. `https://github.com/facebookresearch/mmf`.

Weijie Su, Xizhou Zhu, Yue Cao, Bin Li, Lewei Lu, Furu Wei, and Jifeng Dai. 2019. Vl-bert: Pre-training of generic visual-linguistic representations. *arXiv preprint arXiv:1908.08530*.

Bertie Vidgen, Alex Harris, Josh Cowls, Ella Guest, and Helen Margetts. 2021. *An agenda for research into online hate*. The Alan Turing Institute, London.

Bertie Vidgen, Alex Harris, Dong Nguyen, Rebekah Tromble, Scott Hale, and Helen Margetts. 2019. Challenges and frontiers in abusive content detection. In *Proceedings of the Third Workshop on Abusive Language Online*, pages 80–93, Florence, Italy. Association for Computational Linguistics.

Zeerak Waseem, Thomas Davidson, Dana Warmsley, and Ingmar Weber. 2017. Understanding Abuse: A Typology of Abusive Language Detection Subtasks. In *Proceedings of the First Workshop on Abusive Language Online*, pages 78–84.

Zeerak Waseem, James Thorne, and Joachim Bingel. 2018. Bridging the gaps: Multi task learning for domain transfer of hate speech detection. In *Online harassment*, pages 29–55. Springer.

Ellery Wulczyn, Nithum Thain, and Lucas Dixon. 2017. Ex Machina: Personal Attacks Seen at Scale. In *Proceedings of the International World Wide Web Conference*, pages 1391–1399.

Marcos Zampieri, Shervin Malmasi, Preslav Nakov, Sara Rosenthal, Noura Farra, and Ritesh Kumar. 2019. Predicting the type and target of offensive posts in social media. In *Proceedings of NAACL HLT 2019*, volume 1, pages 1415–1420.

Ron Zhu. 2020. Enhance multimodal transformer with external label and in-domain pretrain: Hateful meme challenge winning solution. *arXiv preprint arXiv:2012.08290*.

VL-BERT+: Detecting Protected Groups in Hateful Multimodal Memes

Piush Aggarwal, Michelle Espranita Liman, Darina Gold, and Torsten Zesch*
Language Technology Lab
University of Duisburg-Essen

Abstract

This paper describes our submission (winning solution for Task A) to the Shared Task on Hateful Meme Detection at WOAH 2021. We build our system on top of a state-of-the-art system for binary hateful meme classification that already uses image tags such as race, gender, and web entities. We add further metadata such as emotions and experiment with data augmentation techniques, as hateful instances are underrepresented in the data set.

1 Introduction

In this work, we present our submission to the Shared Task on Hateful Memes at WOAH 2021: Workshop on Online Abuse and Harms.[1] Detecting hateful memes that combine visual and textual elements is a relatively new task (Kiela et al., 2020). However, research can build on earlier work on the classification of hateful, abusive, or offending textual statements targeting individuals or groups based on gender, nationality, or sexual orientation (Basile et al., 2019; Burnap and Williams, 2014).

Shared Task Description We only tackle Task A, which is predicting fine-grained labels for protected categories that are attacked in the memes, namely RACE, DISABILITY, RELIGION, NATIONALITY, and SEX. The memes are provided in a multi-label setting. Table 1 shows the label distribution of the provided data set.[2]

Our System Our system is built on top of the winning system (Zhu, 2020) of the Hateful Memes Challenge (Kiela et al., 2020), which was a binary hateful meme detection task. Zhu (2020) fine-tuned a visual-linguistic transformer-based pre-trained model called *VL-BERT*$_{LARGE}$ and showed that metadata information of meme images such as race, gender, and web entity tags (recommended textual tags for the image based on data collected from the web) improved the performance of the hateful meme classification system. We replicate this system for a more fine-grained categorization of hateful memes, as proposed by the current shared task. Considering the data scarcity in this novel task, we also propose several data augmentation strategies and examine the effects on our classification problem. The evaluation metric used by the shared task is the (micro-averaged) area under the receiver operating characteristic curve *AUROC*.

In addition, we consider **emotion tags** which are extracted from facial expressions available in the

Labels	Train	Dev	%
NONE	5495	394	64.4
RELIGION	888	78	10.6
RACE	801	59	9.4
SEX	552	44	6.5
NATIONALITY	191	19	2.3
DISABILITY	184	16	2.2
RACE+SEX	66	4	0.8
RELIGION+SEX	52	2	0.6
RACE+RELIGION	53	10	0.7
NATIONALITY+RELIGION	38	3	0.4
DISABILITY+SEX	36	4	0.4
NATIONALITY+RACE	52	2	0.6
NATIONALITY+RELIGION	20	1	0.2
DISABILITY+RACE	16	1	0.2
Other	56	3	0.5
Total	8,500	640	100

Table 1: Overview of categories in WOAH 2021 data set. 'Other' refers to the remaining (very infrequent) instances annotated with different combinations of protected group labels.

*Equal contribution of the first two authors

[1] https://www.workshopononlineabuse.com/cfp/shared-task-on-hateful-memes

[2] In the data set, memes are labeled as PC_EMPTY if they are not hateful and none of the protected categories can be applied. In this paper, we use NONE instead of PC_EMPTY for better intuition.

Proceedings of the Fifth Workshop on Online Abuse and Harms, pages 207–214
August 6, 2021.

(a) (b) (c)

Figure 1: Image pre-processing: Recovering the original image of the meme (a) Original meme image (b) Easy-OCR masking (c) Image inpainting

meme images. Based on experimental results and the shared task leaderboard scores, the inclusion of emotion tags along with VL-BERT$_{\text{LARGE}}$ model equipped with race, gender, and web entity tags exhibits the best performance for Task A. We make our source code publicly available.[3]

2 Related Work

Multi-modal hateful meme detection is the task of identifying hate in the combination of textual and visual information.

Textual Information In most previous works, hate speech detection has been performed solely in textual form. Despite many challenges (Vidgen et al., 2019), there have been several automatic detection systems developed to filter hateful statements (Waseem et al., 2017; Benikova et al., 2017; Wiegand et al., 2018; Kumar et al., 2018; Nobata et al., 2016; Aggarwal et al., 2019). One state-of-the-art model is BERT (Devlin et al., 2019). BERT is a contextualized transformer (Vaswani et al., 2017) based on a pre-trained language model which can be further fine-tuned for downstream applications such as hate speech classification.

Visual Information For hateful meme classification, the Facebook challenge team[4] proposed a unimodal training where a ResNet (He et al., 2015) encoder is used for image feature extraction. Apart from this, there has been a plenitude of work on extracting information from images, which is potentially useful for hateful meme detection. Image processing systems such as Faster R-CNN or Inception V3 models (Ren et al., 2016; Szegedy et al., 2015) are useful for detecting available objects in images. Smith (2007) and EasyOCR[5] can optically recognize the text embedded in an image.

Visual-linguistic Information There have been several ML-based approaches to solve the task of hateful meme detection. Blandfort et al. (2018) extracted textual features such as n-grams, affine dictionary along with local (Faster R-CNN) and global (Inception V3) visual features to train the SVM-based classification model. Sabat et al. (2019) proposed the fusion of vgg16 Convolutional Neural Network (Simonyan and Zisserman, 2015) based image features with BERT (Devlin et al., 2019) based contextualized text features to train a Multi-Layer Perceptron (MLP) based model. Earlier work (Liu et al., 2018; Gomez et al., 2019) proposed either early or late fusion strategies for the integration of textual and visual feature vectors. However, Chen et al. (2020); Li et al. (2020); Su et al. (2020); van Aken et al. (2020) and Yu et al. (2021) extracted visual-linguistic relationships by introducing cross-attention networks between textual transformers and transformers trained on visual features. Such networks deliver promising results on a variety of visual-linguistic tasks such as Image Captioning, Visual Question Reasoning (VQR), and Visual Commonsense Reasoning (VCR). Zhu (2020) and Lippe et al. (2020) exploited these networks for the binary classification of memes as hateful or non-hateful. The incorporation of additional metadata information as race, gender, and

[3] https://github.com/aggarwalpiush/HateMemeDetection

[4] https://ai.facebook.com/blog/hateful-memes-challenge-and-data-set/

[5] https://github.com/JaidedAI/EasyOCR

web entity tags, which are extracted from meme images, increased performance significantly in hateful meme classification (Zhu, 2020).

Hitherto, meme classification, having been introduced only recently, has been a binary task. Except for the VisualBERT (Li et al., 2019) based baseline[6] provided by the WOAH 2021 Shared Task, to our knowledge, there has been no work on detecting protected groups in hateful memes.

3 System Description

In this paper, we exploit the analysis proposed by Zhu (2020) for the fine-grained categorization of hateful memes.

3.1 Pre-processing

Both the visual and the textual parts of the memes are pre-processed. The data provided by the shared task consist of memes with their corresponding meme text. In this paper, we follow the steps proposed by Zhu (2020) to pre-process the provided input memes.

Text Pre-processing For text pre-processing, a BERT-based tokenizer (Devlin et al., 2019) is applied. This is also an integral part of the VL-$\text{BERT}_{\text{LARGE}}$ system (Su et al., 2020) (see Section 3.3).

Image Pre-processing The image part of the memes poses several challenges. First, meme images may consist of multiple sub-images, so-called *patches*. In this case, we segregate these patches using an image processing toolkit (Chen et al., 2019). Second, the text embedded in the images may add noise to the image features. Therefore, we aim to recover the original meme image before the text was added. To do so, we first apply EasyOCR-based Optical Character Recognition, which results in an image with black masked regions corresponding to the meme text as shown in Figure 1b. Then, *inpainting*, a process where damaged, deteriorating, or missing parts are filled in to present a complete image, is applied to these regions using the MMediting Tool (Contributors, 2020) (see Figure 1c).

3.2 Metadata

Understanding memes often requires implicit knowledge (e.g. cultural prejudice, clichés, historical knowledge) that human readers must have to understand the content. Such knowledge might be a big help for the classifier if explicitly provided. Zhu (2020) used meme image metadata, such as race, gender, and web entity tags to enhance binary classification performance on hateful memes. We utilized the same metadata and, in addition to that, emotion tags for the fine-grained categorization into protected groups.

Race and Gender We apply the pre-trained FairFace (Karkkainen and Joo, 2021) model to the provided meme images to extract the bounding boxes of detected faces with their corresponding race and gender metadata.

Web Entities Web entities are web-recommended textual tags associated with an image. They add contextual information to the images, making it easier for the model to establish the relationship between the meme text and image. We use Google's Web Entity Detection service[7] to extract these web entities.

Emotion Emotions are promising features for hate speech detection (Martins et al., 2018). Awal et al. (2021) investigated the positive impact of emotions in textual hate speech detection where emotion features are shared using a multi-task learning network. We exploit this in our system by extracting emotions based on facial expressions available in the meme image together with their corresponding bounding boxes. For this purpose, we use the Python-based emotion detection API[8] which classifies a face into the seven universal emotions described by Ekman (1992)—ANGER, FEAR, DISGUST, HAPPINESS, SADNESS, SURPRISE, and CONTEMPT.

3.3 VL-$\text{BERT}_{\text{LARGE}}$

VL-$\text{BERT}_{\text{LARGE}}$ (Su et al., 2020) demonstrates state-of-the-art performance on binary hateful meme classification Zhu (2020). Therefore, we investigate it for the detection of protected groups in hateful memes. VL-$\text{BERT}_{\text{LARGE}}$ is a transformer (Vaswani et al., 2017) back-boned visual-linguistic model pre-trained on the Conceptual Captions data set (Sharma et al., 2018) and some other text corpora (Zhu et al., 2015). It provides generic representations for visual-linguistic downstream tasks.

[6] https://github.com/facebookresearch/mmf/tree/master/projects/hateful_memes/fine_grained

[7] https://cloud.google.com/vision/docs/detecting-web

[8] https://pypi.org/project/facial-emotion-recognition

(a) (b) (c) (d) (e)

Figure 2: Data augmentation: (a) Original meme (b) Image augmentation with effects (c) Image augmentation with a visually similar image (d) Text augmentation (e) Image and text augmentation

One of the model training requirements is to identify objects and their location in the image. To do that, we use Google's Inception V2 Object Detection model.[9]

We extract features from both modalities (image and text) in the provided data set to fine-tune the pre-trained VL-BERT$_{\text{LARGE}}$ representation. Afterward, these features are used to train a multi-layer feedforward network (also called a downstream network) to generate the final classifier. We train the model for a maximum of 10 epochs with the other default hyperparameters provided by Su et al. (2020).

3.4 Data Augmentation

Data scarcity often leads to model overfitting. As shown in the training set distribution in Table 1, non-hateful memes comprise the majority of the data set. The non-uniform distribution of labels makes this data set quite small for model training. Therefore, we artificially augment the samples labeled with the protected groups. For image augmentation, we use the image augmentation toolkit by Jung et al. (2020) which alters images by adding effects like blur, noise, hue/saturation changes, etc. Additionally, we use Google's Web Entity Detection service to obtain visually similar images. For text augmentation, we generate semantically related statements using *nlpaug* (Ma, 2019). Furthermore, since we have original and augmented versions of images and texts, we combine them in three different ways: i) the original image with augmented text, ii) augmented image with the original text, and iii) augmented image with augmented text (see Figure 2).

[9] https://tfhub.dev/google/faster_rcnn/openimages_v4/inception_resnet_v2/1

3.5 Ensemble

The predictions of a single system may not be generalized enough to be used on unseen data due to high variance, bias, etc. However, relying on multiple systems can overcome these technical challenges. Therefore, we choose our best three systems based on their *AUROC* scores. We apply the majority voting scheme on the prediction labels provided by each system. The label with the highest number of votes will be selected as the final prediction for the ensemble system. In cases when all systems disagree, we choose the label with the highest prediction probability.

4 Results and Discussion

Table 2 shows the results for Task A on the provided development data set. We also compare our results with the VisualBERT (Li et al., 2019) based baseline as provided by the shared task organizers. Among the different configurations of our system, VL-BERT$_{\text{LARGE}}$ model with race, gender, emotion, and web entity tags (called +W,RG,E in the table) achieves the best *AUROC* score. We find that the inclusion of emotion tags has a positive effect on the overall performance when compared to other systems. To analyze the statistical significance among the approaches, we apply the Bowker test (Bowker, 1948) on the contingency matrices created on the number of agreements and disagreements between the systems. To compensate for the chance significance, we apply the Bonferroni correction (Abdi, 2007) on p value. We find that approaches marked with * are statistically significant compared to the best-performing solution.

When the model is trained on the train set along with augmented data, hardly any significant performance improvement is encountered. This is

Approach	sign.	Protected Groups RACE	SEX	REL.	DIS.	NAT.	NONE	Overall F1	AUROC	Leader Board AUROC
Baseline	*	.71	.84	.75	.84	.70	.78	.62	.85	
+W		.79	.86	.87	.90	.92	.71	.64	.91	
+W,RG	–	.81	.87	.91	.91	.85	.80	.70	.92	.912
+W,E		.77	.85	.90	.89	.77	.75	.68	.91	
+W,RG,E		.76	.89	.91	.94	.81	.79	.70	.92	**.914**
U | +W	*	.81	.87	.90	.90	.91	.71	.60	.87	
U | +W,RG	*	.83	.88	.90	.91	.87	.74	.62	.90	
I | +W		.79	.86	.89	.93	.91	.74	.67	.91	
I | +W,RG		.81	.86	.91	.88	.88	.77	.68	.92	
T | +W		.75	.82	.90	.84	.83	.76	.70	.91	
T | +W,RG		.75	.86	.86	.91	.83	.78	.70	.90	
IT | +W	*	.72	.80	.89	.81	.87	.75	.70	.88	
IT | +W,RG	*	.77	.88	.83	.79	.84	.77	.68	.90	
Ensemble		.75	.89	.92	.93	.79	.80	.71	.92	

Table 2: Classification results of hateful memes target (protected groups) classes on provided development data set. Abbreviations are as follows: RG: Race and Gender, W: Web Entities, E: Emotion, T: Text Augmentation, I: Image Augmentation, IT: Image and Text Augmentation, and U: Undersampling. * denotes that the approach is significantly different from the best performing system (+W,RG,E)) using the Bowker significance test, considering $p < 0.004$ after Bonferroni correction.

contrary to our expectations. We analyze the approaches with image and text augmentation (IT| +W and IT| +W,RG) (statistically significant from the best-performing system) and found a notable increase in False Negative errors, especially for RELIGION.

During post-experiment analysis, we find that the predictions for DISABILITY and RELIGION labels are better compared to others when the model is at a low False Positive rate. However, NATIONALITY performs relatively well at a high False Positive rate (see Figure 3). From the confusion matrices (Table 3), we find that the number of False Negatives is dominant in all classes. We believe that class imbalance is responsible for this behavior. To verify this, we train models on the undersampled training data set and found significant improvement on labels with low sample size. However, we also find a huge performance drop on the NONE label.

For the final submission, we generate predictions on the test set using our two best-performing models based on their *AUROC* score — VL-BERT$_{\text{LARGE}}$ +W,RG,E (**winning solution**) and +W,RG (2nd rank) (see Table 2 for Shared Task leaderboard scores).

5 Summary

In this paper, we presented our approach to identify and categorize attacked protected groups in hateful memes. We performed experiments using

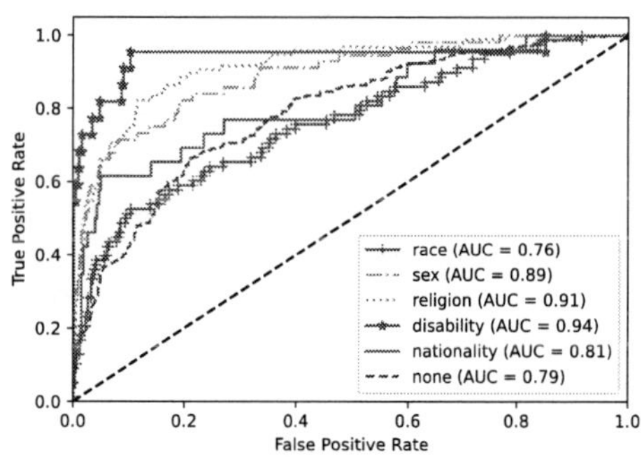

Figure 3: AUROC analysis for individual protected groups for configuration VL-BERT$_{\text{LARGE}}$ (+W,RG,E).

a visual-linguistic pre-trained model called VL-BERT$_{\text{LARGE}}$ along with metadata information extracted from the meme image and text. Results show that the inclusion of metadata helps to improve system performance. However, the final system still lacks a robust understanding of hateful memes targeting protected groups.

Acknowledgments

This work was supported by the Deutsche Forschungsgemeinschaft (DFG) under grant No. GRK 2167, Research Training Group "User-Centred Social Media".

(a) RELIGION

Gold Values \ Predictions	False	True	Total
False	531	14	545
True	43	52	95
Total	574	66	640

(b) RACE

Gold Values \ Predictions	False	True	Total
False	546	16	562
True	56	22	78
Total	602	38	640

(c) NATIONALITY

Gold Values \ Predictions	False	True	Total
False	608	6	614
True	22	4	26
Total	630	10	640

(d) SEX

Gold Values \ Predictions	False	True	Total
False	579	5	584
True	37	19	56
Total	616	24	640

(e) DISABILITY

Gold Values \ Predictions	False	True	Total
False	617	1	618
True	13	9	22
Total	630	10	640

(f) NONE

Gold Values \ Predictions	False	True	Total
False	108	138	246
True	40	354	394
Total	148	492	640

Table 3: Confusion matrices for configuration VL-BERT$_{\text{LARGE}}$ (+W,RG,E).

References

Hervé Abdi. 2007. The bonferonni and Šidák corrections for multiple comparisons. *Encyclopedia of measurement and statistics*, 3.

Piush Aggarwal, Tobias Horsmann, Michael Wojatzki, and Torsten Zesch. 2019. LTL-UDE at SemEval-2019 task 6: BERT and two-vote classification for categorizing offensiveness. In *Proceedings of the 13th International Workshop on Semantic Evaluation*, pages 678–682, Minneapolis, Minnesota, USA. Association for Computational Linguistics.

Betty van Aken, Benjamin Winter, Alexander Löser, and Felix A. Gers. 2020. Visbert: Hidden-state visualizations for transformers.

Md Rabiul Awal, Rui Cao, Roy Ka-Wei Lee, and Sandra Mitrovic. 2021. Angrybert: Joint learning target and emotion for hate speech detection.

Valerio Basile, Cristina Bosco, Elisabetta Fersini, Nozza Debora, Viviana Patti, Francisco Manuel Rangel Pardo, Paolo Rosso, and Manuela Sanguinetti. 2019. Semeval-2019 task 5: Multilingual detection of hate speech against immigrants and women in twitter. In *13th International Workshop on Semantic Evaluation*, pages 54–63.

Darina Benikova, Michael Wojatzki, and Torsten Zesch. 2017. What does this imply? Examining the Impact of Implicitness on the Perception of Hate Speech. In *Proceedings of the International Conference of the German Society for Computational Linguistics and Language Technology*, pages 171 – 179, Berlin, Germany.

Philipp Blandfort, Desmond Patton, William R. Frey, Svebor Karaman, Surabhi Bhargava, Fei-Tzin Lee, Siddharth Varia, Chris Kedzie, Michael B. Gaskell, Rossano Schifanella, Kathleen McKeown, and Shih-Fu Chang. 2018. Multimodal social media analysis for gang violence prevention.

Albert H. Bowker. 1948. A test for symmetry in contingency tables. *Journal of the American Statistical Association*, 43(244):572–574. PMID: 18123073.

P. Burnap and M. Williams. 2014. Hate speech, machine classification and statistical modelling of information flows on twitter: interpretation and communication for policy decision making.

Kai Chen, Jiaqi Wang, Jiangmiao Pang, Yuhang Cao, Yu Xiong, Xiaoxiao Li, Shuyang Sun, Wansen Feng, Ziwei Liu, Jiarui Xu, Zheng Zhang, Dazhi Cheng, Chenchen Zhu, Tianheng Cheng, Qijie Zhao, Buyu Li, Xin Lu, Rui Zhu, Yue Wu, Jifeng Dai, Jingdong Wang, Jianping Shi, Wanli Ouyang, Chen Change Loy, and Dahua Lin. 2019. MMDetection: Open mmlab detection toolbox and benchmark. *arXiv preprint arXiv:1906.07155*.

Yen-Chun Chen, Linjie Li, Licheng Yu, Ahmed El Kholy, Faisal Ahmed, Zhe Gan, Yu Cheng, and Jingjing Liu. 2020. Uniter: Universal image-text representation learning.

MMEditing Contributors. 2020. Openmmlab editing estimation toolbox and benchmark. https://github.com/open-mmlab/mmediting.

Jacob Devlin, Ming-Wei Chang, Kenton Lee, and Kristina Toutanova. 2019. Bert: Pre-training of deep bidirectional transformers for language understanding.

Paul Ekman. 1992. Are there basic emotions? *Psychological Review*, 99(3):550–553.

Raul Gomez, Jaume Gibert, Lluis Gomez, and Dimosthenis Karatzas. 2019. Exploring hate speech detection in multimodal publications.

Kaiming He, Xiangyu Zhang, Shaoqing Ren, and Jian Sun. 2015. Deep residual learning for image recognition.

Alexander B. Jung, Kentaro Wada, Jon Crall, Satoshi Tanaka, Jake Graving, Christoph Reinders, Sarthak Yadav, Joy Banerjee, Gábor Vecsei, Adam Kraft, Zheng Rui, Jirka Borovec, Christian Vallentin, Semen Zhydenko, Kilian Pfeiffer, Ben Cook, Ismael Fernández, François-Michel De Rainville, Chi-Hung Weng, Abner Ayala-Acevedo, Raphael Meudec, Matias Laporte, et al. 2020. imgaug. https://github.com/aleju/imgaug. Online; accessed 01-Feb-2020.

Kimmo Karkkainen and Jungseock Joo. 2021. Fairface: Face attribute dataset for balanced race, gender, and age for bias measurement and mitigation. In *Proceedings of the IEEE/CVF Winter Conference on Applications of Computer Vision*, pages 1548–1558.

Douwe Kiela, Hamed Firooz, Aravind Mohan, Vedanuj Goswami, Amanpreet Singh, Pratik Ringshia, and Davide Testuggine. 2020. The hateful memes challenge: Detecting hate speech in multimodal memes. In *Advances in Neural Information Processing Systems*, volume 33, pages 2611–2624, Virtual. Curran Associates, Inc.

Ritesh Kumar, Atul Kr. Ojha, Shervin Malmasi, and Marcos Zampieri. 2018. Benchmarking Aggression Identification in Social Media. In *Proceedings of the First Workshop on Trolling, Aggression and Cyberbullying (TRAC-2018)*, pages 1–11. Association for Computational Linguistics.

Liunian Harold Li, Mark Yatskar, Da Yin, Cho-Jui Hsieh, and Kai-Wei Chang. 2019. Visualbert: A simple and performant baseline for vision and language.

Xiujun Li, Xi Yin, Chunyuan Li, Pengchuan Zhang, Xiaowei Hu, Lei Zhang, Lijuan Wang, Houdong Hu, Li Dong, Furu Wei, Yejin Choi, and Jianfeng Gao. 2020. Oscar: Object-semantics aligned pre-training for vision-language tasks.

Phillip Lippe, Nithin Holla, Shantanu Chandra, Santhosh Rajamanickam, Georgios Antoniou, Ekaterina Shutova, and Helen Yannakoudakis. 2020. A multimodal framework for the detection of hateful memes.

Kuan Liu, Yanen Li, Ning Xu, and Prem Natarajan. 2018. Learn to combine modalities in multimodal deep learning.

Edward Ma. 2019. Nlp augmentation. https://github.com/makcedward/nlpaug.

Ricardo Martins, Marco Gomes, João Almeida, Paulo Novais, and Pedro Henriques. 2018. Hate speech classification in social media using emotional analysis. pages 61–66.

Chikashi Nobata, Joel Tetreault, Achint Thomas, Yashar Mehdad, and Yi Chang. 2016. Abusive Language Detection in Online User Content. In *Proceedings of the 25th International Conference on World Wide Web*, WWW '16, pages 145–153, Republic and Canton of Geneva, Switzerland. International World Wide Web Conferences Steering Committee.

Shaoqing Ren, Kaiming He, Ross Girshick, and Jian Sun. 2016. Faster r-cnn: Towards real-time object detection with region proposal networks.

Benet Oriol Sabat, Cristian Canton Ferrer, and Xavier Giro i Nieto. 2019. Hate speech in pixels: Detection of offensive memes towards automatic moderation.

Piyush Sharma, Nan Ding, Sebastian Goodman, and Radu Soricut. 2018. Conceptual captions: A cleaned, hypernymed, image alt-text dataset for automatic image captioning. In *Proceedings of the 56th Annual Meeting of the Association for Computational Linguistics (Volume 1: Long Papers)*, pages 2556–2565, Melbourne, Australia. Association for Computational Linguistics.

Karen Simonyan and Andrew Zisserman. 2015. Very deep convolutional networks for large-scale image recognition.

R. Smith. 2007. An overview of the tesseract ocr engine. In *Ninth International Conference on Document Analysis and Recognition (ICDAR 2007)*, volume 2, pages 629–633.

Weijie Su, Xizhou Zhu, Yue Cao, Bin Li, Lewei Lu, Furu Wei, and Jifeng Dai. 2020. Vl-bert: Pre-training of generic visual-linguistic representations.

Christian Szegedy, Vincent Vanhoucke, Sergey Ioffe, Jonathon Shlens, and Zbigniew Wojna. 2015. Rethinking the inception architecture for computer vision.

Ashish Vaswani, Noam Shazeer, Niki Parmar, Jakob Uszkoreit, Llion Jones, Aidan N. Gomez, Lukasz Kaiser, and Illia Polosukhin. 2017. Attention is all you need.

Bertie Vidgen, Alex Harris, Dong Nguyen, Rebekah Tromble, Scott Hale, and Helen Margetts. 2019. Challenges and frontiers in abusive content detection. In *Proceedings of the Third Workshop on Abusive Language Online*, pages 80–93, Florence, Italy. Association for Computational Linguistics.

Zeerak Waseem, Thomas Davidson, Dana Warmsley, and Ingmar Weber. 2017. Understanding Abuse: A Typology of Abusive Language Detection Subtasks. In *Proceedings of the First Workshop on Abusive Language Online*, pages 78–84. Association for Computational Linguistics.

Michael Wiegand, Melanie Siegel, and Josef Ruppenhofer. 2018. Overview of the GermEval 2018 Shared Task on the Identification of Offensive Language.

Fei Yu, Jiji Tang, Weichong Yin, Yu Sun, Hao Tian, Hua Wu, and Haifeng Wang. 2021. Ernie-vil: Knowledge enhanced vision-language representations through scene graph.

Ron Zhu. 2020. Enhance multimodal transformer with external label and in-domain pretrain: Hateful meme challenge winning solution.

Yukun Zhu, Ryan Kiros, Richard Zemel, Ruslan Salakhutdinov, Raquel Urtasun, Antonio Torralba, and Sanja Fidler. 2015. Aligning books and movies: Towards story-like visual explanations by watching movies and reading books.

Racist or Sexist Meme? Classifying Memes beyond Hateful

Haris Bin Zia
Queen Mary
University of London
United Kingdom
h.b.zia@qmul.ac.uk

Ignacio Castro
Queen Mary
University of London
United Kingdom
i.castro@qmul.ac.uk

Gareth Tyson
Queen Mary
University of London
United Kingdom
g.tyson@qmul.ac.uk

Abstract

Memes are the combinations of text and images that are often humorous in nature. But, that may not always be the case, and certain combinations of texts and images may depict hate, referred to as *hateful memes*. This work presents a multimodal pipeline that takes both visual and textual features from memes into account to (1) identify the protected category (e.g. race, sex etc.) that has been attacked; and (2) detect the type of attack (e.g. contempt, slurs etc.). Our pipeline uses state-of-the-art pre-trained visual and textual representations, followed by a simple logistic regression classifier. We employ our pipeline on the Hateful Memes Challenge dataset with additional newly created fine-grained labels for protected category and type of attack. Our best model achieves an AUROC of 0.96 for identifying the protected category, and 0.97 for detecting the type of attack. We release our code at https://github.com/harisbinzia/HatefulMemes

1 Introduction

An internet meme (or simply "meme" for the remainder of this paper) is a virally transmitted image embellished with text. It usually shares pointed commentary on cultural symbols, social ideas, or current events (Gil, 2020). In the past few years there has been a surge in the popularity of memes on social media platforms. Instagram, which is a popular photo and video sharing social networking service recently revealed that over 1 million posts mentioning "meme" are shared on Instagram each day.[1] We warn the reader that this paper contains content that is racist, sexist and offensive in several ways.

Although memes are often funny and used mostly for humorous purposes, recent research suggests that they can also be used to disseminate hate (Zannettou et al., 2018) and can therefore emerge as a multimodal expression of online hate speech. Hateful memes target certain groups or individuals based on their race (Williams et al., 2016) and gender (Drakett et al., 2018), among many other protected categories, thus causing harm at both an individual and societal level. An example hateful meme is shown in Figure 1.

Figure 1: An example of a hateful meme. The meme is targeted towards a certain religious group.

At the scale of the internet, it is impossible to manually inspect every meme. Hence, we posit that it is important to develop (semi-)automated systems that can detect hateful memes. However, detecting hate in multimodal forms (such as memes) is extremely challenging and requires a holistic understanding of the visual and textual material. In order to accelerate research in this area and develop systems capable of detecting hateful memes, Facebook recently launched The Hateful Memes Challenge (Kiela et al., 2020). The challenge introduced a new annotated dataset of around 10K memes tagged for hatefulness (i.e. hateful vs. not-hateful). The baseline results show a substantial dif-

[1] https://about.instagram.com/blog/announcements/instagram-year-in-review-how-memes-were-the-mood-of-2020

Proceedings of the Fifth Workshop on Online Abuse and Harms, pages 215–219
August 6, 2021.

ference in the performance of unimodal and multimodal systems, where the latter still perform poorly compared to human performance, illustrating the difficulty of the problem.

More recently, a shared task on hateful memes was organized at the Workshop on Online Abuse and Harms[2] (WOAH), where the hateful memes dataset (Kiela et al., 2020) was presented with additional newly created fine-grained labels[3] for the protected category that has been attacked (e.g. race, sex, etc.), as well as the type of attack (e.g. contempt, slurs, etc.). This paper presents our multimodal pipeline based on pre-trained visual and textual representations for the shared task on hateful memes at WOAH. We make our code publicly available to facilitate further research.[4]

2 Problem Statement

There are two tasks with details as follows:

- *Task A*: For each meme, detect the Protected Category (PC). Protected categories are: race, disability, religion, nationality, sex. If the meme is not-hateful, the protected category is: pc_empty

- *Task B*: For each meme, detect the Attack Type (AT). Attack types are: contempt, mocking, inferiority, slurs, exclusion, dehumanizing, inciting violence. If the meme is not-hateful, the protected category is: attack_empty

Note, Tasks A and B are multi-label because memes can contain attacks against multiple protected categories and can involve multiple attack types.

3 Dataset

The dataset consists of 9,540 fine-grained annotated memes and is imbalanced, with large number of non-hateful memes and relatively small number of hateful ones. The details of different splits[5] are given in the Table 1 and the distribution of classes are given in Table 2. The majority of memes in the dataset are single-labeled. Figure 2 and Figure 3 present the distribution of memes with multiple protected categories and types of attacks respectively. For the evaluation, we use the standard AUROC metric.

	# memes		
split	**hateful**	**not-hateful**	***total***
train	3007	5493	8500
dev (seen)	246	254	500
dev (unseen)	199	341	540

Table 1: Dataset statistics.

	classes	train	dev (seen)	dev (unseen)
PC	pc_empty	5495	254	341
	religion	1078	95	77
	race	1008	78	63
	sex	746	56	46
	nationality	325	26	20
	disability	255	22	17
AT	attack_empty	5532	257	344
	mocking	378	35	29
	dehumanizing	1318	121	104
	slurs	205	6	4
	inciting violence	407	26	23
	contempt	235	10	6
	inferiority	658	49	35
	exclusion	114	13	8

Table 2: Distribution of classes in splits.

4 Model & Results

This section describes our model, the visual & textual embeddings, as well as the results.

4.1 Embeddings

We use the following state-of-the-art pre-trained visual and textual representations:

- CLIP[6]: OpenAI's CLIP (Contrastive Language Image Pre-Training) (Radford et al., 2021) is a neural network that jointly trains an image encoder and a text encoder to predict the correct pairings of a batch of (image, text) examples. We use pre-trained CLIP image encoder (hereinafter CIMG) and CLIP text

[2]https://www.workshoponlineabuse.com

[3]https://github.com/facebookresearch/fine_grained_hateful_memes

[4]https://github.com/harisbinzia/HatefulMemes

[5]Note, at the time of writing, the gold annotations were available only for train, dev (seen) and dev (unseen) sets. We used train for training, dev (seen) for hyperparameter tuning and dev (unseen) to report results. We also report the results on a blind test set as released by the organizers of WOAH.

[6]https://github.com/OpenAI/CLIP

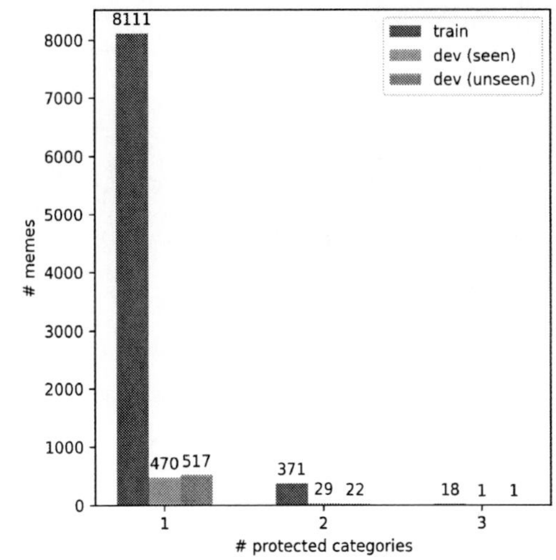

Figure 2: Count of memes with multiple protected categories.

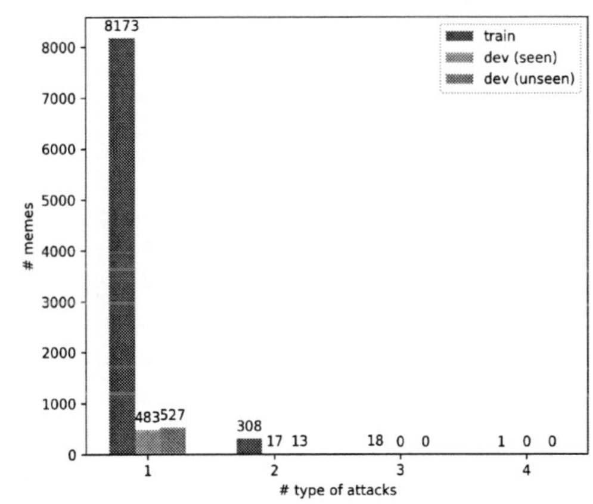

Figure 3: Count of memes with multiple attack types.

encoder (hereinafter CTXT) to embed meme images and text respectively.

- LASER[7]: Facebook's LASER (Language Agnostic SEntence Representations) (Artetxe and Schwenk, 2019) is a BiLSTM based seq2seq model that maps a sentence in any language to a point in a high-dimensional space with the goal that the same statement in any language will end up in the same neighborhood. We use LASER encoder to obtain embeddings for the meme text.

- LaBSE: Google's LaBSE (Language agnostic BERT Sentence Embedding) (Feng et al., 2020) is a Transformer (BERT) based embedding model that produces language-agnostic cross-lingual sentence embeddings. We use the LaBSE model to embed meme text.

4.2 Pipeline

Exploiting the above models, we employ a simple four step pipeline as shown in Figure 4:

1. We extract text from the meme.
2. We embed the meme image and the text into visual and textual representations (Section 4.1).
3. We concatenate the visual and textual embeddings.
4. We train a multi-label Logistic Regression classifier using scikit-learn (Pedregosa et al., 2011) to predict the protected category attacked in the meme (Task A) and the type of attack (Task B).

4.3 Results

The results are shown in Table 3, where we contrast various configurations of our classifier. We observe that the vision-only classifier, which only uses visual embeddings (CIMG), performs slightly better than the text-only classifier, which only uses textual embeddings (CTXT, LASER or LaBSE). The multimodal models outperform their unimodal counterparts. Our best performing model is multimodal, trained on the concatenated textual (CTXT, LASER and LaBSE) and visual (CIMG) embeddings.[8] Class-wise performance of best model is given in Table 4.

5 Conclusion & Future Work

This paper has presented our pipeline for the multilabel hateful memes classification shared task organized at WOAH. We show that our multimodal classifiers outperform unimodal classifiers. Our best multimodal classifier achieves an AUROC of 0.96 for identifying the protected category, and 0.97 for detecting the attack type. Although we trained our classifier on language agnostic representations, it was only tested on a dataset of English memes. As a future direction, we plan to extend our work

[7] `https://github.com/facebookresearch/LASER`

[8] On a blind test set of 1000 memes our best model achieves an AUROC of 0.90 for Task A and 0.91 for Task B

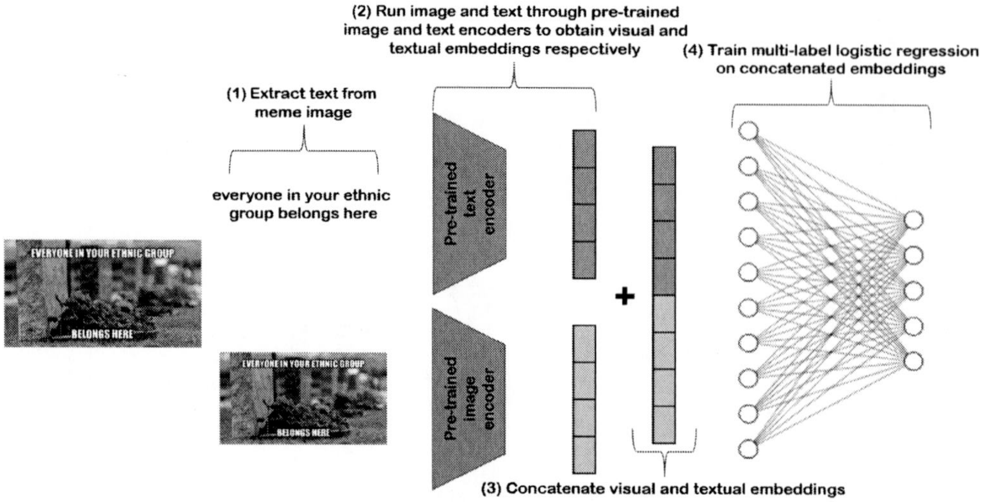

Figure 4: Multimodal pipeline for multi-label meme classification.

		AUROC	
Type	**Embedding**	**Task A**	**Task B**
Unimodal	CTXT	0.56	0.67
	LASER	0.88	0.91
	LaBSE	0.89	0.92
	CIMG	0.93	0.94
Multimodal	CIMG + CTXT	0.95	0.96
	CIMG + LASER	0.94	0.95
	CIMG + LaBSE	0.94	0.95
	CIMG + CTXT + LASER + LaBSE	**0.96**	**0.97**

Table 3: Model performance.

	classes	Precision	Recall	F1
PC	pc_empty	0.74	0.82	0.78
	religion	0.78	0.61	0.69
	race	0.57	0.49	0.53
	sex	0.85	0.61	0.71
	nationality	0.65	0.75	0.70
	disability	0.94	0.88	0.91
AT	attack_empty	0.74	0.82	0.78
	mocking	0.77	0.79	0.78
	dehumanizing	0.68	0.44	0.53
	slurs	0.80	1.00	0.89
	inciting violence	0.67	0.61	0.64
	contempt	1.00	0.33	0.50
	inferiority	0.73	0.31	0.44
	exclusion	1.00	1.00	1.00

Table 4: Class-wise performance of best model.

to multilingual settings, where we evaluate the performance of our classifier on multilingual memes.

References

Mikel Artetxe and Holger Schwenk. 2019. Massively multilingual sentence embeddings for zero-shot cross-lingual transfer and beyond. *Transactions of the Association for Computational Linguistics*, 7:597–610.

Jessica Drakett, Bridgette Rickett, Katy Day, and Kate Milnes. 2018. Old jokes, new media–online sexism and constructions of gender in internet memes. *Feminism & Psychology*, 28(1):109–127.

Fangxiaoyu Feng, Yinfei Yang, Daniel Cer, Naveen Arivazhagan, and Wei Wang. 2020. Language-agnostic bert sentence embedding. *arXiv preprint arXiv:2007.01852*.

Paul Gil. 2020. Examples of memes and how to use them.

Douwe Kiela, Hamed Firooz, Aravind Mohan, Vedanuj Goswami, Amanpreet Singh, Pratik Ringshia, and Davide Testuggine. 2020. The hateful memes challenge: Detecting hate speech in multimodal memes. *arXiv preprint arXiv:2005.04790*.

F. Pedregosa, G. Varoquaux, A. Gramfort, V. Michel, B. Thirion, O. Grisel, M. Blondel, P. Prettenhofer, R. Weiss, V. Dubourg, J. Vanderplas, A. Passos,

D. Cournapeau, M. Brucher, M. Perrot, and E. Duchesnay. 2011. Scikit-learn: Machine learning in Python. *Journal of Machine Learning Research*, 12:2825–2830.

Alec Radford, Jong Wook Kim, Chris Hallacy, Aditya Ramesh, Gabriel Goh, Sandhini Agarwal, Girish Sastry, Amanda Askell, Pamela Mishkin, Jack Clark, et al. 2021. Learning transferable visual models from natural language supervision. *arXiv preprint arXiv:2103.00020*.

Amanda Williams, Clio Oliver, Katherine Aumer, and Chanel Meyers. 2016. Racial microaggressions and perceptions of internet memes. *Computers in Human Behavior*, 63:424–432.

Savvas Zannettou, Tristan Caulfield, Jeremy Blackburn, Emiliano De Cristofaro, Michael Sirivianos, Gianluca Stringhini, and Guillermo Suarez-Tangil. 2018. On the origins of memes by means of fringe web communities. In *Proceedings of the Internet Measurement Conference 2018*, pages 188–202.

Multimodal or Text? Retrieval or BERT? Benchmarking Classifiers for the Shared Task on Hateful Memes

Vasiliki Kougia
Stockholm University
vasiliki.kougia@dsv.su.se

John Pavlopoulos
Stockholm University
ioannis@dsv.su.se

Abstract

The Shared Task on Hateful Memes is a challenge that aims at the detection of hateful content in memes by inviting the implementation of systems that understand memes, potentially by combining image and textual information. The challenge consists of three detection tasks: hate, protected category and attack type. The first is a binary classification task, while the other two are multi-label classification tasks. Our participation included a text-based BERT baseline (TxtBERT), the same but adding information from the image (ImgBERT), and neural retrieval approaches. We also experimented with retrieval augmented classification models. We found that an ensemble of TxtBERT and ImgBERT achieves the best performance in terms of ROC AUC score in two out of the three tasks on our development set.

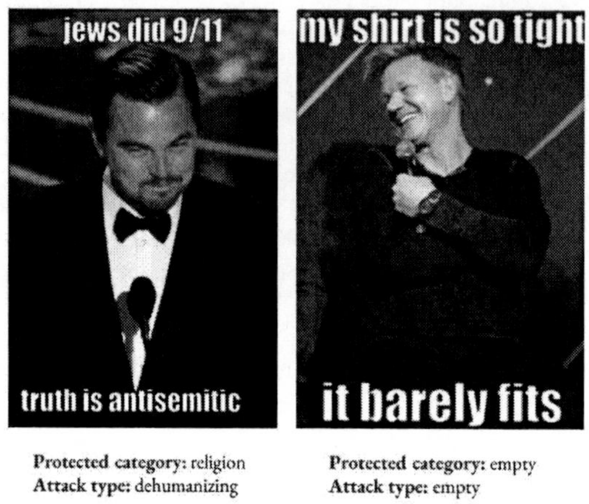

Figure 1: An example of a hateful (left) and a not hateful (right) meme. ©Getty Images

1 Introduction

Multimodal classification is an important research topic that attracts a lot of interest, especially when combining image and text (Li et al., 2019; Lu et al., 2019; Chen et al., 2020; Gan et al., 2020; Su et al., 2019; Yu et al., 2020; Li et al., 2020). Humans understand the world and make decisions, by using many different sources. Hence, it is reasonable to infer that Artificial Intelligence (AI) methods can also benefit by combining different types of data as their input (Gomez et al., 2020; Vijayaraghavan et al., 2019). The Hateful Memes Challenge and dataset were first introduced by Facebook AI in 2020 (Kiela et al., 2020). The goal was to assess multimodal (image and text) hate detection models. The dataset was created in a way such that models operating only on the text or only on the image would not have a good performance, giving focus to multimodality (see Section 2). The winning system used an ensemble of different vision and language transformer models, which was further enhanced with information from input objects detected in the image and their labels (Zhu, 2020). The Hateful Memes shared task extends this competition by adding fine-grained labels for two multi-label tasks (see Fig. 1). The first task is to predict the protected category and the second to predict the attack type.

2 Dataset

The provided dataset comprises images and text. First, Kiela et al. (2020) collected real memes from social media, which they called source set and then, used them to create new memes. For each meme in the source set, the annotators searched for images that had similar semantic context with the image of the meme and replaced the image of the meme with the retrieved images.[1] The newly developed memes were then annotated as hateful or not by the annotators. For the hateful memes, counterfactual examples were created and added to the dataset

[1]The similar images come from Getty Images (https://www.gettyimages.com/).

Proceedings of the Fifth Workshop on Online Abuse and Harms, pages 220–225
August 6, 2021. ©2021 Association for Computational Linguistics

by replacing the image or the text. Following this process a dataset of 10,000 memes was created.

For the Shared Task on Hateful Memes at WOAH 2021, the same dataset was used, but with additional labels. New fine-grained labels were created for two categories: protected category and attack type. Protected category indicates the group of people that is attacked in a hateful meme and consists of five labels: race, disability, religion, nationality and sex. The attack type refers to the way that hate is expressed and consists of seven labels: contempt, mocking, inferiority, slurs, exclusion, dehumanizing, inciting violence . If a meme is not hateful, then the pc_empty label is assigned for the protected category task and the attack_empty label for the attack type task. A meme can have one or more labels, leading to a multi-label classification setting.

Participants of the shared task were provided with a training set comprising 8,500 image-text pairs and two development datasets with 500 and 540 image-text pairs. In our work, we merged these sets and split the total of 9,140 unique pairs to 80% for training, 10 % for validation and 10 % as a development set. The unseen test set for which we submitted our models' predictions consisted of 1,000 examples. The dataset was imbalanced, with approximately 64% of the memes being not hateful.

3 Methods

The methods we implemented for this challenge comprise image and text retrieval, BERT-based text (and image) and retrieval-augmented classification (RAC). The following subsections describe the implemented methods.

3.1 Retrieval

Multimodal Nearest Neighbour (MNN) employs image and text retrieval. In specific, for an unseen test meme, MNN retrieves the most similar instance from a knowledge base (here, the training dataset) and assigns its labels to the unseen meme.

We used two MNN variants, which differed in the way they encode the text. For the encoding of images, each variant used a DenseNet-121 Convolutional Neural Network (CNN), pre-trained on ImageNet (Deng et al., 2009). Each CNN was fine-tuned for the corresponding task independently on our data. For the encoding of text, the first variant uses the centroid of Fasttext word embeddings for English pre-trained on Common Crawl (Grave et al., 2018) (MNN:base).[2] The second variant employs three BERT models, each fine-tuned on one of our tasks (see subsection 3.2), from which we extracted the CLS tokens as the representation of memes' texts (MNN:BERT).

The similarity between the query embeddings (both, image and text) and the knowledge base is computed using the cosine similarity function. During inference, given a test meme, we find the most similar training image to the meme image and the most similar training text to the meme text. Then, we retrieve the labels of these two retrieved training examples. If a label appears in both examples, it is assigned a probability of 1. If it appears in only one example it is assigned the cosine similarity of that example. The rest of the labels, are assigned a zero probability.

3.2 BERT-based

For this method we also tried two text and one multimodal approach. The first text-based approach (TxtBERT) takes as input only the text of the meme. The second, dubbed CaptionBERT, takes as input the meme text and the image caption, separated with the [SEP] pseudo token. We employed BERT base for both and fine-tuned it on our data (one for each task). The image captions were generated by the Show and Tell model (S&T) (Vinyals et al., 2015), which was trained on MS COCO (Lin et al., 2014). In both approaches we extract the [CLS] pseudo-token and feed it to a linear layer that acts as our classifier.

The multimodal approach (ImgBERT) combines TxtBERT above with image embeddings, which are extracted by the same CNN encoder that was used for MNN (see subsection 3.1). We concatenate each image embedding with the BERT representation of the [CLS] pseudo token and feed the resulting vector to the classifier.

The outputs of the classifier correspond to the labels for the multilabel classification tasks and each output is passed through a sigmoid function, in order to obtain one probability for each label. In the binary classification task the output is one probability, where 1 means the text is hateful and 0 means it is not. The BERT-based models are trained using binary cross entropy loss and the Adam optimizer with learning rate 2e-5. Early stopping is applied

[2] https://fasttext.cc/docs/en/crawl-vectors.html

during training with patience of three epochs.

3.3 RAC-based

Inspired by retrieval-augmented generation (RAG) (Lewis et al., 2020), we experimented with Retrieval Augmented Classification (RAC), in order to expand the knowledge of our BERT-based models and improve their performance. To do that we combined TxtBERT and ImgBERT with MNN retrieval and call the two new methods TxtRAC and Txt+Img RAC respectively. The most similar text obtained by MNN:BERT is concatenated to the text of the meme, separated with the [SEP] pseudo-token, and it is passed to TxtBERT (in TxtRAC) and ImgBERT (in Txt+Img RAC). The training setup is the same as the one in the BERT-based models described above (see Section 3.2).

3.4 Ensemble

An ensemble was created combining visual and textual information, based on ImgBERT and TxtBERT. For each label of each task, the ensemble averages the two scores, one per system.

4 Experimental Results

The official evaluation measure of the shared task is the ROC AUC score. Hence, we provided the output probability distribution over the labels of each task from a model in order to evaluate it. The classifiers of our models did not output a probability for the corresponding empty label (meaning that the meme is not hateful) of each task. In order to assign a probability to the not hateful label of the binary classification task we compute 1 - hateful probability. To the pc_empty and attack_empty labels of the corresponding task, we assign the probability of 1 - maximum probability of the other labels. The provided evaluation script computes the ROC AUC score micro averaged and with the one-vs-rest method. It also computes the micro F1 score by applying a threshold (0.5) to the predicted probabilities.

Each team participating in the Shared Task on Hateful Memes could submit predictions from two systems on the unseen test set. We chose to submit the TxtBERT and the ensemble of TxtBERT and ImgBERT.[3] In Table 4 we present the results on the hidden test set. The organizers provided us

Model	F1	AUC
TxtBERT	0.755	0.821
CaptionBERT	0.724	0.780
MNN:base	0.674	0.617
MNN:BERT	0.704	0.663
ImgBERT	0.689	0.755
TxtRAC	0.702	0.799
Txt+Img RAC	0.712	0.796
Ensemble	**0.765**	**0.863**

Table 1: Micro F1 and ROC AUC scores of our models for the binary classification "hateful or not" task. In this task the ensemble of TxtBERT and ImgBERT outperforms all other methods.

Model	F1	AUC
TxtBERT	**0.729**	**0.931**
CaptionBERT	0.724	0.920
MNN:base	0.566	0.783
MNN:BERT	0.578	0.794
ImgBERT	0.640	0.818
TxtRAC	0.717	0.927
Txt+Img RAC	0.640	0.840
Ensemble	0.694	0.920

Table 2: Micro F1 and ROC AUC scores of our models for the protected category task. TxtBERT is the best performing model in this task.

Model	F1	AUC
TxtBERT	**0.681**	0.929
CaptionBERT	0.656	0.914
MNN:base	0.559	0.798
MNN:BERT	0.600	0.825
ImgBERT	0.666	0.928
TxtRAC	0.665	0.925
Txt+Img RAC	0.662	0.928
Ensemble	0.670	**0.932**

Table 3: Micro F1 and ROC AUC scores of our models for the attack type task. The ensemble achieves the best AUC and TxtBERT the best F1 score.

the ROC AUC scores for the protected category and the attack type tasks. Since we do not have the gold labels of the test set in order to evaluate all the models we implemented, we report their results on the development set we created. Table 1 presents the evaluation scores for the hate task on our development set, Table 3 for the attack type task, and Table 1 for the protected category task. Moreover, in Tables 5 and 6 we report the F1 and ROC AUC scores for each label of the protected category and attack type tasks respectively.

[3]The code for our two submitted models is available at: https://github.com/vasilikikou/hateful_memes

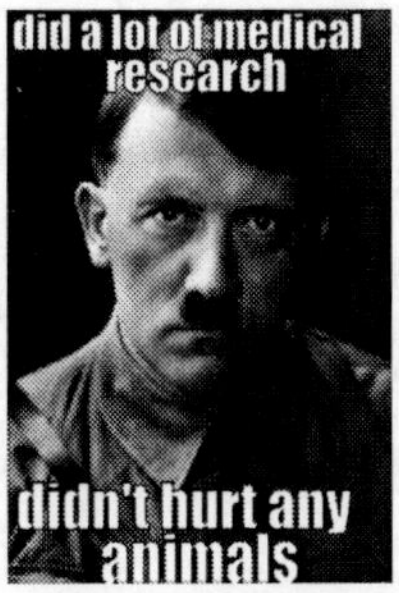

(a) 'hateful', 'religion', 'mocking'

(b) 'hateful', 'religion', 'dehumanizing'

(c) 'hateful', 'religion;nationality', 'exclusion'

(d) 'hateful', 'nationality', 'dehumanizing

Figure 2: The two memes on top (a, b) were better classified by ImgBERT while the two memes below (c, d) by TxtBERT. Ground truth in captions. ©Getty Images

Model	Protected category	Attack type
TxtBERT	**0.876**	0.881
Ensemble	0.865	**0.890**

Table 4: ROC AUC scores of our two submissions for the protected category and attack type tasks as provided by the organizers.

5 Discussion

MNN:BERT outperforms MNN:base in all three tasks. This is probably due to the fact that a simple centroid of word embedding ignores word order, by contrast to a BERT-based representation, which also encodes the position of the word. Interestingly, CaptionBERT outperformed ImgBERT both in hate and protected category detection. This means that integrating the automatically generated caption of the image, instead of the image itself, was beneficial for two out of three tasks. In attack type detection, however, this didn't apply. We also observe that employing the most similar text in the TxtBERT model (TxtRAC), leads to a worse performance, showing that the retrieved text does not help the text classification model as expected. This probably occurs due to the diversity of the texts in the dataset. However, TxtRAC outperforms CaptionBERT in all tasks in terms of ROC AUC, maybe because generated captions from S&T, which is only trained on MS COCO can contain errors.

The ensemble model, that averages the predictions of TxtBERT and ImgBERT, outperformed the rest of the models, in ROC AUC, for hate and attack type detection. However, we note that for a fair comparison we should have created also checkpoint-based ensembles per model. That is, we can't be certain whether the superior performance of the ensemble stems from the combination of textual and visual information or from the reduction of the variance of the models that are used by the ensemble.

In the ROC AUC scores for the hidden test set (see Table 4), we observe similar performance of the models as in the development set. In particular, TxtBERT achieves the best score for the protected category task, while the Ensemble is the best for the the attack type task.

For the two multilabel tasks we also evaluated our models per label in order to obtain a better understanding of their performance. We observe that even though the dataset is imbalanced containing more not hateful memes, the scores of the models for the empty label are lower than the ones for the other labels in both tasks. This means that the models do not achieve a very high performance on the empty label as expected. Also, we see that there

Model	empty		religion		sex		race		disability		nationality	
	F1	AUC	F1	AUC	F1	AUC	F1	AUC	F1	AUC	F1	AUC
TxtBERT	0.808	0.776	0.609	**0.875**	**0.663**	**0.913**	**0.595**	0.873	**0.400**	**0.843**	**0.351**	0.912
CaptionBERT	**0.824**	0.746	0.406	0.869	0.634	0.909	0.479	0.854	0.158	0.765	0.061	0.895
MNN:base	0.767	0.530	0.354	0.678	0.313	0.649	0.224	0.566	0.244	0.635	0.138	0.564
MNN:BERT	0.787	0.590	0.348	0.663	0.282	0.624	0.234	0.574	0.217	0.608	0.096	0.536
ImgBERT	0.789	0.414	0.000	0.661	0.000	0.609	0.000	0.385	0.000	0.632	0.000	0.544
TxtRAC	0.803	**0.794**	**0.631**	0.871	0.630	0.907	0.610	**0.879**	0.000	0.773	0.154	0.859
Txt+Img RAC	0.789	0.606	0.000	0.633	0.000	0.670	0.000	0.573	0.000	0.723	0.000	0.573
Ensemble	0.821	0.759	0.107	0.858	0.422	0.890	0.380	0.838	0.000	0.837	0.000	**0.927**

Table 5: F1 and ROC AUC scores per label for the protected category task. There are five labels for this task and the empty label for not hateful memes.

Model	empty		mock.		deh.		viol.		cont.		excl.		inf.		slurs	
	F1	AUC	F1	AUC	F1	AUC	F1	AUC	F1	AUC	F1	AUC	F1	AUC	F1	AUC
TxtBERT	**0.811**	**0.778**	**0.491**	0.870	0.416	0.814	0.000	0.815	0.000	0.926	0.000	0.678	**0.354**	0.756	0.829	**0.986**
CaptionBERT	0.804	0.708	0.449	**0.883**	0.242	0.779	0.000	0.774	0.000	0.848	0.000	0.645	0.200	0.695	0.087	0.949
MNN:base	0.770	0.521	0.303	0.703	0.295	0.578	0.172	0.577	0.237	0.661	0.111	0.552	0.265	0.628	0.277	0.695
MNN:BERT	0.793	0.571	0.326	0.707	0.332	0.600	**0.220**	0.609	**0.351**	0.741	**0.114**	0.552	0.283	0.635	0.557	0.886
ImgBERT	0.791	0.750	0.444	0.841	0.427	0.803	0.207	0.852	0.000	0.931	0.000	**0.724**	0.350	0.747	0.837	0.971
TxtRAC	0.797	0.775	0.444	0.873	0.403	0.799	0.000	0.816	0.000	0.817	0.000	0.661	0.148	0.751	0.821	0.972
Txt+Img RAC	0.795	0.773	0.440	0.859	**0.457**	0.813	0.000	**0.858**	0.000	0.841	0.000	0.675	0.304	**0.760**	0.829	0.984
Ensemble	0.801	0.774	0.436	0.863	0.398	**0.820**	0.115	0.841	0.000	**0.933**	0.000	0.704	0.336	0.756	**0.857**	0.980

Table 6: F1 and ROC AUC scores per label for the attack type task. The labels for this task are seven: mocking (mock.), dehumanizing (deh.), inciting_violence (viol.), contempt (cont.), exlusion (excl.), inferiority (inf.), slurs and the emply label.

is not a clear winner, since for each label different models can have the best score. Besides TxtBERT and Ensemble, which have the best performance in the micro averaging setting, we see that other models can be better on specific labels. In particular, in the protected category task TxtRAC achieves the best ROC AUC score for the empty and race labels, showing that RAC can benefit these two categories. Interestingly, in the attack type task, retrieval also works well for the inciting_violence and inferiority labels, where Txt+Img RAC has the best ROC AUC score. CaptionBERT and ImgBERT have the best scores for the mocking label and the eclusion label respectively.

Error analysis

TxtBERT outperforms ImgBERT in all three tasks. In order to explain this observation in a meaningful way we compare the ROC AUC scores of several cases from the development set and see in which the image helped the classifier. We studied this for the hateful memes in our development set and saw that ImgBERT outperformed TxtBERT in only 8% of these memes. In Figure 2 we see two memes that ImgBERT predicted with a score closer to the ground truth than TxtBERT (above) and two memes that TxtBERT was closer to the ground truth (below). Indeed for the top two memes (a, b) we observe that the text on its own is not hateful, but when combined with the image a hateful meme is resulted. The third meme (c) has a text that contain slurs, which probably makes it easier for BERT to predict that it is hateful, while the image on its own is not. In the fourth meme (d), it is not clear that the text is hateful, but still TxtBERT is better in detecting this.

6 Conclusions

We participated in the Shared Task on Hateful Memes with the aim of detecting memes with hateful content, as well as the protected categories and the attack types in hateful memes. We experimented with models that employ only the text, that employ the text and image, and with models that also add information from retrieved texts. TxtBERT, a BERT for sequence classification that uses only the text, achieves very good performance. An ensemble of TxtBERT and a multimodal BERT (ImgBERT) outperforms all other methods on our development set in two out of the three tasks. We found that retrieval methods based on both the image and the text do not work well on this dataset, probably due to its complex context and diversity. In future work we plan to experiment with large pre-trained vision and language transformer models, different sources for retrieval and explainability approaches for multimodal methods.

References

Y-C Chen, L. Li, L. Yu, A. El Kholy, F. Ahmed, Z. Gan, Y. Cheng, and J. Liu. 2020. Uniter: Universal image-text representation learning. In *European Conference on Computer Vision*, pages 104–120, held online.

J. Deng, W. Dong, R. Socher, L.-J. Li, K. Li, and L. Fei-Fei. 2009. ImageNet: A Large-Scale Hierarchical Image Database. In *IEEE Conference on Computer Vision and Pattern Recognition*, pages 248–255, Miami Beach, FL, USA.

Z. Gan, Y-C Chen, L. Li, C. Zhu, Y. Cheng, and J. Liu. 2020. Large-scale adversarial training for vision-and-language representation learning. *arXiv:2006.06195*.

R. Gomez, J. Gibert, L. Gomez, and D. Karatzas. 2020. Exploring hate speech detection in multimodal publications. In *Proceedings of the IEEE/CVF Winter Conference on Applications of Computer Vision*, pages 1470–1478, Aspen, CO, USA.

E. Grave, P. Bojanowski, P. Gupta, A. Joulin, and T. Mikolov. 2018. Learning word vectors for 157 languages. In *Proceedings of the International Conference on Language Resources and Evaluation (LREC 2018)*, pages 3483–3487, Miyazaki, Japan.

D. Kiela, H. Firooz, A. Mohan, V. Goswami, A. Singh, P. Ringshia, and D. Testuggine. 2020. The hateful memes challenge: Detecting hate speech in multimodal memes. In *34th Conference on Neural Information Processing Systems (NeurIPS)*, Vancouver, Canada.

P. Lewis, E. Perez, A. Piktus, F. Petroni, V. Karpukhin, N. Goyal, H. Küttler, M. Lewis, W-t Yih, T. Rocktäschel, et al. 2020. Retrieval-augmented generation for knowledge-intensive nlp tasks. *arXiv:2005.11401*.

L. H. Li, M. Yatskar, D. Yin, C-J Hsieh, and K-W Chang. 2019. Visualbert: A simple and performant baseline for vision and language. *arXiv:1908.03557*.

X. Li, X. Yin, C. Li, P. Zhang, X. Hu, L. Zhang, L. Wang, H. Hu, L. Dong, F. Wei, et al. 2020. Oscar: Object-semantics aligned pre-training for vision-language tasks. In *European Conference on Computer Vision*, pages 121–137, held on-line.

T-Y Lin, M. Maire, S. Belongie, J. Hays, P. Perona, D. Ramanan, P. Dollár, and C L Zitnick. 2014. Microsoft coco: Common objects in context. In *European Conference on Computer Vision*, pages 740–755, Zurich, Switzerland.

J. Lu, D. Batra, D. Parikh, and S. Lee. 2019. Vilbert: Pretraining task-agnostic visiolinguistic representations for vision-and-language tasks. *arXiv:1908.02265*.

W. Su, X. Zhu, Y. Cao, B. Li, L. Lu, F. Wei, and J. Dai. 2019. Vl-bert: Pre-training of generic visual-linguistic representations. *arXiv:1908.08530*.

P. Vijayaraghavan, H. Larochelle, and D. Roy. 2019. Interpretable multi-modal hate speech detection. In *International Conference on Machine Learning, AI for Social Good Workshop*, Long Beach, CA, USA.

O. Vinyals, A. Toshev, S. Bengio, and D. Erhan. 2015. Show and tell: A neural image caption generator. In *IEEE Conference on Computer Vision and Pattern Recognition*, pages 3156–3164, Boston, MA, USA.

F. Yu, J. Tang, W. Yin, Y. Sun, H. Tian, H. Wu, and H. Wang. 2020. Ernie-vil: Knowledge enhanced vision-language representations through scene graph. *arXiv:2006.16934*.

R. Zhu. 2020. Enhance multimodal transformer with external label and in-domain pretrain: hateful meme challenge winning solution. *arXiv:2012.08290*.

Author Index

Association for Computational Linguistics
209 N. Eighth Street
Stroudsburg, Pennsylvania 18360

ISBN 978-1-7138-3391-8

CURRAN ASSOCIATES INC.
proceedings.com